Writing Research Papers

A Complete Guide

Seventh Edition

James D. Lester

Austin Peay State University

**HarperCollins*College*Publishers*

Acquisitions Editor: Patricia Rossi
Developmental Editor: Marisa L. L'Heureux
Project Coordination: Benjamin Production Services
Cover Design: Sally Bindari, Designworks
Cover Photos: Robert Schoen Photography
Production/Manufacturing: Michael Weinstein/Paula Keller
Compositor: Black Dot Graphics
Printer and Binder: R. R. Donnelley & Sons Company
Cover Printer: The Lehigh Press, Inc.

Photo credit: Cover photo (Webster's Ninth New Collegiate Dictionary) by permission of
Merriam-Webster Inc., publishers of the Merriam-Webster dictionaries.

For permission to use copyrighted material, grateful acknowledgment is made to the
copyright holders on p. 382, which are hereby made part of this copyright page.

WRITING RESEARCH PAPERS: A COMPLETE GUIDE, Seventh Edition

Library of Congress Cataloging-in-Publication Data

Lester, James D.
    Writing research papers: a complete guide / James D. Lester.—
7th ed.
        p.   cm.
    Includes bibliographical references and index.
    ISBN (Student Edition) 0-673-46643-4
    ISBN 0-673-46644-2 (Instructor's Edition)
    1. Report writing.   I. Title
LB2369.L4   1993
808'.02—dc20   92-24556
                                                                      CIP

        93 94 95 9 8 7 6 5

Contents

3   *Organizing Ideas and Setting Goals* 71

6 *Writing the Paper*   135

Preface

We celebrate the 25th anniversary of *Writing Research Papers: A Complete Guide* with this seventh edition. During these years, documentation has changed from footnotes to in-text citations, and the content of research papers has shifted from a topic on literature to a topic from across the curriculum. Through the years, I have revised the text to keep students up to date. I've continued that tradition in the seventh edition, which brings improvements in several areas. The first you may notice is the addition of colored tabs and section numbers to make the text easier to use.

Electronic Sources   The nature of research has changed rapidly in recent years, and *Writing Research Papers* has kept the pace by providing information on the public access catalog (PAC), national data-bases, locally loaded compact discs (CD-ROM), and computer mail in programs such as BITNET. The text explains how to use electronic sources and also how to cite information gathered from them, both in the text and in the bibliography.

Computer-generated Papers   This new edition provides specific guidance to the many students who now write with word processors. The storage and retrieval capacities of the computer have changed the way writers work. Thus, *Writing Research Papers* explains techniques for entering notes and text, maintaining files, writing, merging, and revising the drafts, and printing the finished work.

Writing Across the Curriculum   Throughout, the text makes reference to topics from many disciplines, and the topics for the sample papers show the same wide-ranging point of view. A new chapter (Chapter 10) on APA style gives a comprehensive explanation to a documentation format that has gained universal application for research papers in several academic fields, not just psychology. The chapter shows students how to design the sources to APA style, both in the text and in the bibliography entries. The chapter also provides a sample paper in APA style.

Chapter 11 explains documentation for other disciplines across the curriculum, specifying both the style for in-text citations and also the form required for bibliography entries. Samples demonstrate the "number" style for the applied sciences and the "footnote" style for certain courses in the fine arts and the humanities (other than language and literature).

In addition, students in cross-curriculum programs will benefit by using the appendix, "List of Reference Sources by Discipline," which provides a list of the best reference sources for each major discipline. It lists reference guides, bibliographies, data-bases, and journals. The critically important sources for each discipline are marked with asterisks and explained with annotations.

Drafting a Research Proposal The research proposal is a preliminary exercise for launching the project. A new section in Chapter 1 discusses the role and scope of the writer, the writer's sense of an audience, the paper's purpose, and the preliminary thesis sentence. It provides several examples. Many instructors require an acceptable research proposal before students may begin serious note-taking because it helps young researchers to stay focused on essential matters.

Selection, Evaluation, and Critical Reading of the Sources A new Chapter 4 gives detailed attention to the methods for finding the best sources and responding to them with a critical eye. It cuts to the heart of the matter: How can I find the best sources? Should I read all or just part of a source? How do I respond to it? The chapter will help students use journal articles and scholarly books rather than copy indiscriminately from magazines, trade books, and encyclopedias. Chapter 4 also features two sample papers: an annotated bibliography and a review of the literature on a topic.

Plagiarism The text devotes a full section in Chatper 5 to explain the role of a researcher, who must cite sources honestly and accurately in order to share with the reader the fundamental scholarship of a narrowed topic. Rather than merely warn students against plagiarism in a negative sense, the text encourages critical thinking so that students learn to assimilate ideas in their notes and to incorporate them in the manuscript in clear, well-documented progression. It displays methods for achieving correct citations, it explains the rules, and it condemns blatant disregard for scholarly conventions. The text also explains the gray area of "common knowledge" facts.

Sample Papers The text includes many sample papers so that students can see how to write and format their own manuscripts:
- research proposals
- an annotated bibliography
- a review of the literature on a topic
- abstracts in MLA and APA style
- two research papers in MLA style
- a research paper in APA style
- a research paper in the number style
- a portion of a paper in footnote style

Additional sample papers appear in the Instructor's Manual.

Collecting Data Outside the Library Many instructors now require students to search for material beyond the library, so the text features a comprehensive section on citing from and documenting information from these types of sources: interviews, letters, questionnaires, local government documents, television programs, and original tests and experiments.

The Writing Process The writing process serves as the structuring feature of the text, carrying students from discovery of a topic to research, note-taking, writing, and formatting the finished manuscript to a specific style. The text moves systematically from one stage to the next, and a new arrangement of eleven chapters, instead of seven, clearly defines the process in its logical sequence and focuses precisely on specific tasks.

Chapter 1 now features methods for developing a research proposal. Chapter 2 highlights electronic sources as well as traditional printed materials. Chapter 3 is now a separate section on setting goals and organizing the material. Chapter 4 adds new material on critical reading so that students might select the best sources and make intelligent responses. Chapter 5 focuses on note-card design, including computer-generated notes. Chapter 6, on writing the manuscript, has an expanded section on techniques for building the body of the paper and continues to provide plenty of methods for developing a full introduction and an effective closing.

Chapter 7 gathers in one place the rules and methods for blending reference material into one's writing. Chapter 8 is a nuts and bolts chapter on format and mechanics, and it includes two sample papers—the short essay that uses sources and the long, formal research paper. Chapter 9 provides specific rules for the Works Cited page in MLA style. Chapter 10 shows APA style, which has gained universal application in the social sciences. Chapter 11 provides rules for citations and documentation in other fields across the curriculum to show several styles: the name and year system for business and the natural sciences, the number system for the applied sciences, and the traditional footnote system for some humanities courses.

Acknowledgments   Almost three million students have used this text since its publication 25 years ago. Hundreds of them, along with faculty and editorial professionals, have contributed to the book's success. Several students deserve special mention: Patricia Bracy, Kim Wells, Pamela Howell, Glenda Durdin, Jo Walker, and Jay Wickham. Anne May Berwind, Head of Library Information Services at Austin Peay State University, revised the list of references in the appendix and also annotated selected works on the list.

Professional reviewers for the seventh edition offered many helpful ideas; they were Lynda G. Adamson, Prince George's Community College; Karen D. Bowser, Pennsylvania State University, Harrisburg; Lynn Bryce, Saint Cloud State University; Donella Eberle, Mesa Community College; Karen W. Gainey, University of Tulsa; Margaret Gwathmey, Skyline College; Kathy Howlett, Northeastern University; Kim Brian Lovejoy, Indiana University, Indianapolis; Elizabeth Nelson, St. Peter's College; Eugene L. Shiro, University of the District of Columbia; Michael W. Shurgot, South Puget Sound Community College; Hassell B. Sledd, Slippery Rock University; James D. Stokes, University of Wisconsin, Stevens Point; John D. Wills, Luzerne County Community College; Matthew Wilson, Pennsylvania State University, Harrisburg.

I appreciate also the support of my family, so I thank Martha, Jim, Mark, and Debbie for their unending enthusiasm and encouragement.

James D. Lester

Introduction

RATIONALE FOR RESEARCH WRITING

As you begin this important task of writing a research paper, you may feel overwhelmed about defending a thesis and conforming to all sorts of documentation rules. This writing manual will help you by providing a step-by-step explanation of the research-writing process. It will encourage you to approach the assignment one step at a time—from selecting a significant topic to producing a polished manuscript. You will develop confidence as you complete each stage of the process and begin the next one. You will become adept at several skills.

1. Narrowing your focus to a manageable topic
2. Locating source materials and taking notes
3. Analyzing, evaluating, and interpreting materials
4. Arranging and classifying materials
5. Writing the paper with a sense of purpose, as well as with clarity and accuracy
6. Handling problems of quoting and properly documenting your sources

In time, you will come to understand that knowledge is not always something conveyed by experts in books and articles to novice writers who merely copy the ideas of the experts onto the pages of their research papers. In truth, you will want to generate new ideas about the issues and defend your position with the weight of your argument, as well as with the strength of your evidence. You will want to cite the sources that support *your* ideas, not cite the sources just because they relate to your subject.

Creating a long, scholarly paper is seldom a neat, logical progression. The task, spread over several weeks, often demands that you work both forward and backward in various starts and stops. One way to succeed is to follow the order of this text: Choose a topic, gather data, plan and write a draft, revise and polish the manuscript, and develop a final bibliography. Word processing makes each of these tasks easier, and this manual explains computer technology as appropriate to the task.

Chapter 1 will help you find a topic that has merit as a scholarly issue or research question. The chapter shows how to search library sources for a topic. It also helps you examine your own experience, reconsider your cultural background, and evaluate issues within your favorite academic disciplines.

Chapters 2, 3, 4, and 5 carry you into the library for critical reading, research, and the writing of note cards. Included is a discussion of plagiarism, which afflicts many students who think proper scholarly credit is unnecessary or who become confused about proper placement of references.

Chapters 6 and 7 provide details about writing the paper—from title and outline to introduction, body, and conclusion. In particular, Chapter 6 will help you frame the argument in the introduction, develop it in the body, and discuss it in the conclusion. You will also be reminded of three vital phases: revising, editing, and proofreading. Chapter 6 also includes a section on adapting your writing to the demands and the rewards of word processing. Chapter 7 explains the value of in-text citations to help you distinguish your own comments from paraphrases and quotations borrowed from the source materials.

Chapter 8 explains matters of format and mechanics. It discusses matters of style and design, from title page to works cited page and from underlining to abbreviations. Sample papers in the Modern Language Association (MLA) style are provided on pages 231–49.

Chapter 9 explains the necessary ingredients of individual bibliography entries so that you can fully document all of your sources on the works cited page.

Chapter 10 explains the American Psychological Association (APA) style and correlates its features with the MLA style. You will need to use the APA style for papers in several disciplines outside the English class, such as psychology, education, political science, and sociology.

Chapter 11 explains the documentation style for disciplines other than those for English and the social sciences. It explains in detail how to document with the *name and year system* for papers in business and the physical or biological sciences. It explains the *number system* for use with papers in the applied sciences and medical sciences. It explains the *footnote* and *endnote* systems for use with some papers in the liberal arts. Samples of writing using each of these systems are provided in Chapter 11.

Finally, the appendix contains an exhaustive subject list to reference works and journals in many fields of study. For every discipline listed, it provides a list of study guides, the important data-bases, the appropriate printed bibliographies, and the most useful indexes to literature in the journals. Consult it as you begin research in a specific discipline, such as drama, home economics, geology, or women's studies.

1   Finding a Topic

Choosing a topic for the research paper is fairly easy (any topic will serve) and yet very complicated (an informed choice is crucial). Select a person, a person's work, or a specific thing to study, for example, General Colin Powell, John Steinbeck's *Of Mice and Men,* or Nintendo games. Select from any area that interests you. Such areas might include the following:

Current events (high salaries for sports personalities)
Education (bilingualism in the classroom)
Social issues (the high cost of shoplifting)
Science (poisonous drugs from the Aconite flower)

However, the subject for a research paper must meet three demands.

1. It must examine a significant issue.
2. It must address a knowledgeable reader and carry that reader to another plateau of knowledge.
3. It must have a serious purpose, one that demands analysis of the issues, argues from a position, and explains complex details.

> **Choose a topic with a built-in issue so that you can interpret the issue and cite the opinions of outside sources.**

You need not abandon a favorite topic, such as "Fishing at Lake Cumberland" or "The Cartoon Strip *Calvin and Hobbes.*" Just be certain that you give it a serious, scholarly perspective, such as "The Effects of Toxic Chemicals on the Fish of Lake Cumberland" or "The Role of Fantasy in *Calvin and Hobbes.*" When your paper examines a problem or raises an issue, you have a reason for sharing outside sources with the reader and you give yourself the opportunity to write a meaningful conclusion.

1a GENERATING IDEAS FOR A RESEARCH-PAPER PROJECT

Many students find selecting an effective topic to be the most difficult part of the research-paper process. You need both a topic and an issue:

| The addiction of some people to video games. |

This topic raises two questions: Do children *and* adults get addicted to video games? With what results?

| Andrew Jackson and the Trail of Tears |

This topic addresses a controversial issue: What was Andrew Jackson's role as president during the Trail of Tears?

Three techniques will help you with topic selection before you enter the library.

1. Reflect on your personal experiences for a topic that touches your life-style or career.
2. Talk with other people because collaborative learning can broaden your vision of the issues.
3. Speculate about the subject and discover ideas by listing issues, asking questions, free writing, and other techniques.

These steps will not only help you find a primary topic but also help you produce a secondary list of issues, terms, questions, and a few written notes.

Using Personal Experience for Topic Discovery

Most people have special interests as demonstrated by their television viewing and their choice of magazines, clubs, and activities. You might decide to combine a topic of personal interest with some aspect of your academic studies:

A personal interest in skiing and a study of sports medicine
An interest in children and a study of childhood psychology
Concern about your personal checkbook and a study of govern-
ment economic policies
The contaminated well water on your family's farm and a study
of chemical toxins

You can also combine your special interests to narrow a general subject to a specific topic. Assume, for instance, that three writers all select the same general subject—latchkey children:

The first writer, who plans a career in law enforcement, focuses
on criminal dangers for latchkey children who must return
from school to empty houses and apartments.

The second writer combines the subject of latchkey children
with an interest in television to investigate programming during after-school hours for the lonely child.

The third writer, majoring in economics, conducts a cost/benefit
analysis of different child-care options for schoolchildren.

The three writers can use personal interests to guide them into research
and into their differing discussions on the same topic.

Your cultural background may prompt you to research your roots, your
culture, and the mythology and history of your ethnic background. You
might, for example,

1. Write about the Indian Wars from the Native American's point
   of view.
2. Examine Chinese theories on the roles of women.
3. Research your bicultural experiences as a Hispanic or
   Japanese-American.
4. Discuss pride as motivation for the behavior of young African-
   Americans.

Caution: Do not become too emotional in your personal response to
your heritage; research writing must maintain objectivity.

Talking with Others to Find a Subject

Like some researchers, you may need to start your research by sitting on
a park bench with a friend or across the coffee table from a colleague or
relative. Ask people in your school and community for ideas and topics that
need investigation. If you have a subject, ask colleagues questions about
the subject. Then listen.

One writer, for example, wanted to argue for more liberal arts courses
in high school curriculums. Before spending hours reading sources,
however, she talked by phone with her former high school teachers. She
discovered that a liberal-arts curriculum was in place; the problem was
something different: how to motivate students toward liberal-arts courses in
a marketplace that demands utilitarian skills, such as typing, auto mechanics, or computer programming. In the end, the writer developed a different
sort of paper, all because she took time to consult with others.

Collaborative learning of this sort sometimes occurs in the classroom
through use of the following steps:

1. Consult with three or four students about your topic.
2. Listen to the concerns of others.
3. Take careful notes.
4. Adjust your research accordingly.

You may need additional explanation and definition, or you may want to
build a stronger argument.

Speculating About Your Subject to Discover Ideas

At some point, you may need to sit back, relax, and use your imagination to contemplate the issues. Out of meditation may come topics and subtopics worthy of investigation. Generate ideas in the following ways.

Keeping a Research Journal

Unlike a diary of personal thoughts about your daily activities and also unlike a journal of creative ideas (poems, stories, or scenarios), the research journal is one that stores ideas and materials on specific issues. In this notebook, you should list issues, do some free writing, paste in photocopied materials, ask questions, and make notes. In effect, you can keep all your initial ideas and materials in one notebook rather than on cards and individual sheets. If you buy a notebook that has pockets on the inside jacket, you will have a place to store any miscellaneous items.

Free Writing

To free write, merely focus on a topic and write whatever comes to mind. Continue writing with your mind on the topic. Do not worry about grammar, style, or penmanship. The result? You have started writing. Your brain is engaged and ideas flow forth. The exercise requires nonstop writing for a page or so to develop valuable phrases, comparisons, episodes, and specific thoughts that help focus issues of concern. Note this brief example:

```
     Global communication networks seem to be changing the
world order and the attitudes of the common people, who now
have a better grasp of events at home and abroad.  News
networks were able to respond instantly when East and West
Germany were reunited, when armed forces attacked Baghdad
in the Desert Storm war, and when the rebirth of the
Russian states occurred. International communication
networks like CNN now link us into a global community.
Dictators cannot perform brazen acts of violence and
oppression without the focus of television cameras and
instant transmission worldwide.  Immediate response by the
world to an act of violence can usually end it before the
power structure can get entrenched.--Emmie Alexander
```

This free writing has set the path for this writer's investigation into world politics and the glare of the television cameras.

Listing Key Words

During your search for a subject, keep a sharp eye out for fundamental terms and concepts that might focus the direction of your research. One student, while considering a topic for his Native American Studies course, listed several terms and phrases about oral traditions of the Blackfoot tribe:

boasting	invoking spirits	singing
making medicine	story telling	reciting history
war chants	jokes and humor	

The key words set the stage for writing the rough outline, as explained in the following section.

Arranging Key Words into a Rough Outline

As you develop ideas and begin listing key terms and subtopics, you should recognize the hierarchy of major and minor issues.

Native American Oral Traditions

Chanting	Narrating	Singing
for war	history	hymns
for good health	stories	folk songs
for religion	jokes	
	boasts	

This arrangement shows an initial ranking of ideas, one that can and should change during the research process.

Clustering

Another method for discovering the hierarchy of your primary topics and subtopics is to cluster ideas around a central subject. The cluster of related topics can generate a multitude of ideas, which are all joined and interconnected, as shown in the following illustration.

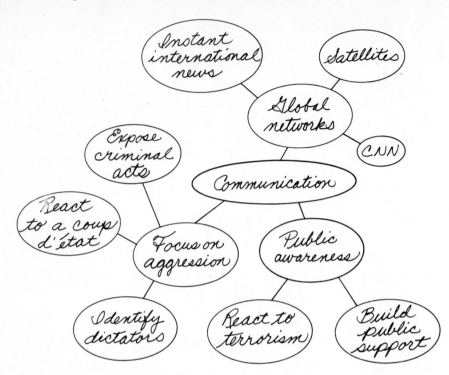

Asking Questions

Stretch your imagination with questions. They can suggest issues of concern and help you locate a workable topic. Having read Henry Thoreau's essay "Civil Disobedience," one writer asked:

What is "civil disobedience"?

Is dissent legal? Is it moral? Is it patriotic?

Is dissent a liberal activity? Conservative?

Should the government encourage or stifle dissent?

Is passive resistance effective?

Answering the questions can lead the writer to a central issue and even produce a thesis statement to govern the entire project.

Another student framed questions by using the rhetorical modes, as illustrated:

Comparison: How does a state lottery compare with horse

racing?

Definition: What is a lottery in legal terms? In

religious terms?

Cause/Effect: What are the consequences of a state lottery on funding for education, highways, prisons, and social programs?

Process: How are winnings distributed?

Classification: What types of lotteries exist and which are available in this state?

Evaluation: What is the value of a lottery to the average citizen? What are the disadvantages?

Any one of these questions can identify a key issue worthy of research.

A third student framed questions for a study across the curriculum on the subject of *sports gambling:*

Economics: Does gambling benefit a college's athletic budget? The national economy?

Psychology: What is the effect of gambling on the mental attitude of the college athlete who knows huge sums hang in the balance on his/her performance?

History: Does gambling on sporting events have an identifiable tradition?

Sociology: What compulsion in human nature prompts people to gamble on athletic prowess?

Such questions help to identify a working topic.

1b USING SOURCE MATERIALS TO DISCOVER AND EVALUATE A TOPIC

After listing, free writing, and clustering have produced a promising topic, go to the library for exploratory reading in reference books, biographies, or periodicals. Look to see how that topic is being talked about in the literature. Read carefully the titles of articles and record key words. Look for tips on how to focus the topic, be it *medical trauma centers, the role of women in Robert Browning's poetry,* or *automobile emissions control.* In addition, speed up the process by using the new computer technology.

Using the Public Access Catalog

Most college libraries now have a *public access catalog* (PAC), which is a computer version of the card catalog files. Early in your work, it will guide you quickly from general subjects to subtopics and, finally, to specific books.

First, type in a general subject at the PAC.

```
TELEVISION
```

Second, examine on the screen a set of subtopics, a list of perhaps 20 topics or 200.

```
SUBJECT HEADING GUIDE--377 HEADINGS FOUND

1 TELEVISION
2 --ANTENNAS
3 --BIBLIOGRAPHY
4 --BIOGRAPHY
5 --EQUIPMENT AND SUPPLIES
```

Third, scan the list looking for an interesting topic. Item 86, TELEVISION AND CHILDREN, has such additional subdivisions as the following:

```
86 TELEVISION AND CHILDREN
87 --ABSTRACTS
88 --ADDRESSES ESSAYS LECTURES
89 --BIBLIOGRAPHY
90 --CONGRESSES
91 --CROSS-CULTURAL STUDIES
```

If you enter item 88, ADDRESSES ESSAYS LECTURES, you will find a more specific list:

```
88 TELEVISION AND CHILDREN --ADDRESSES ESSAYS
   LECTURES

1. TV interactive toys  Tuchscherer, Pamela
   (1988)
2. Television and the aggressive child (1986)
3. Television and social behavior (1980)
4. Children and the faces of television (1980)
5. Television and children  Howe, Michael J.
   (1970)
```

The PAC has carried you to specific titles of books and to the contemporary issues.

Fourth, if one book looks interesting, you can enter the number and get a complete description of the book:

```
BIBLIOGRAPHIC RECORD--No. 1 of 4 Entries Found

Tuchscherer, Pamela.
  TV interactive toys: the new high tech threat to
children.  Fight back without a gun, arm your
child with knowledge / Pamela Tuchscherer; 1st ed.
Bend, Or.: Pinnaroo Pub; Distributed by Gryphon
House, 1988.
  219 p.: ill.; 22cm.
  Bibliography: p. 209-214.
LOCATION; Education stacks
CALL NUMBER: HQ 784/.T4/T83/1988
  04/21/91  Not charged to a user.
```

In effect, the PAC has rapidly identified a specific issue about a broad topic and provided a printout of bibliographic data for a book for preliminary reading.

> **Use a computer search to control the size of the project. If the computer lists 50 or 60 books or lists 200 or more articles, the topic is too broad; narrow it. If it provides one book and only two or three articles, you must broaden the topic.**

Using CD-ROM Files on Computers

In addition to a PAC, most college libraries now have compact disc (CD-ROM) facilities, which means that data-base files, such as *Readers' Guide to Periodical Literature* or *Psychological Abstracts,* are located on a compact disc stored as read only memory in the computer. ROM means the computer can read the files for you, but nobody can write into the files to change them. One system, for example, is *InfoTrac,* which contains files to *Readers' Guide* mingled with files to the *Social Sciences Index* and to the *Humanities Index,* plus others. Libraries will vary in their CD-ROM holdings, so it is important for you to develop a working relationship with the reference librarians. CD-ROM systems have different names, but their function is the same: to help you work from a general subject to specific topics and, finally, to the reading materials.

1. Type in a general subject.

   WOMEN

2. Read the list of subtopics provided on the screen and narrow your search to one.

```
WOMEN IN POPULAR CULTURE
WOMEN IN PRISON
WOMEN IN PUBLIC LIFE
WOMEN AND MEN (BOOK)
```

3. Enter a choice, WOMEN IN POPULAR CULTURE, to get a list of articles.

```
     "Material girl": the effacements of
postmodern culture.  (The Female Body) by
Susan Bordo v29 Michigan Quarterly Review
Fall '90 p.653(25)

     Feminism and pornography.  by Kate
Ellis, Barbara O'Dair and Abby Tallmer
Feminist Review  Autumn '90 p.15(4)

     Feminist myths and Greek mythology.
(column) by Mary Lefkowitz  Times Literary
Supplement  July 22 '88 p.804(2)
```

4. Use these article titles to narrow your own work. If one seems appropriate, read it for ideas and terminology.
5. Use PAC and CD-ROM to begin research with two or three topics at once.

```
BASKETBALL and VIOLENCE

ANCONITE and DRUGS and POISON
```

The computer will search and list only those articles that match the terms, thereby narrowing the search considerably.

6. Use CD-ROM to search the Bible, the complete works of Shakespeare, a 21-volume encyclopedia, or the full text of 107 different books on U.S. history. CD-ROM makes available the entire volumes of major works on one diskette. New diskettes are being produced every day, such as the *Oxford English Dictionary,* the *Oxford Textbook of Medicine,* and *Countries of the World.* CD-ROM technology is changing the way scholars conduct their research.

Inspecting a Book's Table of Contents to Find and Evaluate a Subject

A book's table of contents will subdivide a general subject for you, so scan one for a topic of interest and then investigate it.

Figure 1: Table of contents from *The Universe* by Isaac Asimov

Table of Contents:

CHAPTER 1 – *The Earth*

Introduction	1
The Flat Earth	2
The Spherical Earth	4
The Size of the Earth	7

CHAPTER 2 – *The Solar System*

The Moon	11
The Sun	14
Parallax	17
The Size of the Solar System	21

Is size stable or increasing?

CHAPTER 3 – *The Stars*

The Vault of the Sky	27
A Multiplicity of Suns	33
The Search for Stellar Parallax	35
The Distance of the Nearer Stars	39

As shown above, the student has found a challenging topic, one that provokes a question and one that might launch an exploratory investigation.

Examining a Book's Index to Discover a Subject

Most books contain an index that will list alphabetically the book's contents. Such listings have investigative possibilities, as with "colliding" or "exploding" galaxies found in the index below:

Figure 2: Index from *The Universe* by Isaac Asimov

Galaxies
antimatter and, 257
classes of, 176-178
clusters of, 194-195, 284, 300-301
colliding, 288
continuous formation of, 224-225
distances of, 188, 201-203
electric charge on, 224
expanding Universe and, 193
exploding, 288-293
gravitation and, 193-194
microwave energies of, 288-298

How does an entire galaxy explode?

A logical follow-up involves reading the designated pages to consider issues and to find a general subject. Also, feel free to shift topics during this stage; for example, investigation of "microwave energies" might change your focus from galaxies and astronomy to microwave technology in communications, factories, and home appliances.

Scanning an Encyclopedia Article

An encyclopedia contains not only an alphabetical list of topics but also in-depth discussions that can trigger your own ideas. Note how one student made critical comments on this photocopied article in order to evaluate a possible topic:

Figure 3: Encyclopedia article from *Encyclopedia Americana*, 1989 edition

What did he write his dissertation on?

Was it a rich family?

What did Gandhi write? Passive resistance was Thoreau's idea.

> **KING, Martin Luther, Jr.** (1929–1968), American clergyman and Nobel Peace Prize winner, who led the civil rights movement in the United States for much of the 1950s and 1960s. He was born in Atlanta, Ga., on Jan. 15, 1929, the son and grandson of Baptist ministers. In 1948, King graduated from Morehouse College at the age of 19. Three years later he earned the bachelor of divinity degree at Crozer Theological Seminary, and in 1955 he was awarded a Ph.D. at Boston University. While studying in Boston he met and married Coretta Scott; they had four children.
>
> As the son of "substantial" black parents, young Martin was protected to some degree from the more scarifying experiences of segregation and racial hostility. But he was not completely immune, for there were inevitable personal experiences through which he came to a tardy awareness and a summary rejection of the oppressive prejudice and discrimination that so troubled his sense of moral propriety and social justice.
>
> At Crozer he developed a fascination for Mahatma Gandhi, whose life and teachings were ultimately to influence his own destiny as a leading apostle of passive resistance.

Any one of this student's marginal notes could become the central focus of research.

Searching the Headings in the Printed Indexes

Any index of the reference room, such as *Readers' Guide, Bibliographic Index,* or *Humanities Index,* categorizes and subdivides topics in alphabetical order. A key word or phrase will often enable you to find an issue about the general subject. A portion of *Social Sciences Index* is shown below with a student's marginal notation.

Figure 4:
Example from
the *Social*
Sciences Index

What does this mean—
word superiority?

Why do consonant
clusters cause
spelling errors?

Dyslexia
Abstract letter identities and developmental dyslexia. P. Bigsby. bibl *Br J Psychol* 81:227–63 My '90
A developmental, interactive activation model of the word superiority effect. C. H. Chase and P. Tallal. bibl *J Exp Child Psychol* 49:448–87 Je '90
Phonological awareness and spelling in normal children and dyslexics: the case of initial consonant clusters. M. Bruck and R. Treiman. bibl *J Exp Child Psychol* 50:156–78 Ag '90
Rate and timing precision of motor coordination in developmental dyslexia. P. H. Wolff and others. bibl *Dev Psychol* 26:349–59 My '90
Word-recognition skills of adults with childhood diagnoses of dyslexia. M. Bruck. bibl *Dev Psychol* 26:439–54 My '90

This student can now connect the topic *dyslexia* with one of several issues: *word superiority effect, consonant clusters, spelling problems, motor coordination,* and *word recognition.*

> **Topic selection goes beyond choosing a general category (e.g., *football* or *rice farming*); it includes an issue that provokes research (e.g., *proposition 48 denies football scholarships to deserving athletes*).**

1c DRAFTING A RESEARCH PROPOSAL

A research proposal is a short paragraph that identifies four essential ingredients of your work:

1. The purpose of the paper (explain, analyze, and argue)
2. The intended audience (general or specialized)
3. Your voice as the writer (informer or advocate)
4. The preliminary thesis sentence or opening hypothesis

For example, one writer developed this research proposal:

```
This paper will examine communication networks and their

effect on world order.  Satellite technology has made it

possible for C-SPAN, CNN, and others to show events

instantly from any spot on the globe.  The audience is

often universal.  Because the people know the truth, via

international networks, the political, military, and

economic stability of nations is affected.--Emmie Alexander
```

This writer has identified an issue and will go in search of evidence that will show the effects of communication upon world order.

Explaining Your Purpose in the Research Proposal

Research papers accomplish different tasks:

1. Explain and define the topic.
2. Analyze the specific issues.
3. Persuade the reader with the weight of your evidence.

Usually, one of these purposes will dominate the paper, but you will probably employ all of the purposes in one way or another. For example, a writer who argues against the recreational use of drugs must also explain the products and analyze both the types of drugs and the different dangers.

1. Use the *explanatory purpose* to review and itemize factual data. One writer defined cocaine and explained how it came from the coca shrub of South America. Another writer explained how advertisers have gained entrance into classrooms by providing free educational materials. The explanatory purpose helps those who review books or articles to summarize and briefly discuss one work in order to explain its contribution to a particular field of knowledge. (See Section 4e, 102–04, for a sample annotated bibliography and Section 4f, 104–09, for a sample literature review paper.)

2. Use the *analytical purpose* to classify various parts of the subject and to investigate each one in depth. One writer examined the effects of cocaine on the brain, the eyes, the lungs, the heart, and so on. Another writer classified and examined the methods used by advertisers to reach schoolchildren with their messages. One writer examined the role of the trickster in Native American mythology, another explored the image of women in Shakespeare's sonnets, and a third analyzed the effects of television on the language development of children. Use analysis for discovery, examination, deliberation, and speculation.

3. Use the *persuasive purpose* to defend your argument convincingly. One writer condemned the use of cocaine and warned of its dangers.

Another writer argued that advertisers have enticed children into bad habits: eating improperly, smoking cigarettes, drinking alcohol, or behaving violently. Persuasion enables you to reject the general attitudes about a problem and affirm new theories, advance a solution, recommend a course of action, or—at the least—invite the reader into an intellectual dialogue. For example, condemning violence on television is a worthy but inadequate argument because most people will agree with you. However, you can argue that television, like the movies, should govern itself with ratings (e.g., G, PG, PG-13, and R) and with late-night time slots for R-rated programs.

Consequently, you will need to explain the subject, classify and analyze the issues, anticipate the reader's objections and questions, and reach a conclusion. Be aware that bias and prejudice will be your enemies, not your allies, because the scholarly research paper, unlike a position paper, should be reasonable, not strident, cautious in assertions, not rash, and well defended by your use of the sources.

Identifying Your Audience in the Research Proposal

You will want to design your research paper for an audience of interested readers who expect a depth of understanding on your part and evidence of your background reading on this special topic. A discourse community is a body of readers with special needs.

Readers of a paper on social issues (such as working mothers, latchkey children, or overcrowded prisons) expect analysis that points toward a social theory or answer.

Readers of an academic interpretation of a novel expect to read literary theories on the novel's symbolism, narrative structure, or characterization.

Readers of a business report on outdoor advertising expect statistical evidence that will defend a general proposition.

Therefore, the nature of the audience affects a thesis proposal, an interpretation of literature, or a report of investigative research. The audience determines whether you will give an analysis or an explanation, or provide special charts and tables on your findings. Keep in mind three essential elements:

1. Identify your audience and respond accordingly. It will affect your topic, your development, your voice and style, and even your choice of words.
2. Meet the needs of your readers. Are you telling them everything they need to know without insulting their intelligence? Are you saying something worthwhile? Something new? Do not bore them or insult their intelligence by retelling known facts from an encyclopedia. (This latter danger is the reason

many instructors discourage your use of an encyclopedia as a
source.)

3. Invite your readers into the discussion by approaching the
topic from an interesting and different point of view; that is,
address literature students with an economic interpretation of
a novel, address marketing students with a biological study of
human behavior in the marketplace, or address history students with a geographical study of a nation's destiny.

Identifying Your Role as a Researcher in the Proposal

Your voice should reflect the investigative nature of your work, so try to
display your knowledge. Refer to authorities that you have consulted; do
not hide them. Offer quotations. Provide charts or graphs that you have
created or copied from the sources. Your instructors will give you credit for
using the sources in your paper. Be certain that you give in-text citations to
the sources to reflect your academic honesty. Your role is to investigate,
explain, defend, and argue the issue at hand, all at the same time in the
same paper.

Speak from your specialized point of view. You must appear to be at
ease with the subject, writing from a well-grounded knowledge base and
citing the source material to augment and highlight the discourse. In short,
make it *your* discourse, not a collection of quotations from experts in the
books and journals.

Expressing Your Thesis Sentence in the Research Proposal

A thesis sentence expands your topic into a scholarly proposal, one that
you will try to prove and defend in your paper. It does not state the obvious,
such as "Too much television is harmful to children." That sentence will
not provoke an academic discussion because your readers know that *excess*
in anything is harmful. The writer must narrow and isolate one issue by
finding a critical focus, such as:

```
Violence in children's programming echoes an adolescent's

fascination with brutality.
```

This sentence advances an idea that the writer can develop fully and defend
with the evidence. The writer has made a connection between the subject,
television violence, and the focusing agent, *adolescent psychology.* Look at
two more examples:

Thesis: `The elasticity of children's eyes makes it`

                `perfectly safe for them to sit close to the`

                `television screen.`

Thesis: `Television cartoons can affect a child's attitude`

                `toward violence.`

In the first example, the writer uses expertise in physical development to provide a critical focus. In the second, the writer combines television viewing with psychological development.

Accordingly, a writer's critical approach to the subject affects the thesis. One writer's social concern for battered wives will generate a thesis different from that of another person with a psychological interest and of a third person's biological approach:

Social approach: `Public support of "safe" houses for`

                      `battered wives seems to be public`

                      `endorsement of divorce.`

Psychological approach: `The masochism of some women traps`

                      `them in a marriage of painful love.`

Biological approach: `Battered wives may be the victims`

                      `of their own biological`

                      `conditioning.`

Each thesis will provoke a response from the reader, who will demand a carefully structured defense in the body of the paper.

Your thesis is not your conclusion or your answer to a problem. Rather, the thesis anticipates your conclusion and sets in motion the examination of facts so that you can reach, in the conclusion, the special idea of your paper.

Your thesis is part of the research proposal because it sets in motion your examination of facts so that you can reach a conclusion, one that shows the specific, distinctive nature of your paper. Note below how four writers developed different thesis sentences even though they had the same topic, "Santiago in Hemingway's *The Old Man and the Sea*."

Note: This novel narrates the toils of an old Cuban fisherman named Santiago who has not caught a fish for many days. He desperately needs the money to be gained by returning with a good catch of fish. On this day he catches a marlin, which pulls him far out to sea. Finally, Santiago ties the huge marlin to the side of his small boat. However, during the return in the darkness, sharks attack the marlin so that he arrives home with only a skeleton of the fish. He removes his mast and carries it, like a cross, up the hill to his home.

Thesis: Poverty forced Santiago to venture too far and
struggle beyond reason in his attempt to land the
marlin.

This writer will examine Santiago's poverty and the economic conditions of his trade.

Thesis: The giant marlin is a symbol for all of life's
obstacles and hurdles, and Santiago is a symbol
for all suffering humans.

This writer will examine the religious and social symbolism of the novel.

Thesis: Santiago represents a dying breed, the person who
confronts alone the natural elements without
modern technology.

This writer will explore the history of fishing equipment and explain both Santiago's grandeur and his failure in that light.

Thesis: Hemingway's portrayal of Santiago demonstrates the
author's deep respect for Cuba and its stoic
heroes.

This writer takes a social approach in order to examine the Cuban culture and its influence on Hemingway.

Each preliminary thesis sentence above serves a writer who knows the specific nature of the paper and thereby knows what types of sources to consult. Later, each writer can frame a final thesis sentence, one to serve the reader (see Section 6b, 136–38).

Make the preliminary thesis sentence a part of your research proposal:

This paper will interpret a novel, The Old Man and the Sea,
by Ernest Hemingway. My purpose is to explain to fellow
literature students the novel's setting and the social
conditions of the old Cuban. I suspect that poverty forced
Santiago to venture too far and struggle beyond reason in
his attempt to land the marlin.—Ramon Lopez

This writer and his instructor now have an understanding of the paper's purpose; its audience; the role of the student, Ramon Lopez, as literary interpreter; and the paper's narrow focus on Santiago's economic status.

The next research proposal demonstrates one student's plan for interviewing and charting the social attitudes of a target audience.

> The NIMBY syndrome now prevails across the nation in rural as well as urban neighborhoods. People know that we must give health care to AIDS victims, store toxic wastes, build prisons, but they cry, "Not in my backyard." This paper will examine the social attitudes of the people as based on interviews of 20 people in two neighborhoods. The report will examine responses in three areas--social responsibility, self-reliance, and self-protection.
> --Virginia Forte

1d NARROWING THE GENERAL SUBJECT TO A SPECIFIC TOPIC

As explained above, you should narrow your focus to a specific issue, such as "The Role of the Narrator in 'The Raven'" or "The Symbolic Blackness of Poe's Raven." Research requires accurate facts and evidence in support of a specific proposition. Drafting a research proposal (as explained in Section 1c) will narrow the topic, but you should use the following techniques if needed.

Narrowing and Focusing Comparison Topics

Historians compare Robert E. Lee and Ulysses S. Grant. Political scientists compare Ronald Reagan with George Bush. Literary scholars compare the poets John Keats and Thomas Hardy. Any two works, any two persons, any two groups may serve as the basis for a comparative study. However, the study should focus on issues. Note how a rough outline sets up the differences between Alexander Hamilton and Thomas Jefferson on fiscal issues:

National Bank	Currency	Tariffs
Jefferson	Jefferson	Jefferson
Hamilton	Hamilton	Hamilton

Rather than talk about Jefferson's policies and then Hamilton's, this writer will focus on the issues—the national bank, the currency, and tariffs. The plan limits the discussion to specific differences of the two statesmen.

Restricting and Narrowing Disciplinary Topics

Every discipline, whether sociology, geology, or literature, has its analytical categories, which are those areas requiring detailed study, such as the *behavior* of mice (psychology), the *demographics* of a target audience (marketing), or the *function* of loops and arrays (computer science). Literature students soon learn the importance of these terms:

imagery	symbolism	theme
setting	irony	character
plot	structure	genre

Writers on literature must learn to write symbolic studies, image studies, or thematic studies. In contrast, a researcher in psychology must proceed with *observation* of subjects, conduct *tests* on rats, or make a *cognitive approach* to the data. Of course, you cannot overuse the language of the discipline to the point of writing unclearly; yet, do use the terms of the field to help narrow your subject. (See also "Identifying Your Audience in the Research Proposal," Section 1c, 15–16.)

Narrowing the Topic to Match Source Materials

Library sources often determine the fate of research. Your preliminary work should include a brief search for available sources. Will you have enough books and articles on the topic? Are they up to date? What have other writers focused on? For example, one writer started with the general subject of *Texas* and narrowed it to *Texas politics.* She found several catalog cards to *Sam Houston*—books written primarily in the 1950s and 1960s—and she found only one article at the CD-ROM terminal. Although Sam Houston is a good subject, the sources were out of date. The student wanted a topic of contemporary interest. Economic factors in Texas seemed more important in the literature. Accordingly, she began to shift her focus to the financial condition of the state. Could a woman governor, Ann Richards, pull Texas out of its economic slump? How did one of the sunbelt states get into this condition? Could the economy of Texas recover with or without oil and its economic substructure?

In this way, the writer launched her investigation that combined her interest in Texas with a contemporary issue. With a topic firmly in mind, she was then ready to turn her attention to gathering the data she would need for her paper.

2 *Gathering Data*

For most writing projects, you must go to the library to research a specific subject, perhaps *politically correct language, world banking networks,* or *DNA fingerprinting.*

Modern technology has eased the search for sources—card catalogs on computers, data-base information available by telephone transmission, and compact disks within computers that can search thousands of journal articles in *Social Sciences Index, Psychological Abstracts, Business Periodicals Index,* and many other indexes, in accordance with your library's holdings.

This chapter will help you search out the most timely and authoritative materials on a topic, beginning with printouts of sources at the PAC and the CD-ROM computers. If your library does not yet have the new technology, this chapter also explains how to search the printed catalogs and indexes. In addition, the chapter explains how to go beyond the library to collect information from a television program, an interview, a questionnaire, and other sources (see Section 2h, 62–70).

The design and holdings of your library will affect your research as will the demands of instructors, who expect you to do more than make a quick survey of encyclopedia articles; they demand a systematic review of both books and scholarly articles. This chapter is a broad overview, for instructors have a wide variety of assignments.

The search for sources is a serious task that will take time. Some leads will turn out to be dead ends; other leads will provide only trivial information. Some research will be duplicated, and a recursive pattern will develop; that is, you will go back and forth from reading, to searching indexes, and back again to reading. One idea modifies another, connections are discovered, and a fresh perspective emerges.

In every case, try to adjust research to your experience, moving from general reference works to the specialized indexes and abstracts in your field. In particular, examine the appendix, titled "Index to Reference Sources, by Discipline" (336–68). This appendix advises you about the best sources in psychology, art, black literature, myth and folklore, and many other disciplines. For example, it tells writers in the field of physical education to search *Educational Resources Information Center* (ERIC) and *Current Index to Journals in Education,* but it sends computer science students to *Information Services for Physics, Electro-technology, and Control* (INSPEC) and to *Computer Literature Index.* It highlights the best CD-ROM and data-base sources, as well as the best printed indexes. The appendix, then, can serve as a shortcut to sources. See also Section 2f, 49–58, for ways to access the specialized indexes of your discipline.

Your research strategy might conform to the following list, with adjustments for individual needs:

> *Searching available sources:* card catalog, indexes, abstracts, bibliographies, electronic sources, and reference books
>
> *Refining the topic and evaluating the sources:* browsing, reading abstracts, skimming articles, comparing sources, citation searches, and skimming books
>
> *Reading and note-taking:* books, articles, essays, reviews, computer printouts, and government documents

If your library has PACs and locally mounted CD-ROMs, you can accomplish with computers most of the preliminary search and much of the narrowing of your topic. Some sources will appear only on microforms.

Your preliminary work in the library serves several purposes:

1. It gives you an overview of the subject.
2. It provides a beginning set of bibliography cards or computer printouts.
3. It defines and restricts the subject.
4. It suggests the availability of sufficient source materials with diverse opinions and real disagreements.

2a LEARNING THE ORGANIZATION OF YOUR LIBRARY

Because of the sheer numbers of books and magazines, plus the vast array of retrieval systems, it will be to your advantage to tour the library and learn its arrangement—from the circulation desk to the reference room and on to the stacks. Ask about the availability of computer searches; these searches can save valuable time (see Section 2c, 31–37).

Circulation Desk

The circulation desk is usually located at the front of the library where personnel can point you in the right direction and later check out your books for withdrawal. Many libraries now have computerized machines for book checkout and electronic security devices to prevent theft. Whenever you cannot find a book on your own, check with the circulation desk or the computer terminals to determine whether it is checked out, on reserve, or lost. If the book is checked out, you may be able to place a hold order so the librarians will contact you when the book is returned. The circulation desk also handles most general business, such as renewals, collection of fines, and handling of keys and change for video and photocopying machines.

Reference Room

The reference room contains general and specialized encyclopedias, biographical dictionaries, and other general works to help refine your topic. Reference librarians know the best resources for most topics, so take advantage of their expertise. After your subject is set, the reference room provides the bibliographies and indexes for your search of the sources (see Section 2e, 43–49, and Section 2f, 49–59). In the reference room you should develop a set of bibliography cards (see Section 2b, 25–30) that will direct your search in books and articles. New technology, such as the *InfoTrac* system (see Sections 1b, 9–10, and 2c, 32–33), will help you narrow the topic and will provide a printed list of sources.

Card Catalog

Your library places its holdings in the card catalog by call numbers that will locate all books, listing them by author, title, and subject—all interfiled in one alphabetical catalog. Most libraries have updated the card catalog system with microfilm systems or computer terminals, generally referred to as PACs (see Sections 1b, 8–9, and 2c, 31).

CD-ROM and On-Line Data-Base Facilities

A new type of library is emerging, one with access to sources by local computer and also by national networks that dispatch information on almost any topic—bibliographies, abstracts, and even the full text of some articles. (See also Section 2c, 31–37.)

Reserve Desk

Instructors often place books and articles on reserve with short loan periods—two hours or one day—so that large numbers of students will have access to them. This system prevents one student from keeping an important, even crucial, book for two weeks while others suffer its absence. Your library may also place on reserve other valuable items that might otherwise be subject to theft, such as recordings, videotapes, statistical information, or unbound pamphlets and papers.

Stacks

The numerous shelves (stacks) of the library hold books organized by call numbers. Here, you can locate specific books and browse for others that interest you. However, libraries with closed stacks will not permit you into the stacks at all. Rather, you provide the call numbers of the books you want and an attendant will go into the stacks for you.

Interlibrary Loans

One library may borrow from another. The interlibrary loan service thereby supplements a library's resources by making materials available from other libraries. However, receiving a book or article by interlibrary loan may take seven to ten days. Ask your librarian about interlibrary loans available at your library. Networking with other libraries by means of the BITNET (Because It's Time Network) system is growing in popularity (see Section 2c, 36–37).

Photocopiers

Photocopying services provide a real convenience, enabling you to carry home articles from journals and reserve books that cannot be withdrawn from the library. However, copyright laws protect authors and place certain restrictions on the library. You may use the copying machines and duplicating services for your own individual purposes only, but be sure that you give proper credit to the sources (see Section 5h, 128–34, and also "Copyright Law," 213–14).

Nonprint Materials

Libraries serve as a storehouse for recordings, videotapes, film, microfilm, and many other items. These nonprint materials are usually listed in the general catalog or in a special catalog. If you know how to search this overlooked area of scholarly holdings, you may uncover a valuable lecture on cassette tape or a significant microfiche collection of manuscripts. Ask your librarian about vertical files, which contain articles clipped from magazines and newspapers and kept in alphabetical order by topic, not by title.

Archives and Special Collections

You might wish to design your research paper to take advantage of a special collection at your library. Many libraries are government depository libraries and house special collections and archives. Others, through donations and purchases, house collections of special import—the Robert Browning collection at Baylor University, the James Joyce holdings at Tulsa University, and so forth.

2b DEVELOPING A WORKING BIBLIOGRAPHY

A working bibliography is a list of the sources that you will need to read before drafting your paper. It demonstrates that enough source material exists on your topic. Too few sources indicates that your topic is too narrow or obscure. Too many sources indicates that you need a tighter focus.

Handwritten cards are traditional with the research paper assignment, but these have given way to new technology. Computer printouts can easily be substituted for a set of handwritten cards. Either way, you must eventually convert the bibliography material into MLA form (or some other academic form, such as APA style).

The card system (in which each source is recorded on an individual card) enables you to collate items easily into alphabetical order. Use a different system with approval of your instructor. For example, some researchers circle each source used from a computer printout. Others will paste the computer printout onto cards. Other researchers, with their own supply of paper, will have the computer print only one source per page, and then they use the rest of the sheet for transcribing notes from that source. Still others will create a "Works Cited" computer file and type in new sources daily.

A working bibliography has three purposes:

1. It locates articles and books on the subject for note-taking purposes.
2. It provides information for the in-text citations, as in the following example in MLA style:

> The numerous instances of child abuse among stepfathers has been noted by Stephens (31–32) and McCormick (419), which leads Austin to declare, "A mother who brings a non-father male into her home has statistics stacked against her and her children" (14).

3. It provides information for the final works-cited page (see Chapter 9, 250–79). Therefore, you should keep all bibliography cards and computer printouts until you have completed the paper.

Regardless of which method you use to keep track of your sources, each working bibliography entry should contain the following information, with variations, of course, for books, periodicals, and government documents:

1. Author's name
2. Title of the work

3. Publication information
4. Library call number
5. Optional: A note about the contents of the source

The cards displayed here and there throughout this chapter and Chapter 5 show correct MLA form of basic entries. For special bibliography forms (e.g., lecture, letter, or map), consult the index, which will direct you to the appropriate pages of Chapter 9 for examples of almost every imaginable type of bibliography entry. If needed, consult Chapters 10 and 11 for citation forms to fields of study other than literature and language.

Figure 5: Card for a government document cited in *InfoTrac,* in MLA style

```
TV violence antitrust exemption:-hearing
before the Committee on the Judiciary,
United States Senate, Ninety-ninth Con-
gress, second session on S. 2323. . . June
20, 1986
 Washington:-U.S. G.P.O:-1986
 Distributed to some depository libraries
in microfiche. Shipping list no.:86-998-
111, Item 1042-A, 1042-B (microfiche) MC#
87-5646
SenDoc #Y 4.J 89/2:S.hrs.98-925
```

United States. Cong. Senate.
TV Violence Antitrust
Exemption. Microfilm. 99th
Cong., 2nd sess. S. 2323.
Hearing before the Committee
on the Judiciary.
Washington, DC: APO, 1986.

Figure 6: Card for a book cited in the card catalog, in MLA style

PN
1992.8
P38
1988

Palmer, Edward L.
Television and America's children: a crisis of neglect/Edward L. Palmer.
—New York: Oxford University Press, 1988.

xxv, 194 p.; 22 cm.

Bibliography: p. 171–189
ISBN 0-19-505540-3

PN/1992.8/P38

Palmer, Edward L. Television and America's Children: A Crisis of Neglect. New York: Oxford UP, 1988.

Bibliography on pp. 171-89

Figure 7: Card for a magazine article cited in *Readers' Guide to Periodical Literature,* in MLA style (Note: see front of *Readers' Guide* for explanation of abbreviations)

Acid rain
Mapping the benefits of acid-rain controls [National Acid Precipitation Assessment Program] J. Raloff. *Science News* 138:165 S 15 '90

Raloff, J. "Mapping the Benefits of Acid-Rain Controls." Science News 15 Sept. 1990: 165.

Figure 8: Card for a journal article cited in *Social Sciences Index*, in MLA style

Television and children
See also
Television programs—Children's programs
Determinants of children's stereotyping: parental sex-role traits and television viewing. R. L. Repetti. bibl *Pers Soc Psychol Bull* 10:457-68 S '84
Developmental differences in responses to a television character's appearance and behavior. C. Hoffner and J. Cantor. bibl *Dev Psychol* 21:1065-74 N '85
Effect of maternal commentary in reducing aggressive impact of televised violence on preschool children. K. K. Mattern and B. W. Lindholm. *J Genet Psychol* 146:133-4 Mr '85
Effect of television violence on aggressiveness. J. L. Freedman. bibl *Psychol Bull* 96:227-46 S '84
Intervening variables in the TV violence-aggression relation: evidence from two countries. L. R. Huesmann and others. bibl *Dev Psychol* 20:746-75 S '84
Kungfu TV dramas influence children [China] *Beijing Rev* 28:9-10 Jl 15 '85
The relationship between reading and cognitive processing of television and radio. K. Pezdek and others. bibl *Child Dev* 55:2072-82 D '84
The socialization influence of television on black children. C. A. Stroman. bibl *J Black Stud* 15:79-100 S '84
Using a token-actuated timer to reduce television viewing. L. A. Jason. bibl *J Appl Behav Anal* 18:269-72 Fall '85

Pezdek, K., et al. "The Relationship between Reading and Cognitive Processing of Television and Radio." Child Development 55 (1984): 2072-82.

Figure 9: Card for a government document cited in the *Monthly Catalog of United States Government Publications,* in MLA style

> **Child care—United States—Statistics.**
> Who's minding the kids? : child care arrangements, winter 1984-85. (C 3.186:P-70/2/9), 87-13611

87-13611

C 3.186:P-70/2/9

Who's minding the kids? : child care arrangements, winter 1984-85. — Washington, D.C. : U.S. Dept. of Commerce, Bureau of the Census : For sale by Supt. of Docs., U.S. G.P.O., 1987.

IV, 41 p. : ill., 1 form ; 28 cm. — (Current population reports. Series P-70, Household economic studies ; no. 9) "Data from the Survey of Income and Program Participation." Shipping list no.: 87-334-P. "Issued May 1987." Includes bibliographical references. ●Item 142-C-8 S/N 703-088-00008-2 @ GPO, $2.75

1. Child care — United States — Statistics. 2. Children of working mothers — United States — Statistics. 3. Working mothers — United States — Statistics. 4. Day care centers — United States — Statistics. I. United States. Bureau of the Census. II. Series. OCLC 15716214

C3. 186: P-70/2/9

*United States. Dept. of Commerce.
Bureau of the Census. "Who's
Minding the Kids? Child Care
Arrangements." Winter 1984-85.
Washington, DC: GPO, 1987.*

Figure 10: Card for a newspaper article cited in *New York Times Index, 1991,* in MLA style (Note: be sure to record the year because it does not appear in the entries; find the title by reference to the printed issue or the microfilm)

MUSCULAR DYSTROPHY
   Dr. Peter Law of Cell Therapy Research Foundation, Memphis, in first effort to treat underlying genetic cause of muscular dystrophy, plans to inject child suffering from disease with billions of normal muscle cells in hope of providing him with healthy gene; human testing of unproven therapy spurs controversy over ethics and efficacy; photo (M), My 2,B,10:1

Kolata, Gina. "First Effort to Treat Muscular Dystrophy." New York Times 2 May 1991: B10

Figure 11: Card for an essay that appears in a book, cited in *Essay and General Literature Index, 1987,* in MLA style (Note: publisher's city is listed in a separate place)

Teen-agers *See* Youth
Television
   Birkerts, S. Television: the medium in the mass age. (*In* Birkerts, S. An artificial wilderness p369-81)
Telling of stories *See* Storytelling
Telotte, J. P.
   Through a pumpkin's eye; the reflexive nature of horror. (*In* American horrors: ed. by G. A. Waller p114-28)

Birkerts, Sven. An artificial wilderness; essays on 20th-century literature. Morrow 1987 430p ISBN 0-688-07113-9 LC 87-12383

Birkerts, Sven. "Television: The Medium in the Mass Age." An Artificial Wilderness: Essays on 20th Century Literature. Ed. S. Birkerts. Np.: Morrow, 1987. 369-81.

2c USING A COMPUTER SEARCH

During the 1990s, you will witness a major revolution in library reference materials. The bulky printed indexes have begun to disappear because newly created software programs now create files and perform retrospective searches on microcomputers. Do not be intimidated by the new technology; you will catch on quickly and surprise yourself at the increased pace of your research. For instance, rather than search the printed volumes of *Readers' Guide to Periodical Literature, Humanities Index,* and *Social Sciences Index,* you can now scan computer screens and get a bibliographic printout on any source that looks promising. Your library probably has one or more of these sources. You can learn to use the PAC and the CD-ROM facilities by yourself; use DIALOG and BITNET only after special training.

PAC

(See Section 1b, 8–9, for discussion and examples.) The computer will provide a printout similar to this one:

Figure 12: PAC printout
1. Author 2. Title of book
3. Publication facts 4. Physical description
5. Bibliography available
6. Location in the library stacks
7. Call number
8. Status of the book—this one should be on the shelf

```
BIBLIOGRAPHIC RECORD--No. 1 of 4 Entries
Found
Tuchscherer, Pamela.                  1
  TV interactive toys: the new high tech
threat to children. Fight back without a    2
gun, arm your child with knowledge
/ Pamela Tuchscherer: 1st ed.
Bend, Or.: Pinnaroo Pub; Distributed    3
by Gryphon House, 1988.
219 p.: ill.; 22cm.      4
Bibliography: p. 209-214.       5
LOCATION; Education stacks      6
CALL NUMBER: HQ 784/.T4/T83/1988       7
04/21/91 Not charged to a user.       8
```

Figure 13: Card in MLA style for a PAC printout

HQ/784/T4/T83/1988

Tuchscherer, Pamela. TV Interactive Toys: The New High Tech Threat to Children. Bend, OR: Pinnaroo, 1988.

Bibliography on pp. 209-14.

CD-ROM

(See Section 1b, 9–10, for discussion and examples.) Use the new technology to narrow your area of interest by entering your subject and a series of other topics—computers, desktop publishing, graphics; Robert Frost, women, dramatic monologue. The computer will find material that matches the set of three descriptive words and will then provide a printout similar to this one:

Figure 14: CD-ROM printout
1. Subject
2. Subtopics
3. Title of the article 4. Author
5. Volume number 6. Title of the periodical
7. Date 8. Page number 9. Length of the article (two pages)

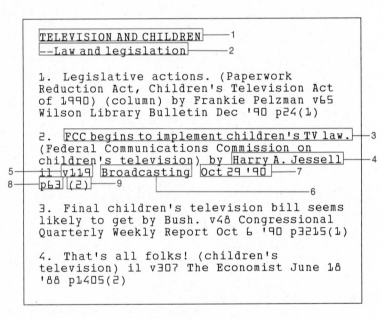

(See Figure 15, 33, for a sample bibliography card.)

Keep in mind that electronic publishing by means of CD-ROM extends beyond indexes and can also provide abstracts and the full text of many kinds of materials. Here is an example of information now available on CD-ROM. (Your library may have these particular diskettes and others.)

U.S. History (The full text of 107 history books with 1,000 images, tables, and maps)
Grolier's Encyclopedia
Shakespeare (complete works)
The Bible
Oxford English Dictionary (over 250,000 key words)
McGraw-Hill Reference Set (100,000 terms; 7,300 articles)

When using such CD-ROM diskettes, you can actually read information from the diskettes and get printouts of material. Mention that fact in your bibliography entry.

Figure 15: Card in MLA style for an article stored on a CD-ROM disk

Williams, T. Harry. *The Military Leadership of the North and South.* U.S. History on CD-ROM. Parsippany, NJ: Bureau Development, 1990.

DIALOG (and Other National Vendors)

DIALOG is an on-line data base using a telephone modem to connect your library with a national vendor. In brief, you or a librarian will connect your library's computer by phone to a national data-base vendor, such as DIALOG, who will transmit by telephone hookup various files. Such files include:

SCISEARCH (articles on scientific topics)
GEOBASE (articles on geology and earth sciences)
ERIC (articles on education and related topics)

(See the appendix, 336–68, for data-base sources for your field.)

Data-base searches for source materials are available at most libraries, but use this search only if you have the necessary experience or if the librarian has time to work with you. There may be a waiting list for users. Generally, librarians discourage undergraduate use of computer searches for small research papers (of eight pages or less) for one reason: the computer is cost effective on *large* retrospective searches, not on narrow research-paper subjects. After all, the data-base vendors charge the library about $75 per hour when logged on. You may be required to pay a fee from $1.00 up to $60.00, or more. Fee schedules vary from university to university because some libraries absorb the cost, while others charge for computer time. Determine these charges *in advance.*

An on-line data-base search involves several steps. First, you must answer a few questions about your search request:

1. What title would best describe your paper's content?
2. List specific topics, synonyms, closely related phrases, and alternate spellings of your subject—using scientific, technical, and common names.

3. List related topics to exclude in order to narrow the search.
4. Do you desire any foreign-language entries? Which languages?
5. Do you wish to limit citations to a specific publication year(s)?

Second, the computer librarian will use your answers to find the key words, called descriptors. (*Note:* To find key words, refer, if necessary, to a computer thesaurus, such as *Thesaurus of ERIC Descriptors* or *Thesaurus of Psychological Index Terms.*) Your three key terms will control a search of citations:

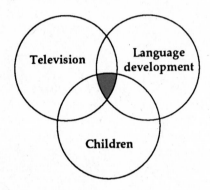

Third, you or the librarian must select an appropriate file, such as ERIC; log on by telephone modem; enter the subject profile; and begin the computer search.

```
File ERIC
    Set    Items      Description
    S1    101810      CHILDREN
    S2      1038      TODDLERS
    S3      6022      INFANTS
    S4     16123      TELEVISION
    S5      8339      LANGUAGE ACQUISITION
    S6      7176      LANGUAGE RESEARCH
    S7        13      (CHILDREN OR TODDLERS OR INFANTS)
                      AND TELEVISION AND LANGUAGE
                      ACQUISITION AND LANGUAGE
                      RESEARCH
```

Fourth, the computer will browse through records to select only those that match the subject profile; that is, articles that include all three descriptors: television, children, and language development. The computer will provide its report. You may then decide to order a copy of the abstract or, in some cases, the full text. (See "Searching an Index to Abstracts" in Section 2f, 52–54, for instructions about using an abstract as one of your sources.)

Figure 16: Two entries of 13 from a DIALOG search of the ERIC data-base

```
7/5/1


EJ338919 FL517179
        Television as a Talking Picture
        Book: A Prop for Language
        Acquisition. Lemish, Dafna; Rice,
        Mabel L. Journal of Child
        Language, v13 n2 p251-74 Jun 1986
        Language: English
        Document Type: JOURNAL ARTICLE
        (080); RESEARCH REPORT (143)


        Provides longitudinal observations
of young children's behaviors while
viewing television in their own homes
when the children were actively involved
in the process of language acquisition.
The observations show an overwhelming and
consistent occurrence of language-related
behaviors among children and parents in
the viewing situation.


7/5/2


EJ3009869 CS730477
        The Verbal Language of Public
        Television.
        Stevens, Kathleen C. Reading
        Horizons, v25 n2 p83-86 Win 1985
        Language: English
        Document Type: JOURNAL ARTICLE
        (080); RESEARCH REPORT (143)


        Analyzes the language of five
popular children's shows on public
television. Suggests that the public
television shows provide a superior
language model than that of commercial
television.
```

At the end of the data-base printout, you will find a summary and estimated cost for the search:

```
07jun91 13:36:59  User0118 Session B1155.1
      $1.98  0.066 Hrs
      $1.30 13 Type(s) in Format 5
  $3.28 Estimated cost File1
  $0.79 Tymnet
  $4.07 Estimated cost this search
Logoff: level 26.04.03 B  13:37:00
```

Your library may require you to pay a fee or it may not charge you at all.
    Again, you will need to convert each citation to MLA style.

**Figure 17: Card
in MLA style for
a data-base
source**

> Lemish, Dafna, and Mabel L. Rice.
> "Television as a Talking
> Picture Book: A Prop for
> Language Acquisition." *Journal
> of Child Language* 13 (1986):
> 251-74.

BITNET

BITNET and systems like it are worldwide electronic networks for the exchange of noncommercial information. If available, BITNET links your school's computer with those at most colleges in the United States and in some foreign countries. In most instances, you will need training, after which you will receive an academic account number and access to your university's mainframe, such as VAX. BITNET extends electronic mail to anyone on the network, so you could collaborate on a research project with somebody at another college, passing information back and forth. It also houses files for various purposes, such as:

```
BIALIK (Brandeis University), a poetry network
BIOSERVE (University of Maryland), a data and
     software network in biotechnology
COMSERVE (Rensselaer Polytechnic Institute), a
     network for users interested in the study of
     human communication
MACSERVE (Princeton University), a software
     repository of utilities, games, notes, and
     graphic items
```

Many files exist, so consult with your local BITNET representative about using the system. A message on BITNET will look similar to this example:

```
From: Glover@PennState.Bitnet 5-Jun-1991
To:  Tom Mitchell <Mitchell@UTAustin.BITNET>
Subj: Steroids and skeletal damage

Since our last correspondence I have interviewed
15 athletes, 12 male and 3 female, who have used
steroids extensively during the past four to six
years.  The subjects all attend a small college
nearby, so I will conduct follow-up interviews
both here and on site.  Only two have refused my
request for additional information.  Six have
agreed to magnetic resonance imaging so that we
```

can search for damage to the soft tissues in the
bones. With these subjects at hand, we can launch
our investigation in earnest.

Pete Glover
Penn State University

If you use a BITNET file in your paper, you will need a special citation (see Chapter 9, 278).

2d USING THE PRINTED CATALOG CARDS

Your library's card catalog may exist as a traditional card bank in file cabinets, not as a PAC computer file. In theory, it will include every book in the library filed by subject, author, and title. In truth, it is not always kept current with the latest holdings, so check with a librarian if you need a recently published work.

Begin your research at the catalog by searching a subject. Theoretically, every book available in the library will be filed together under one or more common headings, which will be printed at the top of the card. Thus, searching under the heading "Television and Children" would produce a number of books with a common heading.

Figure 18:
Subject cards

```
                    TELEVISION AND CHILDREN.
        HQ
        784   Durkin, Kevin.
        .T4      Television, sex roles, and children:
        D88   a developmental social psychological
        1985  account / Kevin Durkin--Milton
              Keynes; Philadelphia; Open University
              Press, c1985
```

```
                    TELEVISION AND CHILDREN.
        HQ
        799.2 Howe, Michael J. A., 1940-
        .T4      Television and children / Michael J.
        H68   A. Howe--London: New University
        1977b Education, 1977.
                 157 p.; 23 cm.
```

```
                    TELEVISION AND CHILDREN.
        HQ
        784   Cullingford, Cedric.
        .T4      Children and television / Cedric
        C84   Cullingford.--New York: St. Martin's
        1984  Press, 1984.
                 x, 239 p.; 23 cm.
                 Includes index.
                 ISBN 0-312-13235-2
```

The next procedure is to record call numbers onto appropriate cards.

Figure 19:
Sample
bibliography
card with call
number

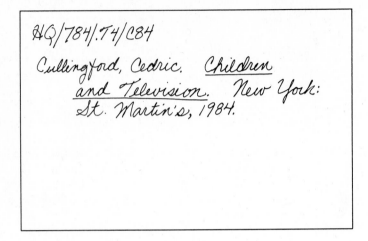

HQ/784/.T4/C84

Cullingford, Cedric. Children and Television. New York: St. Martin's, 1984.

You can also search the catalog by an author's name (the author card) or by the book's title (the title card). Both types are displayed below.

Figure 20: Author card (also called the main-entry card)
1. Library of Congress call number 2. Author 3. Title 4. Joint authors listed together 5. Place of publication 6. Publisher 7. Date of publication 8. Technical description 9. Note on contents of book 10. Separate cards filed under subject heading and under names of coauthor, publisher, and title 11. Library of Congress call number 12. Dewey Decimal number 13. Order number 14. Publisher of this card

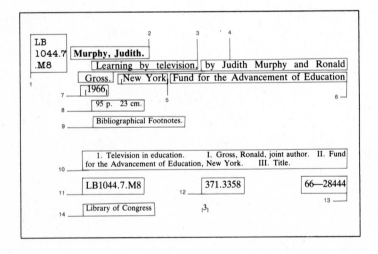

A sample bibliography card for this book follows:

Figure 21: Sample bibliography card

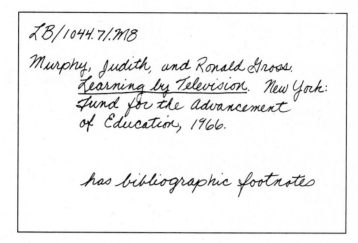

Record the *complete* call number—in this case, LB/1044.7/M8. Use the call number to find similar books. When you find this book in the stacks, you will discover other books on the subject. Also, watch especially for bibliographic notations, which will signal an additional list of sources on the subject.

Figure 22: Title card
1. Title, usually typed in black ink 2. Main-entry card filed under Becker, George J. 3. Subject headings under which you will find this same card

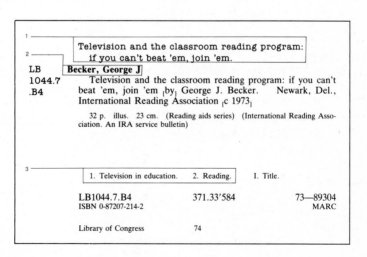

**Figure 22,
continued:
Sample title card**

LB/1044.7/B4

Becker, George. *Television and the Classroom Reading Program: If You Can't Beat 'em, Join 'em.* Newark: IRA, 1973.

Distinguishing the Dewey Decimal System from the Library of Congress System

Your library will classify its books by one of two systems—the Dewey Decimal System or the Library of Congress (LC) system. The Dewey system would list Murphy's *Learning by Television* (see Figure 20) with the number "371.3358/M9541." (The LC system uses "LB 1044.7.M8.") Understanding the system of your library will prove helpful.

Dewey Decimal System

The Dewey system has 100 divisions, as shown in Figure 23. The 300 category, labeled "Social Sciences," lists the subdivision "370 Education." The Murphy book (Figure 20) belongs to this category and is designated "371.3358."

Immediately below the Dewey classification numbers, librarians place a second line of letters and numerals based on the Cutter Three-Figure Author Table. For example, "M9541" is the author number for Murphy's *Learning by Television.* The letter "M" is the initial of the author's last name. Next, the Cutter table subclassifies with the Arabic numerals "954," and the lowercase "l" designates the first important letter in the title to distinguish this entry from similar books by Murphy. Thus, the complete call number for Murphy's book is "371.3358 / M9541." You must use the entire set to locate the book.

Figure 23: From the *Dewey Decimal Classification and Relative Index*

Second Summary*
The Hundred Divisions

000	Generalities	500	Natural sciences & mathematics
010	Bibliography	510	Mathematics
020	Library & information sciences	520	Astronomy & allied sciences
030	General encyclopedic works	530	Physics
040		540	Chemistry & allied sciences
050	General serials & their indexes	550	Earth sciences
060	General organizations & museology	560	Paleontology Paleozoology
070	News media, journalism, publishing	570	Life sciences
080	General collections	580	Botanical sciences
090	Manuscripts & rare books	590	Zoological sciences
100	Philosophy & psychology	600	Technology (Applied sciences)
110	Metaphysics	610	Medical sciences Medicine
120	Epistemology, causation, humankind	620	Engineering & allied operations
130	Paranormal phenomena	630	Agriculture
140	Specific philosophical schools	640	Home economics & family living
150	Psychology	650	Management & auxiliary services
160	Logic	660	Chemical engineering
170	Ethics (Moral philosophy)	670	Manufacturing
180	Ancient, medieval, Oriental philosophy	680	Manufacture for specific uses
190	Modern Western philosophy	690	Buildings
200	Religion	700	The arts
210	Natural theology	710	Civic & landscape art
220	Bible	720	Architecture
230	Christian theology	730	Plastic arts Sculpture
240	Christian moral & devotional theology	740	Drawing & decorative arts
250	Christian orders & local church	750	Painting & paintings
260	Christian social theology	760	Graphic arts Printmaking & prints
270	Christian church history	770	Photography & photographs
280	Christian denominations & sects	780	Music
290	Other & comparative religions	790	Recreational & performing arts
300	Social sciences	800	Literature & rhetoric
310	General statistics	810	American literature in English
320	Political science	820	English & Old English literatures
330	Economics	830	Literatures of Germanic languages
340	Law	840	Literatures of Romance languages
350	Public administration	850	Italian, Romanian, Rhaeto-Romanic
360	Social services; association	860	Spanish & Portuguese literatures
370	Education	870	Italic literatures Latin
380	Commerce, communications, transport	880	Hellenic literatures Classical Greek
390	Customs, etiquette, folklore	890	Literatures of other languages
400	Language	900	Geography & history
410	Linguistics	910	Geography & travel
420	English & Old English	920	Biography, genealogy, insignia
430	Germanic languages German	930	History of ancient world
440	Romance languages French	940	General history of Europe
450	Italian, Romanian, Rhaeto-Romanic	950	General history of Asia Far East
460	Spanish & Portuguese languages	960	General history of Africa
470	Italic languages Latin	970	General history of North America
480	Hellenic languages Classical Greek	980	General history of South America
490	Other languages	990	General history of other areas

*Consult schedules for complete and exact headings

Library of Congress Classification System

The LC system also uses a combination of letters and numerals for its divisions, as shown in Figure 24. Note that "L" designates "Education." Accordingly, Murphy's book is assigned "L" with the subentries "B1044.7." Then, like the Cutter system, LC uses the first letter of the author's last name and a number, "M8."

Figure 24: From
the Library of
Congress system

LIBRARY OF CONGRESS CLASSIFICATION SCHEDULES

For sale by the Cataloging Distribution Service, Library of Congress, Building 159, Navy Yard Annex, Washington, D.C. 20541, to which inquiries on current availability and price should be addressed.

A	General Works
B-BJ	Philosophy, Psychology
BL-BX	Religion
C	Auxiliary Sciences of History
D	History: General and Old World (Eastern Hemisphere)
E-F	History: America (Western Hemisphere)
G	Geography. Maps. Anthropology. Recreation
H	Social Science
J	Political Science
K	Law (General)
KD	Law of the United Kingdom and Ireland
KE	Law of Canada
KF	Law of the United States
L	Education
M	Music
N	Fine Arts
P-PA	General Philology and Linguistics. Classical Languages and Literatures
PA Supplement	Byzantine and Modern Greek Literature. Medieval and Modern Latin Literature
PB-PH	Modern European Languages
PG	Russian Literature
PJ-PM	Languages and Literatures of Asia, Africa, Oceania, American Indian Languages, Artificial Languages
P-PM Supplement	Index to Languages and Dialects
PN, PR, PS, PZ	General Literature, English and American Literature, Fiction in English. Juvenile Belles Lettres
PQ Part 1	French Literature
PQ Part 2	Italian, Spanish, and Portuguese Literatures
PT Part 1	German Literature
PT Part 2	Dutch and Scandinavian Literatures
Q	Science
R	Medicine
S	Agriculture
T	Technology
U	Military Science
V	Naval Science
Z	Bibliography, Library Science

Another example of each of these systems follows:

Library of Congress:
  TD   [Environmental Technology]
  833   [Air Pollution]
  .H48   [Author, Number]

Dewey Decimal:
  628.53   [Engineering and
          Allied Operations]
  H461u   [Author Number]

By using either set of numbers, depending upon your library, you would find this book:

Hesketh, Howard E. *Understanding and Controlling Air Pollution.* 2nd ed. Ann Arbor: Ann Arbor Science, 1974.

2e SEARCHING THE PRINTED BIBLIOGRAPHIES

In the reference section of your library, you will find many types of bibliographies. Some are general guides to a wide range of subjects. Some are bibliographic guides to other bibliographies, listed by subject. Some are specialized for narrow fields. You must make the decision about the research process.

Note: If you have a clearly defined topic, skip to 4*6*, "Using a Shortcut: Searching the Specialized Bibliographies." If you are still trying to formulate a clear focus, begin with general guides and gradually narrow to discipline-specific bibliographies, as discussed next.

Starting the Search with General Bibliographies

If you want to conduct a thorough, comprehensive search, one that reaches back in time, begin with one or two of the following general reference works, which contain bibliographies that direct you to sources on a wide range of subjects:

Besterman, Theodore. *A World Bibliography of Bibliographies.* 4th ed. 5 vols. Lausanne: Societas Bibliographica, 1963.

Hillard, James. *Where to Find What: A Handbook to Reference Service.* Rev. ed. Metuchen, NJ: Scarecrow, 1984.

McCormick, Mona. *The New York Times Guide to Reference Materials.* Rev. ed. New York: Times Books, 1985.

Sheehy, Eugene P., ed. *Guide to Reference Books.* 10th ed. Chicago: ALA, 1986.

These books identify standard, reliable bibliographies, by subject. For more current information, look up your subject in a recent issue or two of this source:

Bibliographic Index: A Cumulative Bibliography of Bibliographies. New York: Wilson, 1938–date.

This work, annually updated, provides page numbers to many different books and journals that contain bibliographies on numerous subjects.

Although *Bibliographic Index* originally covered only the years 1937–42, it is kept current by supplements. Here is an example from *Bibliographic Index* of 1991:

Figure 25: From *Bibliographic Index,* 1991
1. Subject heading 2. Entry of a book that contains a bibliography on children in literature 3. Specific pages on which bibliography is located

1 **Children in literature**
2 Hurst, Mary Jane. The voice of the child in American literature; linguistic approaches to fictional child language. University Press of Ky. 1990 p 154–75 3
Children in poetry *See* Children in literature
Children of alcoholic parents *See* Children of alcoholics
Children of alcoholics
Ackerman, Robert J., and Michaels, Judith A. Children of alcoholics; a bibliography and resource guide. 4th ed Health Communications 1990 141p

The book by Mary Jane Hurst features a 21-page bibliography (pp. 154–75). The entire book by Ackerman and Michaels is a bibliographic guide to source materials. You would need to write a bibliography card for locating this type of source.

Figure 26: Card listing a bibliographic source

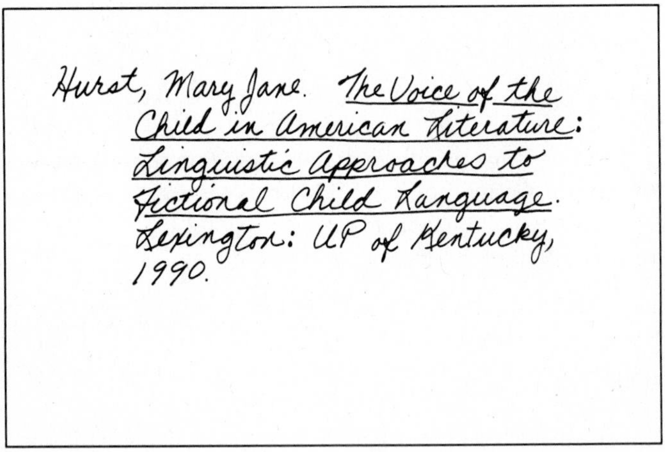
Hurst, Mary Jane. The Voice of the Child in American Literature: Linguistic Approaches to Fictional Child Language. Lexington: UP of Kentucky, 1990.

Using the Trade Bibliographies

Trade bibliographies, intended primarily for use by booksellers and librarians, can help you in three ways: (1) to discover sources not listed in other bibliographies or in the card catalog; (2) to locate facts of publication, such as place and date; and (3) to learn if a book is in print. Start with this work:

Subject Guide to Books in Print. New York: Bowker, 1957–date.

It supplies excellent subject indexes. Here is a sample from the 1990 issue.

Figure 27: From *Subject Guide to Books in Print,* **1990**
1. Subject
2. Author or editor 3. Title
4. Date of publication
5. Price
6. Publisher
7. International Standard Book Number (used when ordering)
8. Paperback book

1 — TELEVISION BROADCASTING–SOCIAL ASPECTS
2 — Adler, Richard, ed | Understanding — 3
Television: Essays on Television As
a Social and Cultural Force | 456p.
4 — 1981 | 49.95 (ISBN 0-275-90575-6, — 5
6 — C0575, Praeger Pubs] . Greenwood.
Arts & Cultural Programs on Radio &
Television (National Endowment for
the Arts Research Division Reports:
No. 4). 92p. 1977, pap. 9.00 (ISBN
7 — 0-89062-091-1 , Pub. by Natl Endow Arts).
Pub Ctr Cult Res.
Baran, Stanley J. The Viewer's
Television Book: A Personal Guide to
Understanding Television & Its
Influence. LC 80-81369. 109p. (Orig.)
8 — 1980. pap 6.95 (ISBN 0-936522-00-3).
Penrith.
Barwise, Patrick & Ehrenberg,
Andrew. Television & Its Audience.
224p. 1989. text ed. 39,95 (ISBN
0-8039-8154-6). pap. text ed. 16.95
(ISBN 0-8039-8155-4). Sage.

Make a note for any promising source (publishers' addresses are located separately).

Figure 28: Sample bibliography card for source found in *Subject Guide to Books in Print.* **The publisher's city will be listed in a separate section of** *Books in Print*

Adler, Richard, ed. Understanding
Television: Essays on Television
As a Social and Cultural
Force. Westport, CT: Praeger,
1981.

You may also use the following trade bibliographies:

Books in Print. New York: Bowker, 1948–date.

> This work provides an author-title index to the *Publishers' Trade List Annual* (New York: Bowker, 1874–date), which lists all books currently in print.

Publishers Weekly. New York: Bowker, 1872–date.

> This journal offers the most current publication data on new books and new editions.

Paperbound Books in Print. New York: Bowker, 1955–date.

> Use this work to locate paperback books on one topic, especially books available at local bookstores rather than the library.

Cumulative Book Index. New York: Wilson, 1900–date.

> Use this work to find complete publication data on one book or to locate *all* material in English on a particular subject.

The National Union Catalog: A Cumulative Author List. Ann Arbor: Edwards, 1953–date.

> Basically, this work is the card catalog in book form, but use it to find titles reported by other libraries.

Library of Congress Catalog: Books, Subjects. Washington, DC: Library of Congress, 1950–date.

> Use this work for its subject classification, which provides a ready-made bibliography to books on hundreds of subjects. Separate volumes are available for the years 1950–54, 1955–59, 1960–64, and annually thereafter.

Union List of Serials in Libraries of the United States and Canada. 3rd ed. New York: Wilson, 1965. Supplements, *New Serial Titles,* Washington, DC: Library of Congress, 1953–date.

> Consult this work to determine if a nearby library has a magazine or journal that is unavailable in a local library.

Ulrich's International Periodicals Directory. Ed. Merle Rohinsky. 15th ed. New York: Bowker, 1973.

> Use this work to locate current periodicals, both domestic and foreign, and to order photocopied reprints of articles.

Using a Shortcut: Searching the Specialized Bibliographies

If you have a well-developed research proposal (see Section 1C, 13–19), you can go directly to reference guides, bibliographies, and indexes for your discipline, as listed in the appendix of this book (336–68). For example, one student narrowed his subject to "The role of female talk show hosts on network television." He looked under the heading "Women's Studies" on page 368 of the appendix and found twenty sources, such as these four:

Women in Popular Culture: A Reference Guide
Womanhood Media: Current Resources about Women
Women in America: A Guide to Information Sources
Women's Studies Abstracts

You can use the appendix in the same manner. It is a shortcut to obtaining essential information for studies in almost any field, from black literature to folklore, to geology, and to many others. It not only lists but also annotates the most important sources.

Another student had narrowed his study to Robert Frost's poetry. The appendix, under "Language and Literature," directed him to *Magill's Bibliography of Literary Criticism,* an index to literary interpretations.

Figure 29: From *Magill's Bibliography of Literary Criticism* 1. Author and dates 2. Title of work 3. Citation to a critical work on the poem

> 1——— **ROBERT FROST (1874-1963)**
>
> 2—— **"After Apple Picking"**
>
> **Brooks, Cleanth.** *Modern Poetry and the Tradition.* Chapel Hill: University of North Carolina Press, 1939, pp. 114–116. Reprinted in *Robert Frost: An Introduction.* Edited by Robert A. Greenberg and James G. Hepburn, New York: Holt, Rinehart, 1961, pp. 3–5.
>
> **Brooks, Cleanth and Robert Penn Warren.** *Understanding Poetry.* New York: Holt, 1950, pp. 389–397.
>
> 3—— **Brower, Reuben A.** *The Poetry of Robert Frost: Constellations of Intention.* New York: Oxford University Press, 1963, pp. 23–27.
>
> **Conder, John J.** "'After Apple Picking': Frost's Troubled Sleep," in *Frost: Centennial Essays.* Edited by the Committee on the Frost Centennial of the University of Southern Mississippi. Jackson: University Press of Mississippi, 1974, pp. 171–181.

> Brower, Reuben A. *The Poetry of Robert Frost: Constellations of Intention.* New York: Oxford UP, 1963.
>
> see pp. 23–27

Works similar to Magill's bibliography are *Poetry Explication* and *Twentieth Century Short Story Explicator.* Language and literature students should also examine the *MLA International Bibliography,* which indexes literary interpretations annually, as demonstrated by the following entry:

Figure 30: From *MLA International Bibliography* 1. Author and dates 2. General articles about Frost's poetry 3. An article about a specific poem

---

FROST, ROBERT (1874-1963)

[8762] Iwayama, Tajiro. "Robert Frost." 439-475 in Ogata, Toshihiko, ed. *America Bungaku no Jikotenkai: 20-seiki no America Bungaku II.* Kyoto: Yamaguchi; 1982. ii, 638 pp.
[8763] Monteiro, George. "'A Way *Out* of Something': Robert Frost's Emily Dickinson." *CentR.* 1983 Summer; 27(3): 192-203. [†Relationship to Dickinson, Emily; includes comment on Bogan, Louise; MacLeish, Archibald; Wilbur, Richard.]

Poetry

[8764] Daniel, Charles L. "Tonal Contrasts in the Imagery of Robert Frost." *WGCR.* 1982 May; 14:12-15. [†Light imagery; dark imagery.]
[8765] Gage, John T. "Humour en Garde: Comic Saying in Robert Frost's Poetic." *Thalia.* 1981 Spring-Summer; 4(1): 54-61. [†Role of humor.]
[8766] Gonzàlez Martín, Jerónimo P. "Approximación a la poesía de Robert Frost." *CHA.* 1983 Apr.; 394: 101-153. [†Includes biographical information.]
[8767] Greenhut, D. S. "Colder Pastoral: Keats, Frost, and the Transformation of Lyric." *MHLS.* 1983; 6: 49-55. [†Lyric poetry. Use of pastoral. Treatment of landscape compared to Keats, John.]
[8768] Marks, Herbert. "The Counter-Intelligence of Robert Frost." *YR.* 1982 Summer; 72(4): 554-578. [†Treatment of revelation, concealment. Sources in Bible; Milton, John: *Paradise Lost.*]
[8769] Slights, William W. E. "The Sense of Frost's Humor." *CP.* 1983 Spring; 16(1): 29-42. [†Humor; comedy; relationship to reader.]
[8770] Sutton, William A. "Some Robert Frost 'Fooling'." *MTJ.* 1983 Spring; 21(3): 61-62. [†Relationship to Clemens, Samuel.]
[8771] Trikha, Manoramma B. *Robert Frost: Poetry of Clarifications.* Atlantic Highlands, NJ: Humanities; 1983. 259 pp. [†Use of metaphor; symbolism. Sources in Emerson, Ralph Waldo; James, William.]

Poetry/"Away"

[8772] Kau, Joseph. "Frost's 'Away!': Illusions and Allusions." *NMAL.* 1983 Winter; 7(3): Item 17.

Poetry/"Beech"

[8773] Will, Norman P. "Robert Frost's 'Beech': Faith Regained." *NMAL.* 1982 Spring-Summer; 6(1): Item 2.

Poetry/A Boy's Will (1913)

[8774] Wordell, Charles B. "Robert Frost from *A Boy's Will* to *North of Boston.*" *SALit.* 1983 June; 19: 1-13. [†*North of Boston.*]

In the reference room, search out encyclopedias for your field, such as *Encyclopedia of Social Work, Encyclopedia of Psychology,* or *Encyclopedia of Geographic Information.* Look especially for bibliographic lists at the end of encyclopedia articles.

Figure 31: Sample bibliography from the end of an article in *Encyclopedia Americana,* 1989 edition

Bibliography

Davis, Lenwood G., *I Have a Dream* (1969; reprint, Greenwood Press 1973).
Fisher, William H., *Free at Last* (Scarecrow 1977).
Garrow, David J., *Bearing the Cross: Martin Luther King, Jr., and the Southern Leadership Conference, 1955–1968* (Morrow 1986)
Lewis, David L., *King: A Critical Biography,* 2d ed. (Univ. of Ill. Press 1978).
Lincoln, C. Eric, ed., *Martin Luther King, Jr.: A Profile* (Hill & Wang 1970).

When you get into the stacks, look for bibliographies at the end of the books. Bibliographies also appear in most scholarly journals at the end of the articles. For example, students of history depend on the bibliographies within various issues of *English Historical Review* and students of literature find bibliographies in *Studies in Short Fiction.*

Skipping back and forth from indexes to periodicals and back to indexes is a normal procedure. In addition, the journals themselves often augment the indexes. For example, having chosen the subject *adoption,* one researcher noticed that a majority of sources was located in a few key journals. In that instance, going straight to a journal was a shortcut that produced a bibliography.

Figure 32: From *Index to Child Welfare* 1. Subject 2. Title of article 3. Author 4. Month and page number to volume 55

Administration
The Director of Professional Services: A Dilemma (Felitto) . . . . D 725

Adoption
Tayari: Black Homes for Black Children (Neilson) . . . . J 41
Another Road to Older Child Adoption (Rooney) . . . . N 665
The Sealed Adoption Record Controversy and Social
    Agency Response (Smith) . . . . F 73
Adoption Trends: 1971–1875 (Haring) . . . . Jy 501

Behavior Modification
Collaboration in Behavior Modification
    in a Day Care Center (Smith, Newcombe) . . . . My 357
Behavior Modification in a Residence and School for Adolescent
    Boys: A Team Approach (Scallon, Vitale, Eschenauer) . . . . . O 561

2f SEARCHING PRINTED INDEXES

An index furnishes the exact page number(s) to specific sections of books and to individual articles in magazines, journals, and newspapers. By tradition, a bibliography is a list of works on a single subject, but even a bibliography often has specific page numbers. Note that *Bibliographic Index* features both words: it *indexes* the page numbers of *bibliographies* to be found in various sources.

Fundamentally, there are five types of indexes: (1) indexes to literature in periodicals, (2) indexes to materials in books and collections, (3) indexes to materials in newspapers, (4) indexes to abstracts, and (5) indexes to pamphlets.

Of course, you can shortcut the process by going directly to the specialized indexes of your discipline, such as *Music Index* or *Philosopher's Index* (see 336–68).

Searching the Printed Indexes to Periodicals

For contemporary views in trade magazines, you can begin with a printed index to general magazines. (Use the CD-ROM facilities if they are available; see Section 2c, 32–33.)

Readers' Guide to Periodical Literature. New York: Wilson, 1900–date.

Although it indexes many nonscholarly publications, such as *Teen, Needle and Craft,* and *Southern Living,* the *Readers' Guide* also indexes important reading for the early stages of research in such magazines as:

Aging	*Foreign Affairs*	*Psychology Today*
American Scholar	*Foreign Policy*	*Science*
Astronomy	*Health*	*Science Digest*
Bioscience	*Negro History Bulletin*	*Scientific Review*
Business Week	*Oceans*	*SciQuest*
Earth Science	*Physics Today*	*Technology Review*

An entry from *Readers' Guide to Periodical Literature* follows.

Figure 33: From
Readers' Guide to
Periodical
Literature
1. Subject
2. Cross-references
3. Title 4. Author
5. Illustrated
6. Name of
periodical and
publication data

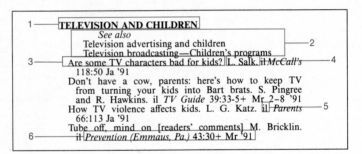

Bibliography cards would be made for any entries that looked promising. See Figure 7, page 27, for an example.

If your study involves a social science, consult the following index:

Social Sciences Index. New York: Wilson, 1974–date.

This work indexes journal articles for 263 periodicals in these fields:

anthropology	geography	political science
economics	law and criminology	psychology
environmental science	medical science	sociology

An example follows.

Figure 34: From
*Social Sciences
Index*
1. Subject
2. Cross-references
3. Title of article
4. Author
5. Name of
periodical and
publication data
6. Contains a
bibliography

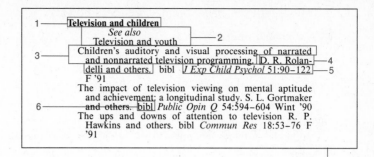

Researchers in the humanities should consult:

Humanities Index. New York: Wilson, 1974–date.

This work catalogs 260 publications in several fields:

archaeology	history	philosophy
area studies	language and literature	political criticism
classical studies	literary criticism	religion
folklore	performing arts	theology

For sources prior to 1974, consult two works that preceded *Humanities Index* and *Social Sciences Index:*

International Index. Vols. 1–18. New York: Wilson, 1907–65.

Social Sciences and Humanities Index. Vols 19–61. New York: Wilson, 1965–74.

Other general indexes of importance are the following:

> *Applied Science and Technology Index.* New York: Wilson, 1958–date.
>> An index for chemistry, engineering, computer science, electronics, geology, mathematics, photography, physics, and other related fields.
>
> *Biological and Agricultural Index.* New York: Wilson, 1947–date.
>> An index for biology, zoology, botany, agriculture, and related fields.
>
> *Education Index.* New York: Wilson, 1929–date.
>> An index for education, physical education, and related fields.
>
> *Business Periodicals Index.* New York: Wilson, 1958–date.
>> An index to many important journal articles for business, marketing, accounting, advertising, and related fields.
>
> *Recently Published Articles.* American Historical Association, 1976–date.
>> An index to journal articles in history and related fields.

In addition to these major indexes, you should examine especially the index for your discipline as listed in the appendix of this book (336–68).

Searching an Index to Abstracts

An index to abstracts, although it requires an extra step in the process, will actually speed your work. You can read an abstract in the reference room and only if the article appears promising will you need to pursue the search.

The appendix (336–68) lists, by discipline, the important indexes to abstracts, such as these:

> *Abstracts of English Studies*
> *Biological Abstracts*
> *Chemical Abstracts*
> *Psychological Abstracts*
> *Sociological Abstracts*

For example, a student with the topic *child abuse* used the index and then searched the appropriate issue of *Psychological Abstracts* for abstract number 9761.

If the source appears useful, this writer should (1) make an appropriate bibliography card and (2) quote from the original journal, *Forensic Reports.* If the journal is not available, the researcher may quote from the abstract and note that fact in the bibliography entry (see 272, 274, and 288). That is, let your readers know that you are citing from an abstract, not from the entire article. You may wish to read the abstracts to the dissertations of graduate students, as listed in this reference source:

> *Dissertation Abstracts International.* Ann Arbor: UMI, 1970–date (formerly *Microfilm Abstracts,* 1938–51, and *Dissertation Abstracts,* 1952–69).

Figure 35: From
Psychological
Abstracts, **1991**
1. Abstract
number
2. Author
3. Affiliation
4. Title of the
article 5. Citation
that tells you
where to find the
full article
6. Abstract of the
article

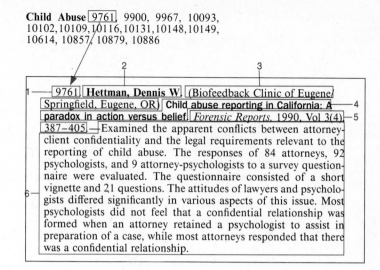

Look for issue No. 12, Part II, of each volume, for it contains the cumulated subject and author indexes for Issues 1–12 of the volume's two sections—*A: Humanities and Social Sciences* and *B: Sciences and Engineering.* For example, the index of *Dissertation Abstracts International A* of May 1991 lists the following entries under the heading "Children":

Figure 36: From
the index to
volume 46 of
Dissertation
Abstracts
International,
1991
1. Title of the
dissertation
2. Author 3. Page
number where
abstract can be
found

> **Children**
> Asking after lived experiences of and with
>   difficulty in physical activity in the life-
>   worlds of children and young people. *Con-*
>   *nolly, Maureen Frances Cecilia,* p.3666A
> Children's construction of meaning in a
>   thematic unit. *Baer McKay, Roberta Anne,*
>   p.3631A
> Growth and transverse line formation in
>   contemporary children, *Magennis, Ann L.,*
>   p.3805A
> Language development and children's un-
>   derstanding of emotion from facial expres-
>   sions. *Gross, Anne Louise,* p.3673A
> Media literacy and children's comprehension
>   of television advertisements and persuasive
>   written text. *Gathercoal, Paul Henry, Jr.*
> p.3617A

The abstract of Paul Gathercoal's dissertation is to be found on page 3617A. It appears as follows:

Figure 37: From *Dissertation Abstracts International*, 1991
1. Title of the dissertation
2. Author, degree earned, school, and date 3. Total number of pages of the dissertation
4. Faculty chair of the dissertation committee
5. Order number, in case you want to order a copy of the complete work 6. Abstract of the dissertation

1— **Media literacy and children's comprehension of television advertisements and persuasive written text.**
2— Gathercoal, Paul Henry, Jr. Ph.D. *University of*
3— *Oregon, 1990.* 258pp. Adviser: Edna P. DeHaven —4
5— **Order Number DA9111111**

The purpose of this study was to measure the effect a media literacy course of instruction had on children's comprehension of television advertisements and persuasive written text. This study differed from previous research inasmuch as a *process* approach to teaching and learning media literacy was implemented and measured for a significant effect on children's comprehension of television advertisements and their comprehension of persuasive written
6— text.

A nonequivalent control group design was used. Fifth grade students and teachers in two elementary schools within one public school district in Oregon participated in the study. One elementary school housed the treatment group and the other housed the control group. There were three separate classes of fifth grade students in each school. All students were pretested for comprehension of television advertisements and persuasive written text. The treatment and control groups' pretest and posttest mean scores were statistically tested for significant differences.

A t-test for independent groups, with alpha set at 0.05, was employed to measure statistical significance. Testing indicated that there was no discernible bias between the treatment and control groups' pretest mean scores for comprehension of television advertisements [$t(119) = .11$, $p = .915$] and persuasive written text [$t(113) = 1.18$, $p = .241$]. However the treatment group's posttest mean scores were significantly higher than the control group's mean scores for comprehension of television advertisements [$t(112) = 3.15$, $p = .001$] and persuasive written text [$t(111) = 2.54$, $p = .0065$]. The findings suggest that a *process* oriented media literacy course of instruction can significantly improve children's comprehension of television advertisements and persuasive written text.

An abstract, of course, only briefly summarizes the entire work. Again, you may cite the abstract in your paper if you include the word "abstract" or the name of the abstraction service in your works cited entry (see 272, 274). If you need the full dissertation and have time, order a copy of the complete work from University Microfilms, Inc., Ann Arbor, MI 48106.

Searching for Essays Within Books

Some essays get lost within collections and anthologies. You can find these essays listed by subject in the following reference work:

> *Essay and General Literature Index, 1900–1933.* New York: Wilson, 1934. Supplements, 1934–date.

This reference work indexes material within books and collections of both a biographical and a critical nature. This index enables you to find essays *within* books that you might otherwise overlook. Here is an example from *Essay and General Literature Index,* June 1991, showing the entry for A. J. Raboteau's article, "Martin Luther King, Jr., and the Tradition of Black Religious Protest," which appears on pages 46–65 of a book titled *Religion and the Life of the Nation,* edited by R. A. Sherrill.

Figure 38: From *Essay and General Literature Index,* 1991
1. Subject
2. Author of article 3. Title of article or chapter in the book
4. Title of the book in which the article appears
5. Editor of the book 6. Page numbers of the article 7. Separate entry for Sherrill's book 8. Separate entry for the publisher

Note: You will need all three citations from *Essay and General Literature Index* in order to write the bibliography entry for the works-cited page (see Chapter 9, 258–59).

Searching the Biographical Indexes for Authors and Personalities

When writing about a specific person, the reference section will provide multiple sources, some specific to a field, such as *American Men and Women of Science: The Physical and Biological Sciences* or *Who's Who in Hard Money Economics.* The appendix of this book (336–68) lists biographical studies by discipline. Several general indexes have value.

Biography Index: A Quarterly Index to Biographical Material in Books and Magazines. New York: Wilson, 1946/47–date.

Biography Index is a starting point for studies of famous persons. It gives clues to biographical information for people of all lands. Note the following short excerpt from *Biography Index:*

Figure 39: From
Biography Index,
1991
1. Subject 2. Dates of subject's birth and death 3. Subject's profession 4. Author of the biography 5. Title of the biography 6. Publisher 7. Date of publication 8. Number of pages 9. Contains a bibliography 10. Illustrated 11. Publication data for a periodical

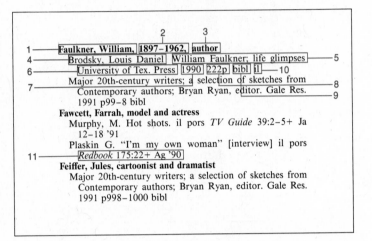

Current Biography Yearbook. New York: Wilson, annually.

This work provides a biographical sketch of important people. Most articles are three to four pages in length and, of importance, they include a short bibliography at the end.

Contemporary Authors. Detroit: Gale, annually.

Use this biographical guide for current writers in fiction, nonfiction, poetry, journalism, drama, motion pictures, television, and a few other fields. It provides a thorough overview of most contemporary writers, giving a list of writings, biographical facts (including a current address and agent); sidelights; and, in many cases, an interview by *CA* with the author. Most entries include a bibliography of additional sources to the writer.

Dictionary of Literary Biography. Detroit: Gale, 1978–date.

In more than 100 volumes, this work provides a profile of thousands of writers under such titles as these:

American Humorists, 1800–1950
Victorian Novelists after 1885
American Newspaper Journalists, 1926–1950

A comprehensive index will help you locate the article on your author. Use *Dictionary of Literary Biography* not only for the profile of the author but also for the bibliography that ends each essay. Shown below is a portion of the bibliography on poet Anne Sexton.

Figure 40:
Sample excerpt
from *Dictionary*
of *Literary*
**Biography*

WORKS OF ANNE SEXTON

POEMS
To Bedlam and Part Way Back. Boston: Houghton Mifflin, 1960.
All My Pretty Ones. Boston: Houghton Mifflin, 1962.
Selected Poems. London: Oxford University Press, 1964.
Live or Die. Boston: Houghton Mifflin, 1966; London: Oxford University Press, 1967.
Poems. London: Oxford University Press, 1968. With Thomas Kinsella and Douglas Livingstone.
Love Poems. Boston: Houghton Mifflin, 1969; London: Oxford University Press, 1969.
Transformations. Boston: Houghton Mifflin, 1971; London: Oxford University Press, 1972.
The Book of Folly. Boston: Houghton Mifflin, 1972; London: Chatto and Windus, 1974.
The Death Notebooks. Boston: Houghton Mifflin, 1974; London: Chatto and Windus, 1975.
The Awful Rowing Toward God. Boston: Houghton Mifflin, 1975; London: Chatto and Windus, 1977.
45 Mercy Street, edited by Linda Gray Sexton. Boston: Houghton Mifflin, 1976; London: Martin Secker and Warburg, 1977.
Words for Dr. Y, edited by Linda Gray Sexton. Boston: Houghton Mifflin, 1978.

CHILDREN'S BOOKS (with Maxine Kumin)
Eggs of Things. New York: Putnam, 1963.
More Eggs of Things. New York: Putnam, 1964.
Joey and the Birthday Present. New York: McGraw-Hill, 1971.
The Wizard's Tears. New York: McGraw-Hill, 1975.

BIBLIOGRAPHY

Northouse, Cameron, and Thomas P. Walsh. *Sylvia Plath and Anne Sexton: A Reference Guide.* Boston: G. K. Hall and Co., 1974

CRITICISM AND REVIEWS

Alvarez, A. *Beyond All This Fiddle: Essays, 1955–57,* New York: Random House, 1969.
Boyers, Robert. *"Live or Die:* The Achievement of Anne Sexton." *Salmagundi,* 2, no. 1:41–71 (Spring 1967). Reprinted in *Anne Sexton, The Artist and Her Critics,* edited by J. D. McClatchy. Bloomington and London: Indiana University Press, 1978 (hereafter referred to as McClatchy).
Dickey, James. "Five First Books." *Poetry,* 97, no. 5:318–19 (February 1961). Reprinted in his *Babel to Byzantium.* New York: Farrar, Straus and Giroux, 1968. Also in McClatchy.
Fields, Beverly. "The Poetry of Anne Sexton." In *Poets in Progress,* edited by Edward Hungerford. Evanston Ill.: Northwestern University Press, 1967. Pp. 251–85.
Gullans, Charles. "Poetry and Subject Matter: From Hart Crane to Turner Cassidy." *The Southern Review,* 7, no. 2:497–98 (Spring 1970). Reprinted in McClatchy.
Howard, Richard. "Anne Sexton: 'Some Tribal Female Who Is Known but Forbidden.'" In his *Alone with America: Essays on the Art of Poetry in the United States Since 1950.* New York: Atheneum, 1971. Pp. 442–50.

You would need to make bibliography cards for any sources that show promise for your research.

Searching the Newspaper Indexes

Newspapers provide contemporary information. One has an index that is especially helpful:

The New York Times Index. New York: New York Times, 1913–date.

It indexes the *New York Times* and thereby indirectly indexes most newspapers by revealing the date on which the same news probably appeared in other newspapers. Many libraries have the *New York Times* on microfilm (see Section 2f, 59). A search for "Water Pollution" produced this list:

Figure 41: From *New York Times Index,* 1991
1. Subject
2. Description of the article
3. Length of the article: (S) short, (M) medium, (L) long 4. Date, section number, page number, and column (February 3, section I, page 14, column 2)

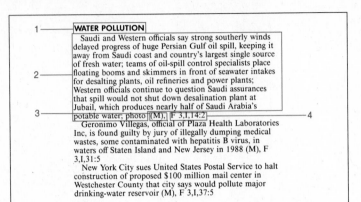

Note: The year is not given in the entries, so get it from the front of the volume you use; in this case, 1991. The title is not listed; you must record it when you read the article. For a sample bibliography entry, see Figure 10, 30. Other important newspaper indexes are:

Wall Street Journal Index. New York: Dow Jones, annually.

Bell and Howell's Index to the Christian Science Monitor. Wooster, OH: Christian Science Publishing Society, annually.

Official Index [to *The London Times*]. London: *Times,* 1907–date.

National Newspaper Index. Belmont, CA: Information Access, 1979–date. Provides a monthly index to the *Christian Science Monitor, Los Angeles Times, New York Times, Wall Street Journal,* and *Washington Post.*

Searching the Pamphlet File and Pamphlet Indexes

Your librarians scan newspapers, bulletins, pamphlets, and miscellaneous materials for items of interest. They clip these and file them alphabetically by subject. You should make the pamphlet file a regular stop during preliminary investigation. Sometimes it is called the vertical file. It will have clippings on many topics, such as:

"Asbestos in the Home"
"Carpel Tunnel Syndrome"
"Everything Doesn't Cause Cancer"
"Medicare and Coordinated Care Plans"

The principal index to published pamphlets is:

> *Vertical File Index: A Subject and Title Index to Selected Pamphlet Material.* New York: Wilson, 1932/35–date.

Your library may not own many of the items listed by this index, but it gives a description of each entry, the price, and the information for ordering the pamphlet. Remember, too, that the federal government publishes many pamphlets and booklets on a vast array of topics (see Section 2g). National publications, such as *SIRS,* collect articles on special topics and reprint them as one unit on a special subject (e.g., abortion, AIDS, prayer in schools, or pollution). With *SIRS* and similar collections, you will have 10 or 12 articles readily available. (See 258–59 for proper citation of such collections.)

Using the Microforms

Libraries have a choice when ordering periodicals: they can buy expensive printed volumes or purchase inexpensive microfilm versions of the same material. Most libraries have a mixture of the two. Your library will specify how journals and magazines are housed.

In particular, most libraries now store national newspapers, weekly magazines, and dissertation abstracts on microfilm. Use a microfilm reader, usually located near the microfilm files, to browse through the articles. Should you need a hard copy of a microfilmed article, the library will have the means to copy it for you.

Your library may also house guides to special microfilm holdings, which carry such titles as *American Culture 1493–1806: A Guide to the Microfilm Collection* or, perhaps, *American Periodicals 1800–1850: A Guide to the Microfilm Collection.* The point is this: every library has its own peculiar holdings of microfilm and microfiche materials.

2g SEARCHING THE INDEXES TO GOVERNMENT DOCUMENTS

All branches of the government publish massive amounts of material. Many documents have great value for researchers, but locating the material can be difficult and frustrating. Look especially for the following:

> U.S. Superintendent of Documents. *Monthly Catalog of United States Government Publications.* Washington, DC: Government Printing Office, 1895–present. Monthly.

It has an index called "Title Keyword" that provides the catalog number:

**Figure 42: Index
to** *Monthly
Catalog of
United States
Government
Publications*
1. Subject
2. Partial title
3. Item number
4. Author 5. Title
6. Publication
facts
7. Description
8. Subject
classifications

1—children	/, Defining the rights of —2	3— **91-12247**
"	:, A report on shortchanging	**91-12490**
"	, Health care for	**91-12529**
"	and youth /, Exceptional Asian	**91-10999**
"	have emotional handicaps /, Taking charge	**91-11012**
"	prior to school entrance /, An Ecological	**91-11004**
"	's outerwear, industries 2341, 2342, 2353,	**91-10738**
"	's underwear; headwear; children's outerwe	**91-10738**
"	, United States, 1988 /, Developmental, le	**91-11399**
"	, Youth, and Families, House of Representa	**91-12379**
"	, Youth, and Families, One Hundred First C	**91-12372**
"	, Youth, and Families, U.S. House of Repre	**91-12379**

91-12247 —3
S 1.71/4:1237
4—Smith, Christopher H. 1953–
5——Defining the rights of children/ Christopher H. Smith.—
6——Washington, D.C. : U.S. Dept. of State, Bureau of Public Affairs,
Office of Public Communication, Editorial Division, [1989]

3 p. ; 28 cm.—(Current policy ; no. 1237) Caption title.
7—Shipping list no.: 90-101-P. "December 1989"—P. 3. ●Item
877-C.

1. Children's rights —International cooperation. 2. Human
rights —International cooperation. I. United States. Dept. of
8—State. Office of Public Communication. Editorial Division. II.
Title. III. Series: United States. Dept. of State. Bureau of Public
Affairs. Current policy ; no. 1237. OCLC 23089524

If you make a bibliography card, include the ordering number because your
library may not have the bulletin. If time permits, you can order it from the
Superintendent of Documents, Government Printing Office, Washington,
DC 20402. (See also Figure 50, 66.)

**Figure 43: Card
for a government
document cited
in the** *Monthly
Catalog of
United States
Government
Publications,* **in
MLA style**

S1.71/4:1237

Smith, Christopher H. Defining
the Rights of Children.
Washington, DC: U.S. Dept.
of State, 1989.

A second place to look for government publications is:

Public Affairs Information Service Bulletin. New York: P.A.I.S., semi-monthly.

A sample entry from this work, known as *PAIS,* is shown below:

Figure 44: From *Public Affairs Information Service Bulletin,* 1991
1. Subject 2. Place 3. Citation to author, title, and date 4. Contains a bibliography and tables 5. Order number 6. Cost 7. Description of article 8. Original source of article

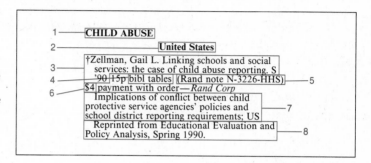

If this 15-page booklet looks promising, record it on a card. If your library does not house that special bulletin, you can write your request to Rand Corporation or to the Superintendent of Documents, Government Printing Office, Washington, DC 20402. Most documents are free and will be shipped immediately.

Search out other indexes in the government documents section of your local library and learn their resources. In many libraries, a separate card catalog lists governmental holdings. The Government Printing Office, like other publishers, is converting to CD-ROM, so look for government documents on a computer if one is available.

The *Congressional Record* is the key publication of Congress. Senate and House bills, documents, and committee reports are published daily with regular indexes. The *Congressional Record* should be available at your library. If not, write the Government Printing Office for free copies of specific legislation.

Public Papers of the Presidents of the United States is the publication of the Executive Branch. All members of the president's cabinet publish enormous amounts of vital information. Again, your best source for information and documents is the Superintendent of Documents. The U.S. Code and the Constitution are the primary publications of the legal branch. The Supreme Court regularly publishes decisions, codes, and other rulings, as do appellate and district courts. State courts also publish rulings and court results on a regular basis.

See Section 9e, 271–72, for correct methods of writing bibliography citations to government documents of all three branches.

2h COLLECTING DATA OUTSIDE THE LIBRARY

Conduct primary research in the laboratory and in the field whenever your topic permits it. Without doubt, the library is an invaluable source of information when writing a research paper, but material exists in other places. Converse with other people in person or by letter, and, if time permits, conduct in-depth interviews or use a questionnaire. Watch for television specials, visit the courthouse archives, and, perhaps, do some empirical research under the guidance of an instructor (see Section 2h, 69–70).

Interviewing Knowledgeable People

Talk to persons who have experience about your subject. Personal interviews are time consuming, but they can elicit valuable in-depth information. It will be information that few others will have.

If necessary, post a notice soliciting help: "I am writing a study of local folklore. Wanted: people who have a knowledge of regional tales." Look to organizations for experienced persons (for example, the writer on folklore might contact the county historian, a senior citizens' organization, or a local historical society).

Prepare in advance several pertinent, focused questions. For accuracy, use a tape recorder (with permission of the person interviewed, of course). Conduct telephone interviews only if you find them necessary, but they will not be as thorough as interviews conducted face to face.

Do not base your conclusions on the evidence of one person; consult with several people and weigh their opinions just as you consider the evidence in various written sources.

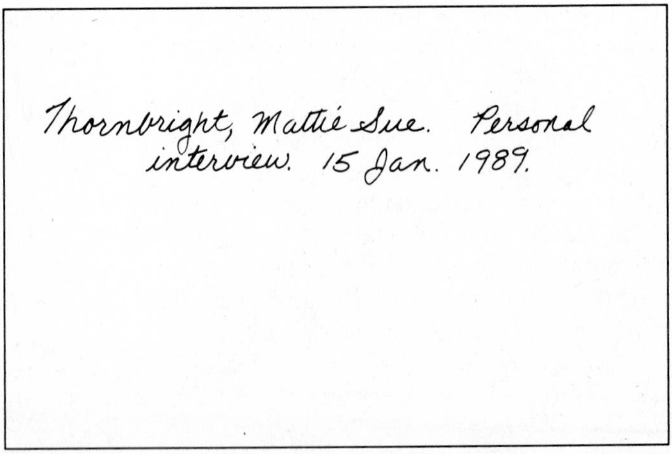

**Figure 45:
Sample
bibliography
card for an
interview**

Thornbright, Mattie Sue. Personal
interview. 15 Jan. 1989.

Keep in mind three criteria for the interview:

1. Consult with experienced persons.
2. Be courteous and on time for interviews.
3. Prepare a set of questions for initiating the interview.

Writing Letters

Correspondence provides a written record for research. Ask pointed questions so that correspondents will respond directly to your central issues. As a courtesy, provide a self-addressed, stamped envelope. Note this example:

```
Mrs. M. W. Beach
512 Meadowlark
Clarksville, TN 37041

Dear Mrs. Beach:

I am a college student conducting research into folklore of
Montgomery County.  In particular, I need specifics on
tales of ghosts.  Do any ghosts haunt homes in this region?
Which homes?  Do the ghosts have names?

I have enclosed a self-addressed, stamped envelope, but you
may telephone me with the information if that method would
be more convenient for you.

Sincerely yours,

Peggy Thompson
560 Thompson Hall
APSU Station
Clarksville, TN 37041
555-4657
```

Figure 46: Sample bibliography card for a letter

Beach, Betty Kay. Letter to the author. 5 Apr. 1988.

Examining Audiovisual Materials

Important data can be found in audiovisual materials: films, filmstrips, music, phonograph recordings, slides, audio cassettes, and video cassettes. You will find these sources both on and off campus. Consult such guides as *Educators Guide* (for films, filmstrips, and tapes), *Media Review Digest* (for nonprint materials), *Video Source Book* (for video catalogs), *The Film File,* or *International Index to Recorded Poetry.*

Figure 47: Sample bibliography card for audiovisual material

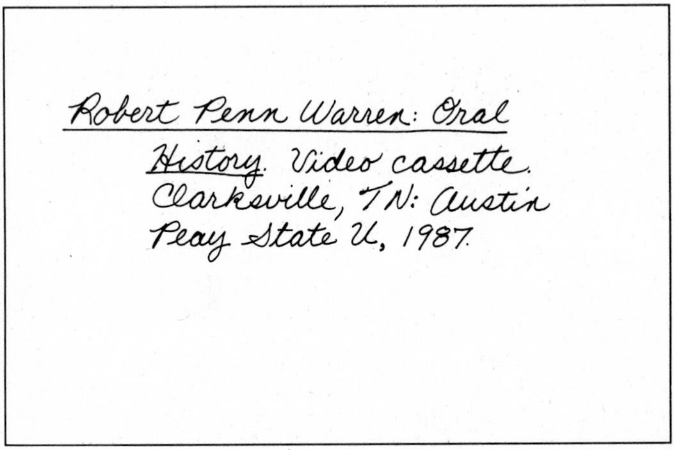

Robert Penn Warren: Oral History. Video cassette. Clarksville, TN: Austin Peay State U, 1987.

Watching Television and Listening to Radio Programs

Numerous programs of quality are available if you watch the schedules carefully. In particular, check the programming of the Public Broadcast System. In addition, national and local talk shows often discuss important issues. Remember to keep accurate notes relating to names, statements, and program title. You will need to cite these sources in a bibliography entry.

In order to have the necessary bibliographic information, make it a habit to record vital information on programs. Since you never know when a program will serve your specific needs, keep a notepad and pencil handy. As a minimum, record title, broadcaster, and date.

Figure 48:
Sample
bibliography
card for a
television
program

"Newsmaker Sunday." CNN News.
CNN, Atlanta. 12 Jan. 1992.

Attending Lectures and Public Addresses

Watch bulletin boards and the newspaper for a featured speaker who might visit your campus. Take careful notes and, if necessary, request a copy of the lecture or speech. Remember, too, that many lectures, reproduced on video, will be available in the library or in departmental files.

Figure 49:
Sample
bibliography
card for a lecture

Petty-Rathbone, Virginia.
"Edgar Allan Poe and the
Image of Ulalume." Lecture.
U. of Kentucky, 1991.

Investigating Local Government Documents

Search the files on three levels of government: county, state, and federal. As a constituent, you are entitled to the services of local, state, and federal officials. If your topic demands it, contact the mayor's office, attend a city council assembly, or search out printed documents.

First, public records in your county will disclose facts on each election, census, marriage, birth, and death. These archives will include wills, tax rolls, military assignments, deeds to property, and much more. A trip to the local courthouse can, therefore, be rewarding, helping you trace the history of the land and its people.

Second, the state will have an archival storehouse for its records. These, too, are available for public review. For example, you might investigate certain legislative documents that have affected your country.

Third, a U.S. senator or representative can send booklets printed by the Government Printing Office. A list of these materials, many of which are free, appears in a monthly catalog issued by the Superintendent of Documents, *Monthly Catalog of United States Government Publications* (Washington, DC: Government Printing Office, 1895–date). In addition, you can gain access to the National Archives Building in Washington, D.C., or to one of the regional branches in Atlanta, Boston, Chicago, Denver, Fort Worth, Kansas City, Los Angeles, New York, Philadelphia, or Seattle. Their archives contain court records and government documents that you can review in two books: *Guide to the National Archives of the United States* and *Select List of Publications of the National Archives and Record Service.* You can borrow some documents on microfilm if you consult *Catalog of National Archives Microfilm Publications.*

Figure 50:
Sample
bibliography
card for a
government
document

S/N 003-001-91481-6

United States. Dept. of Commerce.
Bureau of the Census.
Evaluation of the Population
Estimation Procedures for
Counties, 1980. Washington, DC:
GPO, 1986.

Reading Personal Papers

Search out letters, diaries, manuscripts, family histories, and other personal materials that contribute to your study. In particular, the college library will house private collections. The city library and the county historian may have private papers stored with archival documents. Most towns and cities have private citizens who collect such documents; search them out and take advantage of this rich source of eyewitness accounts.

**Figure 51:
Sample
bibliography
card for personal
papers**

Joplin, Lester. "Notes on
Robert Penn Warren."
Unpublished papers, 1991.

Conducting a Survey with a Questionnaire

Questionnaires can produce accurate data that you can tabulate and analyze quickly. However, various degrees of bias can creep into the questionnaire unless you remain objective. If necessary, let somebody else proofread the questions. Be on guard against your own prejudices, for the results of your questionnaire may prove only what you want them to prove. The loaded question is a common error. Note, for example, this question:

```
Do you believe in supporting the morality of America by

protesting against abortion clinics?
```

The question assumes that a "no" answer will come only from those who have no respect for the morality of America.

Be on guard against questions that are too personal (Do you ever smoke marijuana? How often?). Change them to open-ended questions (Do your friends ever smoke marijuana in your presence? How often?).

Note: Space will not allow this text to explain the necessary techniques of conducting a formal survey. A random sampling, for example, will survey every part of a selected population by age, sex, race, education, income, residence, and so forth. You will need experience with tests and measurements, as well as statistical analysis, if you wish to conduct a formal questionnaire and analysis.

Figure 52:
Sample
bibliography
card for a
questionnaire

> Mason, Valerie, and Sarah
> Mossman. "Child Care
> Arrangements of Parents
> Who Attend College."
> Questionnaire. Knoxville:
> U of Tennessee, 1989.

Writing a Case Study

A case study is a formal report based on your examination of a prearranged subject. For example, it might require you to examine patterns of behavior in order to build a profile of a person as based on biographical data, interviews, tests, and observation. The case study then becomes evidence for your research paper. Space does not permit this text to explore the ways and means of conducting the case study, and you should not begin examining any subject without supervision. Therefore, conduct such work only under the guidance of your instructor or supervisor.

Figure 53:
Sample
bibliography
card for a case
study

> Freed, Gregory. "Johnny Robinette."
> Case Study. Cleveland:
> Case Western Reserve U, 1988.

Conducting Experiments, Tests, and Measurements

Empirical research, usually performed in a laboratory, can determine why and how things exist, function, or interact with one another. Your paper will explain your methods and findings in pursuit of a hypothesis (your thesis). An experiment thereby becomes primary evidence for your paper.

For example, your experiments with a species of reptiles at a test site near Cherokee Lake would require you to write a report that provided four distinct parts:

1. *Introduction* to explain the design of your experiment:

   Present the point of the study.
   State the hypothesis and how it relates to the problem.
   Provide the theoretical implications of the study.
   Explain the manner in which this study relates to previously
      published work.

2. *Method* to describe what you did and how you conducted the study:

   Describe the subjects who participated, whether human or
      animal.
   Describe the apparatus to explain your equipment and how
      you used it.
   Summarize the procedure in execution of each stage of your
      work.

3. *Results* to report your findings:

   Summarize the data that you collected.
   Provide the necessary statistical treatment of the findings with
      tables, graphs, and charts.
   Include findings that conflict with your hypothesis.

4. *Discussion* to explain the implications of your work:

   Evaluate the data and their relevance to the hypothesis.
   Interpret the findings, as necessary.
   Discuss the implications of the findings.
   Qualify the results and limit them to your specific study.
   Make inferences from the results.

Your experiment and the writing of the report will require the attention of your instructor. Seek his or her advice often. Space does not allow this text to explore the many techniques and options available to you for original research.

**Figure 54:
Sample
bibliography
card for test
results**

King, Ralph. "Frequency Graph."
New Brunswick, NJ:
Rutgers U, 1988.

3 *Organizing Ideas and Setting Goals*

Now that you have completed an initial search of library sources, you need to organize your ideas so that reading and note-taking will relate directly to your specific needs. Your notes must grow from carefully drawn plans, which may include a research proposal, a list of ideas or questions, a set of code words, or a rough outline. In addition, the design of your study should match an appropriate academic model, called a *paradigm*. Possible paradigms are discussed in Section 3b, 78–81. This chapter also includes instructions for crafting a final outline to keep your manuscript well ordered.

3a CHARTING A DIRECTION AND SETTING GOALS

Do not plunge too quickly into note-taking. You need to know *what* to look for and *why* you need it. Setting goals by framing your key ideas into a chart or outline will serve you well during both research and writing. Thereby, you can place code words on your notes to fit and fulfill the demands of your manuscript. What follows are various ways to give direction to your research.

Using Your Research Proposal to Direct Your Note-Taking

Your research proposal (see Section 1c, 13–19) may mention several issues and thereby outline the code words for reading and note-taking. The last sentence of this research proposal demonstrates the point:

> I want to address young people who think they need a
> tan in order to be beautiful. Preliminary investigation
> indicates that ultraviolet radiation causes severe skin
> damage that is cumulative; that is, it builds adverse
> effects with each exposure. My role is to investigate the
> facts and explore options for those who desire a good tan.
> I need information on skin types, sun exposure, tanning
> beds, and types of skin damage.

This proposal names four topics that will control the researcher's preliminary search for information. Another writer sketched this research proposal:

> The purpose of my study is to examine the negative and
> positive effects of television viewing on the language
> development of children. Apparently, television viewing
> has both negative and positive effects on language usage,
> reading, and writing. The purpose of my study is to
> examine, classify, and discuss the problem. I may need to
> warn parents and teachers of certain dangers, or I may need
> to explain how to use television effectively (or do both).

In the middle of this proposal, the writer lists three areas affected by television viewing: language usage, reading, and writing. These three terms provide a preliminary list to guide note-taking.

Listing Key Ideas to Set Directions for Note-Taking

To develop a set of code words, follow two fairly simple steps: (1) jot down ideas or words in a rough list, and (2) expand the list to show a hierarchy of major and minor ideas. One researcher started with this set of key words:

> natural sun
>
> tanning beds
>
> sunscreens
>
> time in the sun or under the screen
>
> ultraviolet radiation
>
> skin damage

The writer could begin taking notes with this list and should write one of the code words at the top of each note card.

Ranking Your Major Headings and Their Subheadings

Some ideas will have more value than others, so as early as possible you should arrange the list into a rough outline, which will show the hierarchy of the issues and their relative importance:

```
The tanning process
     Natural sun
     Artificial light at tanning salons
     Time in the sun or under the screen
Effects of radiation on the skin
     Immediate skin damage
     Long-term skin damage
Protection
     Oils
     Sunscreens
     Time control
```

This rough outline, although sketchy, is enough to set goals for note-taking. It provides a set of code words for scanning sources, checking alphabetical indexes, and conducting interviews or questionnaire surveys (see Section 2h, 62–70).

Using Questions to Identify Issues

You might also find it useful to list questions about your topic. The questions will invite you to develop answers on your note cards.

```
Is there such a thing as a healthy tan?
How does a tan differ from "sunburn"?
What causes skin damage?
How prevalent is skin damage?
What are short-term consequences of a sunburn?
What are long-term consequences of a sunburn?
```

You should try to answer every question with at least one note card. One question might lead to others, and your answer to a question might produce a topic sentence for a paragraph.

Skin damage   Rennick 63
One source argues that no
tar is healthy. "Anything
that damages the skin—
and burning certainly does
that—cannot be
considered safe" (Rennick
63).

Setting Goals by Using the Modes of Development

Anticipate the kinds of development you will need and build notes that *define* or *compare* or *explain* a *process*. These are modes of development that usually need expression in sentences or in complete paragraphs. One writer used this method to chart the direction of library research:

<u>Define</u> child abuse.

<u>Contrast</u> child abuse with discipline.

<u>Illustrate</u> abuse with several examples.

Use <u>statistics</u> and <u>scientific data</u>.

Search out <u>causes</u> with a focus on the parents.

Determine <u>consequences</u> with a focus on the children.

Read and use a <u>case study</u>.

Explore the step-by-step stages of the <u>process</u>.

<u>Classify</u> the types and <u>analyze</u> the problem.

Give <u>narrative</u> examples.

With this list in hand, the writer searched for material to develop each idea with a sentence or a paragraph, as shown in the next two sample note cards:

Define child abuse
Abuse corrupts the personalities
of children and brutalizes
their bodies. Magnuson says
it "magnifies normal
discipline into maltreatment
and heightens affection
into sexual molestation"
(23).

Contrast child abuse with discipline
Discipline is training that
develops self-control and
orderliness in children. It may
include forms of punishment,
but it has the best interests
of the child in mind. In
contrast, says Magnuson, "abuse
violates the child for the
gratification of the adult" (25).

Using Approaches Across the Curriculum to Chart Your Major Ideas

Each scholarly discipline can provide valuable insight into any given topic. Suppose, for example, that you wish to examine an event from U.S. history, such as the Battle of the Little Bighorn. The academic disciplines across the curriculum will approach the topic in different ways.

Political science: The political ambitions of General Custer
may have propelled him into hasty action.

Economics: The push to conquer the Indians was, in
part, a push to open the country to
development that would enrich the nation.

Military science: The mathematical numbers were not correct
for success; Custer's troops were divided
at the wrong time and place.

Psychology: General Custer's ego may have precipitated
the massacre, an event that deeply
affected the thinking of most Americans,
many of whom responded with anti-Indian
sentiments.

Geography: The juncture of the Little Bighorn and the
Bighorn was strategically important to
migrating Indians.

Your consideration of topics across the curriculum might produce valuable
paragraphs, such as this one:

> The year 1876 stands as a monument to the western policies
> of Congress and the President, but Sitting Bull and Custer
> seized their share of glory. Custer's egotism and
> political ambitions overpowered his military savvy (Lemming
> 6). Also, Sitting Bull's military tactics (he told his
> braves to kill rather than show off their bravery) proved
> devastating for Custer and his troops who no longer had
> easy shots at "prancing, dancing Indians" (Potter 65).

Using Your Thesis to Chart the Direction of Your Research

If you have a thesis sentence, you can frame a rough outline by listing
topics that need exploration, as shown next:

Thesis: Child abuse reaches beyond the formative years
into the adult life of the abused child.

        Physical impairment
        Psychological disorders
        Marital strife
        Abuse of his/her children

The set of code words above moves the writer from the thesis statement to the specific evidence needed during note-taking. The next writer uses the same technique in a sentence outline:

Thesis: `Television can have positive effects on a child's`
`language development.`

`Television introduces new words.`

`Television reinforces word usage and proper`
`syntax.`

`Literary classics come alive verbally on`
`television.`

`Television provides the subtle rhythms and`
`musical effects of accomplished speakers.`

Revising Your Goals During Research

Your preliminary plans are not a binding contract, so revise the direction of your work periodically to reflect changes in your thinking and your response to the source material. Allow the paper to develop and grow: add new topics and discard others, rearrange the order, identify and develop new code words, and subordinate minor elements.

Writing a research paper is a recursive process, which means that you will examine your goals several times, rechart your direction, and move forward again. The parts of your general plan will expand or shrink in importance as you gather data and write the drafts.

Therefore, use these questions to evaluate your overall plan:

1. What is my role as researcher? Am I reviewing, discovering, interpreting, or theorizing?
2. What is my thesis? Will my notes and records defend and illustrate my proposition? Is the evidence convincing?
3. How specialized is my audience? Do I need to write in a nontechnical language, or may I assume that the audience is knowledgeable in this field and expects in-depth discussion of substantive issues?

Your answers will determine, in part, the type of notes you will need. (See also Section 3c, 81–87.)

3b USING GENERAL MODELS (PARADIGMS) TO STIMULATE YOUR NOTE-TAKING

A paradigm is a universal outline, one that governs most papers of a given type. It is not content specific; rather, it provides a general model or formula. For example, the following paradigm governs reports of original research in the various scientific disciplines (see also Section 2h, 69–70):

Introduction
    The problem
    The background
    The purpose and rationale
Method
    Subjects
    Apparatus
    Procedure
Results
Discussion

Note: A *paradigm,* like the one above, is a broad scaffold and a basic platform of reasoning for all papers of a certain nature, whereas a traditional outline, with its specific detail on various levels of subdivision, is useful for only one paper. To phrase it another way, a paradigm is an ideal pattern for the paper and the outline is a specific, content-oriented plan. They intermingle to form a unified whole.

Paradigm for Advancing Your Ideas and Theories

If you want to advance a theory in your paper, use this next design, but adjust it to fit your needs. Eliminate some items and add new elements as necessary.

Introduction: Establish the problem or question.
                Discuss its significance.
                Provide necessary background information.
                Introduce experts who have addressed the problem.
                Provide a thesis sentence that addresses the problem from a perspective not yet advanced by others.
      Body: Trace issues involved in the problem.
                Develop a past-to-present examination.
                Compare and analyze the details and minor issues.
                Cite experts who have addressed the same problem.

Conclusion: Advance and defend your theory as it grows out of
           evidence in the body.
           Offer directives or a plan of action.
           Suggest additional work and research that is
           needed.

Paradigm for the Analysis of Creative Works

If you plan a literary analysis of poetry, fiction, or drama, use this next
paradigm and adjust it to your subject and purposes:

Introduction: Identification of the work
            Brief summary in one sentence
            Background information that relates to the thesis
            Biographical facts about the author that relate to
               the specific issues
            Quotations and paraphrases of authorities that
               establish the scholarly traditions
            Thesis sentence that establishes your particular
               views of the literary work
     Body: An analysis divided according to such elements as
               imagery, theme, character development,
               structure, symbolism, narration, language, and
               so forth
Conclusion: A fundamental focus on the author of the work, not
               just the elements of analysis as explained in the
               body
            In particular, a conclusion that explores the
               contributions of the writer in concord with your
               thesis sentence

Use this same pattern, with appropriate modifications, for a study of music,
art, nonfiction, and other artistic works.

Paradigm for Position Papers

If you are writing a position paper for philosophy, religion, political
science, or some other field, your paper should conform in general to this
next paradigm.

Introduction: A statement that establishes the problem or
               controversial issue that your paper will examine
            A summary of the issues
            Definition of key terminology

> Quotation and paraphrase of sources to build the
>   controversial nature of the subject
> Background to establish a past/present relationship
> A thesis to establish your position

Body: Arguments in defense of one side
>   Analysis of the issues, both pro and con
>   Evidence from your reading, including quotations as
>   appropriate

Conclusion: Reestablishment of your thesis to make clear your
>   position, which should be one that grows
>   logically from your analysis and discussion of the
>   issues

Paradigm for Analysis of History

If you are writing a historical or political science paper that analyzes events and their causes and consequences, your paper should conform in general to the following plan.

Introduction: Identification of the event
>   The background leading up to the event
>   Quotations and paraphrases from experts
>   A thesis sentence

Body: Thorough analysis of the background events
>   leading up to the event
>   A tracing from one historic episode to another
>   A chronological sequence that explains how one
>   event relates directly to the next
>   Citation of authorities who have also investigated
>   this event in history

Conclusion: The consequences of this event on the course of
>   history
>   Reaffirmation of your thesis and, if possible, an
>   explanation of how the course of history was
>   altered by this one event

Paradigm for a Comparative Study

Writing a comparative study will require you to examine two schools of thought, two issues, or the positions taken by two persons. The paper compares and contrasts the issues, as outlined in the following general plan that offers three arrangements for the body of the paper.

Introduction:	Establish A		
	Establish B		
	Briefly compare the two		
	Introduce the central issues		
	Cite source materials on the subjects		
	Present your thesis		

Body (choose one):	Examine A	Similarities of A & B	Issue 1: Discuss A & B
	Examine B	Differences between A & B	Issue 2 Discuss A & B
	Compare and contrast A & B	Discussion of central issues	Issue 3 Discuss A & B

Conclusion:	Discussion of significant issues
	Conclusion that ranks one over the other
	or
	Conclusion that rates the respective genius of each side

Remember that the formulas provided above are general guidelines, not ironclad rules. Use them in that spirit and adjust each as necessary to meet your special needs.

3c WRITING A FORMAL OUTLINE

Charting a general direction and using an appropriate paradigm will help with your note-taking and with drafting a few paragraphs. However, you may need a more detailed outline for writing the complete paper or for self-evaluation of the rough draft after the initial act of writing.

A formal outline classifies the issues of your study into clear, logical categories with main heads and one or more levels of subheads.

> **A formal outline is not rigid and inflexible; you may, and should, modify it while writing and revising.**

Not all papers require the formal outline, and not all researchers need one. A short research paper can be created from code words or a list of issues. After all, the rough outline and a first draft are preliminary steps to discovering what needs expression. However, most writers benefit by developing a formal outline that classifies the investigation into clear, logical divisions. The formal outline, which can be written before or after the first draft, keeps the final manuscript on track. The outline's service to unity and coherence (see Section 6e, 144–45) can change your rough ideas into polished ones.

Using Standard Outline Symbols

List your major categories and subtopics in this form:

I. _____ First major heading
   A. _____ Subheading of first degree
      1. _____ Subheadings of second degree
      2. _____
         a. _____ Subheadings of third degree
         b. _____
            (1) _____ Subheadings of fourth degree
            (2) _____
               (a) _____ Subheadings of fifth degree
               (b) _____
   B. _____ Subheading of first degree

The degree to which you continue the subheads will depend, in part, on the complexity of the subject. Subheads in a research paper seldom carry beyond the first series of small letters.

An alternative form, especially for papers in business and the sciences, is the *decimal outline,* which divides material by numerical divisions, as follows:

1. _____
   1.1. _____
      1.1.1 _____
      1.1.2. _____
      1.1.3. _____
   1.2. _____
      1.2.1. _____
      1.2.2. _____
2. _____

Writing a Formal Topic Outline

The topic outline is built with balanced phrases. The advantage of the topic outline is the speed with which you can develop it. Note this example that uses noun phrases:

```
II.  Television's effects on children

     A.  Vocabulary development

     B.  Reading ability

     C.  Visual arts appreciation

     D.  Writing efficiency

     E.  Discovery of technology
```

The topic outline may also use gerund phrases (e.g., "Learning a vocabulary" and "Learning to read") or infinitive phrases (e.g., "To develop a vocabulary" or "To learn to read"). Shown next is one outline section in three different forms. The first uses noun phrases:

```
III.  The senses

      A.  Receptors to detect light

          1.  Rods of the retina

          2.  Cones of the retina
```

The second uses gerund phrases:

```
III.  Sensing the environment

      A.  Detecting light

          1.  Sensing dim light with retina rods

          2.  Sensing bright light with retina cones
```

The third uses infinitive phrases:

```
III.  To use the senses

      A.  To detect light

          1.  To sense dim light

          2.  To sense bright light
```

Writing a Formal Sentence Outline

The sentence outline requires full sentences for each heading and subheading. It has two advantages over the topic outline:

1. Many entries in a sentence outline can serve as topic sentences for paragraphs, thereby speeding the writing process.
2. The subject/verb pattern establishes the logical direction of your thinking (for example, the phrase "Vocabulary development" becomes "Television viewing can improve a child's vocabulary").

Consequently, the sentence outline brings into the open any possible organizational problems rather than hiding them as a topic outline might do. The time devoted to writing a complete sentence outline, like writing complete, polished notes (see Section 5a, 111–12), will serve you well when you write the rough draft and revise it. A brief sample follows.

```
II.  Television affects children in the key areas of
     learning.
     A.  Television viewing can improve a child's
         vocabulary.
     B.  Television encourages reading, which, in turn,
         improves language competence.
     C.  The visual arts complement the language arts.
     D.  Writing is enhanced by television viewing.
     E.  Modern communication technology is here to stay
         and children respond to it.
```

Note: Kim Wells (238) chose to work from the brief sentence outline (shown above, in part). She developed fully each section during the drafting stages. Other writers may wish to develop the sentence outline with more subdivisions, as shown below for section II-A of the Wells paper (see the finished text, 237–49). Note how this version includes page citations so that sentences can be transferred easily into the text.

```
II.  Television affects children in key areas of learning.
     A.  Television viewing can improve the vocabulary of
         children.
         1.  Negative comments by Powell and Winkeljohann
             note the simplistic nature of TV language and
             the more important role of the home
             environment.
             a.  Powell fears children will lose the
                 ability to express verbally their deep
                 thoughts and feelings (42).
             b.  Winkeljohann tested TV viewing of sets of
                 children with both good and poor
                 vocabularies, but claims TV was not the
                 "variable" influencing their language
                 levels (100).
```

    2. A study by Rice and Woodsmall and one
       by Singer et al. tested children and
       found improved vocabulary.

       a. Rice and Woodsmall tested 3- and
           5-year-olds who learned "novel"
           words on the basis of a short
           television exposure (425).

       b. Singer et al. demonstrate how
           children retain specialized
           vocabularies after TV viewing (88).

  3. Postman says children gain enormous factual
     knowledge by TV viewing (35).

  4. Surely they accumulate words in the process so
     that television offers a foundation for
     vocabulary development.

Using Notes from a Research Journal to Enrich an Outline

If you have kept a research journal, you have probably developed a number of paragraphs on the topic. Therefore, review the journal and assign each paragraph to a section of your paper. Do this by making a note (such as "put in the conclusion") or by assigning an outline number (for example, "use in II.A.1"). Note this next example:

> Use in section II with the Considine quote
> Modern communication technology is here to stay and cannot be ignored. Fifty years ago we lived in a cocoon of isolation with only the print media and a limited number of radio stations to keep us informed as a nation, but now we live in the information age, an age that bombards us with television and radio in our homes and automobiles, annoys us with ringing telephones, and infatuates us with computers and their modems for networking across the nation.

This journal entry by Kim Wells was eventually used in her paper (237–49).

Using Basic, Dynamic Order to Chart the Course of Your Work

The finished paper should trace the issues, defend and support a thesis, and provide dynamic progression of issues and concepts that point forward to the conclusion. Each section of the paper should move your writing from identification of a problem; to analysis of the issues, with evidence; and, finally, to your interpretation and discussion of the findings. In every case, you will generate the dynamics of the paper by building anticipation in the introduction, by investigating the issues in the body, and by providing a final judgment.

If you have any hesitation about the design of your paper, start with this bare-bones model and expand it with your material:

Title

    I. Identify the subject
       A. Explain the problem
       B. Provide background information
       C. Frame a thesis statement
   II. Analyze the subject
       A. Examine the first major issue
       B. Examine the second major issue
       C. Examine the third major issue
  III. Discuss your findings
       A. Restate your thesis and point beyond it
       B. Interpret the findings
       C. Provide answers, solutions, and a final opinion

Readers, including your instructor, are accustomed to this sequence for research papers. It offers plenty of leeway.

To the introduction, you can add a quotation, an anecdote, a definition, statistics, and other material, which is discussed more specifically in Section 6f, 145–51. Within the body, you can compare, analyze, give evidence, trace historical events, and present many other matters, as explained in Section 6g, 151–57. In the conclusion, you can challenge an assumption, take exception to a prevailing point of view, and reaffirm your thesis, as explained in Section 6h, 157–61. Flesh out each section, adding subheadings as necessary. This next model adds specific content to an introduction:

Advertising in the Schools

I. The quest for a child's money

    A. The past and a new view about children and their
money

        1. Children with money

            a. Allowances and spending money

            b. Effects on the marketplace

        2. Commercial advertising in the schools

            a. Channel One

            b. Educational material from McDonald's

            c. Student clubs that sell merchandise

    B. Problems with advertising in the schools

        1. Advertisers in the classroom

            a. Quotation by Carol Herman

            b. Buying classroom time

        2. Money as the target, not the mind of the child

    C. The thesis statement: The student ought to have
school as a safe zone away from the commercials.

As shown above, you should write the thesis sentence into the outline where it will appear in the paper. The thesis is the main idea of the entire paper, so do not label it as Item I in the outline. Otherwise, you may search fruitlessly for parallel ideas to put in II, III, and IV. (See also Section 6f, 146, on using the thesis in the opening.)

In every case, treat an outline or organizational chart as a tool. Like an architect's blueprint, it should contribute to, not inhibit, the construction of a finished product.

4 *Finding and Reading the Best Sources*

A research paper assignment is a test of your scholarship, especially a test of your ability to find and cite appropriate and relevant sources. Some student researchers photocopy entire journal articles and carry armloads of books from the library. That sort of diligence is misplaced. The quality of your selections outweighs the quantity of your source materials. This chapter will offer tips about selecting and using the sources. It cuts to the heart of the matter: Should I read all or just part of a source? How do I respond to it? How can I find the best sources? This chapter also demonstrates the techniques for writing a summary of one or more sources with either the annotated bibliography or the review of the literature.

4a FINDING THE BEST SOURCE MATERIALS

The card catalog and the indexes can display books and articles for you, but they cannot guarantee the quality of what you find. You must do that yourself. Be skeptical about accepting every printed word as absolute. Constantly review, verify, and double-check the words of your sources. Techniques for finding the most reliable sources do exist, as explained below.

Consulting with Your Instructor and the Librarians

Do not hesitate in asking your instructor or the librarians for help in finding sources. Instructors know the field, know the best writers, and can provide a brief list to get you started. Sometimes instructors will pull books off their office shelves to point the way for you.

Librarians know the resources of the library. Their job is to serve your needs. If you appeal for help, they will walk into the stacks with you to find just the right book or the most appropriate journal article.

Using Recent Sources

A book may look valuable, but if its copyright date is 1938, its content is suspect: time and new developments have probably passed it by (unless, of course, the work is a classic in its field). Scientific and technical topics always require up-to-date research. Learn to depend on monthly and quarterly journals as well as books. (See the appropriate indexes for your field in the appendix, 336–68.)

Using Journals Rather Than Magazines

Beware of biased reporting. In general, scholarly journals offer more reliable evidence than magazines. Magazine writers work for pay, and they may sensationalize some articles to sell magazines. The authors of journals write for academic honor, and they document all sources. In addition, journal writers publish through university presses and academic organizations that require every article to pass the scrutiny of a jury of critics before its publication. A journal article about child abuse found in *Child Development* or in *Journal of Marriage and the Family* should be reliable. A magazine article about child abuse in a Sunday newspaper supplement or in a popular magazine may be less reliable in its facts and opinions.

Using Scholarly Books Rather Than Trade Books and Encyclopedias

Scholarly books, like journal articles, are subjected to careful review before publication. They are published because they give the very best treatment on a subject. They are not published to make money; in fact, many scholarly books lose money for the publishers. Scholarly books treat academic topics with in-depth discussions and careful documentation of the evidence. A college library is a repository, in the main, for scholarly books—technical and scientific works, doctoral dissertations, and publications of the university presses.

Trade books are published to make money for the authors and the publishers. They seldom treat with depth any scholarly subject. *How to Launch a Small Business* and *Landscaping with Rocks* are typical titles of nonfiction trade books to be found in bookstores, not in college libraries (although public libraries often have vast holdings in trade books).

Encyclopedias, by design, contain brief surveys of every well-known person, event, place, and accomplishment. They will serve you well during preliminary investigation, but most instructors prefer that you go beyond encyclopedias in order to cite from scholarly books and journal articles.

Finally, be aware that many organizations publish slanted, biased articles to promote their views. There's nothing wrong with the practice, but you should be aware of such editorial policies. For example, the *New Republic* presents a liberal view of society while the *National Review* remains staunchly conservative. A report on health care may seem reasonable on the surface, but if the publication is sponsored by a health-care insurance company, you must exercise caution.

Reading About the Author

You may need to search out information about an author for several reasons:

1. To provide biographical details in your introduction. The primary topic may be Carl Jung's psychological theories of the unconscious, but some information about Jung's career might be appropriate in the paper.
2. To discuss a creative writer's life in relation to his or her work. For example, Joyce Carol Oates's personal life may shed some light on your reading of her stories or novels.
3. To verify the standing and reputation of somebody that you want to paraphrase or quote in your paper.

You can learn about a writer and the work of that writer in a biography. The librarian can help you find appropriate works, such as these:

Contemporary Authors, a set of biographies on contemporary writers

Dictionary of American Negro Biography, a review of African-American writers and important figures

Who's Who in Philosophy, a list and discussion of the best writers and thinkers in the field

You can find reference works similar to these three books for almost every field. The appendix (336–68) lists many of them.

Conducting a Citation Search

Citation searching discovers the authors whose works have been cited repeatedly in the literature. For example, one writer located the following list of references at the end of two articles on child abuse, and she looked for authors who appeared more than once:

Figure 55: From *Child Development* 1. Authors who appear twice on the list with two different essays

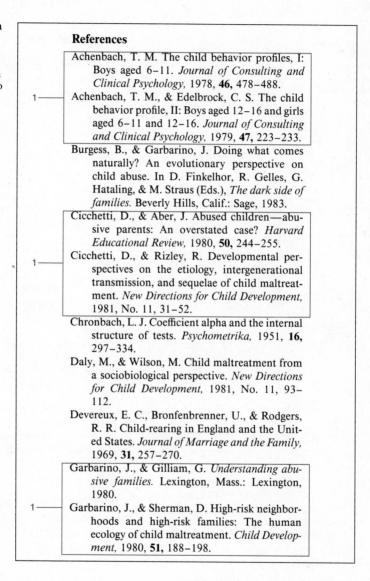

References

Achenbach, T. M. The child behavior profiles, I: Boys aged 6–11. *Journal of Consulting and Clinical Psychology,* 1978, **46,** 478–488.

1 — Achenbach, T. M., & Edelbrock, C. S. The child behavior profile, II: Boys aged 12–16 and girls aged 6–11 and 12–16. *Journal of Consulting and Clinical Psychology,* 1979, **47,** 223–233.

Burgess, B., & Garbarino, J. Doing what comes naturally? An evolutionary perspective on child abuse. In D. Finkelhor, R. Gelles, G. Hataling, & M. Straus (Eds.), *The dark side of families.* Beverly Hills, Calif.: Sage, 1983.

Cicchetti, D., & Aber, J. Abused children—abusive parents: An overstated case? *Harvard Educational Review,* 1980, **50,** 244–255.

1 — Cicchetti, D., & Rizley, R. Developmental perspectives on the etiology, intergenerational transmission, and sequelae of child maltreatment. *New Directions for Child Development,* 1981, No. 11, 31–52.

Chronbach, L. J. Coefficient alpha and the internal structure of tests. *Psychometrika,* 1951, **16,** 297–334.

Daly, M., & Wilson, M. Child maltreatment from a sociobiological perspective. *New Directions for Child Development,* 1981, No. 11, 93–112.

Devereux, E. C., Bronfenbrenner, U., & Rodgers, R. R. Child-rearing in England and the United States. *Journal of Marriage and the Family,* 1969, **31,** 257–270.

Garbarino, J., & Gilliam, G. *Understanding abusive families.* Lexington, Mass.: Lexington, 1980.

1 — Garbarino, J., & Sherman, D. High-risk neighborhoods and high-risk families: The human ecology of child maltreatment. *Child Development,* 1980, **51,** 188–198.

The researcher marked those authors that have more than one article (Achenbach, Cicchetti, and Garbarino). Next, she searched another bibliography and looked for the same names:

Figure 56: From *Child Development*
1. Name of author who participated in writing three articles on the subject 2. Name of the same author who also served as editor of a work on the topic

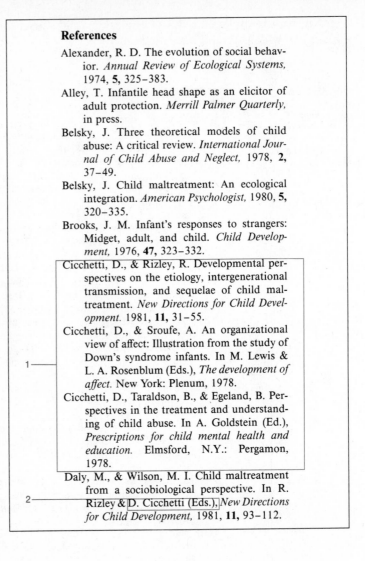

References

Alexander, R. D. The evolution of social behavior. *Annual Review of Ecological Systems,* 1974, **5,** 325–383.

Alley, T. Infantile head shape as an elicitor of adult protection. *Merrill Palmer Quarterly,* in press.

Belsky, J. Three theoretical models of child abuse: A critical review. *International Journal of Child Abuse and Neglect,* 1978, **2,** 37–49.

Belsky, J. Child maltreatment: An ecological integration. *American Psychologist,* 1980, **5,** 320–335.

Brooks, J. M. Infant's responses to strangers: Midget, adult, and child. *Child Development,* 1976, **47,** 323–332.

Cicchetti, D., & Rizley, R. Developmental perspectives on the etiology, intergenerational transmission, and sequelae of child maltreatment. *New Directions for Child Development.* 1981, **11,** 31–55.

Cicchetti, D., & Sroufe, A. An organizational view of affect: Illustration from the study of Down's syndrome infants. In M. Lewis & L. A. Rosenblum (Eds.), *The development of affect.* New York: Plenum, 1978.

Cicchetti, D., Taraldson, B., & Egeland, B. Perspectives in the treatment and understanding of child abuse. In A. Goldstein (Ed.), *Prescriptions for child mental health and education.* Elmsford, N.Y.: Pergamon, 1978.

Daly, M., & Wilson, M. I. Child maltreatment from a sociobiological perspective. In R. Rizley & D. Cicchetti (Eds.), *New Directions for Child Development,* 1981, **11,** 93–112.

The name "Cicchetti" occurs again, which suggests that (1) this person is an authority in this field, and (2) the student should examine his works in detail. In addition, the article by Daly and Wilson appears a second time, which suggests its value.

You should search several bibliographies and mark your bibliography cards with stars or circles each time a source is cited. Two or more stars will suggest *must* reading. The sources themselves have suggested the important books and articles.

Three citation indexes will do some of this work for you:

Arts and Humanities Citation Index (AHCI). Philadelphia: Institute for Scientific Information, 1975–date.

Science Citation Index (SCI). Philadelphia: Institute for Scientific Information, 1955–date.

Social Sciences Citation Index (SSCI). Philadelphia: Institute for Scientific Information, 1956–date.

Examining the Book Reviews

Whenever one book serves as the cornerstone for your research, you can test its critical reputation by reading a review or two. Reviews are hidden here and there in magazines and journals, requiring a search of the following indexes:

Book Review Digest. New York: Wilson, 1905–date.

> Arranged alphabetically by author, this work provides an evaluation of several thousand books each year. It features summaries and brief quotations from the reviews to uncover the critical reception of the work.

Book Review Index. Detroit: Gale, bimonthly.

> This work indexes reviews in 225 magazines and journals.

Index to Book Reviews in the Humanities. Williamston, MI: Thompson, annually.

> This index to reviews in humanities periodicals has entries listed by author, title, and reviewer.

Index to Book Reviews in the Social Sciences. Williamston, MI: Thompson, annually.

> This index to reviews in social science periodicals has entries listed by author, title, and reviewer.

Current Book Review Citations. New York: Wilson, annually.

> This work gives an author-title index to book reviews published in more than 1,000 periodicals.

The Booklist. Chicago: American Library Assn., 1905–date.

> A monthly magazine that reviews new books for librarians, this work includes brief summaries and recommendations.

A sample page of *Book Review Digest* shows the type of information available in a review of books:

Figure 57: From
Book Review
Digest
1. Author, title,
and facts of
publication
2. Dewey call
number and
subject entries for
card catalog
3. Library of
Congress call
number
4. Description of
the work
5. Reviewer's
evaluation of the
book 6. Facts of
publication of the
600-word review:
Annals of the
American Academy
of Political and
Social Science 415
(1974): 275 7. A
review that the
Book Review
Digest has not
quoted

> FONTANA, VINCENT J. Somewhere a child is crying: maltreatment—
> causes and prevention. 268p $6.95 '73 Macmillan Pub. Co. 364.1
> Cruelty to children | Child welfare LC 78-16566
>
> "The author presents numerous case studies of child battering and depri-
> vation, exploring . . . the factors contributing to abusive parental behavior
> as well as the reasons why courts and social welfare agencies often fail to
> protect children. Using the New York City task force on child abuse as an
> example, Fontana shows how better reporting and disposition of abuse
> cases, voluntary self-help groups such as Parents Anonymous, and an ex-
> perimental program of parental retraining have bettered the situation. The
> conclusion calls for a legal statement of children's rights and the machinery
> needed to protect them." (Library J) Index
>
> "The author sketches the long history of child maltreatment . . . [and]
> tells of the increasing rise of conditions which favor [it]. . . . The book
> then becomes one long account of the sufferings of the children, their
> causes, and the barriers against their prevention. . . . [It contains] one ele-
> ment notable in these days of public outcry against any use of punish-
> ment . . . in dealing with violent offenders and those few of the mentally
> deranged who are dangerous to themselves or others. Dr. Fontana does not
> want persons who lose control and harm children to 'get away with it.' . . .
> For the inexpert who may come in contact with children who are being
> abused, Dr. Fontana provides a list of tell-tale indications . . . [He] calls
> for widespread public concern and massive expenditures for the detection of
> child maltreatment in its earliest stages and for the establishment of a na-
> tional system of prevention and remedial services. Let us hope that his
> crusading spirit will prove contagious." E. J. Levinson
>
> Ann Am Acad 415:275 S '74 600w
> "The director of pediatrics at New York's Foundling Hospital and chair-
> man of the Mayor's Task Force on Child Abuse and Neglect presents star-
> tling descriptions and statistics of a major national problem . . . Fontana's
> concern for both child and parent, his plea for recognition of the rights of
> children, and his suggestions for improving both legislation and procedures
> for detecting, investigating, and preventing maltreatment make this book
> vital reading for concerned layman and professional alike." J. M. Marey
> Library J 98:3247 N 1 '73 110w
> Reviewed by George Merrill
> Library J 99:586 F 15 /74 130w [YA]

4b   DECIDING WHETHER TO READ ALL OR PART OF A SOURCE

Many writers have trouble determining the value of a particular article or book. To evaluate an *article* in a periodical, read:

1. The **title.** Look for code words that have relevance to your topic before you start reading the article. For example, "Children and Parents" may look ideal for research on child abuse, until you read the subtitle, "Growing Up in New Guinea."

2. An **abstract.** If an abstract is available on CD-ROM or on an abstracting service (e.g., *Psychological Abstracts*), read it before going in search of the printed article. If a printed article is preceded by an abstract, read it first. Reading an abstract is the best way to ascertain if an essay or a book will serve your specific needs.

3. The **opening paragraphs.** If the opening of an article shows no relevance to your study, abandon the article.

4. The **closing paragraphs.** If the opening of an article seems promising, skip to the closing and read it for relevance. Read the entire article only if the opening and the closing encourage you.

Evaluating a *book,* as explained below, requires a more diligent investigation than does evaluating an article in a periodical. It requires a check of the following additional items:

1. The **table of contents.** A book's TOC may reveal chapters that speak directly on your topic. Often, only one chapter is useful.

2. The **preface** or **introduction.** An author's preface serves as a critical overview of the entire book, pinpointing the primary subject of the text and the peculiar approach of this author. Read an author's preface to find a statement of purpose. One folklore student's reading of a preface put new perspectives on a book titled *A Mysterious Spirit: The Bell Witch of Tennessee* (Nashville: Elder, 1972) in which the author, Charles Bailey Bell, says:

> The name "Bell Witch" has always been resented by the family. They are sensitive to such an appellation. . . . The Author shall relate in this book what was handed down to him by his father, Dr. J. T. Bell, he having the recollections of his father, John Bell, Jr.

The author reveals his built-in bias about the folklore. He is a descendant of one of the principals in the story, which will color his account of what happened. To balance against the Bell book, the student went in search of other sources and found contrasting views in four other books on the Bell Witch by M. V. Ingram, Sharon Shebar, Gladys Barr, and Parks Miller.

3. The **index.** A book's index will list names and terminology with page numbers for all items mentioned within the text. One student, for example, planned to research Andrew Wyeth's 1961 painting "Christina's World." She found Wanda Corn's book, *The Art of Andrew Wyeth,* but neither the preface nor the table of contents mentioned her subject, so she turned to the index and found what she needed:

> *Christina's World,* 38, 39, 40, 55, 74, 78, 93, 95, 143, 144, 164

As a side benefit, she also found at the back of the book a bibliography to Wyeth's letters and interviews and two books and articles about him.

4c RESPONDING TO THE SOURCES

When you find source material relevant to your subject, you must make decisions about your initial response. As you read, you can write note cards to record key ideas or write notations on the margins of photocopied materials. After reading the material, you can locate the key ideas of the source by reducing it to an outline or you can write a précis to summarize the whole.

Selecting Key Ideas

In many instances, you may borrow only one idea from a source, one that you can rephrase into your own words. Figure 58 shows B. N. Raina's original statement; note the highlighted sentences in the middle of this essay:

Figure 58: From
The Explicator
Passage of
importance to the
researcher. From
B. N. Raina,
"Dickinson's
'Because I Could
Not Stop for
Death,'" *The
Explicator* 43.3
(1985): 11–12.

*Use this
idea!*

Dickinson's BECAUSE I COULD NOT STOP FOR DEATH

It has been the general difficulty with critical exegeses of Emily Dickinson's "Because I could not stop for Death—" that (1) "Death" and "Immortality" in the first stanza seem unaccountably syncopated, and (2) that "I first surmised the Horses' Head/Were toward Eternity—" of the end of the poem remains equally enigmatical without derivation. I offer the following interpretive possibility.

The crux of the poem's meanings, I suggest, is in the first two lines, "Because I could not stop for Death—/He kindly stopped for me—". We have tended mechanically to read this to mean that since the narrative subject of the poem finds herself rather too involved in the humdrum of living, with no thought of death, Death like a civil gentleman-suitor stops by in his chaise and four to take the busy persona out for the final ride, paradoxically, to the accompaniment of "Immortality." I think the lines lead us into a simplistic literalness because of the deceptive surface. Read them as you would a prototypical "romantic" utterance and the problem begins to solve itself. To wit, translate the persona's not stopping for death into an imaginative perception of the nonreality of death. Death is death only to those who live within the time-bound finite world outside of the imaginative infinity of consciousness. That being so, the "stopped" of the second line takes on a profoundly rich ambiguity. Whereas clearly the metaphor of Death stopping by is to be retained as one level of courtship, more essentially, since the persona's consciousness has negated death, Death in turn stops, that is, *ceases* to be (the full richness of the initial "because" should now be apparent). And, appropriately, from that dialectic of consciousness is *generated* "Immortality."

The rest of the poem carries forward the poetic journey through a necessary but obviously imagined framework of body-consciousness in which the "chill" of the "Setting Sun" is sensually rendered. Yet, when the carriage comes to the grave—"A Swelling of the Ground—" *entrance* is not made: "we *paused* before a House" merely (emphasis added). So that the "Immortality" achieved at the very beginning remains unthreatened even as death is sensibly confronted. And when the retrospective voice comes back after centuries, the poem only returns to its first accomplished vision of the nonreality of death in an unbroken moment of consciousness:

Since then—'tis Centuries—and yet
Feels shorter than the Day
I first surmised the Horses' Heads
Were toward Eternity.

The "first" surmise recalls how "Immortality" was attained at the start of the poem, and in a remarkable conflation of the romantic and the Christian, the dreaded Horses of the Apocalypse are comfortably perceived as yielding only everlasting life in a grand personal apotheosis: "He kindly stopped for *me*" (emphasis added).

Rather than photocopy the entire piece, the researcher read first, related the reading to her thesis and her own outline, and wrote this note:

Figure 59: Sample note card

> Raina 11-12
>
> B. N. Raina observes that death for this speaker is an "imaginative perception of the nonreality of death" (12) so that death is confronted as a window to everlasting life.
>
> on Dickinson's "Because I Could Not Stop for Death"

This student's note can slide easily into the finished text. A bibliography card with full information on Raina was also prepared.

If you cannot draw from a specific portion of a source, yet the essay has relevance, write a précis to condense the whole into a few words:

Figure 60: Sample précis note

> On death in Dickinson   Raina 11-12
>
> Raina focuses on the idea of stopping, saying that the speaker could not stop, so death ceased to exist and the speaker thereby gained immortality.

See Section 5d, 118–22, for specifics on writing a précis.

Making Notations on Photocopied Materials

Avoid making marks on library books and magazines, but *do* make marginal notes in your own books and magazines or on photocopied materials. Underline sentences, circle key ideas, ask questions, and react with your own comments. Note how the following student expressed his own response to the source:

**Figure 61:
Sample
annotations on
photocopied
material**

*AIDS education
is crucial.*

*AIDS education
may cause
problems.*

*Short programs
and the
pamphlets
themselves
make workers
nervous and
wary.*

*The answer
is longer
sessions by
in-house
speakers.*

AIDS Education May Breed Intolerance

Two thirds of Americans would be concerned about sharing a bathroom with someone who has AIDS. One third would not lend their tools to an infected co-worker. Proximity and casual contact, of course, are not considered to be vectors for the spread of the disease. So education about the modes of transmission and known risk factors should be the best weapon against such worries.

Not necessarily, say researchers at the Georgia Institute of Technology. David M. Herold and John M. Maslyn, who study organizational behavior, believe a little education may be worse than no education at all. They found that some AIDS education programs made workers less tolerant of those with the disease.

The main culprits were programs that provided only a brochure or a presentation from an outside expert that lasted less than 45 minutes. Unfortunately, such education makes up more than half of all types of AIDS schooling in the workplace, according to the study. In contrast, longer programs, those lasting more than two hours, improved the attitudes of employees.

The problem, the researchers say, stems from the educational materials published by public health organizations. These pamphlets emphasize behavioral changes that would reduce the risk of infection. "Most education materials just show little blood cells being attacked by little monsters," Herold observes. And short corporate education sessions never discuss "how to be supportive and deal with others." Employees come away with a "Now-that-I-know-how-you-get-it, why-should-I-help-you attitude," Herold says.

Credibility is also an issue. The study found that 45-minute presentations could improve attitudes, but only if they were given by in-house spokespersons. Insiders, Herold notes, are better able to address fears specific to that workplace.

Providing information about AIDS to workers is "crucially important," Herold asserts. Most problems do not come from those with AIDS but from other workers "who raise hell with their supervisor." Moreover, as improvements in treatment allow infected people to remain healthy longer, Herold notes that more businesses "are going to have to confront the issue of workers with AIDS." —*Philip Yam*

From *Scientific American*, September 1991.

Outlining the Key Ideas of a Source

Most books have a table of contents that outlines the basic ingredients of the book. Consult it for issues that deserve your critical reading. In the case of an essay, you can frame your own outline to capture an author's primary themes; that is, list the main ideas and subtopics to show the hierarchy of issues, to identify parallel parts, and to locate supporting ideas. The goal is to discover the author's primary and secondary ideas.

A rough outline of the Philip Yam essay (reprinted in Figure 61, 98) revealed the central ideas for one researcher.

**Figure 62:
Sample rough
outline**

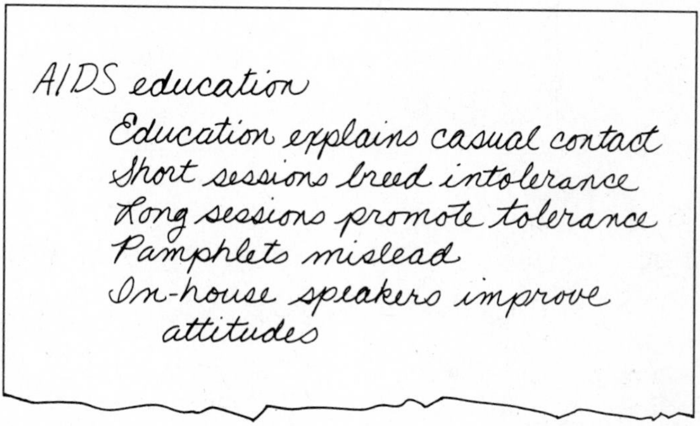

AIDS education
  Education explains casual contact
  Short sessions breed intolerance
  Long sessions promote tolerance
  Pamphlets mislead
  In-house speakers improve
    attitudes

Writing a Summary or a Précis

A *summary* condenses into a brief note the key ideas of a source. More than anything else, it serves to remind you later about the source's relevance to your study. In some cases, you will use the summary in your paper. For further details and examples, see Section 5c, 116–18.

A *précis* is a highly polished summary, one that you can transfer to your paper or use in an annotated bibliography. Use the précis to review a piece of writing or to write a plot summary. For further details and examples, see Section 5d, 118–22.

Here is a quick summary of the Philip Yam article:

**Figure 63:
Sample summary**

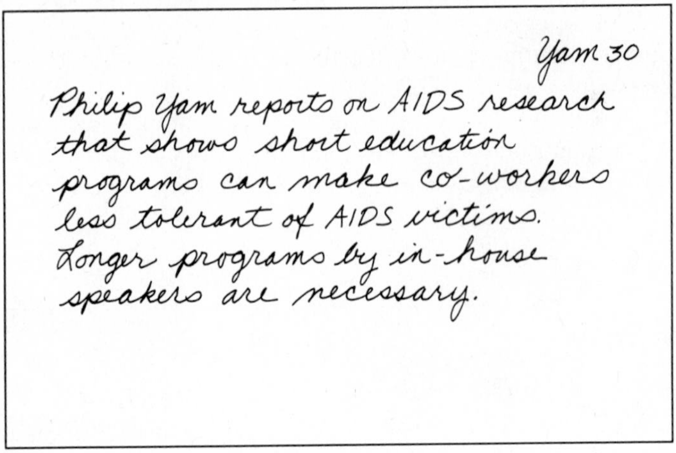

> *Yam 30*
>
> Philip Yam reports on AIDS research that shows short education programs can make co-workers less tolerant of AIDS victims. Longer programs by in-house speakers are necessary.

4d SELECTING A MIX OF BOTH PRIMARY AND SECONDARY SOURCES

Primary sources are the original words of a writer—novel, speech, eyewitness account, letter, autobiography, interview, or results of original research. Feel free to quote often from a primary source because it has direct relevance to your discussion. If you examine a poem by Dylan Thomas, you must quote the poem. If you examine George Bush's domestic policies on the homeless, you must quote from White House documents.

Secondary sources are works about somebody or about somebody's accomplishments. Secondary sources are writings about the primary sources and about the authors who produce primary material. Reporters respond to a presidential speech, reviewers examine new scientific findings, scholars analyze the imagery of a poem. A biography provides a secondhand view of the life of a notable person and a history book interprets events. An evaluation, analysis, or interpretation provides one way of looking at the original.

Do not feel free to quote liberally from secondary sources. Be selective. Use a well-worded sentence, not the entire paragraph. Work a key phrase, not eight or nine lines, into your text. (See "Selecting Key Ideas," 96–97.)

The subject area of a research paper determines, in part, the nature of the source materials. Use the following chart as a guide:

	Primary Sources	**Secondary Sources**
Literature	Novels, poems, plays, short stories, letters, diaries, manuscripts, and autobiographies	Journal articles, reviews, biographies, and critical books about writers and their works
Government, Political Science, History	Speeches, writings by presidents and others, the *Congressional Record,* reports of agencies and departments, and documents written by historic figures	Newspaper reports, news magazines, political journals and newsletters, journal articles, and history books
Social Sciences	Case studies, findings from surveys and from questionnaires, reports of social workers, psychiatrists, and lab technicians	Commentary and evaluations in reports, documents, journal articles, and books
Sciences	Tools and methods, experiments, findings from tests and experiments, observations, discoveries, and test patterns	Interpretations and discussions of test data as found in journals and books (scientific books, which are quickly dated, are less valuable than up-to-date journals)
Fine Arts	Films, paintings, music, and sculptures, as well as reproductions and synopses of these for research purposes	Evaluations in journal articles, critical reviews, biographies, and critical books about the artists and their works
Business	Market research and testing, technical studies and investigations, drawings, designs, models, memoranda and letters, and computer data	Discussion of the business world in newspapers, business magazines, journals, government documents, and books
Education	Pilot studies, term projects, sampling results, tests and test data, surveys, interviews, observations, statistics, and computer data	Analysis and evaluation of educational experimentation in journals, reports, pamphlets, and books

4e PREPARING AN ANNOTATED BIBLIOGRAPHY

One way to evaluate your sources is to write an annotated bibliography. An annotation is a short explanatory note about the contents of a book or article. If you write an annotated bibliography, you must read and evaluate each of your sources. For instructions on writing an annotation, see "Using the Précis to Write an Annotated Bibliography," 121. For instructions on writing the bibliography entries, see Chapter 9 for MLA style, as shown below, or Chapter 10 for APA style.

Annotated Bibliography

Abelman, Robert. "Television Literacy for Gifted

Children." Roeper Review 9 (1987): 166–69.

Television is "a potentially useful and powerful tool"

for classroom teachers. The introduction of

"television literacy" into the curriculum will

encourage critical thinking and imaginative responses,

especially by gifted children.

Note: You may wish to write truncated annotations that omit a subject: "Embraces television as . . ." or "Encourages the introduction of television. . . ."

Blythe, Hal, and Charlie Sweet. "Using Media to Teach

English." Instructional Innovator 28 (1983): 22–24.

Children will watch television, so teachers should

respond to the electronic revolution. Television is

another tool, but it will be an "effective tool" only

if teachers develop a "television consciousness" and

use the media as a supplement to other classroom

methods.

Bryant, Jennings, and Daniel R. Anderson, eds. Children's

Understanding of Television: Research on Attention and

Comprehension. New York: Academic, 1983. Several

essays, including one by the editors, discuss the

effects of television on children. An essay by D.

Anderson and Lorch, chapter one, defends the active

participation of children in answer to those critics who say children are too passive. The essay by J. Anderson, chapter twelve, defends the technical skills required for watching television.

Considine, David M. "Visual Literacy and the Curriculum: More to It Than Meets the Eye." Language Arts 64 (1987): 634-40. The visual media is vital to the education of new generations, according to Considine, who argues that teachers need to "integrate this technology" into their classrooms with "visual literacy training."

Fransecky, Roger B. "Perspectives: Children, Television, and Language Education." Language Arts 58 (1981): 713-20. Rita Brause interviewed Fransecky, who argues that "television is important, universal, and subtle." However, he insists that it becomes "junk food" for children unless teachers actively lead their students into paths of inquiry and critical thinking about what they view on the tube.

Heller, Scott. "Scholars Ponder How to Teach English to Students of a Television Generation." Chronicle of Higher Education 1 July 1987: 9+. This newspaper article reviewed a meeting of teachers who examined the effects of television viewing on their students and the need for change in the structure of education.

Hodge, Robert, and David Tripp. Children and Television: A Semiotic Approach. Stanford UP, 1986. This book on children and television explores the social aspects primarily, and it features one chapter, "Television and Schooling," that discusses television as a "hidden curriculum" that teachers should not ignore.

Moody, Kate. Growing Up on Television: The TV Effect. New York: Times Books, 1980. Moody examines the negative

effects of television on language development. She
compares the imaginative, analytical function of
reading against the "passive act" of television
viewing.

Postman, Neil. Television and the Teaching of English. New
York: Appleton, 1961. In chapter three this author
studies the effects of television to argue that viewing
encourages children to read, provides an "aural-visual
source of information," and adds to their accumulation
or "storehouse" of words. In chapter four the author
defends television for its introduction of literary
classics to children.

4f PREPARING A REVIEW OF THE LITERATURE ON A TOPIC

The review of the literature is a mini-essay about the source material on a narrowed topic. It presents a summary in essay form for two purposes:

1. It sets the context for your investigation of the topic. There-fore, carefully introduce the problem you wish to examine and then show how each source addresses the problem. Do not simply list summaries of the sources without relating each source to your work.
2. It organizes and classifies the sources in some reasonable manner for the benefit of the reader. The essay below classi-fies two types of sources, critics who endorse the use of television in education and critics who condemn its use.

To write brief descriptions of your key sources, see Section 5d, 118–22.
To blend source material into your survey, see Section 7a, 174–76.
To write the bibliography entries, see Chapter 9, 250–79.

Kim Wells

English 1010

May 15, 1988

Selected Review of Literature: Effects of Television

on Children's Language Development

In the late 1940s, researchers began to study the effects of television viewing on children (see, for example, the 1951 book by Shayon). Unfortunately, no definitive answer has surfaced on the central question: Does television have a place in a child's learning development?

Depending on who gathers the statistics and how they are tabulated and interpreted, one undisputed conclusion is that children spend enormous amounts of television time that inevitably affects them for better or worse.

The purpose of this survey is to examine the negative and positive effects of television viewing on children's language development. The literature is split on the issue.

Negative Positions

Several critics see little value, if any, in television's effect on language development of children. Kate Moody in her 1980 text Growing Up on Television: The TV Effect compares the imaginative, analytical function of reading against the "passive act" of television viewing (68). Another drawback to television, according to Moody, is that when viewing television, a child cannot stop the

Wells 2

action, "assimilate the material," and then go on to the
next sequence as one can do while reading. She adds, "A
good story in print will take on new shades of meaning with
each rereading . . ." (56).

Jon Powell, professor of communication at Northern
Illinois University, argues that television tends to speak
in choppy, simplistic, and superficial language in order to
appeal to the widest possible audience. He fears that
children will lose the ability to express verbally deep
thoughts or feelings. He adds that some youngsters may
feel too threatened by the professional examples seen on
the screen to even try, finding it "personally difficult to
imagine one could do as well or better" (41–42).

Sister Rosemary Winkeljohann in 1981 conducted a
limited research project consisting of only eight
kindergarten students at Grand Forks Air Force Base School.
She tested all children for language development, then
chose four who possessed poor language ability and four who
had advanced ability. She then interviewed the parents as
to television viewing. Her conclusion was that "television
was not the variable influencing the children's language
development." She does note that the children with
advanced language ability were exposed at home to more
magazines and books.

Positive Positions

In a 1988 study, Rice and Woodsmall tested groups of
3- and 5-year-old children for ability to learn various new

"novel" words on the basis of a short television exposure.
Both groups learned difficult new words, such as
"gramophone," "nurturant," and "viola." The results
defended the thesis that children "learn new words when
watching television, given an appropriate script" (425).

Two articles published in 1987 defend the role of
television. David Considine embraces the visual media as
vital to the education of new generations and argues that
teachers need to "integrate this technology" into their
classroom with "visual literacy training" (639-40). Robert
Abelman advocates television as "a potentially useful and
powerful tool" for classroom teachers. The introduction of
"television literacy" into the curriculum will encourage
critical thinking and imaginative responses, especially by
gifted children (166).

One of the pioneers in this field is Neil Postman,
whose text Television and the Teaching of English supports
television for its educational values. His third chapter,
"Television and Its Effects," argues that television viewing
encourages children to read, provides an "aural-visual
source of information," and adds to their accumulation or
"storehouse of words" (30-38). His fourth chapter, "The
Literature of Television," defends the media for its
introduction of literary classics to children.

Hal Blyth and Charlie Sweet of Eastern Kentucky
University insist that children will watch television, so
teachers should respond to the electronic revolution. They

argue that television is another tool, but it will be an
"effective tool" only if teachers develop a "television
consciousness" and use the media as a supplement to other
classroom methods (22-24).

    Throughout their discussions, all critics find both
positives and negatives. Roger Fransecky reflects this
duality. He argues that "television is important,
universal, and subtle" (717). However, he insists that
television becomes "junk food" for children unless teachers
actively lead their students into paths of inquiry and
critical thinking about what they view on the tube. As with
any educational tool, the teachers and the parents will
play the key roles in selecting a program, using it wisely,
and--when necessary--turning off the television set.

Wells 5

Works Cited

Abelman, Robert. "Television Literacy for Gifted
    Children." Roeper Review 9 (1987): 166–69.

Blythe, Hal, and Charlie Sweet. "Using Media to Teach
    English." Instructional Innovator 28 (1983): 22–24.

Considine, David M. "Visual Literacy and the Curriculum:
    More to It Than Meets the Eye." Language Arts 64
    (1987): 634–40.

Fransecky, Roger B. "Perspectives: Children, Television,
    and Language Education." Language Arts 58 (1981):
    713–20.

Moody, Kate. Growing Up on Television: The TV Effect. New
    York: Times Books, 1980.

Postman, Neil. Television and the Teaching of English.
    New York: Appleton, 1961.

Powell, Jon T. "What We Don't Know About the Influence of
    Television." Educational Technology 26.8 (1986):
    41–43.

Rice, Mabel L., and Linda Woodsmall. "Lessons from
    Television: Children's Word Learning When Viewing."
    Child Development 59 (1988): 420–29.

Shayon, Robert. Television and Our Children. New York:
    Longmans, 1951.

Winkeljohann, Sister Rosemary. "Queries: What Is the Role
    of Television in the Language Arts Program?" Language
    Arts 58 (1981): 100–02.

5 *Writing Note Cards*

Note-taking is the heart of research, not merely a preliminary step. Chapter 4 explained that your task is not only to find relevant source materials but also to make appropriate selections from them. Note-taking is a careful, thoughtful process. If you write notes of high quality, you will not have to rewrite them for the paper. You cannot quote everything, for only about 10% to 15% of your paper should feature direct quotation of the secondary sources. Therefore, consider the following strategies for taking notes (each is explained fully in this chapter):

Write a **quotation** note to share with your reader the authoritative words and the distinguished syntax of an authority.

Write a **summary** note to make a quick overview of factual data that has marginal value; you can return to the source later if necessary.

Write a **précis** note when you wish to capture the essence of one writer's ideas in capsule form. This type of note includes the plot summary to explain briefly an entire story or novel, the review note, the abstract, and the annotation to a bibliography entry.

Write a **paraphrase** note card when you wish to explain in your own words the prevailing wisdom of a particular scholar. That is, you interpret the source by restating what the authority has said.

Write a **personal** note card for each of your own ideas so that you have a substantial body of individual concepts, not merely a set of borrowed viewpoints.

5a Designing Effective Note Cards

The following tips may prove helpful for attaining accuracy in hand-written notes. (See also Section 5g, 127–28, for tips on writing your notes into a computer.)

1. **Use ink.** Write notes legibly in ink because penciled notes become blurred after repeated shuffling of the cards.

2. **Use index cards.** In general, use either four-by-six- or the smaller three-by-five-inch index cards for recording data. Unlike large sheets of paper, cards are easily shuffled and rearranged.

3. **Write one item per card.** One item of information on each card facilitates shuffling and rearranging the data during all stages of organization.

4. **Write on one side of the card.** Material on the back of a card may be overlooked. Use the back side, if at all, for personal notes and observations, but mark the front with "OVER."

5. **List the source.** Before writing the note, abbreviate the exact source (for example, "Thornton 431") to serve as a quick reference to the full bibliography card. *Note:* Avoid a key number system or other complex plan because you need author and page number, not a key number, for in-text citation. Besides, you might lose your key!

6. **Label each card.** Use code words for labeling cards. Code words at the top of each card will speed arrangement of the notes to fit the design of your paper.

7. **Write a full note.** When you have a source in your hands, write full, well-developed sentences. Full wording in the note will speed the writing of your first draft (see Section 4c, 95–100, for an example). Avoid the temptation to photocopy everything with the hope that materials will fall miraculously into place later on.

8. **Keep everything.** Try to save every card, sheet, scrap, and note in order to authenticate a date, age, page number, or full name.

9. **Label your personal notes.** Write notes to record your own thoughts, but mark them with "my idea," "mine," or "personal note." Later on, you will know that the note is your idea, not something borrowed.

10. **Conform to conventions of research style.** Write complete, well-structured notes the first time so you can incorporate them easily and correctly into your manuscript. This next example demonstrates the correct style for citing sources.

Identifying sources, 7a, 174–175

Using lower case after "that," 7j, 189

Page citations, 7a, 174–76

Punctuation with quotations, 7h, 184–86

Signal your underlining of another's words, 7l, 192–93

    Darrel Abel in his third volume of <u>American Literature</u>
narrates the hardships of the Samuel Clemens family in
Hannibal, yet Abel asserts that "despite such hardships,
and domestic grief which included the deaths of a brother
and sister, young Sam Clemens [Mark Twain] had a happy and
reasonably carefree boyhood" (11–12). Abel acknowledges
the value of Clemens's "rambling reminiscences dictated as
an 'Autobiography' in his old age" (12). Of those days
Clemens says, "In the small town . . . <u>everybody</u> [my
underlining] was poor, but didn't know it; and everybody
was comfortable, and did know it" (qtd. in Abel 12).
Clemens felt at home in Hannibal with everybody at the same
level of poverty.

Underlining, 8b, 229–30

Interpolations, 7l, 192–93

Single quotation marks, 7h, 184–86

Ellipsis points, 7k, 189–92

One source quotes another, 7d, 178–7ª

5b WRITING DIRECT QUOTATION NOTE CARDS

Copying the words of another person is the easiest type of note to write. However, you must be careful to obey a few rules:

1. You cannot copy the words of a source into your paper in such a way that readers will think *you* wrote the material.
2. You must use the exact words of the source.
3. You must provide an in-text citation to author and page number, like this: (Lester 34–35).
4. You may and often should give the author's name at the beginning of the quotation and use the parenthetical citation for page number only, like this:

Fred V. Hein says, "The human body, with its unique blend
of cells, tissues, organs, and systems, is the most complex
and intricate living-machine yet observed on earth" (16).

5. You must begin every quotation with the quotation mark and end it with the quotation mark, as shown immediately above.

6. The in-text citation goes *outside* the final quotation mark but *inside* the period.
7. The quoted material should be important and well phrased, not something trivial or something that is common knowledge. It should *not* be, "John F. Kennedy was a Democrat from Massachusetts" (Rupert 233); rather, "John F. Kennedy's Peace Corps left a legacy of lasting compassion for the downtrodden" (Rupert 233).

Look at this sample note card:

Figure 64:
Sample note card

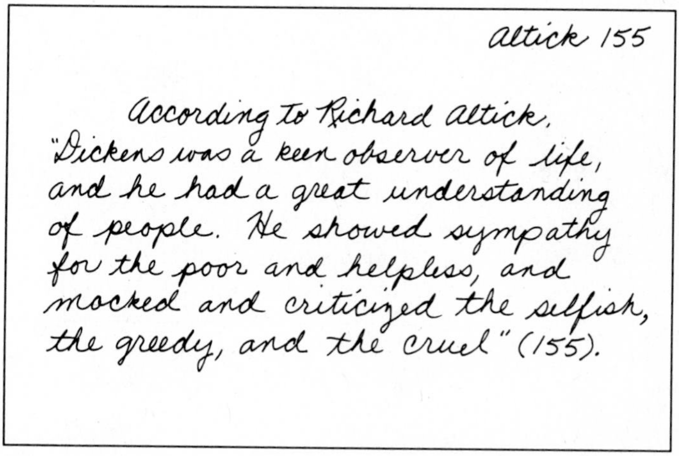

> *Altick 155*
>
> *According to Richard Altick, "Dickens was a keen observer of life, and he had a great understanding of people. He showed sympathy for the poor and helpless, and mocked and criticized the selfish, the greedy, and the cruel" (155).*

This note meets a checklist of requirements:

☑ Uses the exact words
☑ Page citation is outside the final quotation mark but inside the period
☑ Cites author and page
☑ Uses quotation marks
☑ The material is well written and worthy of quotation

Quoting the Primary Sources

Frequent quotation of *primary sources* is necessary because you should cite poetry, fiction, drama, letters, and interviews. In other cases, you may want to quote liberally from a presidential speech, quote a businessperson, or reproduce computer data.

When you quote a primary source, be certain to quote exactly, retaining spacing, margins, and spelling as in the original.

Figure 65:
Sample note
quoting a poem
stanza as a
primary source
(From T. S. Eliot,
"The Love Song
of J. Alfred
Prufrock.")

> *Images of frustration in Eliot's "Prufrock." 5*
> *"For I have known them all already,*
> *   known them all: —*
> *Have known the evenings, mornings,*
> *   afternoons,*
> *I have measured out my life with*
> *   coffee spoons;*
> *I know the voices dying with a*
> *   dying fall*
> *Beneath the music of a farther room.*
> *So how should I presume?"*

The student has copied an entire unit of the poem but may use only a line or two. Having an entire verse (or entire paragraph of prose) assures accuracy in handling the quotation within the body of the research paper.

The following note quotes from a novel:

Figure 66:
Sample note
quoting a
paragraph from a
novel as a
primary source
(From Renzo
Rosso, *The Hard
Thorn*, trans.
William Weaver
(London: Alan
Ross, 1966) 43.)

> *Rosso 43*
>
> *Awakening like being born*
> *"There was the morning's penumbra, the*
> *room, the wind, that beat its swollen*
> *hands against the walls; and it was*
> *as if he had just risen to the surface,*
> *his eyes barely opened. Immersed*
> *in something liquid. This was the*
> *sensation he still had, as if he had*
> *floated up from a deep abyss. Was*
> *it an interrupted dream?"*

Quoting the Secondary Sources

Be selective in quoting *secondary sources*. In particular, avoid lifting huge pieces of a scholarly article over into your paper. Do not copy entire paragraphs from magazines and encyclopedias unless the material is crucial to your discussion. The overuse of direct quotation from secondary sources indicates that (1) you did not have a clear focus and copied verbatim just about everything related to the subject, or (2) you had inadequate evidence and used numerous quotations as padding.

Quote from secondary sources for three specific reasons:

1. To display excellence in ideas *and* expression by the source
2. To explain complex material
3. To set up a statement of your own, especially if it spins off, adds to, or takes exception to the source as quoted

Limit quotations from secondary sources by using only a phrase or a sentence. Quote a phrase by making it a grammatical part of your sentence:

```
The geographical changes in Russia require "intensive

political analysis" (German 611), yet they open the door to

"democratic reforms of the greatest magnitude" (Watts 56).
```

If you quote a sentence, make the quotation a direct object. It tells *what* the authority says.

```
One critic notes, "The American government must exercise

caution and conduct intensive political analysis" (German

611).
```

If you quote more than four lines, set off the material as an indented block (see Section 7i, 186–88).

The following note cards contain quotations from a secondary source:

Figure 67: Sample notes quoting a secondary source

Postman 39-40   TV as literature
"We do not mean to suggest by its use that television is the equivalent of *belles lettres* but rather that certain kinds of television programs employ language and action in ways that duplicate the functions of traditional literary forms."

Postman 41   TV as literature
   He notes the uneven quality of TV by saying, "At its best, it is truthful and artistic. At its worst, it is trivial and formless."

Here is an example of how one researcher worked these two quoted sentences into her paper. Note that rather than lump the sentences together as one long, indented quotation, she works them separately into a meaningful paragraph that fits her style and the MLA format:

> The visual arts complement the language arts, the
> performing arts, and the sense of literature. Neil Postman
> devotes an entire chapter to this issue. In "The
> Literature of Television" he defends the media for its
> introduction of literary classics to children. He modifies
> his point to say, "We do not mean to suggest by its use
> that television is the equivalent of belles lettres but
> rather that certain kinds of television programs employ
> language and action in ways that duplicate the functions of
> traditional literary forms" (39-40). Out of this
> literature of television, surely, children gain not only a
> sense for literary forms but also a feel for the language
> in its best and its worst configurations. Postman notes,
> "At its best, it is truthful and artistic. At its worst,
> it is trivial and formless" (41).

Additional examples of handling quoted materials may be found in Chapter 7 and a discussion of technical matters will be found in Chapter 8.

5c Writing Summary Notes

There are two kinds of summary notes, the quick sketch of material discussed here and the more carefully drawn *précis* (explained in Section 5d).

The summary note is a brief profile of the material without great concern for style or expression. Sometimes you can frame it as an outline. Your purpose is to write quickly and concisely with little concern for careful wording or exact paraphrase. The summary note represents borderline information for your study. If its information is needed, you can rewrite it later in a clear, appropriate prose style and, if necessary, return to the source for revision. Use summary notes for several types of information:

1. Source material that appears to have marginal value
2. Facts that do not fit a code word or an outline heading
3. Statistics that have questionable value for your study

4. The interesting position of a source speaking on a closely related subject but not on your specific topic
5. A reference to several works that address the same issue:

> This problem of waste disposal has been examined in books
>
> by West and Loveless and in articles by Jones et al.,
>
> Coffee and Street, and Abernathy.

The summary gives a quick overview, so select the key information, summarize it, and get on with other matters. A summary card needs documentation to the author, but a page number is seldom cited because the note summarizes the entire article, not a specific passage.

Figure 68:
Sample summary
note card citing
author

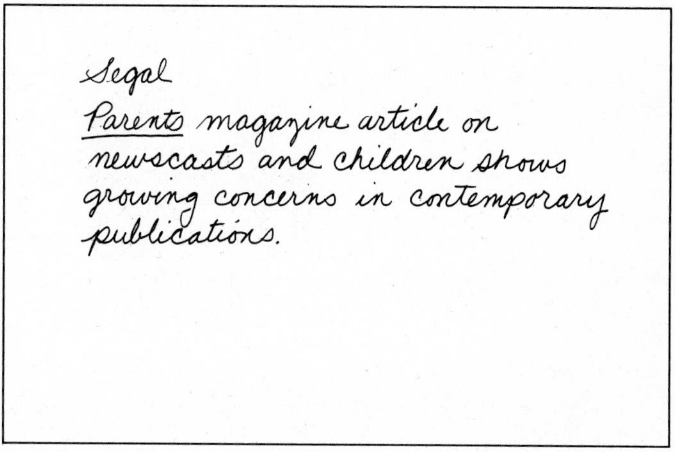

Segal
Parents magazine article on newscasts and children shows growing concerns in contemporary publications.

Eventually, this summary note was incorporated into a final draft for page 7 of the Wells research paper (see 245):

> Popular magazines have begun to address the issues. Julius
>
> and Zelda Segal, in Parents magazine, advise parents on
>
> ways to help children confront news broadcasts showing acts
>
> of violence.

Another note contained this quick summary:

Figure 69: Sample summary note citing author and page number

Winkeljohann 101
Has list of programs, projects, and materials that can be ordered.
Ditto for Fransecky 718+

Eventually, the summary of Winkeljohann resulted in a fully developed endnote in the Wells research paper (see 247):

```
    ²For teacher's guides and special materials, such as
schedules, posters, and author biographies, write to ABC
educational projects, American Broadcasting Company, 1330
Avenue of the Americas, New York, NY 10019.  For special
papers write Committee of Impact of TV on Children,
National Council of Teachers of English, 1111 Kenyon Road,
Urbana, IL 61801.  See Fransecky and Winkeljohann for
additional resource lists.
```

5d WRITING PRÉCIS NOTES

A précis differs from the rough summary by its polished style. It requires you to capture in just a few words the ideas of an entire paragraph, section, or chapter. Usually, a précis serves a specific purpose, so it deserves a polished style for transfer into the paper.

You will need to use the précis for these reasons:

1. To review an article or book
2. To annotate a bibliography entry
3. To provide a plot summary
4. To create an abstract

You serve as the bridge between the source material and the reader, so you must condense (abridge) fairly and without bias. Success with the précis requires the following:

1. Condense the original with precision and directness. Reduce a long paragraph into a sentence, tighten an article into a brief paragraph, and summarize a book into a page.
2. Preserve the tone of the original. If the original is serious, suggest that tone in the précis. In the same way, retain moods of doubt, skepticism, optimism, and so forth.
3. Write the précis in your own language. However, retain exceptional phrases from the original, enclosing them in quotation marks. Guard against taking material out of context.
4. Provide documentation locating the source of your material.

A sample précis note card follows:

Figure 70:
Sample précis
note card

> Powell 41-42
>
> In a section called "Apathy Towards Communication Skills," Powell states that television tends to speak in choppy, simplistic, and superficial language in order to appeal to the widest possible audience. He fears that children will lose the ability to express deep thoughts or feelings verbally.

In only a few sentences, the writer has abridged the essential elements of a long, five-paragraph section. The manner in which this writer used the précis is shown next:

```
      Television can invigorate the vocabulary of children,
although some critics argue otherwise. Jon Powell, for
example, states that television tends to speak in choppy,
simplistic, and superficial language in order to appeal to
the widest possible audience (41-42). In general, he fears
that children will lose the ability to express verbally
deep thoughts or feelings.
```

Accordingly, you will have success with précis notes if you tighten into a sentence or two the essence of a much longer statement.

Using the Précis Note to Review an Entire Work

The précis can condense the entire contents of an article or book, so it is especially useful for writing a review note, which requires you to explain the gist of the whole work in a sentence or two:

**Figure 71:
Sample précis
note reviewing
an entire book**

> The biography <u>Andrew Jackson</u> by James C. Curtis describes a president who was always full of mistrust. Curtis subtitles the book <u>The Search for Vindication</u>, which means that Jackson lived his life trying to justify his public acts and to defend his personal life.

> **A précis usually needs *no* citation to a page number because it reviews the entire work, not a specific passage.**

This next note reviews an entire article in only a few words:

**Figure 72:
Sample précis
note for a
magazine article**

> "Filling" <u>Children Today</u> 32
> This article devotes an entire page to a review of <u>TV News and Children</u>, a booklet published by Action for Children's Television (ACT) to warn that a child's ability to handle news is limited.

Eventually, this note was incorporated into the research paper in this manner:

> Children Today devotes an entire page to a review of TV
> News and Children, a booklet published by Action for
> Children's Television (ACT) to warn that mentally and
> emotionally a child's ability to handle hard news is
> somewhat limited.

Using the Précis to Write an Annotated Bibliography

An annotation is a précis that accompanies a bibliography entry. It explains the contents of a source:

> Blythe, Hal, and Charlie Sweet. "Using Media to Teach
>   English." Instructional Innovator 28 (1983): 22–24.
>
> These scholars insist that children will watch
> television, so teachers should respond to the
> electronic revolution. They argue that television is
> another tool, but it will be an "effective tool" only
> if teachers develop a "television consciousness" and
> use the media as a supplement to other classroom
> methods.

As shown, this annotation briefly clarifies the nature of the work. It seldom extends beyond two or three sentences. Note below how one writer used the annotation as part of her research paper:

> After all, students possess, to use the words of Blythe and
> Sweet (23), a "television consciousness," so teachers
> should take advantage of it.

See also Section 4e, 102–04.

Using the Précis in a Plot Summary Note

Another specialized type of précis is the plot summary. In just a few sentences it summarizes a novel, short story, drama, or similar literary work, as shown by this next example:

**Figure 73:
Sample plot
summary précis
note**

> *Great Expectations* by Dickens describes young Pip, who inherits money and can live the life of a gentleman. But he discovers that his "great expectations" have come from a criminal. With that knowledge his attitude changes from one of vanity to one of compassion.

Furnish a plot summary in your paper as a courtesy to your reader to cue the reader about the contents of a work. *Caution:* Make the plot summary a précis to avoid a full-blown retelling of the whole plot.

Using the Précis to Write an Abstract

An abstract is a brief description that appears at the beginning of an article. Usually written by the article's author, it helps readers decide to read or to skip the article. You will find entire volumes devoted to abstracts, such as *Psychological Abstracts* or *Abstracts of English Studies.* An abstract is required for most papers in the social and natural sciences.

> This study examines the problems of child abuse, especially the fact that families receive attention after abuse occurs, not before. With statistics on the rise, efforts devoted to prevention rather than coping should focus on parents in order to discover those adults most likely to commit abuse because of heredity, their own childhood experiences, the economy, and mental depression. Viewing the parent as a victim, not just a criminal, will enable social agencies to institute preventive programs that may control abuse and hold together family units.

(See also Sections 8a, 196–97, and 10d, 289–90, for instructions about placing the abstract in your paper.)

5e WRITING PARAPHRASED NOTES

A paraphrase is the most difficult note to write. It requires you to restate, in your own words, the thought, meaning, and attitude of someone else. It is not a quick summary but rather an interpretation and careful rewriting of important reference material as developed by careful reading and evaluation of the sources.

Use the paraphrase to maintain the sound of your voice and style and to avoid an endless string of direct quotations. Keep in mind these rules for paraphrase:

1. Rewrite the original in about the same number of words.
2. Provide an in-text citation to author and page number. You may and often should credit the source at the beginning of the paraphrase and put the page number at the end. In that way, your reader will know when the paraphrase begins and when it ends.
3. Retain exceptional words and phrases from the original only if you enclose them within quotation marks.
4. Preserve the tone of the original by suggesting moods of satire, anger, humor, doubt, and so on. Show the author's attitude with appropriate verbs: "Edward Zigler condemns . . . defends . . . argues . . . explains . . . observes . . . defines."

Double-check a finished paraphrase with the original source to be certain that the paraphrase truly rewrites the original and that it uses quotation marks with any retained wording of the original.

To repeat, paraphrasing is a technique for explaining the thought, meaning, and attitude of someone else. In other words, you interpret a statement by rewriting it. As with the précis, you act as a bridge between the source and the reader, but now you must capture the wisdom of the source in approximately the same number of words. That is one of your duties as a researcher—to share prevailing scholarly opinions with your reader. It requires you to name the source (*who*), indicate the source's attitude with your verb (*how*), and rewrite the material (*what*).

Quotation:

Fred Hein explains, "Except for identical twins, each person's heredity is unique" (294).

Paraphrase:

Fred Hein explains that heredity is special and distinct for each of us, unless a person is one of identical twins (294).

Quotation:

> Fred Hein clarifies the phenomenon:
>
>> Since only half of each parent's chromosomes are
>> transmitted to a child and since this half
>> represents a chance selection of those the child
>> could inherit, only twins that develop from a
>> single fertilized egg that splits in two have
>> identical chromosomes. (294)

Paraphrase:

> Fred Hein specifies that identical twins have identical
> chromosomes because they grow from one egg that divides
> after it has been fertilized. He affirms that most
> brothers and sisters differ because of the "chance
> selection" of chromosomes transmitted by each parent (294).

Active verbs, such as *specifies* and *affirms,* will convey your impression of the source's contribution. The verbs indicate the attitudes and the stance of the scholar.

Writing a rough draft goes quickly with paraphrased notes, but not so quickly when shuffling through page after page of photocopied materials. The paraphrased note can be transferred easily into your text. For example, an original interview article about television's influence on children states:

Perspectives: What about writing? Could television be used to aid its development?

Dr. Fransecky: Yes, it could help a lot. Simple things. We always get concerned about kids doing book reports. Why don't we parallel that with video reports, using that critical framework which we have hopefully put in place? Have kids write critical reports of what they've seen, be it television newscasts, sexy jeans commercials, or whatever else. I think we'll be amazed at how perceptive and critical kids are. That's not very new or exciting information, but why shouldn't it be done?

The researcher's paraphrased note, based on this source, is shown next:

Figure 74:
Sample
paraphrased note

> *Fransecky 718*
>
> *In his interview Fransecky responds to these questions: "What about writing? Could television be used to aid its development?" His affirmative answer included the suggestion that children write "video reports" as well as traditional book reports, which could criticize television across the board—from news programs to "sexy jeans commercials."*

Eventually, this paraphrased passage appeared in the final paper, slightly altered, as shown below in MLA style:

```
       Writing is enhanced by television viewing. In a recent

    interview, Roger Fransecky responds to this question:

    "Could television be used to aid [writing] development?"

    He answers in the affirmative to suggest that children

    might write "video reports" in addition to book reports.

    The reports could review a broad spectrum of programming,

    from the news programs to "sexy jeans commercials" (718).
```

To repeat, paraphrasing keeps the length of the note about the same as the original, but converts the original into your language and style. Any specific wording of the source is placed within quotation marks.

5f WRITING PERSONAL NOTE CARDS

During your research, make plenty of personal notes to record your thoughts on the issues. A research journal serves this same purpose. Build your own discourse on the subject. You will need to advance a theory, defend an idea, make a comparison, or discover another point of view. The content of a research paper is not a collection of ideas transmitted by experts in books and articles; your own ideas merit expression. The scholarly evidence is there to support and defend your thesis sentence, your topic sentences, and your fresh view of the issues.

Personal note cards should conform to these standards:

1. The idea on the note card is yours.
2. The card is labeled with "my idea," "mine," or "personal thought" so that later you can be certain that it has not been borrowed.
3. The note is a complete sentence or two so that you can transfer it into your text.
4. The card lists other authorities who address the same issue.
5. The jottings in your research journal are original and not copied from the sources.

Without personal notes, your writing will develop slowly. Let's consider two hypothetical instances. Student A sits down with his outline and note cards drawn entirely from the sources. He faces a major hurdle: how to write his own paper while avoiding the temptation to string together an endless cycle of quotations and paraphrases. Student B uses her personal note cards in combination with notes from the sources in order to write out her argument as supported by the sources. The difference is monumental.

Developing personal notes and writing in a research journal are essential to the process. Personal notes let you personalize your discoveries, reflect on the findings, make connections, and identify prevailing views and patterns of thought. Two samples of personal notes follow:

Figure 75: Sample personal note cards

My note

Reading of sources reveals to me several common knowledge conclusions by all the authorities:

    children watch TV the most
    TV continues to attract the young
    TV affects the kids

My note

TV obviously affects children's language usage for better or worse, so we need to look at – study – how strong a role TV plays in language development.

Eventually, these notes became part of a research paper (see 240):

```
Several propositions seem undisputed by all the
researchers:
        1.   Children are the largest audience for television.
        2.   Television is a continuing interest to children.
        3.   Television can provoke a response in children.
For these reasons, and others as well, parents and teachers
alike must address the role of television in the language
development of young people because it affects language
usage by children for better or worse.  The issues are
complex and controversial.
```

5g USING A COMPUTER FOR NOTE-TAKING

The availability of word processing with a computer offers you an alternative for note-taking. However, you should take advantage of the new technology only if you have the necessary expertise and only if a computer will be available to you throughout the project. *Caution:* Some instructors will collect all note cards, so keep a printout of the notes and make them available to the instructor.

The computer affects note-taking strategies in several ways:

1. You can record the bibliography information for each source you encounter by listing it in a BIBLIO file so that you build the necessary list of references in one alphabetical file. Chapter 9 shows the correct forms.
2. You can enter your notes into the word processor using one of two methods.
   a. Write all notes into a single file, labeled with a short title, such as NOTES. Your notes can then be moved around easily within the one document by BLOCK moves that will transfer them quickly into your TEXT document.
   b. Write each note as a separate temporary file so that each can be moved later into the appropriate section of your TEXT file by a COPY or READ command. With either method, you should print out your notes so that you can see them all at once; then edit them on the printed sheets as well as on the computer monitor.
3. During the drafting stage, you can copy notes directly into your rough draft by moving blocks or by transferring files. However, keep original notes on file in case they are needed again in their original form. That is, you can build and edit

your TEXT and still keep a copy of each note on the disk for proofreading against the finished pages of the TEXT file.

4. Computer notes often approximate the form of a rough draft, so write your computer notes in a complete, fluid writing style because, once keyboarded, the material will not need retyping. You need only move the note into your rough draft and then revise it to fit the context.

5h   Avoiding Plagiarism

Plagiarism (purposely using another person's writing as your own) is a serious breach of ethics. Knowledgeable, ethical behavior is necessary whenever you handle sources and cite the words of other people. A plea of ignorance about plagiarism does not play well with most readers, especially writing instructors, so give credit whenever it is due. Above all, avoid any deliberate effort to deceive instructors and other readers of the research paper.

Documenting Your Sources for a Purpose

The inventor Thomas Edison depended on documented research by others. He once said that he began his inventions where other inventors left off; he built upon their beginnings. How fortunate he was that his predecessors recorded their experiments. Scholarship is the sharing of information. The primary reason for any research paper is to announce and publicize new findings. A botanist explains her discovery of a new strain of ferns in Kentucky's Land Between the Lakes. A medical scientist reports the results of his cancer research. A sociologist announces the results of a two-year pilot study of Native Americans in the Appalachian region.

Similarly, you must explain your findings from a geology field trip, disclose research on illegal dumping of medical waste, or discuss the results of an investigation into overcrowding of school classrooms. A basic ingredient of business and professional life is research, whether by a lawyer, retail merchandiser, or hospital nurse. A management position demands research expertise as well as the ability to examine critically and to write effectively about an issue: a client's liability, a marketing decision, or the design of a nurse's work station.

Like Thomas Edison's, your research in any area begins where others leave off. You will support your thesis sentence by citing the experts in the field, so accuracy in your quotations and paraphrases is essential. When instructors see an in-text citation but no quotation marks, they will assume that you are paraphrasing, not quoting. Be sure that their assumption is true.

Blending the sources into your text is a major part of the assignment. You get credit for borrowing ideas (as long as you cite the source); you get more credit for quoting a well-worded phrase (with appropriate credit to the speaker); and you get credit also for summarizing the best ideas on a topic as expressed by several of the best minds (provided, again, that you name them). This assignment in critical thinking tests your ability to assimilate ideas and then to disseminate them in clear, logical progression.

One of your roles as researcher is to share with the reader the fundamental scholarship on a narrow topic. You are serving the reader by explaining not merely subject matter but also the *literature* of the topic. Therefore, you will strengthen your paper by summarizing an important book, by paraphrasing passages of important articles, and by direct quotation of key authorities. Rather than secretly stuffing your paper with plagiarized materials, announce boldly the name of your sources to let the reader know the scope of your reading on the subject, as in this example:

```
Lamar Alexander, as Secretary of Education, defended his

concept of extended school hours by calling it a "haven"

for children of working parents (23).
```

This sentence serves the reader, who now can identify a key government figure in the movement for extended school hours to benefit working parents and their children. It gives clear evidence of the writer's investigation into the subject. It is intellectually honest.

One way to avoid plagiarism is to develop personal note cards full of your own ideas on a topic. Discover how you feel about the issue. Then, rather than copy sources onto your pages of text, try to synthesize the ideas of the authorities with your own thoughts by using the précis and the paraphrase. Rethink and reconsider ideas gathered by your reading, make meaningful connections, and when you refer to a specific source—as you inevitably will—give it credit.

If you plagiarize, you will abandon critical thinking of your own and become an intellectual cripple. You will never have original ideas because you lean on others—their ideas and their words. On this point, see Section 4c, 95–100, on critical thinking and critical reading.

Understanding Plagiarism So You Can Avoid It

Fundamentally, plagiarism is the offering of the words or ideas of another person as one's own. The worst violation is the use of another student's work. Also flagrantly dishonest are writers who knowingly use sources without documentation and with no remorse (see student version A, 132). These two instances of plagiarism are cause enough for failure in the course and even dismissal from the college. Students who purposely cheat have no place in the college classroom.

A gray area in plagiarism is a student's carelessness that results in an error. For example, the writer fails to enclose quoted material within quotation marks, yet provides an in-text citation (perhaps because the note card was mislabeled or carelessly written); or the writer's paraphrase never quite becomes paraphrase—too much of the original is left intact (see student version B, 132). Although these cases are not flagrant instances of plagiarism, these students face the wrath of instructors who demand precision in citations. The serious consequences of plagiarism, then, require you to exercise caution any time you borrow from the sources.

Admittedly, a double standard exists. Magazine writers and newspaper reporters quote people constantly without documentation. But academic writers must document original ideas borrowed from source materials. The reason goes back to the opening discussion about Thomas Edison. Each scholar builds on previous scholarship. Like Thomas Edison's, your research in any area perpetuates a chain reaction. You begin where others leave off by borrowing from others and by advancing your findings and theory. Then, somebody else, perhaps, continues the research and carries it to another level. Without proper documentation at your station, the research grinds to a halt.

Consequently, you must conform to a few rules of conduct:

1. Acknowledge borrowed material by introducing the quotation or paraphrase with the name of the authority. This practice serves to indicate where the borrowed materials begin.
2. Enclose within quotation marks all quoted material.
3. Make certain that paraphrased material is rewritten into your own style and language. The simple rearrangement of sentence patterns is unacceptable. Do not alter the essential idea of the source.
4. Provide specific in-text documentation for each borrowed item. For example, MLA style requires name and page for all in-text references. Requirements differ for other fields, so see Chapter 10 on APA style and Chapter 11 for other styles.
5. Provide a bibliography entry in the "Works Cited" for every source cited in the paper.
6. Omit sources consulted but not used. This point is important. You do not want your instructor leafing back through the paper trying to find your use of a source that, in truth, was not cited.

These are the rules, but common-knowledge exceptions do exist. For example, most sources on Franklin Pierce will report common-knowledge facts as well as specific perspectives on the facts: his birth and death, 1804–69; his support of the Compromise of 1850; his role at age 48 as 14th president of the United States from 1853–57, and even his political support of the Kansas-Nebraska Act. However, if you use one historian's idea that

Pierce's handling of the slavery issue ruined his effectiveness as president, you must provide an in-text citation to the source. No in-text citation is needed in the following example:

```
Franklin Pierce supported the Compromise of 1850 in an

effort to resolve the slavery issue.  Later, as president,

he gave his support to the Kansas-Nebraska Act, which

allowed slavery to spread west.
```

An in-text citation is required in the following example:

```
An astute statesman would have seen the political peril of

the Kansas-Nebraska Act, but President Pierce supported it

and seriously damaged his political stature (Reiff 409).
```

Common-knowledge information needs no documentation. No in-text citation is needed here:

```
George Bush launched the Desert Storm attack against Iraq

with the support of allies and their troops from several

nations.
```

However, theory, interpretation, or opinion about the facts requires documentation. In-text citation is required in this example:

```
Beyond his victory in the war against Iraq, President Bush

demonstrated great mastery in his diplomatic unification of

a politically diverse group of allies (Wolford 46).
```

The next four examples in MLA style demonstrate the differences between genuine research writing and plagiarism. First is the original reference material; it is followed by four student versions, two of which are plagiarism and two of which are not.

Original Material

Despite the growth of these new technologies and the importance of the mass media in our lives, our schools have failed to do anything in the way of developing a systematic curriculum aimed at helping students to understand the form, content, ownership, and organization of the mass media.—David M. Considine, "Visual Literacy and the Curriculum: More to It Than Meets the Eye," *Language Arts* 64 (1987): 635.

While schools continue to operate as though print were the main means of communication in our culture, an increasingly high-tech society requires a new definition of literacy that encompasses visual, computer, and media literacy.—Considine 639.

Student Version A (Unacceptable)

> Despite new technology that makes the mass media important in our lives, the schools have failed to develop a systematic curriculum aimed at helping students to understand television. In fact, schools operate as though print were the main means of communication in our culture. But young people have a high-tech, visual sense of communication.

This piece of writing is plagiarism in a most deplorable form. Material stolen without documentation is obvious. The writer has simply borrowed abundantly from the original source, even to the point of retaining the essential wording. The writer has provided no documentation whatever and has not named the authority. In truth, the writer implies to the reader that these sentences are an original creation when, actually, nothing belongs to the writer.

The next version is better, but it still demonstrates blatant disregard for scholarly conventions.

Student Version B (Unacceptable)

> Modern communication technology is here to stay and cannot be ignored. We live in the information age, bombarded by television and radio in our homes and automobiles, annoyed by ringing telephones, and infatuated by computers and their modems for networking across the nation. Despite this new technology that makes the mass media important in our lives, the schools have failed to develop a systematic curriculum aimed at helping students to understand television. In fact, schools operate as though print were the main means of communication in our culture. But young people have a high-tech, visual sense of communication (Considine 635–39).

Although this version provides original opening sentences by the student and a citation to the authority, David Considine, it contains two serious errors. First, readers cannot know that the citation "(Considine 635–39)" refers to most of the paragraph; readers can only assume that the citation refers to the final sentence. Second, the borrowed material from Considine is not paraphrased properly; it contains far too much of Considine's language—words that should be enclosed in quotation marks.

The next version is correct and proper.

Student Version C (Acceptable)

> Modern communication technology is here to stay and cannot be ignored. We live in the information age, bombarded by television and radio in our homes and automobiles, annoyed by ringing telephones, and infatuated by computers and their modems for networking across the nation. [David Considine] sees the conflict as chalkboards and talking by teachers versus an environment of electronic marvels [(635)]. He argues, "While schools continue to operate as though print were the main means of communication in our culture, an increasingly high-tech society requires a new definition of literacy that encompasses visual, computer, and media literacy [(639)].

This version represents a satisfactory handling of the source material. The authority is acknowledged at the outset, a key section has been paraphrased in the student's own words with a correct page citation to Considine's articles, and another part has been quoted directly with a page citation at the end.

Let's suppose, however, that the writer does not wish to quote directly at all. The following example shows a paraphrased version:

Student Version D (Acceptable)

> Modern communication technology is here to stay and cannot be ignored. We live in the information age, bombarded by television and radio in our homes and automobiles, annoyed by ringing telephones, and infatuated by computers and their modems for networking across the nation. [David Considine] sees the conflict as chalkboards and talking by teachers versus an environment of electronic marvels [(635)]. He argues our public schools function with print media almost exclusively, while the children possess a complex feel and understanding of modern electronics in their use of computers, television, and other media forms [(639)].

This version also represents a satisfactory handling of the source material. In this case, no direct quotation is employed, and the authority is acknowledged and credited, yet the entire paragraph is paraphrased in the student's own language.

For additional examples, study the sample research paper by Kim Wells, 237–49, and note especially how she weaves back and forth from personal commentary to the sources.

6   *Writing the Paper*

Drafting a long paper involves many starts and stops, and your attention will be diverted by meals, class sessions, dates, and daydreaming. You may lose track of some good thoughts and ideas. Therefore, treat the initial draft as exploratory, one that examines both your knowledge and the strength of your evidence. You will work most effectively if you:

1. Refine your thesis sentence.
2. Write a title that identifies your key terms.
3. Use your outline to keep your ideas in order.
4. Understand your purpose and your role as a writer.

Write without procrastination or fear, reminding yourself that a first draft is a time for discovery. Later, during the revision period, you can strengthen skimpy paragraphs, refine your prose, and rearrange material to maintain the momentum of your argument.

6a Adjusting to the Long, Recursive Nature of Research Writing

Writing the paper will occupy many days, during which you must pull together and transcribe your notes and ideas into a whole. Supporting evidence may be weak, and you may retrace previous steps—reading, researching, and note-taking.

If you get writer's block and find yourself staring at the wall, relax and learn to enjoy the break rather than get frustrated. Lean back in your chair and change depression into prime time for reflecting. Nature has a way of reminding each of us that we need to pause now and then, catch our breath, and rethink our problems. Even if the manuscript is only a page or two, read back over your writing. Rereading might restart your thought processes.

Write portions of the paper when you are ready, not only when you arrive there by outline sequence. For example, when Kim Wells wrote her paper on the effects of television on the language development of children, she realized right away that television technology could not be ignored. She wrote this paragraph and set it aside:

> Modern communication technology improves with
> startling rapidity and cannot be ignored. Fifty years ago,
> people lived in a cocoon of isolation with only newspapers
> and a few radio stations to keep them informed as a nation.
> But now we live in the information age, and it blares at us
> with television and radio in our homes and automobiles,
> annoys us with ringing telephones, and infatuates us with
> computers and their modems for networking across the
> nation.

Wells eventually used the passage on page 6 of her paper (see 244).

Be practical; write what you know and feel, not what you think somebody wants to hear.

Be uninhibited; write the first draft with a controlled frenzy to get words on the page rather than to create a polished document.

Be cautious; treat the sources with respect—citing names, enclosing quotations, and providing page numbers.

6b WRITING A FINAL THESIS SENTENCE

A final thesis sentence will:

1. Control and focus the entire paper.
2. Give order to details of the essay by providing unity and a sense of direction.
3. Specify to the reader the point of the research.

Abandon your preliminary thesis if research leads you to new, different issues. For example, one writer began research on child abuse with this preliminary thesis: "A need for a cure to child abuse faces society each day." Investigation, however, narrowed her focus: "Parents who abuse their children should be treated as victims, not criminals." The writer moved, in effect, to a specific position from which to argue that social organizations should serve abusing parents in addition to their help to abused children.

Use code words from your notes and rough outline to refine your thesis sentence. For example, during your reading of several novels or short stories by Ernest Hemingway, you might have jotted down certain repetitions of image or theme or character. The code words might be "death," "loss of masculinity," "the code of the hero," or other issues that Hemingway explored time and again. These concrete ideas might point you toward a general thesis:

Possible thesis sentence: The tragic endings of Hemingway's
stories force his various heroes
into stoic resignation to their
fate.

Possible thesis sentence: Hemingway's code of the hero
includes a serious degree of
pessimism that clouds the
overstated bravado.

The final thesis should conform to several conventions.

Final Thesis Checklist

1. **It expresses your position in a full, declarative sentence, which is not a question, not a statement of purpose, and not merely a topic.**
2. **It limits the subject to a narrow focus on one issue that has grown out of research.**
3. **It establishes an investigative, inventive edge to your research and thereby gives a reason for all your work.**
4. **It points forward to the conclusion.**
5. **It matches your note-card evidence and your title.**

If you have trouble framing your thesis sentence clearly with a single focus, ask yourself a few questions. One of the answers might serve as the thesis.

What is the point of my research?

Thesis: Recent research demonstrates that self-guilt often
prompts a teenager to commit suicide.

What do I want this paper to do?

Thesis: Blatant sexual images show that advertisers have
little regard for moral scruples and ordinary
decency.

Can I tell the reader anything new or different?

Thesis: The evidence indicates clearly that most well
          water in the county is unsafe for drinking.

Do I have a solution to the problem?

Thesis: Public support for "safe" houses will provide a
          haven for children who are abused by their
          parents.

Do I have a new slant or new approach to the issue?

Thesis: Personal economics is a force to be reckoned with,
          so poverty, not greed, forces many youngsters into
          a life of crime.

Should I take the minority view of this matter?

Thesis: Give credit where it is due: Custer may have lost
          the battle at Little Bighorn, but Crazy Horse and
          his men, with inspiration from Sitting Bull, <u>won</u>
          the battle.

What exactly is my theory about this subject?

Thesis: Trustworthy employees, not mechanical safeguards
          on computers and software, will prevent theft of
          software, sabotage of mainframes, and destruction
          of crucial files.

These sample thesis sentences all use a declarative sentence that focuses the argument toward an investigative issue that will be resolved in the paper's general discussion and conclusion. *Note:* Express your thesis, usually, at the end of your introduction or at the very beginning (see Section 6f, 145–46).

6c WRITING A TITLE

The title of a research paper should provide specific words of identification. A clearly expressed title, like a good thesis sentence, will control your writing and keep you on course. Consider the following strategies for writing a title.

1. Name a general subject, followed by a colon, and followed by a phrase that renames the subject.

> Poor title: Saving the Software
> Better title: Computer Control: Software Safeguards and
>   Computer Theft
>   **Key words: computer theft, software safeguards**

2. Name a general subject and narrow it with prepositional phrases.

> Poor title: Gothic Madness
> Better title: Gothic Madness in Three Southern Writers
>   **Key words: gothic, southern writers**

3. Name a general subject and cite a specific work that will illuminate the topic.

> Poor title: Religious Imagery
> Better title: Religious Imagery in Faulkner's *The Sound and the*
>   *Fury*
>   **Key words: religious imagery, Faulkner, *The Sound and the Fury***

4. Name a general subject, followed by a colon, and followed by a phrase that describes the type of study.

> Poor title: Black Dialect in Maya Angelou's poetry
> Better title: Black Dialect in Maya Angelou's Poetry: A Language
>   Study
>   **Key words: black dialect, Maya Angelou's poetry, language study**

5. Name a general subject, followed by a colon, and followed by a question.

> Poor title: AIDS
> Better title: AIDS: Where Did It Come From?
>   **Key words: AIDS, where**

6. Establish a specific comparison.

> Poor title: A Comparison of Momaday and Storm
> Better title: Religious Imagery in Momaday's *The Names* and
>   Storm's *Seven Arrows*
>   **Key words: religious imagery, Momaday, *The Names,* Storm, *Seven Arrows***

Fancy literary titles may fail to label the issues under discussion. The title "Let There Be Hope" offers no clue for a reader; use such a title with a personal essay or short story, not with a research paper. A better title would be, "Let There Be Hope: A View of Child Abuse." A precise title would be, "Child Abuse: A View of the Victims." For placement of the title on the opening page, see "Opening Page or Title Page" (Section 8a, 195–96).

6d UNDERSTANDING YOUR PURPOSE AND YOUR ROLE AS A WRITER

As you begin writing, ask yourself two basic questions: Why am I writing this paper? What is my purpose? If you hesitate in your answer, review your research proposal (Section 1c, 13–19). Your writing needs to be factual, but it should also be human. Build on the intellectual framework (the facts of the study) and the emotional framework (your feeling about the topic). You can explain a problem with the weight of the evidence, but you cannot afford to be wholly objective, distant, and even cold.

For example, one writer's intellectual position on child abuse predictably condemned the practice, but her emotions responded to the abusers as well as the victims. Should she select an objective approach and, with a degree of detachment, present an analysis of the issues? Or could she become involved, negative in tone at times, positive at others, so that her presentation would persuade readers and call them into action? As an objective writer, she would offer evidence and analysis and keep at a distance from the subject. As a subjective writer, she would argue with flashes of human passion about the subject.

Complete objectivity, then, is unlikely for any research paper, which displays in fact and form an intellectual argument. At the same time, you should avoid the extremes of subjective writing—demanding, insisting, quibbling. Moderation of your voice, even during argument, suggests control of the situation—both emotionally and intellectually.

Writing a research paper affects you as both a researcher and a writer. In fact, most instructors consider the assignment as a learning process, one that features you as principal player in the drama. As a side benefit, your work can influence readers, but only if they see your emotional involvement mixed with scholarly control of the issues and the sources.

Kim Wells, 237–49, wanted to address parents and teachers who might influence changes in television programming, especially its use in improving language growth of children. As a result, she formulated an extended defense of her thesis, arguing that teachers and parents must (1) establish criteria for judging programs, (2) bring television into the curriculum, and (3) learn to use its potential in a beneficial way. She knew her purpose.

6e DRAFTING YOUR PAPER

At some point, you must write a draft of the whole paper. You may work systematically through the outline to keep order and use the note cards for evidence and support. But you may also start anywhere in order to write what you know at the time, keeping the pieces of manuscript controlled by your thesis and overall plan.

Leave plenty of space as you write—wide margins, double-spacing, and blank spaces between some paragraphs. The open areas will invite your editing later on. If available, use word processing so that when the paper is keyboarded one time, you need not rewrite or retype *everything* a second or third time (see Section 6j, 165–72).

Use your note cards and research journal for:

Transferring personal notes directly into the draft
Transcribing précis notes and paraphrase materials directly into
    the text
Quoting primary sources
Quoting secondary sources from notes

Use photocopied pages with caution. Find and quote key phrases and sentences; do not quote an entire paragraph unless it is crucial to your discussion and you cannot easily reduce it to a précis or paraphrase.

You may cite more than one source in a paragraph. The following paragraph cites three sources:

> Without doubt, television influences the mental
> processes and speaking habits of young people who may
> develop their language skills in the family den as much as
> they do in the classroom. Indeed, statistics abound on the
> television habits of children. High school seniors will
> have watched about 15,000 hours of television by the time
> they graduate (1986 Nielson Report as cited in Powell 41). —1
> To gain perspective, Hal Blythe and Charlie Sweet put it
> this way: "By the time the vidkids matriculate at their
> favorite institution of higher learning, almost one-half of
> their waking life will have been spent being Superseted,
> Chromacolored, and Colortaked" (22–23). Sister Rosemary —2
> Winkeljohann reports this incident:
>
>> A few seasons ago, on an episode of "Happy Days,"
>> Fonzie got a library card as a small part of the
>> overall story. The producers thought nothing of
>> it until they later learned that librarians all —3
>> over the country were swamped the next day with
>> children coming to the library. Children who had
>> never used the library facilities now wanted
>> library cards! (100)

```
Most parents and teachers recognize the powerful influence
of television, but too many seem incapable of dealing with
it and, especially, of putting it to good purpose.
```

This sample paragraph illustrates several points; the writer:

1. Weaves the sources effectively into the whole.
2. Cites each source separately, one at a time.
3. Provides three different in-text citations.
4. Indents the long quotation 10 spaces.
5. Makes the use of the sources seem a natural extension of her thinking.

Readers want to discover your thoughts and then examine your sources for contrast, evidence, and defense. You should explain, analyze, and support a thesis, not merely string together research information.

> *Note:* **A paragraph should seldom contain source material only; it needs at least a topic sentence to establish a point for the research evidence.**

Writing in the Proper Tense

Verb tense often distinguishes a paper in the humanities from one in the natural and social sciences. MLA style uses present tense to cite an author's work (e.g., "Johnson *explains*" or "the work of Elmford and Mills *shows*"). In contrast, APA style (see Chapter 10, 280–301) uses past tense or present perfect tense to cite an author's work (e.g., "Johnson *discovered*" or "the work of Elmford and Mills *has demonstrated*").

A paper in the humanities (MLA style) makes universal assertions, so it uses the historical present tense:

```
"It was the best of times, it was the worst of times,"
writes Charles Dickens about the eighteenth century.

Johnson argues that sociologist Norman Wayman has a
"narrow-minded view of clerics and their role in the
community" (64).
```

In contrast, a paper in APA style shows what has been accomplished:

```
Matthews (1989) designed the experiment and, since that
time, several investigators have used the method (Thurman,
1990; Jones, 1991).
```

APA style *does* require present tense when you discuss the results; for example, *the results confirm* or *diuretic therapy helps control hypertension.* See Chapter 10, "Using APA Style," for additional discussion.

MLA style requires that you use the present tense for comments by you and by the sources because the ideas and the works remain in print and continue to be true in the universal present. MLA usage demands "Richard Ellmann argues" or "Eudora Welty writes" rather than past tense verb forms: "argued" or "wrote."

Use the past tense only for reporting historical events. In the next example, past tense is appropriate for all sentences except the last:

```
The year 1963 was dramatic for America in several ways.
John F. Kennedy died in Dallas, about 200,000 marched on
Washington where Martin Luther King proclaimed, "I Have a
Dream."  The Atomic Test-Ban Treaty was signed by the
United States, Russia, and other countries.  Black student
Harvey Gantt enrolled at Clemson University to begin
integration of South Carolina schools.  Gantt's story is a
lesson in courage, one worthy of study.
```

Using the Language of the Discipline

Many words and phrases will be peculiar to your topic. Therefore, while reading and taking notes, jot down words and phrases relevant to the study. Get comfortable with them so that you can use them effectively. For example, a topic on child abuse requires the language of sociology and psychology, thereby demanding an acquaintance with:

social worker	maltreatment	battered child
aggressive behavior	poverty levels	recurrence
behavioral patterns	incestuous relations	formative years
hostility	stress	guardians

In like manner, a poetry paper might require *symbolism, imagery, rhythm, persona,* or *rhyme.* Every discipline and every topic has its own language. In fact, many writers compose a terminology list to strengthen noun and verb usage. However, nothing will betray a writer's ignorance of the subject matter more quickly than awkward and distorted usage of technical terminology. For example, the following sentence uses big words, but it misuses the language:

```
The impediment of maltreatment documents the national
compulsion toward crippling economically deprived children.
```

What does the passage mean? This writer is attempting to impress the reader, not communicate.

Writing in the Third Person

Write your paper with a third-person voice that avoids "I believe" or "It is my opinion." See the sample paper, 231–36, for use of the correct voice. Attribute human functions to yourself, not to nonhuman sources:

Correct: This writer considered the findings of several

sources.

Wrong: The total study considered several findings.

Writing with Unity and Coherence

Unity gives writing a single vision; coherence connects the parts. Your paper has *unity* if it explores one topic in depth, with each paragraph carefully expanding upon a single aspect of the narrowed subject. A good organizational plan will help you achieve unity (see Chapter 3, 71–87). The next passage moves with unity through a series of citations on a central comparison of television and reading:

Unity

The view that television encourages reading is not

universally supported. Kate Moody in her 1980 text Growing

Up on Television: The TV Effect compares the imaginative,

analytical function of reading against the "passive act" of

television viewing (66–76). Another drawback to

television, according to Moody, is that when viewing

television, a child cannot stop the action, "assimilate the

material," and then go on to the next sequence as one can

do while reading. She stresses the idea that "a good story

in print will take on new shades of meaning with each

rereading . . ." (56). Her comparisons of reading and

television viewing emphasize the active nature of reading

and a passive intake of television where a child cannot

exercise the imagination that the printed word demands

(68). However, the concept of $\boxed{\text{passive intake}}$ is disputed
by Daniel Anderson and Elizabeth Lorch, who argue that "the
viewer does not passively incorporate any and all content
. . ." but "applies his or her own experience and
understanding to that content" (29–30).

Your paper has *coherence* if the parts are connected logically by repetition of key words, the judicious use of pronouns and synonyms, and effective placement of transitional words and phrases (e.g., *also, furthermore, therefore, in addition,* and *thus*). Pay special attention to the progression of ideas and to the incorporation of quoted materials, as shown below:

Coherence

$\boxed{\text{Television}}$ must not be vicarious living in an
artificial world that avoids the drama of life; $\boxed{\text{rather}}$, it
must serve as a stimulus to active involvement. $\boxed{\text{In like}}$
$\boxed{\text{manner}}$, parents and teachers cannot avoid the drama of
$\boxed{\text{television}}$ that infects every preschool youngster and, like
a living virus, remains in their systems for the remainder
of their lives. $\boxed{\text{For example}}$, Abelman insists that
"$\boxed{\text{television}}$ is the first curriculum; a method of learning
that is well established before the children's initiation
into formal education" (168). Hodge and Tripp $\boxed{\text{add}}$ this
thought: "The school is a site where $\boxed{\text{television}}$ should be
thoroughly understood, and drawn into the curriculum in a
variety of positive ways" (218). For the parents, Singer
et al. warn that too many parents refused to participate in
their workshops and seemed unconcerned about $\boxed{\text{television's}}$
effects on their children (92).

6f WRITING THE INTRODUCTION OF THE PAPER

Use the first few paragraphs to establish the nature of your study, but keep the introduction short and directed toward the issues.

Subject.   Identify your specific topic, and then define, limit, and narrow it to one issue.

Background.   Provide relevant historical data. Discuss a few key sources that touch on your specific issue. If writing about a major figure, give relevant biographical facts, but not an encyclopedia-type survey. (See "Providing Background Information," 147.)

Problem.   The point of a research paper is to explore or resolve a problem, so identify and explain the complications that you see. The examples shown below demonstrate this technique.

Thesis Sentence.   Within the first few paragraphs, establish the direction of the study and point toward your eventual conclusions. (See below, "Opening with Your Thesis Statement.")

How you work these essential elements into the framework of your opening will depend on your style of writing. They need not appear in this order. You should not cram all these items into a short, opening paragraph. Feel free to write two or three paragraphs for the introduction and use more than one of the following techniques.

Opening with Your Thesis Statement

Generally, the thesis statement will appear near the end of the introduction, although it sometimes begins a research paper, as in this next example:

Thesis—
```
          Parents who abuse their children are victims and
should be treated as such, not as criminals.  Granted, they
are not battered like the youngsters, but society must
understand that child abuse can be a symptom of the
parent's economic condition and social background.
Reaching out to the parent before a child appears in an
emergency room may prove difficult, yet theoretically
solving the causes, not just treating the effects, may be
the only way to stop this escalating maltreatment of
America's greatest resource, the children.
```

Relating to the Well Known

This opening suggests the *significance* of the subject as it appeals to the popular interest and knowledge of the reader:

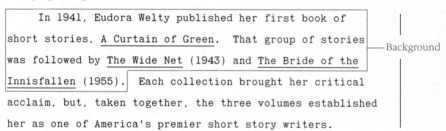

Television flashes images into our living rooms, radios invade our automobiles, and local newspapers flash their headlines to us daily. However, one medium that has gained great popularity and influence within the past decade is the specialized magazine.

— Popular appeal

Providing Background Information

This opening offers essential background matter, not information that is irrelevant to the thesis. For example, explaining that Eudora Welty was born in Jackson, Mississippi, in 1909 would contribute little to the following opening:

In 1941, Eudora Welty published her first book of short stories, A Curtain of Green. That group of stories was followed by The Wide Net (1943) and The Bride of the Innisfallen (1955). Each collection brought her critical acclaim, but, taken together, the three volumes established her as one of America's premier short story writers.

— Background

Reviewing the Literature

This opening cites only books and articles relevant to the specific issue. It distinguishes your point of view by identifying previous works and by explaining the logical connections between previous research and the present work:

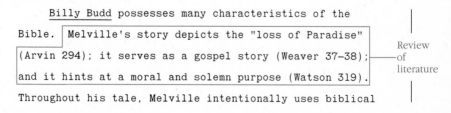

Billy Budd possesses many characteristics of the Bible. Melville's story depicts the "loss of Paradise" (Arvin 294); it serves as a gospel story (Weaver 37–38); and it hints at a moral and solemn purpose (Watson 319). Throughout his tale, Melville intentionally uses biblical

Review of literature

references as a means of portraying and distinguishing
various characters, ideas, and symbols, and of presenting
different moral principles by which people may govern their
lives. In brief, it explores the biblical passions of one
man's confrontation with good and evil (Howard 327-28;
Mumford 248).

Reviewing and Quoting the Literature

This method combines the background review with quotations and
paraphrases from the sources:

Family troubles will most likely affect the delicate
members of our society, the children. The recognition of
causes for their mistreatment and a need for a cure face
this society each day if we are to defeat what one critic
calls "the greatest crippler and killer of our
children--child abuse and neglect" (Fontana xvi). Another
writer argues that "the greatest impediment to our
improving the lives of America's children is the myth that
we are a child-oriented society" (Zigler 39). This

Review
of   sociologist suggests that too many Americans will not
literature
respond to documented findings about child abuse (39). Yet
the death rate from cruelty exceeds that from infectious
disease (Fontana 196). The situation is so bad that
Kratcoski warns parents to prepare for their children to
turn on them and to become parent abusers (437).

Taking Exception to Critical Views

This opening identifies the subject, establishes a basic view taken by
the literature, and then differs from or takes exception with the critical
position of other writers:

Lorraine Hansberry's popular and successful play <u>A
Raisin in the Sun</u>, which first appeared on Broadway in
1959, is a problem play of a black family's determination

to escape a Chicago ghetto to a better life in the suburbs. There is agreement that this escape theme explains the drama's conflict and its role in the black movement (e.g., Oliver, Archer, and especially Knight, who describes the Youngers as "an entire family that has become aware of, and is determined to combat, racial discrimination in a supposedly democratic land" [34]). Yet another issue lies at the heart of the drama. Hansberry develops a modern view of black matriarchy in order to examine both the cohesive and conflict-producing effects it has on the individual members of the Younger family.

Exception to prevailing views

Challenging an Assumption

This opening establishes a well-known idea or general theory in order to question and analyze it, challenge it, or refute it:

Christianity dominates the religious life of most Americans to the point that many Christians mistakenly assume that it dominates the world population as well. However, despite the denominational missionaries who have reached out to every corner of the globe, only one out of every four people on the globe is a Christian, and far fewer than that practice their faith.

Challenge to an assumption

Providing a Brief Summary

When the subject is a novel, long poem, book, or other work that can be summarized, refresh the memory of the reader:

Ernest Hemingway's novel The Old Man and the Sea narrates the ordeal of an old Cuban fisherman, Santiago, who manages to endure a test of strength, first when he is locked in a tug of war with a giant marlin that he hooks and, second, when he fights sharks who attack his prize catch. The heroic and stoic nature of this old hero reflects the traditional Hemingway code.

Summary

Supplying Data, Statistics, and Special Evidence

This opening uses special evidence both to attract the reader and to establish the subject:

> Severe abuse of children is on the rise. Each year more and more children suffer the trauma of physical and emotional abuse. Although the exact number remains unknown, the Education Commission of the States reports that some 60,000 cases occur annually (Cohen and Sussman 433). Boys outnumber the girls in suffering from abuse until the teen years (Chase 104). The death rate from cruelty exceeds that from infectious disease (Fontana 196). In truth, few young persons reach maturity without a severe spanking from an angry parent.

Statistics and evidence

Defining Key Terms

Some openings explain difficult terminology, as shown with the following example:

> Black matriarchy, a sociological concept with origins in slavery, is a family situation, according to E. Earl Baughman, in which no husband is present or, if he is present, in which the wife and/or mother exercises the main influence over family affairs (80–81). Hansberry develops a modern view of black matriarchy in order to examine the conflict-producing effects it has on the individual members of the Younger family.

Definition

Avoiding Certain Mistakes in the Opening

Avoid a purpose statement, such as "The purpose of this study is . . . ," unless your writing reports empirical research, in which case you *should* explain the purpose of your study (see Chapter 10, "Using APA Style").

Avoid repetition of the title, which should appear on the first page of the text anyway.

Avoid complex or difficult questions that may puzzle the reader. However, general rhetorical questions are acceptable.

Avoid simple dictionary definitions, such as "Webster defines *monogamy* as marriage with only one person at a time." See above (150) for an acceptable definition opening, and see 153–54 for defining key terminology.

Avoid humor, unless the subject deals with humor or satire.

Avoid artwork and cute lettering unless the paper's nature requires it (for example, "The Circle as Advertising Symbol").

6g WRITING THE BODY OF THE RESEARCH PAPER

The body of the paper should feature a logical analysis of the major issues in defense of the thesis sentence. The presentation of ideas in well-reasoned statements with proper documentation may seem an ideal but distant dream. Just remember, however, that writing is the act of discovery, an act of thought that demands a mode of expression. The thought and the expression will differ with every writer. Your unique view and expression have validity. As you write, then, your ideas and your notes will experience a metamorphosis, which is a transformation from scribbled notations to a series of neat, typewritten paragraphs. The transformation continues until the rough manuscript stops crawling or limping along and marches boldly to carry the banner of the argument. When finished, you will have traced, classified, compared, and analyzed the various issues.

The sample research paper (237–49) may prove helpful in demonstrating how one writer built a body of substantive paragraphs to explore her complex topic.

Using Chronology and Plot Summary to Relate a Time Sequence

Use *chronology* and *plot summary* to trace historical events and to survey a story or novel. You should discuss the significance of the events.

> John Updike's "A & P" is a short story about a young grocery clerk named Sammy, who feels trapped by the artificial values of the small town where he lives. The store manager, Lengel, is the voice of the conservative values in the community. For him, the girls in swimsuits pose a disturbance to his store, so he expresses his displeasure by reminding the girls that the A & P is not the beach (1088). Sammy, a liberal, believes the girls may be out of place in the A & P only because of its

Quick summary

"Fluorescent lights," "stacked packages," and "checkerboard green-and-cream-rubber-tile floor," all artificial things (1086).

> *Note:* **Keep the plot summary short and relate it to your thesis, as shown by the first sentence in the passage above. Do not allow the plot summary to extend beyond one paragraph; otherwise, you may retell the entire story. Your task is to make a point, not retell the story.**

Comparing or Contrasting Issues, Critics, and Literary Characters

Employ *comparison* and *contrast* to show the two sides of a subject, to compare two characters, to compare the past with the present, or to compare positive and negative issues:

Comparison and contrast

> To burn or not to burn the natural forests in the national parks is the question. The pyrophobic public voices its protests while environmentalists praise the rejuvenating effects of a good forest fire. It is difficult to convince people that not all fire is bad. The public has visions of Smokey the Bear campaigns and mental images of Bambi and Thumper fleeing the roaring flames. Perhaps the public could learn to see beauty in fresh green shoots, like Bambi and Faline as they returned to raise their young. Chris Bolgiano explains that federal policy evolved slowly "from the basic impulse to douse all fires immediately to a sophisticated decision matrix based on the functions of any given unit of land." Bolgiano declares that "timber production, grazing, recreation, and wilderness preservation elicit different fire-management approaches" (23).--Marcia Minkus

Developing Cause and Effect

Write *cause and effect* paragraphs to develop the reasons for a circumstance or to examine the consequences:

To see how the Hubble Law implies uniform, centerless expansion of a universe, imagine that you want to make a loaf of raisin bread. As the dough rises, the expansion pushes the raisins away from each other. Two raisins that were originally about one centimeter apart separate more slowly than raisins that were about four centimeters apart. The uniform expansion of the dough causes the raisins to move apart at speeds proportional to their distances. Helen Wright, in explaining the theory of Edwin Powell Hubble, says the farther the space between them, the faster two galaxies will move away from each other. This is the basis for Hubble's theory of the expanding universe (369).
--Robyn Elliott

Cause and effect

Drafting a paragraph or two on each method of development is one way to build the body of your paper, but only if each part fits the purpose and design of your work. Write a comparison paragraph, classify and analyze one or two issues, show cause and effect, and ask a question and answer it. Sooner than you think, you will draft the body of the paper.

Defining Your Key Terminology

Use *definition* to expand on a complex subject:

Football players and weightlifters often use anabolic steroids to "bulk out." According to Oakley Ray, "Steroids are synthetic modifications of testosterone that are designed to enhance the anabolic actions and decrease the

Definition

"androgenic effects." He says the anabolic substance, which
improves the growth of muscles, is an action caused by
testosterone, a male sex hormone.   Anabolism, then,
increases the growth of muscle tissue (Ray 81).--Patti
Murphey

Showing a Process

Draft a *process* paragraph that explains stage by stage the steps
necessary to achieve a desired end:

Process—

    Blood doping is a process for increasing an athlete's
performance on the day of competition. To perform this
procedure, technicians drain about one liter of blood from
the competitor about 10 months prior to the event. This
time allows the "hemoglobin levels to return to normal"
(Ray 79). Immediately prior to the athletic event, the
blood is reintroduced by injection to give a rush of blood
into the athlete's system. Ray reports that the technique
produces an "average decrease of 45 seconds in the time it
takes to run five miles on a treadmill" (80).--Patti
Murphey

Asking Questions and Providing Answers

Framing a *question* as a topic sentence gives you the opportunity to
develop a thorough answer with specific details and evidence:

Question
with
answers

    Does America have enough park lands? The lands now
designated as national and state parks, forests, and
wildland total in excess of 33 million acres. Yet
environmentalists call for additional protected land. They
warn of imbalances in the environment. Dean Fraser, in his
book, The People Problem, addresses the question of whether
we have enough park land:

    Yosemite, in the summer, is not unlike Macy's the
    week before Christmas. In 1965 it had over 1.6

> million visitors; Yellowstone over 2 million.
> The total area of federal plus state-owned parks
> is now something like 33 million acres, which
> sounds impressive until it is divided by the
> total number of annual visitors of something over
> 400 million. . . . (33)

We are running short of parks and playgrounds, which must
give way to highways, housing projects, and industrial
development.--Marcia Minkus

Citing Evidence from the Source Materials

Cite the various authorities on the subject. Provide quotations, paraphrases, and summaries in support of your topic sentences:

> Several critics reject the impression of Thomas Hardy
> as a pessimist. He is instead a realist who tends toward
> optimism. Thomas Parrott and Willard Thorp make this
> comment about Hardy in Poetry of the Transition:
>
>> There has been a tendency in the criticism of
>> Hardy's work to consider him as a philosopher
>> rather than as a poet and to stigmatize him as a
>> gloomy pessimist. This is quite wrong. (413)
>
> The author himself felt incorrectly labeled, for he writes:
>
>> As to pessimism. My motto is, first correctly
>> diagnose the complaint--in this case human
>> ills--and ascertain the cause: then set about
>> finding a remedy if one exists. The motto of
>> optimists is: Blind the eyes to the real malady,
>> and use empirical panaceas to suppress the
>> symptoms. (Life 383)
>
> Hardy is dismayed by these "optimists" and has little
> desire to be lumped within such a narrow perspective.
> --Laurina Isabella Lyle

Quotation of secondary source

Quotation of primary source

Many other methods exist for developing paragraphs; among them are *description, statistics, symbolism, point of view, scientific evidence, history, character, setting,* and others. You must make the choices, basing your decision on your subject and your notes. Here are a few examples.

Use *classification* to identify several key issues of the topic, and then use *analysis* to examine each issue in detail. For example, you might classify several types of fungus infections and do an analysis of each, such as athlete's foot, dermatophytosis, and ringworm.

Use specific *criteria of judgment* to examine performances and works of art. For example, analyze the films of George Lucas by a critical response to story, theme, editing, photography, sound track, special effects, and so forth.

Use *structure* to control papers on architecture, poetry, fiction, and biological forms. For example, a short story might have six distinct parts that you can examine in sequence.

Use *location* and *setting* for arranging papers in which geography and locale are key ingredients. For example, examine the settings of several novels by William Faulkner or build an environmental study around land features (e.g., lakes, springs, or sinkholes).

Use *critical responses to an issue* to establish a paragraph. For example, an examination of President Harry Truman's decision to use the atom bomb at the end of World War II would invite you to consider several minor reasons and then to study Truman's major reason(s) for his decision.

Dividing the body by important *issues* is standard fare in many research papers. Kim Wells, 237–49, uses the body of her paper to develop major issues of television viewing by children (see also her outline, 238).

Building the body by *cause and effect* has merit in many papers. Kim Wells, for example, explores the effects of television on the language development of children.

Writing Paragraphs of Substance for the Body of the Paper

Give the reader sufficient evidence to support each of your topic sentences. The paragraphs in the body of a research paper ought to be about one-half page in length or longer. You can accomplish this task only by writing good topic sentences and by developing them fully, as shown below:

```
If shoplifters with sticky fingers are looting retail

stores in ever larger numbers, a simple question is this

one: Who pays? Well, the bill comes to you and the other

honest shoppers who must make up the difference. Consumers
```

pay not only for shoplifting but also for the cost of
security measures. Jack Fraser, a retail executive,
states: "Stores are losing 1.94 percent of sales per
year—and that doesn't even include the expense of
maintaining the security staff and equipment. That's a lot
of cash. It cuts into profits" (qtd. in Schneider 38).

The writer of the paragraph above has used a question-answer sequence to build the paragraph, asking the question, "Who pays?" She answers it, "consumers pay," and she defends that answer with a quotation from an authority on the subject.

Almost every paragraph you write in the body of the research paper is, in one way or another, explanatory. You must state your position in a good topic sentence and then list and evaluate your evidence. Notice how the following writer defends his topic sentence with specific details. The accumulation of evidence builds a paragraph of substance.

Let the real world into the public schools. Channel
One furnishes a satellite dish for every school and a
television set for every classroom. We should use this
technology. It can bring PBS programs and other news and
features to the students. We should use videotapes,
camcorders, audio cassettes with "walkmen," electronic
piano keyboards, and computers. Some students have better
electronic equipment at home in their bedrooms than in
their schools. A teacher, a desk, and a book are not
adequate anymore. The Apple corporation has made gifts of
computers to schools for many years now. They had a profit
motive, but so what? Look at the trade-off. Worse, look
at the alternative—no computers at all in the schools.
—Lawrence Thompson

6h WRITING THE CONCLUSION OF THE PAPER

Build a conclusion that goes beyond mere summary and repetition of the thesis. It should reach a judgment to endorse one side of an issue, to discuss findings, or to offer directives. To put it succinctly, it should say something worthwhile. After all, the reader who stays with a long research paper has a right to a concluding statement. The following techniques suggest ways to build a comprehensive conclusion.

Restating the Thesis and Reaching Beyond It

As a general rule, restate your thesis; however, do not stop and assume that your reader will generate final conclusions about the issues. Instead, establish the essentials of your study:

A literary study might turn from analysis of the work to a discussion of the author's accomplishments.

A business paper might establish guidelines and directives.

A sociology study might explain the social ramifications of your findings.

Note how the next example expresses first the thesis and second a judgment:

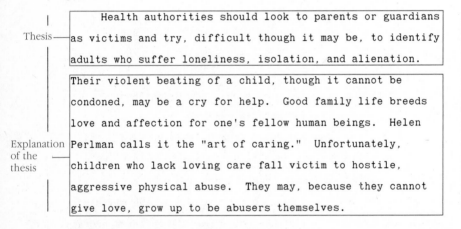

Thesis—
> Health authorities should look to parents or guardians as victims and try, difficult though it may be, to identify adults who suffer loneliness, isolation, and alienation.

Explanation of the thesis—
> Their violent beating of a child, though it cannot be condoned, may be a cry for help. Good family life breeds love and affection for one's fellow human beings. Helen Perlman calls it the "art of caring." Unfortunately, children who lack loving care fall victim to hostile, aggressive physical abuse. They may, because they cannot give love, grow up to be abusers themselves.

Closing with an Effective Quotation

Sometimes a source may provide a striking commentary that deserves special placement:

Quotation—
> Billy Budd, forced to leave the <u>Rights of Man</u>, goes aboard the <u>Bellipotent</u> where law, not morality, is supreme. His death is an image of the crucifixion, but the image is not one of hope. William Braswell best summarizes the mystery of the novel by suggesting that the crucifixion, for Melville, "had long been an image of human life, more suggestive of man's suffering than of man's hope" (146).

Returning the Focus of a Literary Study to the Author

While the body of a literary paper should analyze the characters, images, and plot, the conclusion should explain the author's accomplishments:

> By her characterization of Walter, Lorraine Hansberry
> has raised the black male above the typical stereotype.
> Walter is not a social problem, nor a mere victim of
> matriarchy. Rather, Hansberry creates a character who
> breaks out of the traditional sociological image that
> dehumanizes the black male. By creating a character who
> struggles with his fate and rises above it, Hansberry has
> elevated the black male. As James Baldwin puts it, "Time
> has made some changes in the Negro face" (24).

Focus on the author, Hansberry

Comparing Past to Present

You can use the conclusion rather than the opening to compare past research to the present study or to compare the historic past with the contemporary scene:

> In the traditional patriarchal family, the child was the
> legal property of the parents. But the idea that children
> are the property of the parents and, therefore, may receive
> whatever punishment seems necessary, no longer holds true.
> Social organizations and governmental agencies now help
> young victims in their search for preventive measures.
> Unlike the past, children today have rights too!

—Comparison

Offering a Directive or Solution

After analyzing a problem and synthesizing issues, offer your theory or solution, as demonstrated below:

> The four points above defend a central theory: the
> troubled parents who were victims in their own childhood
> and those who are victimized by circumstances today need to
> be identified by social agencies and helped to recognize
> their real potential as human beings and parents. The

—Theory

responsibility rests with health professionals who can

prevent abuse before it occurs. Major cities across the

nation and many rural communities are establishing child

abuse centers and parental self-help groups. A few of the

most successful community involvement programs are the

Child Abuse Prevention Center in Toledo, the Johnson County

Coalition for Prevention of Child Abuse in Kansas City, and

the Council for Prevention of Child Abuse and Neglect in

Seattle. More cities should establish such programs.

Discussing the Test Results

Discuss your findings and identify any limitations of a scientific study, as shown:

Findings and
limitations of
the study

The results of this experiment were similar to

expectations, but perhaps the statistical significance,

because of the small subject size, was biased toward the

delayed conditions of the curve. The subjects were,

perhaps, not representative of the total population because

of their prior exposure to test procedures. Another factor

that may have affected the curves was the presentation of

the data. The images on the screen were available for five

seconds, and that amount of time may have enabled the

subjects to store each image effectively. If the time

period for each image were reduced to one or two seconds,

there could be lower recall scores, thereby reducing the

differences between the control group and the experimental

group.

(See also Chapter 10, "Using APA Style.")

Avoiding Certain Mistakes in the Conclusion

Avoid afterthoughts or additional ideas; now is the time to end the paper, not begin a new thought. However, empirical studies often discuss options and possible alterations that might affect test results (see, "Discussing the Test Results," 160).

Avoid the use of "thus," "in conclusion," or "finally" at the beginning of the last paragraph. Readers can see plainly the end of the paper.

Avoid ending the paper without a sense of closure.

Avoid trailing off into meaningless or irrelevant information.

Avoid questions that raise new issues; however, rhetorical questions that restate the issues are acceptable.

Avoid fancy artwork.

6i REVISING, EDITING, AND PROOFREADING

After completing the rough draft, you face three important tasks:

1. *Revising* means altering, amending, and improving the entire work.
2. *Editing* means preparing the draft for final writing by checking your style, word choice, and grammar.
3. *Proofreading* means examining the final typed manuscript to spot any last-minute errors.

Revising Your Various Drafts

Revision can turn a passable paper into an excellent one, and change an excellent one into a radiant one. To revise means cutting out wordiness and irrelevant thoughts, reattaching sentences in new places, and transplanting paragraphs. Delete sentences that contribute nothing to the dynamics of the paper, as painful as that might be. Move sentences from the introduction to the conclusion. Set aside note cards that have become irrelevant. Above all, do not fall in love with anything you have written thus far.

Travel through the paper one time to examine each paragraph for its logical development of one central idea. Some sections will need extra development or more evidence from primary and secondary sources. One or two paragraphs may rely too heavily on sources and not enough on your own input. Some woefully short paragraphs can be combined with others. Long, difficult paragraphs may need to be divided because you crammed too much into them.

For unity, ask yourself, "Does this paper maintain a central proposition from paragraph to paragraph?" For example, the paper by Kim Wells, 237–49, consistently examines television's influence on the language development of children. She does not drift into other areas of influence, such as violence or commercialism.

Meet the needs of your readers, but avoid insulting their intelligence by giving simplistic facts: "It is obvious that television has an important impact on children." If obvious, why tell us? Instead, offer your insight:

> Television must not be a vicarious living in an
>
> artificial world that avoids the drama of life; rather, it
>
> must serve as a stimulus to active involvement.

At some point, reexamine the *introduction* for the presence of several items: a thesis, a clear direction or plan of development, and a sense of your involvement (see also Section 6f, 145–51). Invite the reader into your investigation of a problem. Kim Wells, 237–49, explains the tremendous amount of time devoted by children to television and then launches her investigation of television's impact.

Examine the *body* of the paper for a clear sequence of major statements. Examine it for appropriate and effective evidence in support of your key ideas. Examine it for transitions that move the reader effectively from one block of material to another (see also Sections 6e, 144–45, and 6g, 151–57). For example, Kim Wells, in her research paper, 237–49, provides both the negative and the positive views about television's effects on children and their language.

Examine the *ending* for a conclusion (1) drawn from the evidence, (2) developed logically from the introduction and the body, and (3) determined by your position on the issues (see also Section 6h, 157–61). Kim Wells builds on the evidence to advance her conclusion that the traditional classroom curriculum needs to find harmony with the preschool television curriculum.

When satisfied that the paper flows effectively point by point and fulfills the needs of your intended audience, you can begin editing.

Editing Before You Type the Final Manuscript

After revision, read through the paper again to study your word choices. Check individual words for their effectiveness and appropriateness. The language of a research paper should be slightly formal, so be on guard against trendy expressions, humor, and slang.

Study your sentences, and cut phrases and clauses that do not advance your main ideas or that merely repeat what you or your sources have already stated.

Look at your verbs. Change "to be" verbs (e.g., *is, are, was*) to stronger active verbs. Maintain the present tense in most verbs. Convert passive structures to active, if possible.

Confirm that your paraphrases and quotations flow smoothly within your text (see Chapter 7, 173–93).

6i Revising, Editing, and Proofreading **163**

Check your format, such as margins, headings, and page numbers (see Section 8a, 195–96).

Note the editing by one student in the following example:

> *In some cases* ~~One critic calls~~ television, *is* "junk food" *see* (Fransecky
> 717), and ~~I think~~ excessive viewing ~~does~~ distract*s* from
> *(see esp. Paul Witty as qtd. in Postman 41)*
> other activities, yet television can and does bring
> *and* *of our best* *according to the evidence,*
> cultural programs, some ~~good~~ novels. It does, improve
> children's vocabularies, encourages their reading, and
> *and school*
> inspires their writing. Television, should not be ~~an~~
> *the traditional classroom curriculum should seek*
> antagonist*s*; ~~it should complement school work.~~
> *and find harmony with the preschool television curriculum.*

As shown above, the writer conscientiously edited the paragraph. You, too, should delete unnecessary material, add supporting statements and evidence, relate facts to one another, rearrange for active voice, and rewrite for clarity. Review earlier sections of this text, if necessary, on unity and coherence (144–45) and writing the body (151–57). See also "Revising Your First Drafts on a Computer," 169–71.

Editing to Avoid Discriminatory Language

You must exercise caution against words that may stereotype any person, regardless of gender, race, nationality, creed, age, or disability. Reevaluate words for accuracy; there is no need to avoid gender, for example, when writing about the difficulty of working during the sixth month of pregnancy. Be specific. Unless your writing is precise, readers might make assumptions about race, age, and disabilities. To many people, a reference to a doctor or governor may bring to mind a white male, while a similar reference to a teacher or homemaker may bring to mind a woman. In truth, no characteristic should be assumed for all members of a group. The following are some guidelines to avoid discriminatory language:

1. Review the accuracy of your statements.

   Discriminatory: Old people walk with difficulty.
   1. How old is old?
   2. Do *all* old people walk with difficulty?
   3. Are the elderly the only persons who walk with difficulty?

   Nondiscriminatory: Persons afflicted with severe scoliosis walk with difficulty.

2. Use plural subjects so that nonspecific, plural pronouns are grammatically correct. For example, do you intend to specify that Judy Jones maintains *her* lab equipment in sterile condition or to indicate that technicians, in general, maintain *their* own equipment? Do be careful, though, because the plural is easily overused and often inappropriate. For example, some people now use a plural pronoun with the singular *everybody, everyone, anybody, anyone, each one* in order to avoid the masculine reference (even though it is not correct grammar):

    Sexist: Each author of the Pre-Raphaelite period produced *his* best work prior to 1865.

Colloquial: Each author of the Pre-Raphaelite period produced *their* best work prior to 1865.

    Formal: *Authors* of the Pre-Raphaelite period produced *their* best *works* prior to 1865.

3. Reword the sentence so that a pronoun is unnecessary:

Correct: The doctor prepared the necessary surgical equipment without interference.

Correct: Each technician must maintain laboratory equipment in sterile condition.

4. Use pronouns denoting gender only when necessary to specify gender or when gender has been previously established. *Note:* A new pronoun, *s/he,* has begun to gain popularity in letters and memos. It may become an acceptable academic choice.

The use of a specifier (*the, this, that*) is often helpful. In directions and informal settings, the pronoun "you" is appropriate, but *it is not appropriate in research papers.* Note these sentences:

Specify gender: Mary, as a new laboratory technician, must learn to maintain *her* equipment in sterile condition.

Use a specifier: The lab technician maintains *that* equipment in sterile condition.

Use second person: Each of you should maintain *your* equipment in sterile condition.

5. In general, avoid formal titles (e.g., Dr., Gen., Mrs., Ms., Lt., or Professor). Avoid their equivalents in other languages (e.g., Mme, Dame, Monsieur). First mention of a person requires the full name (e.g., Ernest Hemingway or Margaret Mead) and thereafter requires only use of the surname (e.g., Hemingway or Mead). Use Emily Brontë and thereafter use Brontë, *not* Miss Brontë.

Editing with an eye for the inadvertent bias should serve to tighten up the expression of your ideas. However, beware of the pitfalls. If your attempt to be unbiased draws more attention than your arguments, it will ultimately detract from the paper.

Proofreading the Final Manuscript

After the typed copy is finished, proofread it carefully. Mechanical and stylistic errors suggest carelessness that can seriously weaken your credibility. Typing a paper, or having it typed by somebody else, does not relieve you of the responsibility of proofreading; if anything, it requires you to be doubly careful. Typographical errors often count against the paper just as heavily as other shortcomings. If necessary, make corrections neatly in ink. Marring a page with a few handwritten corrections is better than leaving damaging errors in your text.

Specifically, use a few proofreading strategies, especially those geared to your particular style. Go through the paper several times to check for errors that plague your writing. You know which ones apply to you.

1. Check for errors in sentence structure, spelling, and punctuation, especially the errors in your history as a writer.
2. Check for hyphenation and word division. Remember that no words should be hyphenated at the ends of lines. If you are using a computer, turn off the automatic hyphenation.
3. Read each quotation for accuracy of your own wording and that within your quoted materials. Look, too, for your correct use of quotation marks.
4. Double-check in-text citations to be certain that each one is correct and that each source is listed in the "Works Cited" page at the end of the paper.
5. Read the paper aloud to discover awkward phrasing.
6. Pause at every pronoun—especially those that begin sentences—to be certain that its referent is clear.
7. Double-check the format—the title page, margins, spacing, content notes, and many other elements, as explained in Chapter 8, 194–249.
8. If you have written the paper on a computer, use available software programs to check your spelling, grammar, and style.

6j WRITING WITH A COMPUTER

Word processing has several advantages. It saves time because you will type the text just once, and you can make subsequent revisions quite easily. The computer can store notes and retrieve them instantly, transferring them into your draft with the touch of a few keys. It enables you to move blocks of typed material from one place to another. In many instances, it will review your writing style, check your spelling, and offer a thesaurus of available words.

Storing and Retrieving Notes, Documents, and Bibliography Sources

Methods for writing your notes into a computer are explained in Chapter 5, 127–28, which shows the importance of establishing a BIBLIO document to store full information on your sources. The BIBLIO document will produce your "Works Cited" page. Chapter 5 also explains two methods for writing and storing your notes, one that keeps all notes in a single file and one that creates each note as a separate, temporary file.

Pulling the Text Together On-Screen

Once you learn a few new commands, the word-processing system on any computer functions much like a typewriter. If you did not use the word processor to store your notes, you should now gather all materials and begin typing, much as you would at a regular typewriter. You can transfer your outline to the screen to guide your writing. Do this in one of two ways.

Method one requires the complete outline on file so that you can type information onto the screen under any of the headings as you develop ideas. You can transfer your notes to a specific location of the outline. This technique allows you to work anywhere within the paper to match your interest of the moment with a section of your outline. Kim Wells used the technique in preparing her research paper, 237–49.

Figure 76:
Working with an
outline file on a
word processor

```
                    Outline
1.   Television's influence on
       children
     A.   The problem is television's
     influence on children and, in
     particular, its effects on the
     language development of young
     people.
     B.   It is a significant issue
     because statistics in common
     confirm unconditionally that
     children spend enormous amounts of
     time watching television.

       Without doubt, television
     influences the mental processes and
     speaking habits of young people who may
     develop their language skills in the
```

Method two requires a word-processing system that supports windows; that is, the computer splits the screen so that you can write text while another section of the screen, a window, holds in place a section of your outline or even a section of your notes. (See Chapter 5, 127–28, for tips on developing your notes with a computer.) The window reminds you of content necessary for the text.

Figure 77: Using an outline in a window while writing on a word processor

```
1.   Television's influence on
     children
     A.   The problem is television's
     influence on children and, in
     particular, its effects on the
     language development of young
     people.



     Without doubt, television influences
the mental processes and speaking habits
of young people who may develop their
language skills in the family den as much
as they do in the classroom.
```

Transferring Material from Your Notes to the Text

You can transfer your notes to the text without retyping them only if you used the word processor to write your notes.

If you wrote all your notes into a single file, such as NOTES, begin writing your draft at the beginning of this NOTES file (which will push your notes downward as you type). When you need a certain note, scroll downward to find it, MARK it or CUT it as a block, scroll upward to your text, and MOVE it into place. Then blend it into your textual discussion with necessary rewording. An important alternative for a long set of notes, 12 or more, would be to label each note with a brief heading so that when you need one, you can employ the FIND feature, block the note, and move it into your text. Keep a separate, written list of these special headings.

If you developed each note in a separate file and used a different code word for each, you can pause during your writing and ask the computer to READ or COPY a file into your text. For example, let's suppose you have labeled and filed your notes by number, name of author, or the key words of your outline, such as TVTIME, TVABUSE, THESIS, TV&LANGUage. (*Note:* Names of files are generally limited to eight characters.) You would now retrieve those files and blend them into your rough draft. This system is more rapid than the first because you will not scroll through note after note looking for the right one. However, you must keep a written record of file names and the contents of each file.

Transferring Graphics into the Text

You can create graphic designs and transfer them into your text. Some computers allow you to create bar, line, or pie graphs as well as spreadsheets and other original designs. Some computer software includes ready-made graphics that you can use, as well. Such materials can enhance the quality of your presentation. After you create or locate a graphic, transfer it to the body of your text if it fits easily on the page. Place a full-page graphic design on a separate sheet following a textual reference ("See Table 7"). Place graphics in an appendix only when you have several complex items that would distract the reader from your textual message. In all cases, conform to standard rules for numbering, labeling, and presenting tables and illustrations. (See 216–19 for rules and examples.) Finally, use graphics *only* where appropriate. Do not substitute graphics for good, solid prose or use them to dazzle when your information is shaky.

Safeguarding Your Work on a Computer

During your entry of text into the computer, be sure to SAVE the material every page or so. This command preserves your writing onto the hard disk or floppy diskette. If the computer suddenly shuts down for any reason, your work will not be lost.

When finished with your initial typing, have the computer produce a copy of your paper in double or triple spacing. If you use a 40-character screen, print a DRAFT copy that duplicates screen spacing to ease your revision efforts.

Note: Be aware that some devious and perhaps evil persons have created the computer virus, which is a software program that can destroy a hard disk and all its files. Keep your diskettes or your personal computer free of any virus by using controlled laboratories where every diskette is screened before its use at computers in the laboratory. Or, use a virus-detection program (especially on your personal computer).

Revising Your Drafts on a Computer

The word processor enables you to make major and minor changes in the text and then quickly print various drafts. Consider the following.

Using the Computer for Global Revision of the Whole Work

Once you keyboard the entire paper, you can redesign and realign sentences, paragraphs, and entire pages without bothering to cut pages and paste them back together. You can add, delete, or rewrite material anywhere within the body.

Move and rearrange material with the MOVE or MOVE BLOCK commands. After each move, remember to rewrite and blend the words into your text. Then reformat your paragraph. Use the FIND command to locate some words and phrases in order to eliminate constant scrolling up and down the screen. Use the FIND/REPLACE command to change wording or spelling throughout the document.

Using the Computer to Edit Your Text

In some situations, you may have a software program that examines the *style* of your draft. Such a program provides such information as total number of words, number of sentences, average number of words per sentence, number of paragraphs, or average number of words per paragraph. It provides a list of your most active words and counts the number of monosyllabic and polysyllabic words. It may locate passive constructions, jargon words, and usage errors. Its analysis then suggests, for example, "Your short paragraphs suggest a journalistic style that may not be appropriate for scholarly writing" or "The number of words in your sentences exceeds the norm."

The software program may provide a readability score. For example, the Flesch Reading Ease Score is based on the number of words in each sentence and also the average number of syllables per word. The highest score, 100, represents a 4th grade level. A Flesch score within the range of 40–50 would be acceptable for a research paper. Another program, the Gunning Fox index, examines sentence length, but it looks especially for words of three or more syllables. A score of 6 means an easy reading level, but research papers, because they use a specialized language, usually reflect a higher level, one of 9–12.

After a software program examines the style of your manuscript, you should revise and edit the text to improve certain stylistic weaknesses. However, you must edit and adjust your paper by *your* standards with due respect to the computer analysis. Remember, it is your paper, not the computer's. You may need to use some long words and write some long sentences, or you may prefer the passive voice in one particular sentence.

Some software programs examine your grammar, looking for a parenthesis that you have opened but not closed, unpaired quotation marks, passive verbs, and other specific items that the computer will flag for your correction. Pay attention to the caution flags raised by this type of program.

A spelling checker moves through your text to flag misspelled words and words not in the computer's dictionary, such as proper names. You must then move through the text and correct misspellings. Regardless of the availability of such sophisticated software, you should work through the text on the screen of your monitor and make all necessary editorial changes.

In particular, use the SEARCH function of your computer system. It moves the cursor quickly to troublesome words and common grammatical errors. For example, if your experience with the use of *there, their,* and *they're* has been less than successful, search quickly all instances of these words. By concentrating on one problem and tracing it through the entire paper, you can edit effectively. If your writing history would suggest it, SEARCH and examine especially one or more of the following:

1. **Words commonly misused.**   Do you sometimes use *alot* rather than *a lot* and *to* rather than *too?* If so, order a SEARCH for *alot* and then for *to* and correct errors accordingly. You know your weaknesses, so search out usage problems that plague you:

   accept/except
   adapt/adopt
   advice/advise
   all ready/already
   among/between
   cite/site
   criteria/criterion
   data/datum
   farther/further
   its/it's
   lay/lie
   on to/onto
   passed/past
   suppose to/supposed to
   use to/used to

   These are words a spelling checker will usually ignore, so the SEARCH is necessary.

2. **Contractions.**   Research papers are formal, so avoid contractions. You can easily correct them by a SEARCH for the apostrophe (').

3. **Pronouns.**　Troublesome words are *he, she, it, they, their* because referents can be unclear. For example, SEARCH *he* to be sure you have a clear masculine referent, not ambiguity or bias:

```
Stonewall Jackson served General Lee valiantly in the

battles against Union forces. He was a man of raw courage.
```

The cursor, blinking as it pauses at *He,* encourages a change to:

```
Stonewall Jackson served General Lee valiantly in the

battles against Union forces. Jackson, like Lee, was a man

of raw courage.
```

Here is another example that a SEARCH for the word *this* might uncover:

```
Dr. Himmelweit stresses this point: "Book reading comes

into its own, not despite television but because of it"

(qtd. in Postman 33). This is not universally supported.
```

The first highlighted *this* is correct, but the second needs clarification, as with:

```
This view by Himmelweit is not universally supported.
```

4. **Unnecessary negatives.** SEARCH for *no, not, never* in order to correct obtuse wording:

```
A not unacceptable reading of Hawthorne is Fogle's

interpretation of The Scarlet Letter.
```

Correction makes a positive assertion:

```
Fogle's reading of The Scarlet Letter asserts Hawthorne's

positive view of Hester's moral strength (15).
```

5. **Punctuation.** SEARCH for the comma (,) and the semicolon (;) to establish your accuracy. Consult also Section 7i, 184–86, on punctuation of quotations. If you employ parentheses regularly, SEARCH for the opening parenthesis and check visually for a closing one.

6. **Abbreviations.** Use the SEARCH AND REPLACE function to put into final form any abbreviated words or phrases employed in the early draft(s). For example, you might have saved time in drafting the paper by typing SL for *The Scarlet Letter.* Now is the time to SEARCH for each instance of SL and to replace it automatically with the full title.

Proofreading Before the Final Computer Printout

After you have edited the text to your satisfaction, print a hard copy as formatted by your final specifications, such as double spacing, one-inch margins, page numbers, a running head, and so forth. See 194–98 for details of page format. Proofread this version for correctness of the format and spelling, punctuation, alphabetizing of the page of works cited, and so forth.

If at all possible, print your final version on a laser printer or a typewriter-quality printer. Such printers with sheet-fed paper or razor-cut continuous forms paper will produce a manuscript of the best typewriter quality. Perforated paper in continuous forms will leave ragged edges along the top, sides, and bottom of the sheets. A dot-matrix printer will not give the black sharpness of detail that many instructors require. You can overcome that obstacle by using the double-strike feature available on most dot-matrix printers. This feature commands the printer to strike each letter twice, with the second strike slightly off center, giving letters a darker quality.

Using the Computer to Pull Together Your Works Cited Entries

The computer makes it easy for you to build the "Works Cited" page, especially if you have made bibliography entries for your sources as you developed the notes and drafted the paper. Simply pull them together, put them in alphabetical order, and draft a printout for corrections. In some cases, the software will do the work for you. That is, you can keyboard information to match a template on the computer screen and the computer arranges the list for you. Just keep in mind that you, not the computer, will be responsible for the final product.

7 *Blending Reference Material into Your Writing*

One of your primary tasks is to blend your source material into your writing with unity and coherence. First, the sources contribute to the *unity* of your paper if they are useful to the argument. That is, quotation, paraphrase, and summary must explain and otherwise develop a topic sentence and your thesis. A collection of random quotations, even though they treat the same topic, is unacceptable. Second, the source material contributes to *coherence* only if you relate it directly to the matter at hand. Introductions, transitions, repetition of key words—these tie the paraphrase or the quotation to your exposition. (See also Section 6e, 144–45.)

Your in-text citation should conform to standards announced by your instructor. This chapter explains MLA style, as established by the Modern Language Association. It governs papers in freshman composition, literature, English usage, and foreign languages. Instructors in courses other than these may require a different form of documentation, such as APA style, the number style, or the footnote style (if so, see Chapters 10 and 11). A program that features writing across the curriculum may require you to use MLA style for all your papers or it may expect you to switch styles according to your subject matter, such as APA style for a social issue, the number system for a paper on computer technology, or the footnote system for a history paper.

The MLA style requires you to list an author and a page number in your text, usually within parentheses, and then at the end of your paper to provide a full bibliography entry on a "Works Cited" page (see Section 9a, 250–51). Notice how this next passage uses names and page numbers in two different ways. In the first sentence, the writer uses the name of the authority to introduce the quotation and places the page number after the quotation. In the second, the writer places both the name and the page number at the end:

```
According to  John Hartley,  19th century scientists

"discovered single cells that divided into two identical

offspring cells" (56) .  This finding eventually produced

the cell theory, which asserts, "All organisms are composed

of cells and all cells derive from other living cells"

(Justice 431) .
```

> *Note:* **Do not place a comma between the name and the page number in the parenthetical citation.**

7a BLENDING A REFERENCE INTO YOUR TEXT

An important reason for writing the research paper is to gather and present source material on a topic, so it only follows that you should display those sources prominently in your writing, not hide them or fail to cite them.

As a general policy, provide just enough information within the text to identify a source. Remember, your reader will have full documentation to each source on the "Works Cited" page. Sometimes you will need no parenthetical reference, as with: "Baird has devoted his entire text to the subject of Melville's mythology" (if Baird has only one book in the "Works Cited"). However, if you cite a specific part of a book, add page numbers:

```
James Baird argues convincingly that Melville shaped a new

"symbolistic literature  (19) .
```

Try always to use this standard citation because it informs the reader of the beginning and the end of borrowed materials, as explained next.

Beginning with the Author and Ending with a Page Number

Introduce a quotation or a paraphrase with the author's name and close it with a page number, placed inside parentheses:

```
Herbert Norfleet states that the use of video games by

children improves their hand and eye coordination  (45) .
```

This paraphrase makes absolutely clear to the reader when the borrowed idea begins and when it ends.

Notice how unclear the use of the source can become when the writer does not introduce borrowed material:

> The use of video games by children improves their hand and eye coordination. They also exercise their minds by working their way through various puzzles and barriers. "The mental gymnastics of video games and the competition with fellow players are important to young children and their development physically, socially, and mentally" (Norfleet 45).

What was borrowed? Did only the final quotation come from Norfleet? In truth, the entire paragraph, both the early paraphrasing and the quotation, came from Norfleet. Norfleet is the expert for this paragraph, so the paper should mention his name prominently, as shown below:

> Herbert Norfleet defends the use of video games by children. He says it improves their hand and eye coordination and that it exercises their minds as they work their way through various puzzles and barriers. Norfleet states, "The mental gymnastics of video games and the competition with fellow players are important to young children and their physical, social, and mental development" (45).

The above paragraph demonstrates proper usage in the following ways:

1. It credits the source properly and honestly.
2. It correctly uses both paraphrase and quotation.
3. It demonstrates the writer's research into the subject.

(See also student version B, 132, which explains plagiarism.)

Putting the Name and Page Number at the End of Borrowed Material

You can, if you like, put the authority's name with the page number at the end of a quotation or paraphrase, but give your reader a signal to show when the borrowing begins:

One source explains that the DNA in the chromosomes must be
copied perfectly during cell reproduction. "Each DNA
strand provides the pattern of bases for a new strand to
form, resulting in two complete molecules" (Justice, Moody,
and Graves 462).

By opening with "One source explains," the writer signals when the
borrowing begins. In the following example, the reader cannot possibly tell
which ideas are those of the authority and which are not:

Herman Melville used symbols of reincarnation, innocence,
primitive waters, the shadow that haunts all people, and
many others. He shaped a new "symbolistic literature" for
America (Baird 19).

Remember to give the reader a clue about where the borrowing begins:

The book Ishmael explains that Herman Melville used symbols
of reincarnation, innocence, primitive waters, the shadow
that haunts all people, and many others. The writer argues
that Melville shaped a new "symbolistic literature" for
America (Baird 19).

7b CITING A SOURCE WHEN NO AUTHOR IS LISTED

When no author is shown on a title page, cite the title of an article, the
name of the magazine, the name of a bulletin or book, or the name of the
publishing organization.

Note: **Search for the author's name at the bottom of the
opening page and at the end of the article.**

Citing the Title of a Report

One bank showed a significant decline in assets
despite an increase in its number of depositors (Annual
Report 23).

Citing the Title of a Magazine Article

Experts recognize the validity of play and a child's
use of toys. "In one sense toys serve as a child's tools,
and by learning to use the toys the child stimulates
physical and mental development" ("Selling" 37).

> *Note:* **You should shorten magazine titles to a key word for the citation. You will then give the full title in the works cited entry.**

One regional magazine correctly locates the Jesuit
settlement of St. Gall, Texas, as the modern city of Fort
Stockton ("Crossroads" 49).

or

The regional magazine Southern Living correctly locates the
Jesuit settlement of St. Gall as the modern city of Fort
Stockton, Texas ("Crossroads" 49).

The works cited entry would read: "Crossroads of West Texas History."
Southern Living Dec. 1984: 49.

Citing the Name of a Publisher or a Corporate Body

The report by the school board endorsed the use of Channel
One in the school system and said that "students will
benefit by the news reports more than they will be
adversely affected by advertising" (Clarion County School
Board 3-4).

7c IDENTIFYING NONPRINT SOURCES THAT HAVE NO PAGE NUMBER

On occasion, you may need to identify nonprint sources, such as a
speech, the song lyrics from a compact disc, an interview, or a television
program. There is no page number, so omit the parenthetical citation.

Instead, introduce the type of source—i.e., lecture, letter, or interview—so that readers do not expect a page number:

```
Thompson's  lecture  defined  impulse  as "an action triggered

by the nerves without thought for the consequences."
```

```
Mrs. Peggy Meacham said in  a phone interview  that prejudice

against young black women is not as severe as that against

young black men.
```

```
In his  rap song,  Julian Young cries out to young people

with this message: "Stay in the school, man, stay in the

school; learn how to rule, man, learn how to rule."
```

7d USING A DOUBLE REFERENCE TO CITE SOMEBODY WHO HAS BEEN QUOTED IN A BOOK OR ARTICLE

Sometimes the writer of a book or article will quote another person from an interview or personal correspondence, and you will want to use that same quotation. For example, in a newspaper article in *USA Today*, page 9A, Karen S. Peterson writes this passage in which she quotes two other people:

> Sexuality, popularity, and athletic competition will create anxiety for junior high kids and high schoolers, Eileen Shiff says. "Bring up the topics. Don't wait for them to do it; they are nervous and they want to appear cool." Monitor the amount of time high schoolers spend working for money, she suggests. "Work is important, but school must be the priority."
> Parental intervention in a child's school career that worked in junior high may not work in high school, psychiatrist Martin Greenburg adds. "The interventions can be construed by the adolescent as negative, overburdening and interfering with the child's ability to care for himself."
> He adds, "Be encouraging, not critical. Criticism can be devastating for the teen-ager."

Suppose that you want to use the quotation above by Martin Greenburg. You will need to quote the words of Greenburg, and put Peterson's name in the parenthetical citation as the person who wrote the article:

```
After students get beyond middle school, they begin to

resent interference by their parents, especially in school
```

```
activities.  They need some space from Mom and Dad.  Martin
Greenburg says, "The interventions can be construed by the
adolescent as negative, overburdening and interfering with
the child's ability to care for himself" (qtd. in Peterson
9A).
```

As shown above, you need a double reference, one that introduces the speaker and another that includes a clear reference to the book or article where you found the quotation or the paraphrased material. Without the reference to Peterson, nobody could find the article. Without the reference to Greenburg, readers would assume that Peterson spoke the words.

> *Note:* **Peterson's name will appear on a bibliography entry in your list of works cited, but Greenburg's will not because Greenburg is not the author of the article.**

Note: If a person quotes from another writer's published essay or book, you should go in search of the original essay or book and should not use the double reference. Cite the original source if at all possible (see Section 9b, 258–59).

7e CITING FREQUENT PAGE REFERENCES TO THE SAME WORK

When you make frequent references to the same novel, drama, or long poem, you need not repeat the author's name in every instance; a specific page reference is adequate, or you can provide act, scene, and line if appropriate. Note the following example:

```
When the character Beneatha denies the existence of God in
Hansberry's A Raisin in the Sun, Mama slaps her in the face
and forces her to repeat after her, "In my mother's house
there is still God" (37).  Then Mama adds, "There are some
ideas we ain't going to have in this house.  Not long as I
am at the head of the family (37).  Thus Mama meets
Beneatha's challenge head on.  The other mother in the
Younger household is Ruth, who does not lose her temper,
but through kindness wins over her husband (79-80).
```

> *Note:* If you are citing from two or more novels in your paper, let's say John Steinbeck's *East of Eden* and *Of Mice and Men,* provide both title (abbreviated) and page unless the reference is clear: (*Eden* 56) and (*Mice* 12–13).

7f CITING MATERIAL FROM TEXTBOOKS AND LARGE ANTHOLOGIES

Reproduced below is a small portion of a textbook:

METAPHOR

The Skaters

Black swallows swooping or gliding
In a flurry of entangled loops and curves;
The skaters skim over the frozen river.
And the grinding click of their skates as they
      impinge upon the surface,
Is like the brushing together of thin wing-tips
      of silver.

John Gould Fletcher

—From *Patterns in Literature.* Ed. Edmund J. Farrell, Ouida H. Clapp, and Karen Kuehner, eds. Glenview: Scott, 1991. 814.

If you quote from Fletcher's poem, and if that is all you quote from the anthology, cite the author and page in the text and put a comprehensive entry in the list of works cited:

Text

In "The Skaters," John Gould Fletcher compares "the grinding click" of ice skates to "the brushing together of thin wing-tips of silver" (814).

Bibliography Entry

Fletcher, John Gould. "The Skaters." Patterns in
    Literature. Ed. Edmund J. Farrell, Ouida H. Clapp,
    and Karen Kuehner. Glenview: Scott, 1991. 814.

Suppose, however, that you also want to quote not only from Fletcher but also from the authors of the textbook and from a second poem in the book. You can make in-text citations to name and page, but your works cited entries can be shortened by cross references.

In the Text

In "The Skaters," John Gould Fletcher compares "the grinding click" of ice skates to "the brushing together of thin wing—tips of silver" (814). The use of metaphor is central to his poetic efforts. One source emphasizes Fletcher's use of metaphor, especially his comparison of "the silhouettes of a group of graceful skaters to a flock of black swallows" (Farrell et al. 814). Metaphor gives us a fresh look, as when Lew Sarett in his "Requiem for a Modern Croesus" uses coins to make his ironic statement about the wealthy king of sixth century Lydia:

> To him the moon was a silver dollar, spun
>
> Into the sky by some mysterious hand; the sun
>
> Was a gleaming golden coin——
>
> His to purloin;
>
> The freshly minted stars were dimes of delight
>
> Flung out upon the counter of the night.
>
> In yonder room he lies,
>
> With pennies in his eyes. (814)

Note: Center the lines of poetry if necessary rather than indenting 10 spaces (see also Section 7i, 186–88).

In addition, let's suppose that you also decide to cite a portion of Dickens's novel *Great Expectations* from this same anthology. Your list of works cited will require four entries, mixed by alphabetical order with other entries. Dickens, in the example below, comes before Farrell et al. even though the anthology is the primary source. (See also Section 9b, 259.)

Bibliography Entries

Dickens, Charles. Great Expectations. Farrell et al.
675–785.

Farrell, Edmund J., Ouida H. Clapp, and Karen Kuehner, eds.
Patterns in Literature. Glenview: Scott, 1991.

```
Fletcher, John Gould.  "The Skaters."  Farrell et al. 814.
Sarett, Lew.  "Requiem for a Modern Croesus."  Farrell et
     al. 814.
```

Note: **The reference entry to Farrell et al. is primary; the others make cross-references to it.**

7g Adding Extra Information to In-Text Citations

As a courtesy to your reader, add extra information within the citation. Show parts of books, different titles by the same writer, or several works by different writers. For example, your reader may have a different anthology from yours, so a clear reference to *Great Expectations,* "(681; ch. 4)," will enable the reader to locate the passage. The same is true with a reference to *Romeo and Juliet,* "(2.3.65–68)." The reader will find the passage in any edition of Shakespeare's play.

One of Several Volumes

```
In a letter to his Tennessee Volunteers in 1812 General
Jackson chastised the "mutinous and disorderly conduct" of
some of his troops (Papers 2: 348–49).
```

```
Joseph Campbell suggests that man is a slave yet also the
master of all the gods (Masks I: 472).
```

The citations above provide three vital facts: (1) an abbreviation for the title, (2) the volume used, and (3) the page numbers.

Two or More Works by the Same Writer

```
Thomas Hardy reminds readers in his prefaces that "a novel
is an impression, not an argument" and that a novel should
be read as "a study of man's deeds and character" (Tess
xxii; Mayor 1).
```

The writer on the previous page makes reference to two different novels, both abbreviated. Full titles are *Tess of the D'Urbervilles* and *The Mayor of Casterbridge.*

```
Because he stresses the nobility of man, Joseph Campbell

suggests that the mythic hero is symbolic of the "divine

creative and redemptive image which is hidden within us all

. . ." (Hero 39). The hero elevates the human mind to an

"ultimate mythogenetic zone--the creator and destroyer, the

slave and yet the master, of all the gods" (Masks 1: 472).
```

Note: The complete titles of the two works by Campbell are *The Hero with a Thousand Faces* and *The Masks of God,* a four-volume work.

Several Authors in One Citation

```
Several sources have addressed this aspect of gang warfare

as a fight for survival, not just for turf (Robertson

98-134; Rollins 34; Templass 561-65).
```

The citation above refers to three different writers who treat the same topic. Put them in alphabetical order to match that of the works-cited page, or place them in the order of importance to the issue at hand. That is, list first the source that you recommend to the reader.

Additional Information with the Page Number

```
Horton (22, n. 3) suggests that Melville forced the

symbolism, but Welston (199-248, esp. 234) reaches an

opposite conclusion.
```

As a courtesy to your reader, identify notes, sections, or special editions. Classical prose works such as *Moby-Dick* or *Paradise Lost* may appear in two or more editions. Courtesy dictates that you provide extra information to chapter, section, or part so that readers can locate a quotation in any edition of the work.

```
Melville uncovers the superstitious nature of Ishmael by

stressing Ishmael's fascination with Yojo, the little totem

god of Queequeg (71; ch. 16).
```

See also Section 7f, 180-82.

7h PUNCTUATING CITATIONS PROPERLY AND WITH CONSISTENCY

Keep page citations outside quotation marks but inside the final period (exception: long, indented quotations as shown below). Use no comma between name and page within the citation (Jones 16–17 *not* Jones, 16–17). Do not use *p.* or *pp.* with the page number(s).

Commas and Periods

Place commas and periods inside quotation marks unless the page citation intervenes:

> "Modern advertising," says Rachel Murphy, "not only
> creates a marketplace, it determines values." She responds
> to several provocative ads in this manner: "I resist the
> advertiser's argument that they 'awaken, not create
> desires'" (192).

The example above shows (1) how to put the comma inside the quotation marks, (2) how to interrupt a quotation to insert the speaker, (3) how to use single quotation marks within the regular quotation marks, and (4) how to place the period after a page citation.

If the original material states:

> The Russians had obviously anticipated neither the quick discovery of the bases nor the quick imposition of the quarantine. Their diplomats across the world were displaying all the symptoms of improvisation, as if they had been told nothing of the placement of the missiles and had received no instructions what to say about them.—From Arthur M. Schlesinger, Jr., *A Thousand Days* (New York: Houghton, 1965) 820.

Punctuate citations from this source using one of the following methods (MLA style):

> "The Russians," writes Schlesinger, "had obviously
> anticipated neither the quick discovery of the [missile]
> bases nor the quick imposition of the quarantine" (820).

Note: **Use brackets to interpolate explanatory matter; see Section 7l, 192–93.**

> Schlesinger notes, "Their diplomats across the world were
> displaying all the symptoms of improvisation . . ." (820).

> Schlesinger observes that the Russian failure to
> anticipate an American discovery of Cuban missiles caused
> "their diplomats across the world" to improvise answers as
> "if they had been told nothing of the placement of the
> missiles . . ." (820).

This last example correctly changes the capital "T" of "their" to lowercase to match the grammar of the restructured sentence, and it does not use ellipsis points before "if" because the phrase flows smoothly into the text.

Semicolons and Colons

Both semicolons and colons go outside the quotation marks:

> Zigler admits that "the extended family is now rare in
> contemporary society"; however, he stresses the greatest
> loss as the "wisdom and daily support of older, more
> experienced family members" (42).

> Zigler laments the demise of the "extended family": that
> is, the loss of the "wisdom and daily support of older,
> more experienced family members" (42).

> Brian Sutton-Smith says, "Adults don't worry whether their
> toys are educational" (64); nevertheless, parents want to
> keep their children in a learning mode.

The last example above shows how to place the page citation after a quotation and before a semicolon.

Question Marks and Exclamation Marks

When a question mark or an exclamation mark comes at the end of a quotation, keep it inside the quotation mark. Put the citation to a page number up in the text, immediately after the name of the source, as shown below:

> The philosopher Thompson (16) asks, "How should we order our lives?"
>
> "How should we order our lives," asks Thompson (16), when we face "hostility from every quarter"?
>
> Thompson (16) passionately shouted to union members, "We can bring order into our lives even though we face hostility from every quarter!"

Single Quotation Marks

When a quotation appears within another quotation, use single quotation marks with the shorter one. Should a quotation appear also within the shorter one, use double quotation marks for it:

> George Loffler (32) confirms that "the unconscious carries the best of human thought and gives man great dignity, but it also has the dark side so that we cry, in the words of Shakespeare's Macbeth, 'Hence, horrible shadow! Unreal mockery, hence.'"

Place the period inside the quotation marks.

Remember that the period always goes inside the quotation marks unless the page citation intervenes, as shown below:

> George Loffler confirms that "the unconscious carries the best of human thought and gives man great dignity, but it also has the dark side so that we cry, in the words of Shakespeare's Macbeth, 'Hence, horrible shadow! Unreal mockery, hence'" (32).

Place the period after the page citation.

7i INDENTING LONG QUOTATIONS OF PROSE AND POETRY

Set off long prose quotations of four lines or more by indenting 10 spaces. Do not use quotation marks with the indented material. Double-space between your text and the quoted materials. Place the parenthetical citation *after* the final mark of punctuation, as shown below:

> The prophecy, spoken by the angel Gabriel, states:
>
> > Seventy weeks are determined upon thy people and
> > upon thy holy city, to finish the transgression,
> > and to make an end of sins, and to make
> > reconciliation for iniquity, and to bring an
> > everlasting righteousness, and to seal up the
> > vision and prophecy, and to anoint the most Holy.
> >
> > (Dan. 9.24)
>
> Scholars generally agree in their interpretation of this
> prophecy.

> *Note:* **If you quote more than one paragraph, indent all paragraphs three (3) extra spaces unless the first sentence quoted does not begin a paragraph in the original source (see Section 7k, 191).**

Citing Long Passages of Poetry

Set off three or more lines of poetry by indenting 10 spaces, as shown below, or by centering the lines of poetry (see 181).

> The king cautions Prince Henry:
>
> > Thy place in council thou has rudely lost,
> > Which by thy younger brother is supplied,
> > And art almost an alien to the hearts
> > Of all the court and princes of my blood.
> >
> > (3.2.32–35)

Reference to act, scene, and lines is sufficient only after you have established Shakespeare's *Henry IV, Part 1* as the central topic of your study; otherwise, write "(*1H4* 3.2.32–35)." (See also "Arabic Numerals," Section 8b, 207–08.)

Quoting Short Passages of Poetry

Incorporate short quotations of poetry (one or two lines) into your text:

> Eliot's <u>The Waste Land</u> (1922) remains a springtime search
> for nourishing water: "Sweet Thames, run softly, for I
> speak not loud or long" (3.12) says the speaker in "The
> Fire Sermon," while in Part 5 the speaker of "What the
> Thunder Said" yearns for "a damp gust / Bringing rain"
> (5.73–74).

As the example demonstrates:

1. Set off the material with quotation marks.
2. Indicate separate lines by using a virgule (/) with a space before and after the slash mark.
3. Place line documentation within parentheses immediately following the final quotation mark and inside the period.
4. Use Arabic numerals for books, parts, volumes, and chapters of works; acts, scenes, and lines of plays; cantos, stanzas, and lines of poetry (see "Arabic Numerals," Section 8b, 207–08).

Signaling Turnovers for Long Lines of Poetry

Provide a "[t/o]" in the right margin to signal typed turnovers of long lines of poetry. That is, when one line of poetry is too long for your right margin, indent the continuation five spaces more than the longest indentation and type "[t/o]" at the end of the line to indicate that the line is a turnover:

> In the first section of <u>Ash–Wednesday</u> Eliot lets
> despair spill out:
> > Because I cannot drink
> > There, where trees flower, and springs flow, for
> > > there is nothing again   [t/o]
> > Because I know that time is always time
> > And place is always and only place. . . .
> Thus the theme of the exile reaches its low ebb, and Eliot
> turns to the religious theme.

7j ALTERING INITIAL CAPITALS IN SOME QUOTED MATTER

In general, you should reproduce quoted materials exactly, yet one exception is permitted for logical reasons: if the quotation forms a grammatical part of the sentence in which it occurs, you need not capitalize the first word of the quotation, even though it is capitalized in the original. In the following example, "The," which is capitalized as the first word in the original sentence, is changed to lowercase because it continues the grammatical flow of the student's sentence:

```
Another writer argues that "the single greatest impediment

to our improving the lives of America's children is the

myth that we are a child-oriented society" (Zigler 39).
```

Restrictive connectors, such as *that* or *because,* make restrictive clauses and eliminate a need for the comma. Without a comma, the capital letter is unnecessary.

However, when your quotation follows a formal introduction, set off by a comma or colon, you must capitalize the first word as in the original:

```
Another writer argues, "The single greatest. . . ."
```

or

```
Zigler states: "The single greatest. . . ."
```

but

```
Zigler says that "the single greatest. . . ."
```

7k USING ELLIPSIS POINTS TO OMIT PORTIONS OF QUOTED MATTER

Omit quoted material with spaced ellipsis points (. . .). Use a fourth dot to end a sentence. Ellipsis points must *not* be used to change the spirit or essential meaning of the original. Quote your sources in correct grammatical structure.

1. Ellipsis points for material omitted from the middle of a sentence:

```
Phil Withim objects to the idea that "such episodes are

intended to demonstrate that Vere . . . has the       Three spaced
                                                       periods
intelligence and insight to perceive the deeper issue"

(118).
```

2. Ellipsis points for material omitted from the end of a source:

R. W. B. Lewis declares that "if Hester has sinned, she has
done so as an affirmation of life, and her sin is the
source of life . . ." (62).

Ellipsis with
period after the
page citation

or

R. W. B. Lewis (62) declares that "if Hester has sinned,
she has done so as an affirmation of life, and her sin is
the source of life . . . ."

Four spaced
ellipsis points

> *Note:* **As shown in the sample above, at the end of a
> sentence use a period with no space and then three
> spaced ellipsis points.**

3. Ellipsis points for material omitted from the beginning of a source:

He states: ". . . the new parent has lost the wisdom
and daily support of older, more experienced family
members" (Zigler 34).

Caution: The passage would read better without the ellipsis points:

He states that "the new parent has lost the wisdom and
daily support of older, more experienced family members"
(Zigler 34).

4. Ellipsis points for complete sentence(s) omitted from the middle of a source:

Zigler reminds us that "child abuse is found more
frequently in a single (female) parent home in which the
mother is working . . . . The unavailability of quality day
care can only make this situation more stressful" (42).

5. Ellipsis points for line(s) of poetry omitted:

Do ye hear the children weeping, O my brothers,
   Ere the sorrow comes with years?
They are leaning their young heads against their mothers,

```
    And that cannot stop their tears.
  . . . . . . . . . . . . . . . . . . . . . . . . . . . . . . . .
    They are weeping in the playtime of the others,
      In the country of the free.  (Browning 382)
```

6. Ellipsis points for paragraphs omitted:

```
    Zigler makes this observation:
```

Indent three extra spaces

```
          With many others, I am nevertheless optimistic
          that our nation will eventually display its
          inherent greatness and successfully correct the
          many ills that I have touched upon here.
            . . . . . . . . . . . . . . . . . . . . . . . .
          Of course, much remains that could and should
          be done, including increased efforts in the area
          of family planning, the widespread implementation
          of Education for Parenthood programs, an increase
          in the availability of homemaker and child care
          services, and a reexamination of our commitment
          to doing what is in the best interest of every
          child in America.  (42)
```

> *Note:* **If you are quoting two or more paragraphs, indent the first line of each paragraph an extra three (3) spaces in addition to the standard indention of 10 spaces.**

Many times you can be more effective if you incorporate parts of the quotation rather than quote the whole sprinkled with many ellipsis points:

```
    The long-distance marriage, according to William Nichols,
    "works best when there are no minor-aged children to be
    considered," the two people are "equipped by temperament
    and personality to spend a considerable amount of time
    alone," and both are able to "function in a mature, highly
    independent fashion" (54).
```

This writer's grammatical styling handles the omissions smoothly. The phrases fit into the sentence, so ellipsis points would only disturb the reader.

71 USING BRACKETS TO INSERT YOUR WORDS INSIDE QUOTED MATTER

Use brackets for interpolation, which means to insert new matter into a text or quotation. The use of brackets signals the insertion. Note the following:

1. Use brackets to clarify:

This same critic indicates that "we must avoid the temptation to read it [The Scarlet Letter] heretically" (118).

2. Use brackets to establish correct grammar:

"John F. Kennedy . . . [was] an immortal figure of courage and dignity in the hearts of most Americans," notes one historian (Jones 82).

3. Use brackets to note the addition of underlining:

He says, for instance, that the "extended family is now rare in contemporary society, and with its demise the new parent has <u>lost the wisdom</u> [my emphasis] and daily support of older, more experienced family members" (Zigler 42).

4. Use brackets with *sic* to indicate errors in the original:

Lovell says, "John F. Kennedy, assassinated in November of 1964 [sic], became overnight an immortal figure of courage and dignity in the hearts of most Americans" (62).

> *Note:* **The assassination occurred in 1963. However, do not burden your text with the use of "sic" for historical matter in which misspellings are obvious, as with:**
>
> **"Faire seemely pleasauance each to other makes."**

5. Use brackets to enclose parenthetical material within parentheses:

> The escape theme explains the drama's racial conflict
> (see esp. Knight, who describes the Younger family as one
> that opposes "racial discrimination in a supposedly
> democratic land" [34]).

or

> Consult the tables at the end of the report (i.e., the
> results for the experimental group [n = 5] are also listed
> in Figure 3, page 16).

6. Use brackets to present fractions:

a = [(1 + b)/x]$^{1/2}$

To present fractions in a line of text, use a slash mark (/) and parentheses first ( ), then brackets [( )], and finally braces {[( )]}. Some typewriters do not have brackets or braces; if that is the case, leave extra space for the brackets and braces and write them in with ink.

8 *Handling Format*

This chapter addresses your questions about margins, spacing, page numbers, and so forth. Section 8a shows you how to design the final manuscript, and Section 8b explains matters of usage in an alphabetized glossary. In Section 8c you will find a short literary paper that uses just four sources. Section 8d gives an example of a longer, more formal research paper.

8a PREPARING THE FINAL MANUSCRIPT

In its total organization, the format of a research paper consists of the following parts:

1. Title page
2. Outline
3. Abstract
4. The text of the paper
5. Content notes
6. Appendix
7. List of works cited

Items 4 and 7 are required for a paper in MLA style; use other items on the list according to the instructions below or according to the specifications of your instructor.

Note: **A paper in APA style (see Chapter 10) requires items 1, 3, 4, and 7, and the order differs for items 5–7.**

Opening Page or Title Page

Most undergraduate research papers written in MLA style do not need a separate title page. Instead, use the first page of the text to list name and affiliation, as shown next.

You may omit the title page if you have no outline, abstract, or other prefatory matter, in which case you place identification in the upper left corner of your opening page, as shown here:

Figure 78: First page of a paper with no title page

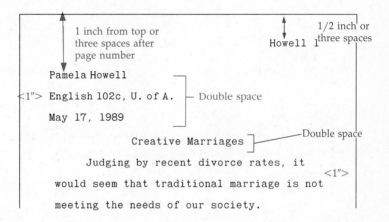

If you include prefatory matter, such as an outline, you will need a title page, which has three main divisions: the title of the paper, the author, and the course identification:

Figure 79: Information to be included on a title page

```
        An Interpretation of Melville's

           Use of Biblical Characters

               In Billy Budd




                        by

                 Doris Singleton




        Freshman English II, Section 108b

                 Mr. Crampton

                April 23, 1992
```

Follow these guidelines for writing a title page in MLA style:

1. Use an inverted pyramid to balance two or more lines.
2. Use capitals and lowercase letters without underlining and without quotation marks. Published works that appear as part of your title will require underlining (books) or quotation marks (short stories). Do not use a period after a centered heading.
3. Place your full name below the title, usually in the center of the page.
4. Employ separate lines, centered, to provide the course information, institution, instructor, date, or program (e.g., Honors Program).
5. Provide balanced, two-inch margins for all sides of the title page.

> *Note:* **APA style requires a different setup for the title page; see 290 for guidelines and an example.**

Outline

Include your outline in the finished manuscript only if your instructor requires it. Place it after the title page on separate pages and number these pages with small Roman numerals, beginning with ii (e.g., ii, iii, iv, v) at the top right-hand corner of the page just after your last name (e.g., Spence iii). For full information on the formal outline, see Section 3c, 81–87, and sample outlines on 82–85 and 238.

Abstract

Include an abstract for a paper in MLA style only if your instructor requires it. (APA style requires the abstract; see Section 10d, 289–90.) An abstract summarizes the essential ideas of the paper in about 100 words. It provides a *brief* digest of the paper's argument. Some of your topic sentences should serve well in the abstract. Use one or two sentences to explain your conclusion(s) or finding(s).

Place the abstract on the first page of text (page 1) one double space below the title and before the first line of the text. Indent it five spaces and use quadruple spacing to set it off from the text, which follows immediately. You may also place the abstract on a separate page between the title page and the first page of text. Remember that the abstract is usually read first and may be the *only* part read; therefore, make it accurate, specific, objective, and self-contained (i.e., so that it makes sense alone without references to the main text). Note this example:

Figure 80:
Sample abstract
on the first page
of a paper

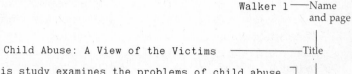

Walker 1——Name
and page

Child Abuse: A View of the Victims ————Title

This study examines the problems of child abuse, especially the fact that families receive attention after abuse occurs, not before. With abuse statistics on the rise, efforts devoted to prevention rather than coping should focus on parents in order to discover those adults most likely to commit abuse because of heredity, their own childhood, the economy, or other causes of depression. Viewing the parent as a victim, not just a criminal, will enable social agencies to institute preventive programs that may control abuse and hold together family units. ——Abstract

Family troubles will most likely affect the delicate members of our society, the children. The recognition of causal elements . . . ——Text

The Text of the Paper

Double-space throughout the entire paper except for title page (195) or opening page (195). See Chapter 6 for a discussion of the three dominant parts of the text: introduction (Section 6f, 145–51), body (Section 6g, 151–57), and conclusion (Section 6h, 157–61). "Drafting Your Paper" (Section 6e, 140–45) explains such matters as tense, voice, and language.

See Section 8a, 195, for details about name, page number, and course identification for your first page of text.

In general, you should *not* use subtitles or numbered divisions for your paper, even if it becomes 20 pages long. Instead, use continuous paragraphing without subdivisions or headings. However, some scientific and business reports demand underlined side headings (see Chapters 10 and 11).

The closing page of your text should end with a period and blank space on the remainder of the page. Do not write "The End" or provide artwork as a closing signal. Do not start "Notes" or "Works Cited" on the final page of text.

Content Endnotes Page

Label this page with the word "Notes" centered and one inch from the top edge of the sheet. Continue your page numbering sequence in the upper right corner. Double-space between the "Notes" heading and the first note. Number the notes in sequence with raised superscript numerals to match those within your text. Double-space all entries and double-space between them. See below, "Content Endnotes," 210–13, and see the sample "Notes" page, 247.

Appendix

Place additional material, if necessary, in an appendix immediately preceding the works-cited page. It is the logical location for numerous tables and illustrations, computer data, questionnaire results, complicated statistics, mathematical proofs, or detailed descriptions of special equipment. Double-space appendixes and begin each appendix on a new sheet. Continue your page numbering sequence in the upper right corner of the sheet. Label the page with the word "Appendix"; center it and place it one inch from the top edge of the sheet. If you have more than one appendix, use "Appendix A," "Appendix B," and so forth.

Works Cited Page

Label this page "Works Cited," and center it one inch from the top edge of the sheet. Continue your page numbering sequence in the upper right corner. Double-space throughout. Set the first line of each entry flush left and indent subsequent lines five spaces. For samples and additional information see Chapter 9, "Works Cited," 250–79, and also the sample "Works Cited" pages on 236 and 248–49.

8b GLOSSARY: PREPARING THE MANUSCRIPT

The alphabetical glossary that follows will answer your miscellaneous questions about matters of form, such as margins, pagination, dates, and numbers. For matters not addressed below, consult the index, which will direct you to appropriate pages elsewhere in this text.

Abbreviations   Employ abbreviations often and consistently in notes and citations, but avoid them in the text. In your documentation entries, always abbreviate technical terms (anon., e.g., diss.), institutions (acad., assn., Cong.), dates (Jan., Feb.), states (OH, CA), and names of publishers (McGraw, UP of Florida). See also "Names of Persons," 221, for comments on the abbreviation of honorary titles.

Abbreviating Technical Terms and Institutions

abr. abridged

AD *anno Domini* 'in the year of the Lord'; precedes numerals with no space between letters, as in "AD 350" (Note: Use AD in your text, not *anno Domini*)

anon. anonymous

art., arts. article(s)

assn. association

assoc. associate, associated

BC 'Before Christ'; follows numerals with no space between letters, as in "500 BC"

bk., bks. book(s)

ca., c. *circa* 'about'; used to indicate an approximate date, as in "ca. 1812"

cf. *confer* 'compare' (one source with another); not, however, to be used in place of "see" or "see also"

ch., chs., chap., chaps. chapter(s)

col., cols. column(s)

comp. compiled by or compiler

diss. dissertation

doc. document

ed., eds. editor(s), edition, or edited by

e.g. *exempli gratia* 'for example'; preceded and followed by a comma

enl. enlarged, as in "enl. ed."

esp. especially, as in "312–15, esp. 313"

et al. *et alii* 'and others'; "John Smith et al." means John Smith and other authors

etc. *et cetera* 'and so forth'

et pas. *et passim* 'and here and there' (see "passim")

et seq. *et sequens* 'and the following'; "9 et seq." means page nine and the following page; compare "f." and "ff."

f., ff. page or pages following a given page; "8f." means page eight and the following page; but exact references are sometimes preferable, for example, "45–51, 55, 58" instead of "45ff." Acceptable also is "45+."

fig. figure

fl. *floruit* 'flourished'; which means a person reached greatness on these dates, as in "*fl.* 1420–50"; used when birth and death dates are unknown

ibid. *ibidem* 'in the same place'; i.e., in the immediately preceding title, normally capitalized and italicized as in "*Ibid.,* p. 34"

i.e. *id est* 'that is'; preceded and followed by a comma

illus. illustrated by, illustrations, or illustrator

infra 'below'; refers to a succeeding portion of the text; compare "supra." Generally, it is best to write "see below"

intro., introd. introduction (by)

loc. cit. *loco citato* 'in the place (passage) cited'

ms., mss. manuscript(s), as in "(Cf. the mss. of Glass and Ford)"

n., nn. note(s), as in "23, n. 2" or "51n."

narr. narrated by

n.d. no date (in a book's title or copyright pages)

no., nos. number(s)

n.p. no place (of publication)

ns new series

op. cit. *opere citato* 'in the work cited'

p., pp. page(s); do not use "ps." for "pages"

passim 'here and there throughout the work'; e.g., "67, 72, et passim," but also acceptable is "67+"

proc. proceedings

pseud. pseudonym

pt., pts. part(s)

rev. revised, revised by, revision, review, or reviewed by

rpt. reprint, reprinted

sec., secs. section(s)

ser. series

sess. session

sic 'thus'; placed in brackets to indicate an error has been made in the quoted passage and the writer is quoting accurately; see example on 192

St., Sts. Saint(s)

st., sts. stanza(s)

sup., supra 'above'; refers to a preceding portion of the text; it is just as easy to write "above" or "see above"

suppl. supplement(s)

s.v. *sub voce (verbo)* 'under the word or heading'

trans., tr. translator, translated, translated by, or translation

ts., tss. typescript(s)

viz. namely

vol., vols. volume(s), as in "vol. 3"

vs., v. versus 'against'; as used in citing legal cases

Abbreviations for Days and Months

Sun.	Jan.	July
Mon.	Feb.	Aug.
Tues.	Mar.	Sept.
Wed.	Apr.	Oct.
Thurs.	May	Nov.
Fri.	June	Dec.
Sat.		

Abbreviations for States and Geographical Names

AL	Alabama	FL	Florida
AK	Alaska	GA	Georgia
AZ	Arizona	GU	Guam
AR	Arkansas	HI	Hawaii
CA	California	ID	Idaho
CO	Colorado	IL	Illinois
CT	Connecticut	IN	Indiana
DE	Delaware	IA	Iowa
DC	District of Columbia	KS	Kansas

KY Kentucky

LA Louisiana

ME Maine

MD Maryland

MA Massachusetts

MI Michigan

MN Minnesota

MS Mississippi

MO Missouri

MT Montana

NE Nebraska

NV Nevada

NH New Hampshire

NJ New Jersey

NM New Mexico

NY New York

NC North Carolina

ND North Dakota

OH Ohio

OK Oklahoma

OR Oregon

PA Pennsylvania

PR Puerto Rico

RI Rhode Island

SC South Carolina

SD South Dakota

TN Tennessee

TX Texas

UT Utah

VT Vermont

VI Virgin Islands

VA Virginia

WA Washington

WV West Virginia

WI Wisconsin

WY Wyoming

Abbreviation of Publishers' Names   Use the shortened forms below as guidelines. Some of these publishers no longer exist, but their imprints remain on copyright pages of the books.

Abrams	Harry N. Abrams, Inc.
ALA	American Library Association
Allen	George Allen and Unwin Publishers, Inc.
Allyn	Allyn and Bacon, Inc.
Barnes	Barnes and Noble Books
Basic	Basic Books
Beacon	Beacon Press, Inc.
Bobbs	The Bobbs-Merrill Co., Inc.
Bowker	R. R. Bowker Co.
Cambridge UP	Cambridge University Press
Clarendon	Clarendon Press
Columbia UP	Columbia University Press
Dell	Dell Publishing Co., Inc.
Dodd	Dodd, Mead, and Co.
Doubleday	Doubleday and Co., Inc.
Farrar	Farrar, Straus, and Giroux, Inc.
Free	The Free Press
Gale	Gale Research Co.
GPO	Government Printing Office
Harcourt	Harcourt Brace Jovanovich, Inc.
Harper	Harper and Row Publishers, Inc.
HarperCollins	HarperCollins Publishers, Inc.

Harvard UP	Harvard University Press
Heath	D. C. Heath and Co.
Holt	Holt, Rinehart and Winston, Inc.
Houghton	Houghton Mifflin Co.
Indiana UP	Indiana University Press
Knopf	Alfred A. Knopf, Inc.
Lippincott	J. B. Lippincott Co.
Little	Little, Brown and Co.
Macmillan	Macmillan Publishing Co., Inc.
McGraw	McGraw-Hill, Inc.
MIT P	The MIT Press
MLA	Modern Language Association
Norton	W. W. Norton and Co., Inc.
Oxford UP	Oxford University Press
Prentice	Prentice-Hall, Inc.
Putnam's	G. P. Putnam's Sons
Random	Random House, Inc.
St. Martin's	St. Martin's Press, Inc.
Scott	Scott, Foresman and Co.
Scribner's	Charles Scribner's Sons
Simon	Simon and Schuster, Inc.
State U of New York P	State University of New York Press
U of Chicago P	University of Chicago Press
UP of Florida	University Press of Florida
Washington Square P	Washington Square Press

Abbreviation of Biblical Works   Use parenthetical documentation for biblical references in the text—that is, place the entry within parentheses immediately after the quotation, for example:

```
After the great flood God spoke to Noah, "And I will

establish my covenant with you; neither shall all flesh be

cut off any more by the waters of a flood; neither shall

there any more be a flood to destroy the earth" (Gen. 9.11).
```

Do not underline titles of books of the Bible. Abbreviate books of the Bible except one-syllable titles, such as "Mark."

1 and 2 Chron.	1 and 2 Chronicles
Col.	Colossians
1 and 2 Cor.	1 and 2 Corinthians

Dan.	Daniel
Deut.	Deuteronomy
Eccles.	Ecclesiastes
Eph.	Ephesians
Exod.	Exodus
Ezek.	Ezekiel
Gal.	Galatians
Gen.	Genesis
Hab.	Habakkuk
Hag.	Haggai
Heb.	Hebrews
Hos.	Hosea
Isa.	Isaiah
Jer.	Jeremiah
Josh.	Joshua
Judg.	Judges
Lam.	Lamentations
Lev.	Leviticus
Mal.	Malachi
Matt.	Matthew
Mic.	Micah
Nah.	Nahum
Neh.	Nehemiah
Num.	Numbers
Obad.	Obadiah
1 and 2 Pet.	1 and 2 Peter
Phil.	Philippians
Prov.	Proverbs
Ps. (Pss.)	Psalm(s)
Rev.	Revelation
Rom.	Romans
1 and 2 Sam.	1 and 2 Samuel
Song of Sol.	Song of Solomon
1 and 2 Thess.	1 and 2 Thessalonians
1 and 2 Tim.	1 and 2 Timothy
Zech.	Zechariah
Zeph.	Zephaniah

Abbreviation of Literary Works

Shakespeare   In parenthetical documentation, use the abbreviations of titles of Shakespearean plays:

```
Too late, Capulet urges Montague to end their feud, "O
brother Montague, give me thy hand" (Rom. 5.3.296).
```

Ado	*Much Ado About Nothing*
Ant.	*Antony and Cleopatra*
AWW	*All's Well That Ends Well*
AYL	*As You Like It*
Cor.	*Coriolanus*
Cym.	*Cymbeline*
Err.	*The Comedy of Errors*
Ham.	*Hamlet*
1H4	*Henry IV, Part 1*
2H4	*Henry IV, Part 2*
H5	*Henry V*
1H6	*Henry VI, Part 1*
2H6	*Henry VI, Part 2*
3H6	*Henry VI, Part 3*
H8	*Henry VIII*
JC	*Julius Caesar*
Jn.	*King John*
LLL	*Love's Labour's Lost*
Lr.	*King Lear*
Mac.	*Macbeth*
MM	*Measure for Measure*
MND	*A Midsummer Night's Dream*
MV	*Merchant of Venice*
Oth.	*Othello*
Per.	*Pericles*
R2	*Richard II*
R3	*Richard III*
Rom.	*Romeo and Juliet*
Shr.	*The Taming of the Shrew*
TGV	*Two Gentlemen of Verona*
Tim.	*Timon of Athens*
Tit.	*Titus Andronicus*
Tmp.	*The Tempest*
TN	*Twelfth Night*
TNK	*The Two Noble Kinsmen*
Tro.	*Troilus and Cressida*
Wiv.	*The Merry Wives of Windsor*
WT	*Winter's Tale*

Use these abbreviations for Shakespeare's poems:

Luc.	*The Rape of Lucrece*
PhT	*The Phoenix and the Turtle*
PP	*The Passionate Pilgrim*
Son.	*Sonnets*
Ven.	*Venus and Adonis*

Chaucer   In parenthetical documentation, use the following abbreviations:

CkT	The Cook's Tale
ClT	The Clerk's Tale
<u>CT</u>	*The Canterbury Tales*
CYT	The Canon's Yeoman's Tale
FranT	The Franklin's Tale
FrT	The Friar's Tale
GP	The General Prologue
KnT	The Knight's Tale
ManT	The Manciple's Tale
Mel	The Tale of Melibee
MerT	The Merchant's Tale
MilT	The Miller's Tale
MkT	The Monk's Tale
MLT	The Man of Law's Tale
NPT	The Nun's Priest's Tale
PardT	The Pardoner's Tale
ParsT	The Parson's Tale
PhyT	The Physician's Tale
PrT	The Prioress's Tale
Ret	Chaucer's Retraction
RvT	The Reeve's Tale
ShT	The Shipman's Tale
SNT	The Second Nun's Tale
SqT	The Squire's Tale
SumT	The Summoner's Tale
Th	The Tale of Sir Thopas
WBT	The Wife of Bath's Tale

Other Literary Works   Wherever possible in your in-text citations, use the initial letters of the title. A reference to page 18 of Melville's *Moby-Dick: or The Whale* could appear as: (<u>MD</u> 18). Use the following abbreviations as guidelines:

<u>Aen.</u>	*Aeneid* by Vergil
<u>Ag.</u>	*Agamemnon* by Aeschylus
<u>Ant.</u>	*Antigone* by Sophocles
<u>Bac.</u>	*Bacchae* by Euripides
<u>Beo.</u>	*Beowulf*
<u>Can.</u>	*Candide* by Voltaire
<u>Dec.</u>	*Decameron* by Boccaccio
<u>DJ</u>	*Don Juan* by Byron
<u>DQ</u>	*Don Quixote* by Cervantes
<u>Eum.</u>	*Eumenides* by Aeschylus

FQ	*Faerie Queene* by Spenser
Gil.	*Gilgamesh*
GT	*Gulliver's Travels* by Swift
Il.	*Iliad* by Homer
Inf.	*Inferno* by Dante
MD	*Moby-Dick* by Melville
Med.	*Medea* by Euripides
Nib.	*Nibelungenlied*
Od.	*Odyssey* by Homer
OR	*Oedipus Rex* by Sophocles
PL	*Paradise Lost* by Milton
SA	*Samson Agonistes* by Milton
SGGK	*Sir Gawain and the Green Knight*
SL	*Scarlet Letter* by Hawthorne

Accent Marks   When you quote, reproduce accents exactly as they appear in the original. Use ink if your typewriter or word processor does not support the marks.

"La tradición clásica en españa," according to Romana,

remains strong and vibrant in public school instruction.

Acknowledgments   Generally, acknowledgments are unnecessary. Nor is a preface required. Use a superscript reference numeral to your first sentence and then place any obligatory acknowledgments or explanations in a content endnote (see also 213):

[1]I wish here to express my thanks to Mrs. Horace A.

Humphrey for permission to examine the manuscripts of her

late husband.

Note: **Acknowledge neither your instructor nor typist for research papers, though such acknowledgments are standard with graduate theses and dissertations.**

Ampersand   Avoid using the ampersand symbol "&" unless custom demands it, for example, "A & P." Use *and* for in-text citations in MLA style (Smith and Jones 213–14), *but do use* "&" in APA style references (Spenser & Wilson, 1991, p. 73).

Annotated Bibliography   An annotation describes the essential details of a book or article. Place it just after the facts of publication. Follow these suggestions:

1. Explain the main purpose of the work.
2. Briefly describe the contents.
3. Indicate the possible audience for the work.
4. Note any special features.
5. Warn of any defect, weakness, or suspected bias.

Provide enough information in about three sentences for a reader to have a fairly clear image of the work's purpose, content, and special value. Turn to 102–04 to see a complete annotated bibliography.

Apostrophe   To form the possessive of singular nouns add an apostrophe and *s* (e.g., "the typist's ledger"). Use only the apostrophe with plural nouns ending in *s* (e.g., "several typists' ledgers"). Use the apostrophe and *s* with singular proper nouns of people and places even if the noun ends in an *s* (e.g., "Rice's story," "Rawlings's novel," "Arkansas's mountains," *but* "the Rawlingses' good fortune"). Exceptions are *Jesus'* scriptures, *Moses'* words, and hellenized names of more than one syllable ending in *es; Euripides'* dramas. Use apostrophes with the plurals of letters (a's and b's) but not with numbers or with abbreviations (ACTs in the 18s and 19s, the 1980s, sevens, three MDs).

Arabic Numerals   MLA style demands Arabic numerals whenever possible: for volumes, books, parts, and chapters of works; acts, scenes, and lines of plays; and cantos, stanzas, and lines of poetry.

Use Arabic figures to express all numbers 10 and above (such as 154, 1,269, the 10th test, the remaining 12%). Write as Arabic numerals any numbers below 10 that cannot be spelled out in one or two words (such as 3½ or 6.234). Numbers below 10 grouped with higher numbers should appear as Arabic numerals (such as 3 out of 42 subjects or lines 6 and 13, but 15 tests in three categories).

Large numbers may combine numerals and words (such as 3.5 million). For inclusive numbers that indicate a range, give the second number in full for numbers through 99: 3–5, 15–21, 70–96. In MLA style, with three digits or more give only the last two in the second number unless more digits are needed for clarity (e.g., 98–101, 110–12, 989–1001, 1030–33, 2766–854). In APA style, with three digits or more give all numbers (e.g., 110–112, 1030–1033, 2766–2854).

Commas in numbers are usually placed between the third and fourth digits from the right, the sixth, and so on, as with 1,200 or 1,200,000. Exceptions are page and line numbers, addresses, the year, and zip codes: page 1620, at 12116 Nova Road, in 1985, or New York, NY 10012.

Spell out the initial number that begins a sentence (e.g., Thirty people participated in the initial test).

Use the number "1" in every case for numbers, not the lowercase "l" or uppercase "L," especially if you type into a word processor or computer.

Numbers in the Text   Use numbers in your text according to the following examples.

AD 200 *but* 200 BC
in 1991–92 *or* from 1991 to 1992, *but not* from 1991–92
lines 32–34 *but not* 11. 32–34
32–34 *or* pages 32–34 *but not* pp. 32–34
45, *but not* the forty-fifth page
6.213
0.5 *but not* .5
March 5, 1991, *or* 5 March 1991, *but not* both styles
1990s *or* the nineties
one-fifth *but* 153½
eighty-eight errors
thirty-four times
six percent *but* 6 percent and 15 percent were low scores
six o'clock *or* 6:00 p.m.
twentieth century *but* twentieth-century literature *and* 20th century in the list of works cited
three-dimensional
zero-based budget
one response *but* 1 of 15 responses
one fifth of the session
twelve 6-year-olds *or* 12 six-year-olds, *not* 12 6-year olds

Numbers in Documentation Use numerals with in-text citations and
works-cited entries according to the following examples:

(*Ham.* 5.3.16–18)
(*Faust* 2.140)
(2 Sam. 2.1–8)
(Fredericks 23–24) (MLA style)
(Fredericks, 1985, pp. 23–24) (APA and CBE style)
2 vols.
Rpt. as vols. 13 and 14
MS CCCC 210
102nd Cong., 1st sess. S. 2411
16 mm., 29 min., color
Monograph 1962-M2
College English 15 (Winter 1991): 3–6 (MLA style)
Memory and Cognition, 3, 562–590 (APA style)
J. Mol. Biol. 149:15–39; 1990 (CBE style)
Journal of Philosophy 26 (1992): 172–89 (footnote style)

Asterisks Do not use asterisks (*) for content notes or illustrations or
tables (see 216–19). Use numbers for tables and figures (Table 2 or Figure
3) and letters for notes (see Figure 85, 219).

Bible Use parenthetical documentation for biblical references in the
text (2 Chron. 18.13). Do not underline the books of the Bible. For
abbreviations, see 202–03.

Capitalization

Capitalize Some Titles   For books, journals, magazines, and newspapers, capitalize the first word and all principal words, but not articles, prepositions, conjunctions, and the *to* in infinitives, when these words occur in the middle of the title (e.g., *The Last of the Mohicans*). For titles of articles and parts of books capitalize as for books (e.g., "Appendix 2," "Writing the Final Draft"). If the first line of a poem serves as the title, reproduce it exactly as it appears in print ("anyone lived in a pretty how town").

Note: APA style capitalizes only the first word and proper names of reference titles (including the first word of subtitles), as shown below:

```
Baron, J. N., & Bielby, W.  (1980.) Bring the firms back
     in: Stratification, segmentation and the organization of   APA style
     work.  American Sociological Review, 45, 737-765.
```

Study the appropriate style for your field, as found in Chapters 10 and 11.

Capitals After a Colon   When a *complete* sentence follows a colon, MLA style does *not* capitalize the first word, but APA style *does* capitalize the first word after the colon. MLA style:

```
The consequences of this decision will be disastrous: each

division of the corporation will be required to cut twenty

percent of its budget within this fiscal year.
```

APA style:

```
They have agreed on the outcome:  Informed subjects perform

better than do uninformed subjects.
```

> *Note:* **In this one instance, APA style requires two spaces after the colon. In all other situations, both in APA style and MLA style, use one space after a colon.**

Capitalize Some Compound Words   Capitalize the second part of a hyphenated compound word only when it is used in a heading with other capitalized words:

```
Low-Frequency Sound Equipment
```

but

```
Low-frequency sound distortion is caused by several

factors.
```

Capitalize Trade Names   Use capitals for trade names, such as:

```
Pepsi, Plexiglas, Dupont, Dingo, Corvette, Xerox
```

Capitalize Proper Names   Capitalize proper names used as adjectives, *but not* the words used with them:

```
Einstein's theory or Salk's vaccine
```

Capitalize Specific Departments or Courses   Use

```
Department of Psychology, but the psychology department

Psychology 314, but an advanced course in psychology
```

Capitalize Nouns Used Before Numerals or Letters   Capitalize the noun when it denotes a specific place in a numbered series:

```
during Test 6, we observed Group C as shown in Table 5 and

also Figure 2
```

But do not capitalize nouns that name common parts of books or tables followed by numerals:

```
chapter 12          page ix          column 14
```

Content Endnotes   As a general rule, put important matters into the text and omit entirely the unimportant and marginally related items. A *content note* is the place to explain research problems, conflicts in the testimony of the experts, matters of importance that are not germane to your discussion, interesting tidbits, credit to people and sources not mentioned in the text, and other tangential matters that you think will interest the reader.

When circumstances call for content notes, they should conform to these rules:

1. Content notes are *not* documentation notes. Use in-text citations to document your sources. *Note:* Instructors in some fields, especially history, philosophy, and the fine arts, may ask for documentation footnotes; if so, see "Footnotes for Documentation," 214 and 328–35.
2. Place the content notes on a separate page(s) following the last page of text. Do not write them as footnotes at the bottom of pages. See 328–35 for specifications on typing notes.
3. Place superscript numerals within the text by turning the roller of the typewriter so that the Arabic numeral strikes about half a space above the line, like this.[3] At a computer, use a word-processing code to produce superscript numbers. Each superscript numeral should follow immediately the material to which it refers, usually at the end of a sentence,

with no space between the superscript numeral and a word
or mark of punctuation.

Third, a program to advise college students about
politically correct language and campus attitudes[1] may
incite demonstrations against the censorship of free speech
by both faculty and students.

> *Note:* **The superscript numeral above refers to note 1 in
> rule 5 below. See also the sample paper for its use of
> superscript numerals and content endnotes, 243 and
> 247.**

4. Sources mentioned in endnotes must appear in your list of
works cited even if they are not mentioned in your primary
textual discussions.
5. The samples below demonstrate various types of content
notes.

Related Matters Not Germane to the Text

[1] The problems of politically correct language are
explored in Adams, Tucker (4-5), Zalers, and also Young and
Smith (583). These authorities cite the need for caution
by administrators who would impose new measures on speech
and behavior. Verbal abuse cannot be erased by a new set
of unjust laws. Patrick German offers several guidelines
for implementing an effective but reasonable program
(170-72).

Blanket Citation

[2] On this point, see Giarrett (3-4), de Young (579),
Kinard (405-07), and Young (119).

[3] Cf. Campbell (<u>Masks</u> 1: 170-225; <u>Hero</u> 342-45), Frazer
(312), and Baird (300-344).

Literature on a Related Topic

[4] For additional study of the effects of alcoholics on
children, see especially the <u>Journal of Studies on Alcohol</u>
for the article by Wolin et al. and the bibliography on the

topic by Orme and Rimmer (285–87). In addition, group therapy for children of alcoholics is examined in Hawley and Brown.

Major Source Requiring Frequent In-text Citations

[5] All citations to Shakespeare are to the Parrott edition.

[6] Dryden's poems are cited from the California edition of his <u>Works</u> and documented in the text with first references to each poem listing volume, page, and lines and with subsequent references citing only lines.

Reference to Source Materials

[7] Cf. James Baird who argues that the whiteness of Melville's whale is "the sign of the all–encompassing God" (257). Baird states: "It stands for what Melville calls at the conclusion of the thirty–fifth chapter of <u>Moby–Dick</u> 'the inscrutable tides of God'; and it is of these tides as well that the great White Whale himself is the quintessential emblem, the iconographic representation" (257).

[8] On this point, see also the essay by Patricia Chaffee in which she examines the "house" as a primary image in the fiction of Eudora Welty.

Explanation of Tools, Methods, or Testing Procedures

[9] Water samples were drawn from the identical spot each day at 8 a.m., noon, 4 p.m., and 8 p.m. with testing done immediately on site.

[10] The control group continued normal dietary routines, but the experimental group was asked to consume nuts, sharp cheeses, and chocolates to test acne development of its members against that of the control group.

[11] The initial sample was complete data on all twins born in Nebraska between 1920 and 1940. These dates were selected to provide test subjects 60 years of age or older.

> *Note:* **A report of an empirical study in APA style would require an explanation of tools and testing procedures in the text under "Methods." See Section 3b, 78, and Chapter 10, 280–301.**

Statistics   See also "Illustrations and Tables," 216–19.

    12 Data-base results show 27,000 pupil-athletes in 174
high schools with grades 0.075 above another group of
27,000 nonathletes at the same high schools. Details on
the nature of various reward structures are unavailable.

Acknowledgments for Assistance or Support

    13 Funds to finance this research were graciously
provided by the Thompson-Monroe Foundation.

    14 This writer wishes to acknowledge the research
assistance of Pat Luther, graduate assistant, Department of
Physics.

Variables or Conflicts in the Evidence

    15 Potlatch et al. included the following variables:
the positive acquaintance, the equal status norm, the
various social norms, the negative stereotypes, and sexual
discrimination (415-20). However, racial barriers cannot
be overlooked as one important variable.

    16 The pilot study at Dunlap School, where sexual
imbalance was noticed (62 percent males), differed sharply
from test results compared with those of other schools.
The male bias at Dunlap thereby eliminated those scores
from the totals.

Copyright Law   Your "fair use" of the materials of others is permitted without the need for specific permission as long as your use is noncommercial for purposes of criticism, scholarship, or research, which means you can quote from sources and reproduce artistic works within reasonable limits. The law is vague on specific amounts that can be borrowed, suggesting only the "substantiality of the portion used in relation to the copyrighted work as a whole." You should be safe in reproducing the work of another as long as the portion is not substantial. To protect your own work, if necessary, you need only type in the upper right-hand corner of your manuscript, "Copyright © 19__ by _____." Fill in the blanks with the proper year and your name. Then, to register a work, order a form from the U.S. Copyright Office, Library of Congress, Washington, DC 20559.

Note: It is not legal under "fair use" laws to copy computer software, even if the purpose in showing it is purely educational.

Corrections   Make corrections neatly and keep them to a minimum. Use correction fluid, correction paper, or tape to cover and type over any errors. Add words or short phrases directly above a line (not in your margins). Retype pages that require four or more corrections. *Do not* strike over a letter, paste inserts onto the page, write vertically in the margins, or make handwritten notes on the manuscript pages.

Dates   See "Arabic Numerals," 207–08.

Definitions   For definitions and translations within your text, use single quotation marks without intervening punctuation; for example:

```
The use of et alii 'and others' has diminished in scholarly
writing.
```

Endnotes for Documentation of Sources   An instructor or supervisor may prefer traditional superscript numerals within the text and documentation notes at the end of the paper. If so, see Chapter 11, 302–35.

Etc.   *Et cetera* 'and so forth'; avoid using this term by adding extra items to the list or by saying "and so forth."

Footnotes for Documentation   Footnotes are still used by some instructors in the fields of fine arts and humanities. If your instructor requires you to use footnotes, see Chapter 11, Sections 11h, 11i, and 11j, 328–35, for discussion and examples.

Foreign Cities   In general, spell the names of foreign cities as they are written in original sources. However, for purposes of clarity, you may substitute an English name or provide both with one in parentheses:

```
Köln (Cologne)        Braunschweig (Brunswick)
München (Munich)      Praha (Prague)
```

Foreign Languages   Underline foreign words used in an English text:

```
Like his friend Olaf, he is aut Caesar, aut nihil, either
overpowering perfection or ruin and destruction.
```

Do not underline quotations of a foreign language:

```
Obviously, he uses it to exploit, in the words of Jean
Laumon, "une admirable mine de thèmes poétiques."
```

Do not underline foreign titles of magazine or journal articles, but do underline the names of the magazines or journals:

```
Arrigoitia, Luis de.  "Machismo, folklore y creación en
     Mario Vargas Llosa."  Sin nombre 13.4 (1983): 19-25.
```

Do not underline foreign words of places, institutions, proper names, or titles that precede proper names:

```
Racine became extremely fond of Mlle Champmeslé, who
interpreted his works at the Hôtel de Bourgogne.
```

For titles of French, Italian, and Spanish works, capitalize the first word and the proper nouns, but not adjectives derived from proper nouns:

```
La noche de Tlatelolco: Testimoniosde historia oral
```

and

```
Realismo y realidad en la narrativa argentina
```

Titles of German works: capitalize the first word, all nouns, and all adjectives derived from names of persons:

```
Über die Religion: Reden an die Gebildeten unter ihren
Verächtern
```

Headings   Begin every major heading on a new page of your paper (title page, opening page, notes, appendix, works cited). Center the heading with major words capitalized one inch from the top of the sheet. Use a double space between the heading and your first line of text. (APA style also requires double spaces between headings and text, but see Chapter 10, 291–92, for use of triple spacing before side headings and before and after illustrations.) Number *all* text pages, including those with major headings. (See also "Spacing," 227.) Most papers will need only major headings (A-level), but the advent of desktop publishing makes it possible for some research papers to gain the look of professional typesetting. Use the following guideline for writing subheads in your paper:

```
                 Writing a Research Paper◄───────A heading
       Writing the First Draft ◄───────────────B heading
       Revising and editing the manuscript◄────C heading
           Proofreading.  Every researcher . . .◄──────D heading
```

Illustrations and Tables A table is a systematic presentation of materials, usually in columns. An illustration is any nontext item that is not a table: blueprint, chart, diagram, drawing, graph, photograph, photostat, map, and so on. Note the following samples:

Figure 81: Sample illustration in a paper

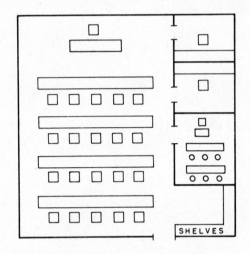

Fig. 4: Audio Laboratory with Private Listening

Rooms and a Small Group Room

Figure 82: Sample table in a paper

Table 1

Response, by Class, on Nuclear Energy Policy

	Freshmen	Sophomores	Juniors	Seniors
1. More nuclear power	150	301	75	120
2. Less nuclear power	195	137	111	203
3. Present policy is acceptable	87	104	229	37

When you present an illustration or table in your paper, conform to the following guidelines:

1. Present only one kind of information in each illustration, and make it as simple and as brief as possible. Frills and fancy artwork may distract rather than attract the reader.
2. Place small illustrations and tables within your text; place large illustrations, sets of illustrations, or complex tables on separate pages in an appendix (see "Appendix," 198).

3. Place the figure or table as near to your textual discussion as possible, but the illustration should not precede your first mention of it.

4. Make certain that the text adequately explains the significance of the illustration. Follow two rules: (1) label the illustration so that your reader can understand it without reference to your discussion; and (2) write the description of the illustration so that your reader may understand your observations without reference to the illustration, but avoid giving too many numbers and figures in your text.

5. In the text, refer to illustrations by number (e.g., "Figure 5" or "Table 4, 16"), not by vague reference (e.g., "the table above," "the following illustration," or "the chart below").

6. Number illustrations consecutively throughout the paper with Arabic numerals, preceded by "Fig." or "Figure" (e.g., "Figure 4"), placed one double space *below* the illustration as shown below:

Figure 83: Sample illustration with clear labels and caption

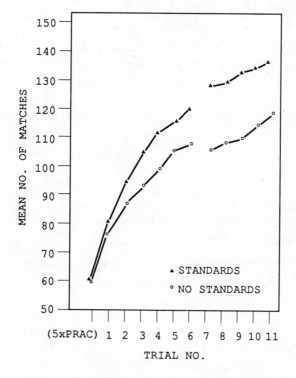

Fig. 6: Mean Number of Matches by Subject with and without Standard (by Trial). Source: Locke and Bryan (289).

Figure 84:
Sample
illustration with
explanatory
caption

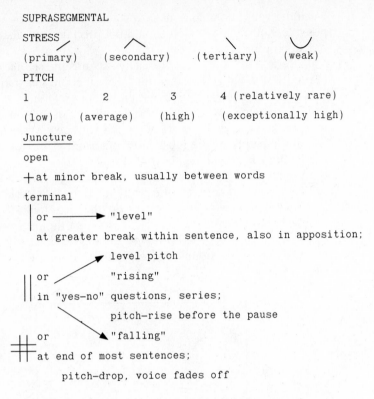

SUPRASEGMENTAL

STRESS

(primary)   (secondary)   (tertiary)   (weak)

PITCH

1   2   3   4 (relatively rare)

(low)   (average)   (high)   (exceptionally high)

Juncture

open

+ at minor break, usually between words

terminal

or ────► "level"

   at greater break within sentence, also in apposition;

       level pitch

or   "rising"

in "yes—no" questions, series;

      pitch—rise before the pause

or   "falling"

at end of most sentences;

    pitch—drop, voice fades off

Figure 9: Phonemes of English. Generally, this figure
follows the Trager—Smith system, used widely in
American linguistics. Source: Anna H. Live (1066).

7. Number tables consecutively throughout the paper with Arabic numerals, preceded by "Table" (for example, "Table 2"), placed one double space above the caption and flush left on the page *above* the table.

8. Always insert a caption that explains the illustration, placed *above* the table and *below* the illustration, flush left, in full capital letters or in capitals and lowercase, but do not mix forms in the same paper.

9. Insert a caption or number for each column of a table, centered above the column or, if necessary, inserted diagonally or vertically above it.

10. When inserting an explanatory or reference note, place it below both a table and an illustration; then use a lowercase letter, not an Arabic numeral, as the identifying superscript (see Figures 85 and 86).

11. Sources are abbreviated as in-text citations, and full documentation must appear in the list of works cited.

Figure 85:
Sample table with in-text citation

Table 2[a]

Mean Scores of Six Values Held by College Students, According to Sex

All Students		Men		Women	
Pol.	40.61	Pol.	43.22	Aesth.	43.86
Rel.	40.51	Theor.	43.09	Rel.	43.13
Aesth.	40.29	Econ.	42.05	Soc.	41.62
Econ.	39.45	Soc.	37.05	Econ.	36.85
Soc.	39.34	Aesth.	36.72	Theor.	36.50

[a]Carmen J. Finley et al. (165).

Figure 86:
Sample table with in-text citations and notes

Table 3

Inhibitory Effects of Sugars on the Growth of Clostridium Histoylticum (11 Strains) on Nutrient Agar[a]

Sugar added 2%	Aerobic incubation (hr)		Anaerobic incubation (hr)	
	24	48	24	48
None	11[b]	11	11	11
Glucose	0	0	11	11
Maltose	0	0	11	11
Lactose	1	1	11	11
Sucrose	3	6	11	11
Arabinose	0	0	0	0
Inositol	0	0	11	11
Xylose	0	0	0	0
Sorbitol	2	7	11	11
Mamnitol	9	10	11	11
Rhamnose	0	0	11	11

[a] Nishida and Imaizumi (481).

[b] No. of strains that gave rise to colonies in the presence of the sugar.

Indention Indent paragraphs of your text five spaces. Indent long quotations 10 spaces. The opening sentence to a long, quoted paragraph receives no extra indention even though it is indented in the original; however, if you quote two or more paragraphs, indent the beginning of each paragraph an extra three spaces (see 191). Indent entries in the list of works cited five spaces on the second and succeeding lines. Indent the first line of content footnotes five spaces. Other styles (APA or CBE) have different requirements (see Chapters 10 and 11, 280–335).

Italics If your word-processing system and your printer will reproduce italic lettering, use it. Otherwise, show italics in a typed manuscript, if necessary, by underlining (see "Underlining Titles," 229–30, and "Underlining for Emphasis," 230).

Length of the Research Paper A reasonable length is 10 pages, but setting an arbitrary length for a research paper is difficult. The ideal length for your work will depend on the nature of the topic, the reference material available, the time allotted to the project, and your initiative as the researcher and writer. Your instructor or supervisor may set definite restrictions concerning the length of your paper. Otherwise, try to generate a paper of 2,000 to 3,000 words, about 10 typewritten pages, excluding the title page, outline, endnotes, and pages of works cited.

Margins A basic one-inch margin on all sides is recommended. Place your page number one-half inch down from the top edge of the paper and one inch from the right edge. You should then triple-space (MLA style) between the page number and your text so that you place the first line of text one inch from the top of the page. If you use your name as a running head (MLA style), place both name and page number on the same line, flush with the right margin (for examples, see 231–49). Word processing may enable you to print automatically the page numbers and the running head.

Monetary Units Spell out percentages and monetary amounts only if you can do so in no more than two words. Conform to the following:

$10 *or* ten dollars
$14.25 *but not* fourteen dollars and twenty-five cents
$4 billion *or* four billion dollars
$10.3 billion *or* $10,300,000,000
$63 *or* sixty-three dollars
the fee is one hundred dollars ($100) *or* the fee is one hundred (100) dollars
two thousand dollars *or* $2,000
thirty-four cents

Names of Persons   As a general rule, first mention of a person requires the full name (e.g., Ernest Hemingway or Margaret Mead) and thereafter requires only use of the surname, such as Hemingway or Mead. (APA style uses last name only.) Omit formal titles (e.g., Mr., Mrs., Dr., Hon.) in textual and note references to distinguished persons, living or dead. Convention suggests that certain prominent figures (e.g., Lord Byron, Dr. Johnson, Dame Edith Sitwell) require the title while others, for no apparent reason, do not (e.g., use Tennyson, Browne, and Hillary rather than Lord Tennyson, Sir Thomas Browne, or Sir Edmund Hillary). Where custom dictates, you may employ simplified names of famous persons (e.g., use Dante rather than the surname Alighieri and use Michelangelo rather than Michelangelo Buonarroti). You may also use pseudonyms where custom dictates (e.g., George Eliot, Maxim Gorky, Mark Twain). Refer to fictional characters by names used in the fictional work (e.g., Huck, Lord Jim, Santiago, Capt. Ahab).

Numbering (Pagination)   Number your pages in the upper right-hand corner of the page, one-half inch down from the top edge of the paper and one inch from the right edge. Precede the number with your last name. Triple-space between the page number and a heading or the first line of text so that your top margin is one inch from the top of the sheet.

Any pages that precede your text require lowercase Roman numerals (ii, iii, iv).

If you have a separate title page, count it as a page "i," but do not type the number on the page. You *should* put a page number on your opening page of text, even if you include course identification (see 231). Your last name should precede the page number unless anonymity is required, in which case you may use a shortened version of your title rather than your name, as in APA style (see 290).

> *Note:* **If your computer printer numbers pages automatically at the bottom of the sheet and you don't know how to change the configuration, leave the numbering at the bottom and put only your name in the upper right corner.**

Numbering a List of Items   Incorporate a list of items into the text with parenthetical numbers:

```
College instructors are usually divided into four ranks:
(1) instructors, (2) assistant professors, (3) associate
professors, and (4) full professors.
```

Present longer items in tabular form:

> 1. Full professors generally have 15 or more years of
> experience, have the Ph.D. or other terminal degree, and
> have achieved distinction in teaching and scholarly
> publications.
>
> 2. Associate professors. . . .

Paper   Type on one side of white bond paper, 16- or 20-pound weight, 8½ by 11 inches. On rare occasions, instructors will accept a handwritten paper if it is legible and written on ruled theme paper. If you write the paper by word processor or computer, use the best quality paper available, and use the letter-quality switch on dot-matrix printers. Avoid erasable paper.

Percentages   Use numerals with appropriate symbols (3%, $5.60); otherwise use numerals only when they cannot be spelled out in one or two words:

percent *not* per cent
one hundred percent *but* 150 percent
a two point average *but* a 2.5 average
one metric ton *but* 0.907 metric ton or 3.150 metric tons
forty-five percent *but* 45½ percent *or* 45½%

In business, scientific, and technical writing that requires frequent use of percentages, write all percentages as numerals with appropriate symbols:

100%   45½   12%   6@15.00   £92 $99.45

Proofreading Symbols   Be familiar with the most common proofreading symbols so that you can correct your own copy or mark your copy for a typist. (See Figure 87, 223.)

Punctuation   Consistency is the key to punctuation. Careful proofreading of your paper for punctuation errors will generally improve the clarity and accuracy of your writing.
Commas appear in a series of three or more before *and* or *or.*

> Reader, Scott, and Wellman (615–17) agree with Steinbeck on
> this point (34).

Never use a comma and a dash together. The comma follows a parenthesis if your text requires the comma:

Figure 87: Common proofreading symbols

⸝	error in spelling (m**e**stake) with correction in the margin
lc or /	lower/case (mis⧸take)
⌣	close up (mis ͡take)
⌶	delete and close up (mis͡take)
├───┤	delete and close up more than one letter (the ⧸mistakes and⧸ errors continue)
∧	insert (mi∧take) with s above
∾	transpose elements (the⧢ir)
◯	material to be corrected or moved, with instructions in the margin, or material to be spelled out, (corp.)
Caps or ☰	capitalize (Huck ̲f̲inn and Tom Sawyer)
¶	insert paragraph
ℓ	delete (a mistake⧸s)
#	add space
⊙	period
⸒	comma
⸕	semicolon
⸝	apostrophe or single closing quotation mark
⸌	single opening quotation mark
⸌⸍ ⸜⸝	double quotation marks
(*bf*)	boldface
stet	let stand as it is; ignore marks

> How should we order our lives, asks Thompson (22–23), when
> we face "hostility from every quarter"?

The comma goes inside single quotation marks as well as double quotation marks:

> Such irony is discovered in Smith's article, "The Sources
> of Franklin's 'The Ephemera,'" but not in most textual
> discussions.

Colons introduce examples or further elaboration on what has been said in the first clause. **Semicolons** join independent clauses. (For proper usage of colons and semicolons within quotations, see Sections 7h and 7i, 184–88, and for usage within documentation see Section 9b, 253.) Skip only one space after the colon or semicolon. Do not capitalize the first word after a colon or semicolon, but see 209 for an exception to this rule. Do not use a colon where a semicolon is appropriate for joining independent clauses. Here, a colon is used to introduce an elaboration or definition:

```
Weathers reminds us of crucial differences in rhetorical

profiles that no writer should forget: colloquial wording

differs radically from formal wording and a plain texture

of writing differs greatly from a rich texture.
```

Next, a semicolon is used to separate two distinct sentences:

```
Weathers reminds us of crucial differences in rhetorical

profiles that no writer should forget; the writer who does

forget may substitute colloquial wording where formal is

appropriate or may use a plain texture where a rich texture

is needed.
```

Dashes are formed with your typewriter by typing two hyphens with no blank space before or after, as shown here:

```
Two issues--slow economic growth and public debt--may

prevent an early recovery for the banking industry.
```

Exclamation marks should be avoided. Research writing is not supposed to be emotional or subjective, so avoid the use of exclamation marks. A forceful declarative sentence is preferable.

Hyphens: Both MLA style and APA style discourage division of words at the end of a line, asking instead that you leave the lines short, if necessary, rather than divide a word. You can usually disengage the automatic hyphenation of a word processor.

If you *do* hyphenate or if the computer does it automatically, you should always double-check word division by consulting a dictionary. Do not hyphenate proper names. Avoid separating two letters at the end or beginning of a line (e.g., use "depend-able," not "de-pendable").

When using hyphenated words, follow a few general rules.

1. Do not hyphenate unless the hyphen serves a purpose:

   a water treatment program *but* a water-powered turbine

2. Compound adjectives that *precede* a noun usually need a hyphen, but those that follow do not:

   same-age children *but* children of the same age

3. When a common base serves two or more compound modifiers, omit the base on all except the last modifier, but retain the hyphens on every modifier:

   right- and left-hand margins *or* 5-, 10-, and 15-minute segments

4. Write most words with prefixes as one word:

overaggressive, midterm, antisocial, postwar

But there are exceptions:

self-occupied, anti-intellectual, ex-husband, post-1980

Consult a dictionary regularly to resolve doubts on such narrow problems as anti-Reagan *but* antisocial.

5. Use a hyphen between pairs of coequal nouns:

scholar-athlete *or* trainer-coach

Periods signal the end of complete sentences of the text, endnotes, footnotes, and all bibliography entries. Use two spaces after a period. Periods between numbers indicate related parts (e.g., 2.4 for act 2, scene 4). The period normally follows the parenthesis. (The period is placed within the parentheses only when the parenthetical statement is a complete sentence, as in this instance.) See also Section 7k, 189–92, for explanation of the period in conjunction with ellipsis points.

Use **brackets** to enclose phonetic transcription, mathematical formulas, and interpolations into a quotation. An interpolation is the insertion of your words into the text of another person. Insert them by hand if these figures are not on your keyboard (see Section 7l, 192–93, for examples).

Use **quotation marks** to enclose all quotations used as part of your text except for long, indented quotations (the indention signals the use of a quotation). Quotations require proper handling for stylistic effects; they also require precise documentation (see examples and discussions in Chapter 7, 173–93).

Use quotation marks for titles of articles, essays, short stories, short poems, songs, chapters of books, unpublished works, and episodes of radio and television programs.

Use quotation marks for words and phrases that you purposely misuse, misspell, or use in a special sense:

> The "patrons" turned out to be criminals searching for a
> way to launder their money.

However, a language study requires underlining for all linguistic forms (letters, words, and phrases) that are subjects of discussion and requires single quotation marks for definitions that appear without intervening punctuation (for example, *nosu* 'nose').

> José Donoso's <u>El jardin de al lado</u> 'The Garden Next Door'
> dramatizes an artistic crisis that has ethical and
> political implications.

In other cases, use double quotation marks for foreign phrases and sentences and single quotation marks for your translation:

> It was important to Bacon that the 1625 collection appear
> in France as "un oeuvre nouveau" 'a new work' (14:536).

Use **parentheses** to enclose these items:

1. In-text citations:

> Larson (23–25) and Mitchell (344–45) report. . . .

2. Independent matter:

> The more recent findings (see Figure 6) show. . . .

3. Headings for a series:

> The tests were (a) . . ., (b) . . ., and (c). . . .

4. First use of an abbreviation:

> The test proved reaction time (RT) to be. . . .

Roman Numerals   Use capital Roman numerals for titles of persons (Elizabeth II) and major sections of an outline (see 82). Use small Roman numerals for preliminary pages of text, as for a preface or introduction (iii, iv, v). Otherwise, use Arabic numerals (e.g., Vol. 5, Act 2, Ch. 16, Plate 32, 2 Sam. 2.1–8, or *Iliad* 2.121–30), *except* when writing for some instructors in history, philosophy, religion, music, art, and theater, in which case you may need to use Roman numerals (e.g., III, Act II, I Sam. ii.1–8, *Hamlet* I.ii.5–6). Here is a list of Roman numerals:

	Units	Tens	Hundreds
1	i	x	c
2	ii	xx	cc
3	iii	xxx	ccc
4	iv	xl	cd
5	v	l	d
6	vi	lx	dc
7	vii	lxx	dcc
8	viii	lxxx	dccc
9	ix	xc	cm

Thus, xxi equals 21, cx equals 110, and clv equals 155.

Running Heads   Repeat your name in the upper right corner of every page just in front of the page number. MLA style requires that your name precede page numbers on all pages after the first (see the sample paper, 231–36). APA style requires a short title at the top of each page just above the page number (see "Short Titles in the Text," immediately below).

Short Titles in the Text   Use abbreviated titles of books and articles mentioned often in the text after a first, full reference. For example, *Backgrounds to English as Language* should be shortened, after initial usage, to *Backgrounds* in the text, notes, and in-text citations (see also 183), but not in the bibliography entry. Mention *The Epic of Gilgamesh* and thereafter use *Gilgamesh.* (*Note:* Be certain to underline the shortened title when referring to the work.)

When typing a manuscript according to APA style, shorten your own title to the first two or three words and place it at the top right corner of each page for identification purposes (e.g., "Discovering Recall Differences of the Aged" should be shortened to "Discovering" or "Discovering Recall Differences"). See 290–301 for examples of the short title as page heading.

Slang   Avoid the use of slang terminology. When using it in a language study, enclose in double quotation marks any words to which you direct attention. Words used as words, however, require underlining (see 214 and 230).

Spacing   As a general rule, double-space everything—the body of the paper, all indented quotations, and all reference entries. Footnotes, if used, should be single-spaced, but endnotes should be double-spaced (see Chapter 11, 302–35). APA style (see 290–301) double-spaces after all headings and separates text from indented quotes or figures by double-spacing; however, APA advocates quadruple-spacing above and below statistical and mathematical expressions, and allows a triple space above a side heading and before and after an illustration or table.

Space after punctuation according to these stipulations:

- one space after commas, semicolons, and colons (exception: APA style uses two spaces when a complete sentence follows the colon (see "Capitals After a Colon," 209)
- two spaces after punctuation marks at the end of sentences in both MLA and APA styles
- two spaces after periods that separate parts of a reference citation in both MLA and APA styles (see 285n)
- no space before or after periods within abbreviations (i.e., e.g., a.m.)
- one space between initials of personal names (M. C. Bone)
- no space before or after a hyphen (a three-part test) *but* one space before and after a hyphen used as a minus sign ($a - b + c$)
- no space before or after a dash (the evidence—interviews and statistics—was published)

Spelling   Spell accurately. When in doubt, always consult a dictionary. If the dictionary says a word may be spelled in two separate ways, be consistent in the form employed, as with *theater* and *theatre,* unless the variant form occurs in quoted materials. Use American (as opposed to

English) spelling throughout. Use the computer to check spelling if the software is available. In addition, proofread carefully for errors of hyphenation.

Statistical and Mathematical Copy   Use the simplest form of equation that can be made by ordinary mathematical calculation. If an equation cannot be reproduced entirely by keyboard, type what you can and fill in the rest with ink. As a general rule, keep equations on one line rather than two:

Acceptable: $\dfrac{a + b}{x + y}$ Better: $(a + b)/(x + y)$

Superscript Numerals in the Text   Place the raised note numerals, like this,[14] into the text (see Chapter 11, 302–35), by turning the roller of the typewriter so that the Arabic numeral strikes about half a space above the line. Do not skip a space with superscript numerals that come after a word or a mark of punctuation. Compare with numerals that precede a line (see Chapter 11). On a computer, use the appropriate keys as explained in the printed manual (e.g., Shift-F1, Control key-PY, and so forth). See also "Using the Footnote System," Chapter 11.

Table of Contents   A table of contents is unnecessary for a research paper. Do write a table of contents for a graduate thesis or dissertation (see immediately below).

Theses and Dissertations   The author of a thesis or dissertation must satisfy the requirements of the college's graduate program. Therefore, even though you may use MLA style or APA style, you must abide by certain additional rules with regard to paper, typing, margins, and introductory matter, such as title page, approval page, acknowledgment page, table of contents, abstract, and other matters. Use both the graduate school guidelines and this book to maintain the appropriate style and format.

Titles Within Titles   For a title to a book that includes another title indicated by quotation marks, retain the quotation marks:

| `O. Henry's Irony in "The Gift of the Magi"` |

For a title of an article within quotation marks that includes a title to a book, as indicated by underlining, retain the underlining:

| `"Great Expectations as a Novel of Initiation"` |

For a title of an article within quotation marks that includes another title indicated by quotation marks, enclose the shorter title within single quotation marks:

| `"A Reading of O. Henry's 'The Gift of the Magi'"` |

For an underlined title to a book that incorporates another title that normally receives underlining, do not underline the shorter title or place it within quotation marks:

<u>Interpretations of</u> Great Expectations

<u>Using Shakespeare's</u> Romeo and Juliet <u>in the Classroom</u>

Typing Submit the paper in typed form. Only on rare occasions will instructors accept handwritten manuscripts. Type only on one side of the page. Avoid typewriters with script or other fancy print. If you use a computer, get permission before using the typefaces supported by a laser printer (Helvetica, Times Roman, Gothic, and others). Keep in mind that you are responsible for correct pagination and accuracy of the manuscript. Right justification (expanding print) is not acceptable because it creates incorrect spacing. Use no hyphens at the ends of lines. Use special features—boldface, italics, graphs, color—with discretion. The writing, not the graphics, will earn the credits and the better grades. See also "Revising, Editing, and Proofreading," 161–65.

Underlining Titles Underlining takes the place of italics in a typed manuscript. Use a continuous line for titles with more than one word. Always use the italics on your computer printer or underline the titles of the following types of works:

aircraft	<u>Enola Gay</u>
ballet	<u>The Nutcracker</u>
book	<u>Earthly Powers</u>
bulletin	<u>Production Memo 3</u>
drama	<u>Desire Under the Elms</u>
film	<u>Treasure of the Sierra Madre</u>
journal	<u>Journal of Sociology</u>
magazine	<u>Newsweek</u>
newspaper	<u>The Nashville Banner</u>
novel	<u>The Scarlet Letter</u>
opera	<u>Rigoletto</u>
painting	<u>Mona Lisa</u>
pamphlet	<u>Ten Goals for Successful Sales</u>
periodical	<u>Scientific American</u>
play	<u>Cat on a Hot Tin Roof</u>
poem	<u>Idylls of the King</u> (only if book length)
radio show	<u>Grand Ole Opry</u>
recording	<u>The Poems of Wallace Stevens</u>
sculpture	<u>David</u>
ship	<u>Titanic</u>
short novel	<u>Billy Budd</u>

symphony	Beethoven's <u>Eroica</u>
	but
	Beethoven's Symphony no. 3 in A
	(to identify form, number, and key)
television	Tonight <u>Show</u> (program title,
	not a single episode)
yearbook	The Pegasus

In contrast, place quotation marks around: articles, essays, chapters, sections, short poems, stories, songs, lectures, sermons, reports, and individual episodes of television programs.

If separately published, underline titles of essays, lectures, poems, proceedings, reports, sermons, and stories. However, these items are usually published as an anthology of sermons or a collection of stories, in which case you would underline the title of the anthology or collection.

Do not underline sacred writings (Genesis or Old Testament), series (The New American Nation Series), editions (Variorum Edition of W. B. Yeats), societies (Victorian Society), courses (Greek Mythology), divisions of a work (preface, appendix, canto 3, scene 2), or descriptive phrases (Nixon's farewell address or Reagan's White House years).

Underlining for Emphasis   On occasion, you may use underlining to emphasize certain words or phrases in a typed paper, but positioning the key word accomplishes the same purpose:

Expressed emphasis: Perhaps an answer lies in <u>preventing</u> abuse, not in makeshift remedies after the fact.

Better: Prevention of abuse is a better answer than makeshift remedies after the fact.

Some special words and symbols require underlining.

1. Species, genera, and varieties:

<u>Penstemon caespitosus</u> subsp. <u>thompsoniae</u>

2. Letter, word, or phrase cited as a linguistic sample:

the letter <u>e</u> in the word <u>let</u>

3. Letters used as statistical symbols and algebraic variables:

trial <u>n</u> of the <u>t</u> test or <u>C</u>(3, 14) = 9.432

Word Division   Avoid dividing any word at the end of a line. Leave the line short rather than divide a word (see "Hyphens," 224–25).

8c SAMPLE PAPER: A SHORT ESSAY WITH DOCUMENTATION

The following paper demonstrates the correct form for short papers that use only two or three secondary sources. Keep in mind that short papers, like the long, formal research paper, require correct in-text citations and a list of references.

Wickham 1

Jay Wickham

Heritage 1020

March 5, 1991

    Same Construction, Different Walls: Structural

        Similarities in the Short Stories of

                Flannery O'Connor

    Flannery O'Connor uses a recurring structural pattern in the development of the main characters in four short stories: "Greenleaf," "Good Country People," "Revelation," and "Everything That Rises Must Converge." The pattern consists of three stages: (1) the author makes use of the omniscient point of view, allowing the reader to be privy to all the characters' thoughts and motives; (2) then a disconcerting and jolting climax occurs, usually very harsh for the character; and (3) readers finally discover how this climax affects the characters.

    The five main characters of these stories (Mrs. May, Hulga, Mrs. Turpin, Julian, and his mother) are all based on a common denominator in their character makeup—that of emotional contempt for the world they inhabit and, even more, contempt for themselves. O'Connor sets up these characters with inflated egos; then she pulls the rug out from under the characters in a climactic moment. Ironically, each character is smashed by something he or she held in contempt.

Use an inverted pyramid style for the title (see Section 8a, 195).

Identify the literary work early in the paper (see Section 6f, 145–46).

Use parenthetical numbers to list three or more ideas.

Provide a thesis sentence to control the analysis of the literary works (see Sections 1c, 16–19, and 6b, 136–38).

Introduce
quotations with
the speaker's
name and end
them with the
parenthetical
citation (see
Section 7a,
174–76).

The citation
means that
Poirer was
quoted in the
book
*Contemporary
Authors,* a book
that the writer
properly
abbreviates in
the textual
citations (see
205–06).

The writer uses
brackets to
interpolate his
own word,
religion, into the
quoted material
(see 192–93).

Use three
ellipsis dots to
indicate the
omission of
words from a
quotation (see
189–92).

CS in the
citation refers to
O'Connor's *The
Complete
Stories* (see
205–06).

Critic Richard Poirer, writing on O'Connor's structure

of climax, argues that "she propels her characters towards

the cataclysms where alone they can have a tortured glimpse

of the need and chance for redemption" (qtd. in <u>CA</u> 721).

The aftermath of those destructive moments is rather grim.

The character dies or withdraws in shame and despair.

In "Greenleaf" Mrs. May is (1) a woman with two lazy

and ungrateful sons; (2) a woman who encourages her sons to

go to church, even though she herself "did not, of course,

believe any of [religion] was true" (<u>CS</u> 316); and (3) a

woman who envies her despised neighbors, the Greenleafs,

who become successful. Most frustrating to her is the fact

that the Greenleafs succeed because she made it possible.

The Greenleafs have made good in the wake of her failures.

Mrs. May is gored by the Greenleafs' bull, just as

they have served as the thorn in her side. Mrs. May dies

almost instantly, but not before O'Connor describes her as

"leaning over . . . as if to whisper some final discovery

into the bull's ear" (<u>CS</u> 334). This final sentence

suggests that Mrs. May had learned something, but the story

gives no hint as to what that might be, and just as well.

Robert Drake calls it a "dark vision of modern damnation

and redemption" (<u>CA</u> 721).

In "Good Country People," Hulga is a misanthropic

Ph.D. with a wooden leg. Hulga is not satisfied with the

quality of her life and perhaps justifiably so; a real leg

would be nice, just as helpful sons would be nice for Mrs.

May. Hulga takes her emotional pain out on others around

her, scoffing at them for the miserable people they are,

not realizing her own inadequacies.

Being a conceited intellectual, she has lived with the

idea that the people around her, including her mother, are

Wickham 3

simpletons. Hulga regards her mother as a woman who
refuses to use her mind, and would likely try to solve
heartache with a peanut-butter and jelly sandwich; but when
Manley Pointer pulls out his flask and his condoms, she is
left with the realization that she, the self-acknowledged
brilliant one, has been undone by a simple country boy who
steals her wooden leg. He departs and says (CS 291),
"Hulga, you ain't so smart. I been believing in nothin'
ever since I was born!" Her contempt does her no good now.

In "Revelation," Mrs. Turpin is a pious and prejudiced
woman, yet she is another character who looks down on
others around her. She takes comfort in the knowledge that
people less important than herself exist so that she can
look down on them, including the ugly girl in the waiting
room.

At this point in the story, Mrs. Turpin has been
prattling on for quite some time, to anyone in the waiting
room who will converse with her, lauding all the while the
many gifts a gracious God has given her. As she goes on
and on, the ugly girl gets angry, and finally explodes in a
furious attack on Mrs. Turpin. The girl, finally
restrained by orderlies, shouts to Mrs. Turpin, "Go back to
hell where you came from, you old wart hog" (CS 500).

About this scene, Robert Brinkmeyer says, "Human
pretensions are not merely undercut but utterly destroyed;
they are shown to be worthless and insignificant if not
terribly evil" (57). "Revelation," true to its title, is
the only story of the four where O'Connor lets the reader
follow the main character home to see the long-term
effects. Mrs. Turpin's self-image has been destroyed by
the insults of the girl, whose attack she takes to heart.
It causes Mrs. Turpin to scream and shake her fist at God,

Put a page citation in front of a quotation to avoid interfering with an exclamation point or a question mark (see 186).

Leave a line short rather than use the hyphen to divide a word at the end of a line (see 224).

to question for the first time why she is what she is. Her
answer is life-shattering, for she turns her high-powered
and pious contempt on herself. She begins to feel her own
worthlessness.

Of her themes concerning piety, O'Connor writes:

> If other ages felt less, they saw more, even
> though they saw with the blind, prophetical,
> unsentimental eye of acceptance, which is to say,
> of faith. In the absence of this faith, now, we
> govern by tenderness. It is a tenderness, which
> long cut off from the person of Christ, is
> wrapped in theory. When tenderness is detached
> from the source of tenderness, its logical
> outcome is terror. (Qtd. in Morrow 145)

In "Everything That Rises Must Converge," Julian is a
college graduate and, like Hulga, is overly proud of his
intellect. He is misanthropic, especially toward his
mother. Alienated from others, he has an insensitive
personality, one that hates easier than it loves. His
mother, on the other hand, is a friendly lady unaccustomed
to questioning the feelings or impulses in her heart. She
judges the right and wrong of situations by what Julian
believes to be a worn-out set of values.

Both Julian and his mother are also characterized by
their racial prejudices. Julian is respectful of blacks,
but he has no notion of how to interact. His mother,
having grown up on a plantation, presumes to know how to
treat blacks. However, a black woman strikes Julian's
mother with a heavy purse when Julian's mother offers a
penny to a black child. The blow causes Julian's mother to
have a stroke, and she soon collapses. She has been
destroyed by her own prejudices, in the sense that she
could not anticipate that a black woman would be offended
by her condescending offer. She never saw the blow coming.

Wickham 5

In a domino effect, her stroke becomes Julian's moment of destruction. After taunting his mother, then realizing her serious condition, he runs from the scene into the night. The guilt of the moment follows close behind. The person he most condemned—his mother—has been eradicated. Perhaps that is why he ran; he cannot face the fact that he truly held his mother in contempt. He discovers "his own ignorance and cruelty" (Brinkmeyer 71). Thus "the tide of darkness seemed to sweep him back to her, postponing from moment to moment his entry into the world of guilt and sorrow" (CS 420).

Every author has a different method of creating characters. O'Connor seems to have decided for these four stories that if something works well once, it will work well again. In terms of character development, these stories are structurally the same because all four correspond to the same theme in terms of characterization: live by the sword, die by the sword. The jolting climax of each story "produces a shock for the reader," says O'Connor, who adds, "and I think one reason for this is that it produced a shock for the writer" (qtd. in Brinkmeyer 39).

Blend quotations into your sentences smoothly, as shown in these two examples (see Section 7a, 174–76).

Works Cited

Brinkmeyer, Robert. The Art and Vision of Flannery

    O'Connor. Baton Rouge: Louisiana State UP, 1989.

Contemporary Authors. First Rev., vols. 1-4, Detroit: Gale, 1967.

Morrow, Suzanne P. Flannery O'Connor: A Study of the Short

    Fiction. Boston: Twayne, 1988.

O'Connor, Flannery. The Complete Stories. New York:

    Farrar, 1962.

Remember to include the primary source, the collection of stories, as well as the secondary sources (see Section 9a, 250–51).

8d SAMPLE PAPER: A FORMAL RESEARCH PAPER

The following paper illustrates the style and form of the fully developed research paper. It includes a title page, outline pages, a variety of in-text citations, superscript numerals to content endnotes, and a fully developed works-cited page. Notations in the margins signal special circumstances in matters of form and style.

The Effects of Television on the Language

Development of Children

by

Kim Wells

Professor James D. Lester

Composition 1010

18 November 1992

The following marginal comments clarify the form of the research paper and explain specific problems you may encounter.

The title page is a three-part balance of title, author, and course information (see 195–96).

See also the preliminary papers: "Annotated Bibliography," 102–04, and "Selected Review of Literature," 104–09.

Wells ii

Use lowercase
Roman
numerals for
preliminary
pages (see 121).

This writer uses
the sentence
outline (see
83–85).

Repeat your
thesis at the
beginning of the
outline,
although it may
take a different
form in the
paper itself (see
16–19).

Use standard
outline symbols
(see 82).

The headings
for both the
introduction (I)
and conclusion
(III) are
content-oriented
like other
outline entries
(see 81–85).

Outline

Thesis: Parents and teachers alike must address the role of television in the language development of young people because, for better or worse, it affects the way children use language.

I.   Television influences children.

   A.   The problem is television's influence on children and its effects on language development.

   B.   It is a significant issue because statistics confirm unconditionally that children spend enormous amounts of time watching television.

   C.   Experts have debated the effects of this visual medium upon the minds of young people, both to condemn it and to endorse it.

   D.   The role of television in the language development of young people must be addressed by parents and teachers alike.

II.   The issues are serious and worthy of study.

   A.   Television viewing can augment vocabulary.

   B.   Television encourages reading, which, in turn, improves language competence.

   C.   The visual arts complement the language arts.

   D.   Modern communication technology provides educational tools that cannot be ignored.

   E.   Television viewing enhances writing.

III.   Television enhances language development.

   A.   Teachers should take advantage of the students' television consciousness.

   B.   Teachers should develop criteria for judging the worth of television programming.

   C.   Parents must not allow television to produce passive children; rather, they must use it to stimulate learning activities.

The Effects of Television on the Language

Development of Children

    Without doubt, television influences the mental
processes and speaking habits of young people who may
develop their language skills in the family den as much as
they do in the classroom. Indeed, statistics abound on the
television habits of children. High school seniors will
have watched about 15,000 hours of television by the time
they graduate (1986 Nielson Report as cited in Powell 41).
To gain perspective, Hal Blythe and Charlie Sweet put it
this way: "By the time the vidkids matriculate at their
favorite institution of higher learning, almost one-half of
their waking life will have been spent being Superseted,
Chromacolored, and Colortaked" (22-23). Sister Rosemary
Winkeljohann reports this incident:

> A few seasons ago, on an episode of "Happy Days,"
> Fonzie got a library card as a small part of the
> overall story. The producers thought nothing of
> it until they later learned that librarians all
> over the country were swamped the next day with
> children coming to the library. Children who had
> never used the library facilities now wanted
> library cards! (100)

Most parents and teachers recognize the powerful influence
of television, but they seem hesitant about putting it to
good purpose. It took an entrepreneur like Chris Whittle
to bring television (Channel One) into the school for a
profit.

    Since the late 1940s, researchers have studied the
effects of television viewing on children (see, for
example, the 1951 study by Shayon). Some condemn it
outright; others endorse it conditionally. Unfortunately,
definitive answers are not yet available despite complete

Both running
head and page
number are
given (but see
226).

Repeat the title
on the first
page of text.

For tips on
building
opening
paragraphs, see
145–51.

Use
parenthetical
citations to
your sources
(see Section
7a, 174–76).

This writer
identifies the
issue, but a
thesis comes
later (see the
next page).
Note: Most
research
papers have
openings that
extend over
several
paragraphs.

Long quotes are
introduced by a
colon, indented,
without
quotation
marks, double
spaced, with
source cited at
the end (see
186–88).

This writer
begins
narrowing her
topic about
television's
influence on
language
development of
children.

books on the subject, such as the texts by Healy (1990);
Bryant and Anderson (1983), which presents 13 essays by
different writers; and the current efforts of Mabel Rice
and Linda Woodsmall at the University of Kansas.

Several propositions seem undisputed by all the
researchers:

1. Children are the largest audience for television.

2. Television is a continuing interest for most
   children.

3. Television can provoke a response in children.

For these reasons, and others as well, parents and teachers
alike must address the role of television in the language
development of young people. The issues are complex and
controversial, but the impact is certain.

Television can invigorate the vocabulary of children,
although some critics argue otherwise. Jon Powell, for
example, states that television tends to speak in a choppy,
simplistic, and superficial language in order to appeal to
the widest possible audience (41-42). Child psychologist
Lee Salk is more blunt, saying that "children will pick up
crude language or rudeness if such behavior is introduced
into the home on a TV show" (50). And David Rolandelli
suggests that children must look more than listen "because
the linguistic information is often incomprehensible" (75).

Jane Healy has serious doubts about television's role
in educating children. In her 1990 study, Healy condemns
television as a "poor teacher," arguing that television
programming does not offer "interactive engagement" in
which children can enter a dialogue rather than just
listen. Healy notes that refinements of grammar,
vocabulary, and social usage "depend on the quality and

The writer
enumerates
specific issues.

The thesis
comes late in
the opening; it
could also
appear early
(see 146).

The writer uses
paraphrase
effectively (see
123-25).

This section
develops
negative/positive
viewpoints. For
tips on building
the body of
your paper, see
151-57, and the
section on
paradigms,
78-81.

Wells 3

quantity of interactions in both preschool and elementary years" (<u>Endangered</u> 88–89).

These negative views stand in contrast to a 1988 study by Mabel Rice and Linda Woodsmall, who tested groups of three- and five-year-old children for ability to learn various new "novel" words on the basis of a short television exposure. Both groups learned difficult new words, such as <u>gramophone</u>, <u>nurturant</u>, and <u>viola</u>. The results defended the thesis that children "learn new words when watching television, given an appropriate script" (425).

In like manner, the study by Singer et al. demonstrates that an experimental group of children exposed to selective viewing quickly learned such words as <u>video</u>, <u>fiction</u>, <u>animation</u>, <u>sponsor</u>, and <u>prejudice</u> (88). Figure 1 demonstrates how the children retained the specialized vocabulary.

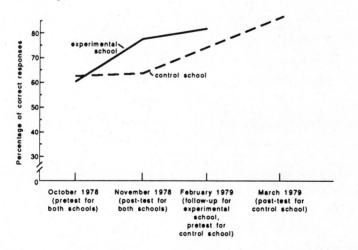

Figure 1: Percentages of correct responses by children in experimental and control schools to questions on lesson-related vocabulary words. Source: Singer et al. (89).

Note the blend of paraphrase and quotation so that text follows smoothly with proper introductions and in-text citations (see Section 7a, 174–76).

See 216–19 for guidelines on the use of tables and illustrations.

See 252 on the use of "et al." to substitute for multiple authors.

Neil Postman supports television for children because they "may accumulate . . . a fund of knowledge that was simply inaccessible to pre-television children" (35). Surely, as children accumulate factual knowledge, they also accumulate words. Four-year-olds today must have a vast vocabulary in comparison with children of the 1930s. Whether they can transfer the visual-auditory influence to their reading is another matter, as discussed later in the paper. Nevertheless, the value of educational programs, such as <u>Sesame Street</u>, is in their power or ability to provide a foundation of words that parents and teachers can then supplement, despite Healy's recent argument that <u>Sesame Street</u> has sold children on letters and numbers but "underemphasized the verbal and reasoning skills necessary to make them meaningful" ("10 Reasons" 63).

Television encourages reading, which in turn improves language competence. Beyond the one-time motivation of children who responded to Fonzie's request for a library card, research indicates that good programming improves reading and can increase library lendings. The Himmelweit study in Great Britain, <u>Television and the Child</u>, confirms that "television in the long run encourages children to read books, a conclusion that can be reinforced by evidence from libraries, book clubs, and publishing companies." Dr. Himmelweit stresses this point: "Book reading comes into its own, not despite television but because of it" (qtd. in Postman 33).

This view by Himmelweit is not universally supported. Kate Moody, in her 1980 text <u>Growing Up on Television: The TV Effect</u>, compares the imaginative, analytical function of reading against the "passive act" of television viewing (66-76). Another drawback to television, according to

The writer effectively summarizes the basic problem, then moves to the next issue.

The writer shifts to a new issue in accordance with her outline (see Section 3c, 81-87).

Note the form used for a quote within another writer's work (see Section 7d, 178-79).

Wells 5

Moody, is that when viewing television, a child cannot stop the action, "assimilate the material," and then go on to the next sequence as one can do while reading. She stresses the idea that "a good story in print will take on new shades of meaning with each rereading . . ." (56). Her comparisons of reading and television viewing emphasize the active nature of reading and the passive intake of television (68). Mark Bricklin echoes Moody's argument, saying that time spent watching television is not as bad as the "passive" nature of it (143).

However, the concept of passive intake is disputed by Daniel Anderson and Elizabeth Lorch, who argue that "the viewer does not passively incorporate any and all content . . ." but "applies his or her own experience and understanding to that content" (29–30). In addition, the work of Rice and Woodsmall, while focusing on word acquisition, nevertheless notes that children who acquire a new word often "identify the grammatical role, and putative meaning of the unfamiliar adjective and noun" (426). Thereby, they structure words within a mental sentence to guide their reading of it at a later time. If children do learn new words, as research indicates, it seems reasonable to assume that children assign the new words not only to a lexical reservoir but to a grammatical one as well.[1]

Television at its best is literature, and writing is enhanced by literature. If it ranks as literature, then surely it will invite children into the world of rich language usage. Robert Oliphant argues that nonreaders can benefit from their extensive "dramatic awareness" from television viewing in order to develop and perform their own plays (48). In an interview, Roger Fransecky responds to this question: "Could television be used to aid [writing] development?" He answers in the affirmative and

---

Blend quotations into your text smoothly (see Chapter 7, 173–93).

See Section 7k, 189–92, on the use of ellipsis points.

Superscript numerals signal content endnotes (see 210–13). Do not use superscript numerals and endnotes for documentation of sources unless you need to cluster several sources.

Use parentheses to add clarifying words to your own text, but use brackets to insert your words into a quotation (see Section 7l, 192–93).

Wells 6

suggests that children might write "video reports" in
addition to book reports (718).

Composition in the classroom, enhanced by television,
makes good sense. Children identify with television
programming. They know the characters, the plots, and the
subtle language particulars of their favorite programs. To
deny them an opportunity of writing about a medium that
preoccupies every waking day is to ignore a powerful
resource of information. Postman says television provides
awesome quantities of factual data and suggests that
schools can now have purposes other than merely supplying
information (36). Writing about facts learned on
television, even the tragedies, might have an importance.

The shift into past tense is correct, but regular text should use historical present tense (see 142–43).

Modern communication technology is here to stay and
cannot be ignored. Fifty years ago we lived in a cocoon of
isolation with only the print media and a limited number of
radio stations to keep us informed as a nation, but now we
live in the information age, an age that bombards us with
television and radio in our homes and automobiles, annoys
us with ringing telephones, and infatuates us with
computers and their modems for networking across the
nation. David Considine sees the conflict as chalkboards
and talking by teachers versus an environment of electronic

Some lines may appear extremely short, but do *not* hyphenate words at the end of lines (224–25).

marvels (635). He argues, "While schools continue to
operate as though print were the main means of
communication in our culture, an increasingly high-tech
society requires a new definition of literacy that

Even paraphrased materials should be introduced and documented in the text (see Section 5e, 123–25).

encompasses visual, computer, and media literacy" (639).
James Anderson, while admitting that reading "dominates"
any sense of media literacy, admonishes us to remember that
television, like reading, requires children to collect,
interpret, test, and then apply the accumulated data (297).

Wells 7

This point brings us back to the original thesis. The role of television in the language development of young people must be addressed by parents and teachers alike, for children's language is, for better or worse, affected by the medium. After all, students possess, to use the words of Blythe and Sweet (23), a "television consciousness," so teachers should take advantage of it. Considine pulls no punches on this point:

> Teachers who fail to integrate this technology into the instructional process limit their own teaching strategies, ignore the iconic world in which their students live, and retard the language development of their students by denying them an understanding of the form and content of the visual media. (635)

If television affects children, and it does, then parents and teachers should begin building positive reinforcement to complement television learning and to develop a child's intellectual curiosity. Popular magazines have begun to address the issue. Julius and Zelda Segal in <u>Parents</u> magazine advise parents on ways to help children confront news broadcasts that show various acts of violence, and <u>Children Today</u> devotes an entire page to the review of <u>TV News and Children</u>, a booklet published by Action for Children's Television ("Filling" 32).

If selecting the proper program is vital to language enhancement, teachers should train children in what to watch and how to evaluate it. Teachers can correspond with national groups, such as The Committee of Impact of TV on Children or the ABC Education Projects.[2]

Parents must not allow television to produce passive children (the "couch potato" syndrome). Parents and

---

The writer reasserts her thesis. The conclusion now officially begins. Note how the writer develops a full judgment on the issue and does not merely summarize the paper.

For tips on writing paragraphs of the conclusion, see Section 6h, 157–61.

This paragraph blends personal observations with paraphrase, short quotations, and a long, indented quotation (see 173–93).

Reference to an entire article needs no in-text citation to a page number (see 120–21).

teachers must know that television infects every preschool
youngster and, like a living virus, it remains in their
systems for the remainder of their lives.

In some cases, television is "junk food" (see
Fransecky 717), and excessive viewing distracts from other
activities (see esp. Paul Witty as quoted in Postman 31),
yet television can and does bring cultural programs and
some of our best literature into homes and schools. A
recent book by Cecilia Tiché examines the television
culture and argues, "Kids can handle all the
sources—friends, stereos, television, reading
materials—much better than adults" (qtd. in "Vandy
Professor," B5). In truth, television does, according to
the evidence, improve children's vocabularies, encourage
their reading, and inspire their writing. Television and
school should not be antagonists; the traditional
classroom curriculum should seek and find harmony with the
preschool television curriculum.

Wells 9

otes

sed in more detail in Hodge and

explain N. Chomsky's theory

yntax and the child as a

resses through a series of

pp also explain here the theories

y.

ides and special materials, such as

d author biographies, write to ABC

American Broadcasting Company, 1330

New York, NY 10019. For special papers

Impact of TV on Children, National

of English, 1111 Kenyon Rd., Urbana, IL

61801. See cky and Winkeljohann for additional

resource lists.

Content notes appear on a separate page. For tips on writing content notes, see 210–13.

This note offers additional literature on a point (see 212).

Start the "Works
Cited" on a new
page.

Works Cited

For tips on
writing the
bibliography
entries, see
250–79.

Anderson, Daniel R., and Elizabeth Pugzles Lorch.   "Looking

    at Television: Action or Reaction?"   Bryant and

    Anderson 1–33.

A
cross-reference
entry (see 259).

Anderson, James A.   "Television Literacy and the Critical

    Viewer."   Bryant and Anderson 297–330.

An entry for
two authors (see
257).

Blythe, Hal, and Charlie Sweet.   "Using Media to Teach

    English."   <u>Instructional Innovator</u> 28 (1983): 22–24.

Bricklin, Mark.   "Why Johnny Can't Learn."   <u>Prevention</u> Nov.

    1990: 143+.

A book entry
(see 253).
Include any
subtitles
separated
from the
main title
by a colon.

Bryant, Jennings, and Daniel R. Anderson, eds.   <u>Children's</u>

    <u>Understanding of Television: Research on Attention and</u>

    <u>Comprehension</u>.   New York: Academic, 1983.

Considine, David M.   "Visual Literacy and the Curriculum:

    More to It Than Meets the Eye."   <u>Language Arts</u> 64

    (1987): 634–40.

Entry for a
review of
another work
(see 268).

"Filling the News Gap."   Rev. of <u>TV News and Children</u>.

    <u>Children Today</u> 17.2 (Mar.–Apr. 1988): 32.

A typical entry
for a journal
article (see 267).

Fransecky, Roger B.   "Perspectives: Children, Television,

    and Language Education."   <u>Language Arts</u> 58 (1981):

    713–20.

Healy, Jane M.   <u>Endangered Minds: Why Our Children Don't</u>

    <u>Think</u>.   New York: Simon, 1990.

———.   "10 Reasons 'Sesame Street' Is Bad News for Reading."

    <u>Education Digest</u> Feb. 1991: 63–66.

Note
abbreviation for
a university
press (see
201–02).

Hodge, Robert, and David Tripp.   <u>Children and Television: A</u>

    <u>Semiotic Approach</u>.   Stanford UP, 1986.

Moody, Kate.   <u>Growing Up on Television: The TV Effect</u>.   New

    York: Times Books, 1980.

Oliphant, Robert.   "From Television to Writing."   <u>Education</u>

    <u>Digest</u> Oct. 1988: 46–48.

Wells 11

Postman, Neil. <u>Television and the Teaching of English</u>.
New York: Appleton, 1961.

Powell, Jon T. "What We Don't Know About the Influence of
Television." <u>Educational Technology</u> 26 (Aug. 1986):
41–43.

Rice, Mabel L., and Linda Woodsmall. "Lessons from
Television: Children's Word Learning When Viewing."
<u>Child Development</u> 59 (1988): 420–29.

Rolandelli, David R. "Children and Television: The Visual
Superiority Effect Reconsidered." <u>Journal of
Broadcasting & Electronic Media</u> 33 (1989): 69–81.

Salk, Lee. "Are Some TV Characters Bad for Kids?"
<u>McCall's</u> Jan. 1991: 50.

Segal, Julius, and Zelda Segal. "As They Grow / 5 and 6:
Helping Children Deal With the News." <u>Parents</u> Nov.
1987: 265.

Shayon, Robert. <u>Television and Our Children</u>. New York:
Longmans, 1951.

Singer, Dorothy G., Diana M. Zuckerman, and Jerome L.
Singer. "Helping Elementary Children Learn About TV."
<u>Journal of Communication</u> 30.3 (1980): 84–93.

"Vandy Professor Says TV Can Be a Positive Influence."
<u>Leaf Chronicle</u> [Clarksville, TN] 2 July 1992: B5.

Winkeljohann, Sister Rosemary. "Queries: What Is the Role
of Television in the Language Arts Program?" <u>Language
Arts</u> 58 (1981): 100–02.

Entry for a magazine (see 268).

An entry with three authors (see 257).

A journal entry may include the issue number (see 267).

9 *Works Cited*

After writing your paper, you should prepare a "Works Cited" page to list your reference materials. List only the ones actually used in your manuscript, including works mentioned within content endnotes or in captions of tables and illustrations. If you carefully developed your working bibliography cards and kept them up to date (see 25–30), preparing the "Works Cited" page will be relatively simple. Your cards, arranged alphabetically, provide the necessary information.

Your heading indicates the nature of your list.

Label the page "Works Cited" if your list includes only those printed works quoted and paraphrased in the paper.

Label the page "Sources Cited" if your list includes nonprint items (e.g., interview or speech) as well as printed works.

Reserve the heading "Bibliography" for a complete listing of *all* works related to the subject, an unlikely prospect for undergraduate papers.

Works pertinent to the paper, but not quoted or paraphrased, such as an article on related matters, can be mentioned in a content endnote (210–13) and then listed within the "Works Cited." On this point, see especially the "Notes" page of the sample paper, 247.

Type your "Works Cited" page according to the MLA standards that follow. (For the format in other disciplines, see Chapters 10 and 11.)

9a FORMAT FOR THE WORKS CITED PAGE

Arrange items in alphabetical order by the surname of the author. When no author is listed, alphabetize by the first important word of the title. Imagine lettered spelling for unusual items, such as "#2 Red Dye" (entered as though "Number 2 Red Dye"). Place the first line of each entry flush with the left margin and indent succeeding lines five spaces. Double-space each entry and also double-space between entries. Set the title "Works Cited" one inch down from the top of the sheet and double-space between it and the first entry. A sample page follows (see also the sample "Works Cited" pages on 236 and 248–49):

Figure 88:
Sample "Works
Cited" page

Works Cited

The Bible. Revised Standard Version.

Bulfinch, Thomas. Bulfinch's Mythology. 2 vols. New
    York: Mentor, 1962.

Campbell, Joseph. The Hero With a Thousand Faces.
    Cleveland: Meridian, 1956.

---. The Masks of God. 4 vols. New York: Viking, 1970.

Henderson, Joseph L., and Maud Oakes. The Wisdom of the
    Serpent: The Myths of Death, Rebirth, and
    Resurrection. New York: Collier, 1971.

Homer. The Iliad. Trans. Richmond Lattimore. Chicago: U
    of Chicago P, 1951.

Laird, Charlton. "A Nonhuman Being Can Learn Language."
    College Composition and Communication 23 (1972):
    142-54.

Lévi-Strauss, Claude. "The Structural Study of Myth."
    Myth: A Symposium. Ed. Thomas A. Sebeok.
    Bloomington: Indiana UP, 1958.

Robinson, Lillian S. "Criticism--and Self-Criticism."
    College English 36 (1974): 436-45.

9b BIBLIOGRAPHY FORM: BOOKS

Enter information for books in the following order. Items 1, 3, and 8 are
required; add other items according to the instructions that follow.

1. Author(s)
2. Chapter or part of book
3. Title of the book
4. Editor, translator, or
   compiler
5. Edition

6. Name of the series
7. Number of volumes
8. Place, publisher, and date
9. Volume number of this
   book
10. Page numbers

Name of the Author(s)   The author's name, surname first, followed by
a comma, followed by given name or initials, followed by a period:

Bellow, Saul. The Bellaros Connection. New York: Penguin,
    1989.

Always give authors' names exactly as shown on the title page; for example, "Cosbey, Robert Cord" or "Cosbey, Robert C." However, APA style (see Chapter 10, 251–52) requires last name and initials only (Cosbey, R. C.).

When an author has two or more works, do not repeat the name with each entry. Rather, insert a continuous three-dash line flush with the left margin, followed by a period:

> Hansberry, Lorraine. <u>A Raisin in the Sun</u>. New York:
>
>   Random, 1959.
>
> ---. <u>To Be Young, Gifted and Black</u>. Ed. Robert Nemiroff.
>
>   Englewood Cliffs, NJ: Prentice, 1969.

List two works by the same author alphabetically by the title (ignoring *a, an,* and *the*); in this case "R" precedes "T." *Remember:* The hyphens stand for exactly the same name(s) as in the preceding entry, so do not substitute three hyphens for an author who has two or more works in the bibliography when one is written in collaboration with someone else:

> Lagarsfeld, Paul F., et al., eds. <u>Continuities in the</u>
>
>   <u>Language of Social Research</u>. Rev. ed. New York:
>
>   Free, 1972.
>
> Lagarsfeld, Paul F., and E. Katz. <u>Language of Social</u>
>
>   <u>Research: A Reader in the Methodology of Social</u>
>
>   <u>Research</u>. New York: Free, 1965.

A Chapter or Part of a Book   List the chapter or part of a book in "Works Cited" only when it is separately edited, translated, or written, or if it demands special attention. For example, if you quote from a specific chapter of a book, let's say Lewis Thomas's chapter entitled "The Music of This Sphere" from his book *The Lives of a Cell,* the entry should read:

> Thomas, Lewis. <u>The Lives of a Cell</u>. New York: Viking,
>
>   1974.

Your in-text citation will have listed specific page numbers, so there is no reason to mention a specific chapter even though it is the only portion of Thomas's book that you read.

Anthologies, however, contain works by many authors or different works by the same author. Because readers will search your list for the person cited in the text, not an editor, you need specifics in the "Works Cited," as follows:

1. If you paraphrase or quote portions of an essay by Lonne Elder, write this entry:

> Elder, Lonne. "Ceremonies in Dark Old Men." <u>New Black</u>
>
>   <u>Playwrights: An Anthology</u>. Ed. William Couch, Jr.
>
>   Baton Rouge: Louisiana State UP, 1968. 55–72.

2. If you cite lines from Aristophanes' drama *The Birds* in your paper, write this entry:

> Aristophanes. <u>The Birds</u>. <u>Five Comedies of Aristophanes</u>.
>
>   Trans. Benjamin B. Rogers. Garden City, NY:
>
>   Doubleday, 1955. 110–54.

3. If you cite material from a chapter of one volume in a multivolume set, write this entry:

> Saintsbury, George. "Dickens." <u>The Cambridge History of</u>
>
>   <u>English Literature</u>. Ed. A. W. Ward and A. R. Waller.
>
>   14 vols. New York: Putnam's, 1917. 13: 336–76.

In cases where you cite several different authors from the same anthology, you should make cross-references in the bibliography (see 259).

The Title of the Book   Show the title of the work, underlined, followed by a period. Separate any subtitle from the primary title by a colon and one space even though the title page has no mark of punctuation or the card catalog entry has a semicolon:

> Budd, Richard W., and Brent D. Ruben. <u>Beyond Media: New</u>
>
>   <u>Approaches to Mass Communication</u>. Rev. ed. New
>
>   Brunswick, NJ: Transaction, 1991.

If a title includes the title of another article or book, special rules apply (see "Titles Within Titles," 228–29). You may need to omit underlining, as in this next example:

> Schilling, Bernard N. <u>Dryden and the Conservative Myth: A</u>
>
>   <u>Reading of</u> Absalom and Achitophel. New Haven: Yale
>
>   UP, 1961.

Name of the Editor or Translator   Mention an editor of a collection or a translator after the title, "Ed." or "Trans.":

> Dante. <u>The Purgatorio</u>. Trans. John Ciardi. New York:
>
>   NAL, 1961.
>
> Yeats, W. B. <u>The Poems</u>. Ed. Richard J. Finneran. New
>
>   York: Macmillan, 1983.

However, if your in-text citation refers to the work of the editor or translator (e.g., "The Ciardi edition caused debate among Dante scholars") use this form:

```
Ciardi, John, trans.  The Purgatorio.  By Dante.  New York:

     NAL, 1961.
```

Edition of the Book   Indicate the edition used, whenever it is not the first, in Arabic numerals (e.g., "3rd ed."), without further punctuation:

```
Emery, Michael, and Edwin Emery.  The Press and America: An

     Interpretive View of the Mass Media.  6th ed.

     Englewood Cliffs, NJ: Prentice, 1988.
```

Name of a Series   If the book is one in a published series, show the name of the series, without quotation marks and not underlined, followed by a comma, followed by the number of this work in the series in Arabic numerals (e.g., "vol. 3," "no. 3," or simply "3"), followed by a period:

```
Brown, J. R., and Bernard Harris.  Restoration Theatre.

     Stratford-upon-Avon Studies 6.  London: Arnold, 1965.

Fowler, David.  Piers the Plowman.  U of Washington Publ.

     in Lang. and Lit. 16.  Seattle: U of Washington P,

     1961.
```

Number of Volumes with This Title   Show the number of volumes with this particular title, if more than one, in Arabic numerals (e.g., "4 vols."):

```
Horecek, Leo, and Gerald Lefkoss.  Programmed Ear Training.

     4 vols.  New York: Harcourt, 1970.
```

Place, Publisher, and Date   Indicate the place, publisher, and date of publication:

```
Ronell, Avital.  The Telephone Book.  Lincoln: U of

     Nebraska P, 1989.
```

If more than one place of publication appears on the title page, the first city mentioned is sufficient. If successive dates of copyright are given, use the most recent (unless your study is specifically concerned with an earlier, perhaps definitive, edition). A new printing does not constitute a new edition. For example, if the text has a 1940 copyright date, but a 1975 printing, use 1940 unless you have other information, such as "facsimile printing" or "1975 third printing rev."

```
Bell, Charles Bailey, and Harriett P. Miller.  The Bell
     Witch: A Mysterious Spirit.  1934; facsim. ed.
     Nashville: Elder, 1972.
Lewes, George Henry.  The Life and Works of Goethe (1855).
     2 vols.  Rpt. as vols. 13 and 14 of The Works of J. W.
     von Goethe.  Ed. Nathan Haskell Dole.  14 vols.
     London: Nicolls, n.d.
Weaver, Raymond.  Introduction.  The Shorter Novels of
     Herman Melville.  1928; New York: Premier-Fawcett,
     1960.  v-xxi.
```

If the place, publisher, or date of publication is not provided, insert either "n.p." or "n.d." as shown above. Include the abbreviation for the state only if necessary for clarity:

```
Forliti, John E.  Program Planning for Youth Ministry.
     Winona, MN: St. Mary's College P, 1975.
```

Provide the publisher's name in a shortened form, such as Bobbs rather than Bobbs-Merrill Co., Inc. (See 201–02 for a list of abbreviations of publishers.) A publisher's special imprint name should be joined with the official name: Anchor-Doubleday, Jove-Berkley, Ace-Grossett, Del Rey-Ballantine, Mentor-NAL:

```
Faulkner, William.  "Spotted Horses."  Three Famous Short
     Stories.  New York: Vintage-Random, 1963.  3-76.
```

If you borrow materials from CD-ROM or data-base printouts, special rules apply. See 32–33 for explanation of this type of entry:

```
Williams, T. Harry.  The Military Leadership of the North
     and the South.  1960.  US History on CD-ROM.
     Parsippany, NJ: Bureau Development, 1990.
```

Volume Number of the Book Used When citing one entire volume of a multivolume work, use the following form:

```
Durant, Will.  The Age of Faith.  Vol. 4 of The Story of
     Civilization.  7 vols.  New York: Simon, 1950.
```

If you cite from part of one volume in a multivolume work, show the volume number, in Arabic numerals, followed by a colon and page numbers:

Child, Harold.   "Jane Austen."   The Cambridge History of
        English Literature.   Ed. A. W. Ward and A. R. Waller.
        14 vols.   London: Cambridge UP, 1927.   12: 231–44.

Page Numbers to a Section of a Book   Cite pages to help a reader find
a particular section of a book. List pages with a volume number (shown
above) or alone (shown below).

Knoepflmacher, U. C.   "Fusing Fact and Myth: The New
        Reality of Middlemarch."   This Particular Web: Essays
        on Middlemarch.   Ed. Ian Adam.   Toronto: U of Toronto
        P, 1975.   55–65.

See also "A Chapter or Part of a Book," 252–53.

Sample Bibliography Entries: Books

Author

McMurtry, Larry.   Buffalo Girls.   New York: Simon, 1990.

Author, Anonymous

The Song of Roland.   Trans.   Frederick B. Luquines.   New
        York: Macmillan, 1960.

Author, Anonymous But Name Supplied

[Madison, James.]   All Impressments Unlawful and
        Inadmissible.   Boston: Pelham, 1804.

Author, Pseudonymous, But Name Supplied

Slender, Robert [Freneau, Philip].   Letters on Various and
        Important Subjects.   Philadelphia: Hogan, 1799.

Author, Listed by Initials with Name Supplied

A[lden], E[dmund] K.   "Alden, John."   Dictionary of
        American Biography.   1928 ed.

Author, More Than One Work by the Same Author

Hansberry, Lorraine.   A Raisin in the Sun.   New York:
        Random, 1959.

———. To Be Young, Gifted and Black. Ed. Robert Nemiroff.

    Englewood Cliffs, NJ: Prentice, 1969.

Authors, Two

Hooper, Henry O., and Peter Gwynne. Physics and the

    Physical Perspective. New York: Harper, 1977.

Authors, Three

Chenity, W. Carole, Joyce Takano Stone, and Sally A.

    Salisbury. Clinical Gerontological Nursing: A Guide

    to Advanced Practice. Philadelphia: Saunders, 1991.

Authors, More Than Three

Lewis, Laurel J., et al. Linear Systems Analysis. New

    York: McGraw, 1969.

Use "et al.," as shown in the previous entry, which means "and others," or list all the authors, as shown below:

Balzer, LeVon, Linda Alt Berene, Phyllis L. Goodson, Lois

    Lauer, and Irwin L. Slesnick. Life Science.

    Glenview, IL: Scott, 1990.

Author, Corporation or Institution

Committee on Telecommunications. Reports on Selected

    Topics in Telecommunications. New York: NAS, 1970.

List a committee or council as the author even when the organization is also the publisher, as in this example:

American Council on Education. Annual Report, 1991.

    Washington, DC: ACE, 1991.

Alphabetized Works, Encyclopedias, and Biographical Dictionaries

Dickinson, Robert E. "Norman Conquest." The World Book

    Encyclopedia. 1976 ed.

Well-known encyclopedias, as shown above, need only edition date, but less familiar works need a full citation:

Perrin, Porter G. "Puns." Writer's Guide and Index to

    English. 4th ed. Glenview, IL: Scott, 1968.

The Bible

```
The Bible.  [Denotes King James version]
The Bible.  CD-ROM Dataset-The Old Testament.  Parsippany,
     NJ: Bureau Development, 1990.
The Bible.  Revised Standard Version.
The Geneva Bible.  1560; facsim. rpt.  Madison: U of
     Wisconsin P, 1961.
The Four Translation New Testament.  Minneapolis: World
     Wide, 1966.
```

Classical Works

```
Homer.  The Iliad.  Trans. Richmond Lattimore.  Chicago: U
     of Chicago P, 1951.
```

Committee Report, Published as a Book

```
National Committee on Careers for Older Americans.  Older
     Americans: An Untapped Resource.  Washington, DC: AED,
     1979.
```

See also "Author, Corporation or Institution," 257.

Component Part of an Anthology or Collection. In general, works in an anthology have been published previously, but the prior publication data may not be readily available; therefore, use this form:

```
Updike, John.  "A & P."  Fiction 100.  Ed. James H.
     Pickering.  4th ed.  New York: Macmillan, 1982.
     1086-89.
```

But use the following if you can quickly identify original publication information:

```
Updike, John.  "A & P."  Pigeon Feathers and Other Stories.
     New York: Knopf, 1962.  Rpt. in Fiction 100.  Ed.
     James H. Pickering.  4th ed.  New York: Macmillan,
     1982.  1086-89.
```

If you use several works from the same anthology, you can shorten this citation by citing the short work and by making cross-references to the larger one (see "Cross-References," 259, for specific details).

Note also the following sample entries:

```
Hoy, Cyrus.  "Fathers and Daughters in Shakespeare's
     Romances."  Shakespeare's Romances Reconsidered.  Ed.
     Carol McGinnis Kay and Henry E. Jacobs.  Lincoln: U of
     Nebraska P, 1978.  77-90.
Hawthorne, Nathaniel.  The Scarlet Letter.  The Scarlet
     Letter and Other Writings by Nathaniel Hawthorne.  Ed.
     H. Bruce Franklin.  Philadelphia: Lippincott, 1967.
     22-233.
Scott, Nathan, Jr.  "Society and the Self in Recent
     American Literature."  The Broken Center.  New Haven:
     Yale UP, 1966.  Rpt. in Dark Symphony: Negro
     Literature in America.  Ed. James A. Emanuel and
     Theodore L. Gross.  New York: Free, 1968.  539-54.
```

Cross-References   If you are citing several selections from one anthology or collection, cite the main work and then cite individual pieces from it with cross-references to the editor(s) of the main collection:

```
Emanuel, James A., and Theodore L. Gross, eds.  Dark
     Symphony: Negro Literature in America.  New York:
     Free, 1968.
Hughes, Langston.  "Mulatto."  Emanuel and Gross, 204-06.
Scott, Nathan, Jr.  "Society and the Self in Recent
     American Literature."  Emanuel and Gross, 539-54.
```

These three sources, above, may not appear together on your "Works Cited" page. Other sources will mingle among the three because of alphabetical order. Note also the following in which the first entry refers to the one that follows:

```
Eliot, George.  "Art and Belles Lettres."  Westminster
     Review.  U.S.A. ed.  April 1856.  Partly rpt. Eliot, A
     Writer's Notebook.
---.  A Writer's Notebook, 1854-1879, and Uncollected
     Writings.  Ed. Joseph Wiesenfarth.  Charlottesville:
     UP of Virginia, 1981.
```

Edition Note any edition beyond the first, as shown below:

Keith, Harold. Sports and Games. 6th ed. Scranton:

    Crowell, 1976.

Stone, Lawrence. The Crisis of the Aristocracy: 1558–1660.

    Abridged ed. London: Oxford UP, 1971.

Indicate that a work has been prepared by an editor, not the original author:

Melville, Herman. Moby-Dick. Ed. with Intro. by Alfred

    Kazin. Riverside ed. Boston: Houghton, 1956.

Editor List the editor first only if your in-text citation refers to the work of the editor (e.g., the editor's introduction or notes):

Bevington, David, ed. The Complete Works of Shakespeare.

    4th ed. New York: HarperCollins, 1992. 56n.

Bryant, Jennings, and Daniel R. Anderson, eds. Preface.

    Children's Understanding of Television: Research on

    Attention and Comprehension. New York: Academic,

    1983. iii-v.

Electronic Sources (CD-ROM, BITNET, Data Bases) New technology makes it possible for you to have access to 100 or more books on one compact disk. You can copy sections of these books onto your floppy disk or to a hard disk, and then you can incorporate the material into your paper without having to retype the information. However, you must cite the electronic source that you have used:

The Bible. CD-ROM Dataset-The Old Testament. Parsippany,

    NJ: Bureau Development, 1990.

"Alexander Hamilton." Academic American Encyclopedia.

    1981 ed. CompuServe, 1983, record no. 1816.

Shakespeare, William. Hamlet. Shakespeare on CD-ROM.

    N.p.: CMC ReSearch, 1989.

    "N.p." indicates that the researcher could not locate a place of publication.

Williams, T. Harry. The Military Leadership of the North

    and the South. 1960. US History on CD-ROM.

    Parsippany, NJ: Bureau Development, 1990.

Bailey, Charles W., Jr. "Overview." BAILEY PRV1N1.

    BITNET 5 Mar. 1991: PACS-L@UHUPVM1.

This last entry for a BITNET printout provides (1) the name of the sender; (2) the title of the message; (3) the file name (Bailey private file 1N1), which you will need to access the message; (4) the BITNET designation and the date; and (5) the program name within the BITNET system (Public Access Computer Systems-List at the University of Houston with access code UPVM1). *Note:* This electronic network is developing at a rapid pace, so this form will provide necessary information for anyone who wishes to use the source.

Encyclopedia

```
Garrow, David J.  "Martin Luther King, Jr."  World Book
     Encyclopedia.  1990 ed.

"King, Martin Luther, Jr."  Current Biography Yearbook.
     1965 ed.
```

Introduction, Preface, Foreword, or Afterword

If you are citing the person who has written the introduction to a work by another author, use the following form:

```
Lester, Julius.  Introduction to This Edition.  The Negro
     Caravan.  Ed. Sterling A. Brown, Arthur P. Davis, and
     Ulysses Lee.  Rpt. ed.  Salem: Ayer, 1991.  v-vii.
Lowell, Robert.  Foreword.  Ariel.  By Sylvia Plath.  New
     York: Harper, 1966.  vii-ix.
```

Note: When you quote part of a book, provide page numbers to the specific section. If the author, not an editor, has written the prefatory matter, use only the author's last name after "By."

```
Vonnegut, Kurt.  Prologue.  Jailbird.  By Vonnegut.  New
     York: Delacorte, 1979.  ix-xxxviii.
```

Note: Use the form above when you cite the prologue only and not the main text.

Manuscript Collections in Book Form

```
Cotton Vitellius.  A. XV.  British Museum.
```

See also "Manuscripts and Typescripts," 276.

Play, Classical

```
Shakespeare, William.  Macbeth.  Shakespeare: Twenty-Three
     Plays and the Sonnets.  Ed. T. M. Parrott.  New York:
     Scribner's, 1953.  828-58.
```

Racine, Jean. Phaedra. Trans. Robert Lowell. World
   Masterpieces. Continental edition. 2 vols. Ed.
   Maynard Mack, et al. New York: Norton, 1956. 2:
   102–46.

Play, Modern

Greene, Graham. The Complaisant Lover. New York: Viking,
   1959.

Eliot, T. S. The Cocktail Party. The Complete Poems and
   Plays: 1909–1950. New York: Harcourt, 1952. 295–387.

Poem, Classical

Dante. The Divine Comedy. Trans. Lawrence G. White. New
   York: Pantheon, 1948.

Ciardi, John, trans. The Divine Comedy. By Dante. New
   York: Norton, 1977. 189–23.

Note: Use the form immediately above only if the citation is to Ciardi's
prefatory matter or notes to the text.

Poem, Modern Collection   Use this form if you cite one short poem:

Eliot, T. S. "The Love Song of J. Alfred Prufrock." The
   Complete Poems and Plays 1909–1950. New York:
   Harcourt, 1952. 3–7.

Use this next form if you cite one book-length poem:

Eliot, T. S. Four Quartets. The Complete Poems and Plays
   1909–1950. New York: Harcourt, 1952. 115–45.

Use this next form if you cite several different poems of the collection:

Eliot, T. S. The Complete Poems and Plays 1909–1950. New
   York: Harcourt, 1952.

Republished Book

Arnold, Matthew. "The Study of Poetry." Essays: English
   and American. Ed. Charles W. Eliot. 1886. New York:
   Collier, 1910. Originally published as the General
   Introduction to The English Poets. Ed. T. H. Ward.
   1880. 314–75.

Hooker, Richard. <u>Of the Lawes of Ecclesiasticall Politie</u>.

    1594. Facsim. rpt. Amsterdam: Teatrum Orbis

    Terrarum, 1971.

Lowes, John Livingston. <u>The Road to Xanadu: A Study in the</u>

    <u>Ways of the Imagination</u>. 1930. New York:

    Vintage-Knopf, 1959.

      Use this last form in citing a republished book, such as a paperback
version of a cloth-bound edition.

Series, Numbered and Unnumbered

Commager, Henry Steele. <u>The Nature and the Study of</u>

    <u>History</u>. Social Science Seminar Series. Columbus,

    OH: Merrill, 1965.

Jefferson, D. W. "'All, all of a piece throughout':

    Thoughts on Dryden's Dramatic Poetry." <u>Restoration</u>

    <u>Theatre</u>. Ed. J. R. Brown and Bernard Harris.

    Stratford-upon-Avon Studies 6. London: Arnold, 1965.

    159-76.

Wallerstein, Ruth C. <u>Richard Crashaw: A Study in Style and</u>

    <u>Poetic Development</u>. U of Wisconsin Studies in Lang.

    and Lit. 37. Madison: U of Wisconsin P, 1935.

Sourcebooks and Casebooks

Ellmann, Richard. "Reality." <u>Yeats: A Collection of</u>

    <u>Critical Essays</u>. Ed. John Unterecker. Twentieth

    Century Views. Englewood Cliffs, NJ: Prentice, 1963.

    163-74.

If you can identify original facts of publication, include that information
also:

Ellmann, Richard. "Reality." <u>Yeats: The Man and the</u>

    <u>Masks</u>. New York: Macmillan, 1948. Rpt. in <u>Yeats: A</u>

    <u>Collection of Critical Essays</u>. Ed. John Unterecker.

    Twentieth Century Views. Englewood Cliffs, NJ:

    Prentice, 1963. 163-74.

If you cite more than one article from a casebook, use cross-references (see
259).

Title, Foreign   Use lowercase letters for foreign titles except for the first major word and proper names. Provide a translation in brackets if you think it necessary (e.g., *Etranger* [*The Stranger*] or Praha [Prague]). In both titles and subtitles, capitalize only the first words and all words normally capitalized.

Brombert, Victor. <u>Stendhal et la voie oblique</u>. New Haven:

 Yale UP, 1954.

Castex, P. G. Le rouge et le noir <u>de Stendhal</u>. Paris:

 Sedes, 1967.

Levowitz-treu, Micheline. <u>L'amour et la mort chez

 Stendhal</u>. Aran: Editions du Grand Chéne, 1978.

  Compare this form with that for a journal entry (see 269).

Translator

Condé, Maryse. <u>Segu</u>. Trans. Barbara Bray. New York:

 Ballantine, 1982.

List the translator's name first only if the translator's work is the focus of your study:

Shorey, Paul, trans. <u>The Republic</u>. By Plato. Cambridge:

 Harvard UP, 1937. ii-iv.

Volumes, a Work of Several Volumes

Parrington, Vernon L. <u>Main Currents in American Thought</u>.

 3 vols. New York: Harcourt, 1927-32.

Ruskin, John. <u>The Complete Works of Ruskin</u>. 26 vols. New

 York: Bryan, 1894.

Volumes, One of Several Volumes

Dryden, John. <u>Poems 1649-1680</u>. Vol. 1 of <u>The Works of

 John Dryden</u>. Ed. Edward Niles Hooker et al. 4 vols.

 Berkeley: U of California P, 1956.

Volumes, Component Part of One of Several Volumes

Daiches, David. "The Restoration." <u>A Critical History of

 English Literature</u>. 2nd ed. 2 vols. New York:

 Ronald, 1970. 2: 537-89.

Hawthorne, Nathaniel. "My Kinsman, Major Molineaux." <u>The</u>
　　<u>American Tradition in Literature</u>. Ed. Sculley
　　Bradley, R. C. Beatty, and E. Hudson Long. 3rd ed. 2
　　vols. New York: Norton, 1967. 1: 507–22.
Ruskin, John. "Ideas of Truth." <u>The Complete Works of</u>
　　<u>Ruskin</u>. 26 vols. New York: Bryan, 1894. 20: 121–27.

9c Bibliography Form: Periodicals

For journal or magazine articles, use the following order:

1. Author(s)
2. Title of the article
3. Name of the periodical
4. Volume, issue, year, and page numbers (for journals)
5. Specific date, year, and page numbers (for magazines)

Name of the Author(s)　Show the author's name flush with the left margin, without a numeral and with succeeding lines indented five spaces. Enter the surname first, followed by a comma, followed by a given name or initials, followed by a period:

Healy, Jane M. "10 Reasons 'Sesame Street' Is Bad News for
　　Reading." <u>Education Digest</u> 56 (1991): 63–66.

Title of the Article　Show the title within quotation marks, followed by a period inside the closing quotation mark:

Heck, J. K. "Camcorders in the Science Classroom." <u>Media</u>
　　<u>Methods</u> 27 (Mar./Apr. 1991): 26–27.

Name of the Periodical　Give the name of the journal or magazine, underlined, and with no following punctuation:

Boose, Lynda E. "Othello's Handkerchief: 'The Recognizance
　　and Pledge of Love.'" <u>English Literary Renaissance</u> 5
　　(1975): 360–74.

Volume, Issue, and Page Numbers for Journals　In general, journals are paged continuously through all the issues of any given year, so listing the month of publication is unnecessary. Page numbers, 127–37, and volume number, 54, will enable you to find an article in *College English:*

> Haefner, Joel. "Democracy, Pedagogy, and the Personal
>
>   Essay." College English 54 (1992): 127-37.

Therefore, give the volume number, the year within parentheses and followed by a colon, and inclusive pages numbers (see the sample immediately above). If you discover that a journal has separate pagination for each issue, add an issue number following the volume number, separated by a period:

> Frey, John R. "America and Her Literature Reviewed by
>
>   Post-War Germany." American-German Review 20.5
>
>   (1954): 4-6.

Add the month if more information would ease the search for the article: "20.5 (Nov. 1954): 4-6."

Specific Date, Year, and Page Numbers for Magazines   With magazines, the volume number offers little help for finding an article. For example, one volume of *Time* (52 issues) will have page 16 repeated 52 times. You need to insert an exact date to a specific issue; therefore, provide an exact date for weekly and fortnightly publications:

> Klein, Joe. "The Real Deficit: Leadership." New York 22
>
>   July 1991: 20-25.

The month suffices for monthly and bimonthly publications:

> Andrews, Peter. "The Media and the Military." American
>
>   Heritage July/Aug. 1991: 78-85.

Supply inclusive page numbers (202-09, 85-115, or 1112-24), but if an article is paged here and there throughout the issue (for example, pages 74, 78, and 81-88), write only the first page number and a plus sign with no intervening space:

> Gaylin, Jody. "Secrets of Marriages That Last." Parents
>
>   Magazine Aug. 1991: 74+.

Sample Bibliography Entries: Periodicals

Address, Published

> Humphries, Alfred. "Computers and Banking." Address to
>
>   Downtown Kiwanis Club, Nashville, 30 Aug. 1981. Rpt.
>
>   in part in Tennessee Monthly 31 Aug. 1985: 33-34.

U. S. President. "Address to Veterans of Foreign Wars."
     19 Aug. 1974. Rpt. in <u>Weekly Compilation of</u>
     <u>Presidential Documents</u> 10 (26 Aug. 1974): 1045–50.

Author, Anonymous

"The Talk of the Town." <u>New Yorker</u> 29 July 1991: 21–25.

Interview, Published

Hanks, Nancy. Chairperson, National Endowment of the Arts.
     Interview. <u>U.S. News and World Report</u> 7 Oct. 1974:
     58–60.

See also "Interview, Unpublished," 275.

Journal, with All Issues for a Year Paged Continuously

Garrett, N. "Technology in the Service of Language
     Learning." <u>Modern Language Journal</u> 75 (1991): 74–101.

Journal, with Each Issue Paged Anew

Mangan, Doreen. "Henry Casselli: Superb Contradictions."
     <u>American Artist</u> 38.2 (1974): 39–43.

Use the issue number after the volume number because page numbers
alone cannot locate the article within a volume of six or twelve issues when
one issue has separate pagination. As an alternative, use the month or
season to locate the one issue:

Stuart, Jesse. "Love Affair at the Pasture Gate." <u>Ball</u>
     <u>State University Forum</u> 15 (Winter 1974): 306.

If a journal uses only an issue number, treat it as a volume number:

Wilson, Katharina M. "Tertullian's <u>De cultu foeminarum</u> and
     Utopia." <u>Moreana</u> 73 (1982): 69–74.

Journal, Volume Numbers Embracing Two Years

Brooks, Peter. "Freud's Masterplot." <u>Yale French Studies</u>
     55–56 (1977–78): 280–300.

Magazine, Monthly

Hallowell, Christopher. "Water Crisis on the Cape."
Audubon July/Aug. 1991: 65–74.

Nicklin, Flip. "Beneath Arctic Ice." National Geographic
July 1991: 2–31.

Magazine, Weekly

von Hoffman, Nicholas. "The White House News Hole." The
New Republic 6 Sept. 1982: 19–23.

Monograph

LeClercq, R. V. "Crashaw's 'Epithalamium': Pattern and
Vision." Literary Monographs 6. Madison: U of
Wisconsin P, 1975. 73–108.

"Strategies for Children in the 1990s." A UNICEF Policy
Review. New York: United Nations Children's Fund,
1989.

Notes, Queries, Reports, Comments, Letters

"Professional Notes and Comment." PMLA 97 (1982): 724+.

Robinson, Ken. "Does Otway Ascribe Sodom to Rochester? A
Reply." Notes and Queries ns 29 (1982): 50–51.

Seymour, Thom. "Faulkner's The Sound and the Fury." The
Explicator 39.1 (1980): 24–25.

Stoppelmann, Ron. "Letters." New York 23 Aug. 1982: 8.

Reprint of a Journal Article

Hope, A. D. "Anne Killigrew: or, The Art of Modulating."
Southern Review: An Australian Journal of Literary
Studies 1 (1963): 4–14. Rpt. in Hope, The Cave and
the Spring: Essays on Poetry. Adelaide, Australia:
Rigby, 1965. 129–43.

Review, in a Magazine or Journal

Clignet, Remi. Rev. of Urban Poverty in a Cross–Cultural
Context, by Edwin Eames and Judith Granich Goode.
American Journal of Sociology 80 (1974): 589–90.

"Editor's Bookshelf." Rev. of <u>On Broadway</u>, by David W.
    Dunlap. <u>American Heritage</u> July/Aug. 1991: 110-11.
Steck, Richard. "The Next Best Thing to Being There."
    Rev. of <u>Remote Access</u> [Computer software], by Custom
    Software. <u>PC World</u> 1.5 n.d.: 97-99.

Series

Hill, Christopher. "Sex, Marriage and the Family in
    England." <u>Economic History Review</u> 2nd ser. 31 (1978):
    450-63.

Technical Articles

Fisher, E. R., and P. B. Armentrout. "Kinetic Energy
    Dependence of the Reactions of $0\pm$ and $0_2\pm$ with CF_4 and
    C_2F_6." <u>Journal of Physical Chemistry</u> 95 (1991):
    6118-24.

However, a technical paper using this source should probably follow the
guidelines for the number system of the applied sciences (see Section 11e,
316–17).

Title, Foreign

Stivale, Charles J. "Le Vraisemblable temporel dans <u>Le</u>
    <u>rouge et le noir</u>." <u>Stendhal Club</u> 84 (1979): 299-313.

Title, Omitted

Berkowitz, David. <u>Renaissance Quarterly</u> 32 (1979):
    396-493.

Title, Quotation Within the Article's Title

Ranald, Margaret Loftus. "'As Marriage Binds, and Blood
    Breaks': English Marriage and Shakespeare."
    <u>Shakespeare Quarterly</u> 30 (1979): 68-81.

Title, Within the Article's Title

Dundes, Alan. "'To Love My Father All': A Psychoanalytic
    Study of the Folktale Source of <u>King Lear</u>." <u>Southern</u>
    <u>Folklore Quarterly</u> 40 (1976): 353-66.

9d BIBLIOGRAPHY FORM: NEWSPAPERS

Provide the name of the author, title of the article, name of the newspaper as it appears on the masthead, omitting any introductory article (*Wall Street Journal,* not *The Wall Street Journal*), and the complete date—day, month (abbreviated), and year. Omit any volume and issue numbers.

Provide a page number as listed (21, B-6, 14C, D3); for example, *USA Today* uses 6A, but *New York Times* uses A6. There is no uniformity among newspapers on this matter, so list the page accurately as an aid to your reader. If the article is not printed on consecutive pages (e.g., it begins on page 1 and skips to page 8), write the first page number and a plus (+) sign.

Newspaper in One Section

```
Walters, David.   "Redefining Art from the Heart of Africa."
     Christian Science Monitor 22 July 1991: 10-11.
```

Newspaper with Lettered Sections

```
Olivas, Michael A.  "Mr. Justice Marshall, Dissenting."
     Chronicle of Higher Education 17 July 1991: B1-B3.
```

Newspaper with Numbered Sections

```
Telingator, Sue.  "Theater Therapy."  Chicago Tribune 12
     July 1991, sec. 2: 3.
```

Newspaper Editorial with No Author Listed

```
"Fight Against Root Causes of Violence."  Editorial.  USA
     Today 23 July 1991: 10A.
```

Newspaper Article with City Added

```
Powers, Mary.  "Finding Advances Search for Strep Vaccine."
     Commercial Appeal [Memphis] 7 July 1991: C3.
```

Edition Listed

```
"Ohio Curb on Abortions Is Struck Down."  New York Times 13
     Aug. 1988, natl. ed.: 1+.
```

Foreign Newspaper

Richard, Michel Bole, and Frédéric Fritscher. "Frederick
    DeKlerk, l'homme qui a aboli l'apartheid." <u>Le Monde</u> 3
    Juillet 1991: 1.

9e BIBLIOGRAPHY FORM: GOVERNMENT DOCUMENTS

Since the nature of public documents is so varied, the form of the entry
cannot be standardized. Therefore, you should provide sufficient information so that the reader can easily locate the reference. As a general rule,
place information in the bibliography entry in this order: Government.
Body. Subsidiary body. Title of document. Identifying numbers. Publication facts.

Congressional Papers

United States. Cong. <u>Cong. Rec.</u> 11 July 1991: H5425–26.

> Senate and House sections are identified by an "S" or an "H" with
> the page numbers.

United States. Cong. House. Committee on Interstate and
    Foreign Commerce. <u>Federal Cigarette Labeling and
    Advertising Act.</u> 89th Cong., 1st sess. H. Rept. 449
    to accompany H.R. 3014. Washington, DC: GPO, 1965.

United States. Cong. Senate. <u>Violent Crime Control Act
    1991.</u> 102d Cong., 1st sess. S. 1241. Washington,
    DC: GPO, 1991.

Executive Branch Documents

United States. Dept. of State. <u>Foreign Relations of the
    United States: Diplomatic Papers, 1943.</u> 5 vols.
    Washington, DC: GPO, 1943–44.

United States. President. <u>National Drug Control Strategy.</u>
    Budget Summary. Washington, DC: GPO, 1991.

———. ———. "The President's News Conference" [21 Dec.
    1989]. <u>Public Papers of the Presidents of the United
    States.</u> 2 vols. Washington, DC: Office of the
    Federal Registrar, 1990. 2: 1728–34.

> The hyphens signal repetition of "United States" and "President."

Legal Citations

California. Const. Art. 2, sec. 4.

Environmental Protection Agency et al. v. Mink et al.

    U. S. Reports, CDX. 1972.

15 U. S. Code. Sec. 78h. 1964.

Illinois. Revised Statutes Annotated. Sec. 16-7-81.

    1980.

Noise Control Act of 1972. Statutes at Large. 86. Public

    Law 92-574. 1972.

People v. McIntosh. California 321 P.3d 876, 2001-6.

    1970.

State v. Lane. Minnesota 263 N. W. 608. 1935.

United States. Const. Art 2, sec. 1.

9f BIBLIOGRAPHY FORM: OTHER SOURCES

Abstract

Spezzano, Charles. "What to Do between Birth and Death:

    The Art of Growing Up." Abstract. Psychology Today

    25 (1992): 54+.

Art Work

Wyeth, Andrew. Hay Ledge. [1957]. Illustrated in The Art

    of Andrew Wyeth. Ed. Wanda M. Corn. San Francisco:

    The Fine Arts Museum, 1973. 31.

Use the form shown above for reproductions in books and journals. If you actually experience the work itself, use the form shown next:

Wyeth, Andrew. Hay Ledge. Private Collection of Mr. and

    Mrs. Joseph E. Levine.

BITNET Sources

Bailey, Charles W., Jr. "Overview." BAILEY PRV1N1.

    BITNET 5 Mar. 1991: PACS-L@UHUPVM1.

See 36–37 for an explanation of this citation.

Bulletin

Economic Research Service. <u>Demand and Price Situation</u>.
>   Bulletin DPS-141, 14 pp. Washington, DC: Department
>   of Agriculture, Aug. 1974.

French, Earl. <u>Personal Problems in Industrial Research and</u>
>   <u>Development</u>. Bulletin No. 51. Ithaca: New York State
>   School of Industrial and Labor Relations, 1963.

Cartoon

Lazarus, Mell. "Miss Peach." Cartoon. <u>Tennessean</u>
>   [Nashville] 23 July 1991: 6-D.

Cullum, Leo. Cartoon. <u>New Yorker</u>. 12 Sept. 1988: 30.

Cartoon. <u>New Yorker</u>. 12 Sept. 1988: 30.

> *Note:* Use this last form if you cannot decipher the name of the
> cartoonist.

CD-ROM

Shakespeare, William. <u>Hamlet</u>. Shakespeare on CD-ROM.
>   N.p.: CMC ReSearch, 1989.

> "N.p." indicates that the researcher could not locate a place of
> publication. See also 255.

Computer Data

<u>Purchase Ledger</u>. Computer software. Chamberley, England:
>   Graham Doreian Software, 1982. CPM C-Basic for Apple
>   II.

<u>Scipax</u>. Series 3 computer software. Cleveland: Hunt
>   Information Services, 1982.

Sears, Robert O. <u>Trends in Women's Sports: Factual Data on</u>
>   <u>Participation and Revenue</u>. Computer software.
>   Bowling Green: Western Kentucky State U, 1983.
>   VAX-1419.

<u>Statistics on Child Abuse--Montgomery County, Tennessee</u>.
>   Computer software. Clarksville, TN: Harriett Cohn
>   Mental Health Center, 1983. Apple IIe, Diskette 12.

Data-Base Sources   Write an entry for material obtained from a computer service (DIALOG, BRS, MEAD) like other references to printed materials, but you should also add a reference to the service, the file, and the accession number(s). As shown below, DIALOG has an accession number and the supplier also provides one.

```
                                      MLA Bibliography
                                      Dialog File 71
DIALOG & MLA accession numbers─→      8424847  84-1-3804
Title ──────────────────────────→     Leigh Hunt and Shelley:
                                      A New Letter
Author ─────────────────────────→     Allentuck, Marcia
Journal ────────────────────────→     Keats-Shelley Journal
International Standard
       Serial Number ───────────────→ ISSN 0453-4387
Volume, page, and year   ───────────→ 33:50 1984
Document type ──────────────────────→ journal article
```

In your works cited entry, then, provide the numbers that will give others access to the record:

```
Allentuck, Marcia.  "Leigh Hunt and Shelley: A New Letter."

     Keats-Shelley Journal  33 (1984): 50.  Dialog file 71,

     item 8424847 84-1-3804.
```

Dissertation, Abstract Only

```
Havens, Nancy Bergstrom.  "Verbalized Symbolic Play of

     Pre-School Children in Two Types of Play

     Environments."  DAI 42 (1982): 5058A.  Temple

     University.
```

Use this form when you cite from *Dissertation Abstracts International* (*DAI*). The page number features A, B, or C to designate the series used: A Humanities, B Sciences, C European dissertations.

Dissertation, Published

```
Nykrog, Per.  Les Fabliaux: Etude d'histoire littéraire et

     de stylistique mediévale.  Diss. Aarhus U, 1957.

     Copenhagen: Munksgaard, 1957.
```

Dissertation, Unpublished

```
Havens, Nancy Bergstrom.  "Verbalized Symbolic Play of
     Pre—School Children in Two Types of Play
     Environments."  Diss. Temple University, 1982.
```

Film

```
Robin Hood: Prince of Thieves.  Warner Bros., 1991.
```

Add specific information if your study focuses on one aspect of the film, such as the acting, directing, or screenwriting (see "Performances," 277).

```
Wilets, Bernard, director.  Environment.  Santa Monica, CA:
     BFA Educational Media, 1971.  (16 mm., 29 min., color.)
```

Information Services (ERIC, NTIS)   If you obtain material from an information service, such as Educational Resources Information Center (ERIC), you should provide the appropriate microfiche number at the end of your citation:

```
Hansen, Tom.  "Reclaiming the Body: Teaching Modern Poetry
     by Ignoring Meaning."  ERIC, 1990.  ED 329 992.
```

If the material listed in ERIC has been published previously, provide the details of its original publication, followed by the name of the information service and the number:

```
Van Noate, Judith, comp.  Nathaniel Hawthorne and Herman
     Melville: A Research Guide.  Charlotte: North Carolina
     U, 1990.  ERIC ED 329 985.
```

Interview, Unpublished

```
Page, Oscar.  President, Austin Peay State University.
     Interview.  5 Mar. 1991.
```

For a published interview, see 267.

Letter, Personal

```
Weathers, Walter.  Letter to the author.  5 Mar. 1991.
```

Letter, Published

```
Eisenhower, Dwight.  Letter to Richard Nixon.  20 Apr.
     1968.  Memoirs of Richard Nixon.  By Richard Nixon.
     New York: Grosset, 1978.
```

Manuscripts (ms) and Typescripts (ts)

Alexander, Homer. Journal 3, ms. H. Alexander Private
     Papers, Clarksville, TN.

Tanner. Item 346, ms. Bodleian Library, Oxford.

Williams, Ralph. Notebook 15, ts. Williams Papers.
     Vanderbilt U, Nashville.

Map

County Boundaries and Names. United States Base Map GE–50,
     No. 86. Washington, DC: GPO, 1987.

Virginia. Map. Chicago, Rand, 1987.

Microfilm or Microfiche

Tuckerman, H. T. "James Fenimore Cooper." Microfilm.
     North American Review 89 (1859): 298–316.

Mimeographed Material

Smith, Jane L. "Terms for the Study of Fiction."
     Mimeographed. Cleveland, 1991.

Miscellaneous Materials (Program, Leaflet, Poster, Announcement)

"Earth Day." Poster. Louisville: 23 Mar. 1991.

"Gospel Arts Day." Program. Fisk U. Nashville: 18 June
     1989.

Monograph

NEA Research Division. Kindergarten Practices, 1961.
     Monograph 1962–M2. Washington, DC: 1962.

See 268 for a monograph published in a journal.

Musical Composition

Mozart, Wolfgang A. Jupiter. Symphony No. 41.

Wagner, Richard. Lohengrin.

Pamphlet

United States Civil Service Commission. The Human
     Equation: Working in Personnel for the Federal
     Government. Pamphlet 76. Washington, DC: GPO, 1970.

Performances (Radio, Television, Opera, Recordings, Film)   If your paper cites the contribution of a particular individual, begin the bibliographic entry with that person's name. Other persons who contributed to the production may follow the title if their names have also been mentioned in your text.

Connick, Harry, Jr., vocals and piano. Blue Light. Prod.
    Tracey Freeman. Columbia, CK 48685, 1991.

Lange, Jessica, actress. O Pioneers! Dir. Glenn Jordan.
    Adapted by Robert W. Lenski from the novel by Willa
    Cather. CBS Television. 2 Feb. 1992.

Lerner, Alan Jay, screenwriter. An American in Paris.
    Dir. Vincente Minnelli. Prod. Arthur Freed. Music by
    George Gershwin. Lyrics by Ira Gershwin. With Gene
    Kelly, Leslie Caron, and Oscar Levant. MGM, 1951.

Marguiles, Donald, playwright. Sight Unseen. Dir. Michael
    Bloom. With Dennis Boutsikaris, Jon de Vries, Laura
    Linney, and Deborah Hedwall. Shubert Theatre, New
    York, 1992.

Redford, Robert, actor. The Natural. Dir. Barry Levinson.
    Prod. Mark Johnson. Screenplay Roger Towne and Phil
    Dusenberry. Based on the novel by Bernard Malamud.
    TriStar Pictures, 1984.

Public Address or Lecture

Sarnoff, David. "Television: A Channel for Freedom."
    Address. University of Detroit Academic Convocation.
    Detroit, 1961.

Recording on Record or Tape

Berlioz, Hecter. Symphonie fantastique, op. 14. Cond.
    Georg Solti. Chicago Symphony Orch. London, CS 6790,
    1968.

"Chaucer: The Nun's Priest's Tale." Canterbury Tales.
    Narrated in Middle English by Robert Ross. Caedmon,
    TC 1008, 1971.

John, Elton. "This Song Has No Title." Goodbye Yellow
    Brick Road. MCA, MCA 2-10003, 1974.

Report

Linden, Fabian. "Women: A Demographic, Social and Economic
        Presentation." Report. The Conference Board. New
        York: CBS/Broadcast Group, 1973.

Unbound reports are placed within quotation marks; bound reports are
treated as books:

Coca-Cola Company. 1990 Annual Report. Atlanta: Coca-Cola
        Company, 1991.

Reproductions and Photographs

Blake, William. Comus. Plate 4. Photograph in Irene
        Taylor. "Blake's Comus Designs." Blake Studies 4
        (Spring 1972): 61.

Michener, James A. "Structure of Earth at Centennial,
        Colorado." Line drawing in Centennial. By Michener.
        New York: Random, 1974. 26.

Table, Illustration, Chart

Alphabet. Chart. Columbus: Scholastic, 1984.

Tables or graphs published within works need detailed citation:

Corbett, Edward P. J. Syllogism graph. Classical Rhetoric
        for the Modern Student. New York: Oxford UP, 1965.

Because the graph has no title, the descriptive heading should not be
placed within quotation marks.

Television or Radio Program

The Commanders: Douglas MacArthur. New York: NBC-TV. 17
        Mar. 1975.

Shakespeare, William. As You Like It. Nashville:
        Nashville Theatre Academy, WDCN-TV. 11 Mar. 1975.

Thesis See "Dissertation, Unpublished," 275.

Transparency

Sharp, La Vaughn, and William E. Loeche. <u>The Patient and</u>
<u>Circulatory Disorders: A Guide for Instructors</u>. 54
transparencies, 99 overlays. Philadelphia:
Lippincott, 1969.

Unpublished Paper

Elkins, William R. "The Dream World and the Dream Vision:
Meaning and Structure in Poe's Art." Unpublished
paper, 1981.

Videotape

Thompson, Paul. "W. B. Yeats." Lecture on Videotape.
VHS—MSU 160. Memphis: Memphis State U, 1982.

Sevareid, Eric. <u>CBS News</u>. New York: CBS—TV 11 Mar. 1975;
Media Services Videotape 1975—142. Nashville:
Vanderbilt U, 1975.

10   *Using APA Style*

Your instructor may require you to write the research paper in APA style, which is governed by *The Publication Manual of the American Psychological Association.* This style has gained wide acceptance in academic circles.

> APA style is used in the social sciences, and versions similar to it are used in the biological sciences, business, and the earth sciences.

You need to understand two basic ideas that govern this style. First, a scientific paper attempts to show what has been proven true by research in a narrowly defined area, so it requires the past tense when you cite the work of scientists (e.g., "Johnson stipulated" or "the work of Elmford and Mills showed"). Second, the scientific community considers the year of publication as vital information, so it is featured immediately after any named source in the text, like this: (Johnson & Marshall, 1991). These two primary distinctions, and others, are explained below.

10a WRITING IN THE PROPER TENSE FOR AN APA STYLED PAPER

Verb tense is an indicator that distinguishes papers in the humanities from those in the natural and social sciences. MLA style, as shown in previous chapters, requires you to use present tense when you refer to a cited work ("Johnson *stipulates*" or "the work of Elmford and Mills *shows*"). In contrast, APA style requires you to use past tense or present perfect tense ("Marshall stipulated" or "the work of Elmford and Mills has demonstrated"). APA style *does* require present tense when you discuss the results (e.g., "the results confirm" or "the study indicates") and when you mention established knowledge (e.g., "the therapy offers some hope" or "salt contributes to hypertension").

A paper in the humanities (MLA style) makes universal assertions, so it uses the historical present tense:

```
"It was the best of times, it was the worst of times,"
 writes  Charles Dickens about the eighteenth century.


Johnson  argues  that sociologist Norman Manway has a

"narrow-minded view of clerics and their role in nineteenth

century fiction" (64).
```

A scientific study makes a specific claim and requires the past tense or the present perfect tense with your citations to a scientist's work:

```
Matthews (1989)  designed  the experiment, and since that

time several investigators  have used  the method (Thurman,

1990; Jones, 1991).
```

Note the differences in the verbs of these next two passages whenever the verbs refer to a cited work:

MLA Style:	**APA Style:**
Television encourages reading, which in turn improves language competence. Beyond the one-time motivation of children who responded to Fonzie's request for a library card, research `indicates` that good programming `improves` reading and `can increase` library lendings. The Himmelweit study in Great Britain, <u>Television and the Child</u>, `confirms` that "television	Television encourages reading, which in turn improves language competence. Beyond the one-time motivation of children who responded to Fonzie's request for a library card, research `has` `indicated` that good programming `improved` reading and `increased` library lendings. The Himmelweit study in Great Britain, <u>Television and the Child</u>, `confirmed` that "television

MLA Style: **APA Style:**

in the long run encourages	in the long run encourages
children to read books, a	children to read books, a
conclusion that can be	conclusion that can be
reinforced by evidence from	reinforced by evidence from
libraries, book clubs, and	libraries, book clubs, and
publishing companies"	publishing companies"
(Postman 33). Himmelweit	(Postman, 1961, p. 33).
makes this point: "Book	Himmelweit made this point:
reading comes into its own,	"Book reading comes into its
not despite television but	own, not despite television
because of it" (qtd. in	but because of it" (cited in
Postman 33).	Postman, 1961, p. 33).

As shown above, left, MLA style requires that you use the present tense both for personal comments and for introducing the sources. In MLA style the ideas and the words of the authorities, theoretically, remain in print and continue to be true in the universal present. APA style, above right, requires that you use present tense for generalizations and references to stable conditions, but it requires the past tense for sources cited: the sources *have tested* (present perfect) a hypothesis or the sources *reported* (past tense) the results of the test.

Use present tense for established knowledge (*exists*) and past tense for a citation (*reported*).

The danger of steroid use exists for every age group, even youngsters. Lloyd and Mercer (1991) reported on six incidents of liver damage to 14-year-old swimmers who used steroids.

10b USING IN-TEXT CITATIONS IN APA STYLE

APA style, unlike MLA style, uses these conventions for in-text citations.

1. Cites last names only.
2. Cites the year, within parentheses, immediately after the name of the author.
3. Cites page numbers only with a direct quotation, not with a paraphrase.
4. Uses "p." or "pp." before page numbers.
5. Uses double-spacing throughout, like MLA style, but permits triple-spacing before side headings and permits triple-spacing before and after illustrations and tables.

APA style requires an in-text citation to the last name of the author and the year of publication:

```
The study of Conniff (1990) showed that one federal agency,

the Bureau of Land Management, failed to protect the

natural treasures of public land holdings, and Struble

(1991) offered evidence that BLM serves the needs of

ranchers, not the public.
```

If you do not use the author's name in your text, place the name within the parenthetical citation:

```
It has been shown that the Bureau of Land Management often

sacrifices wildlife and the environment to benefit miners

and ranchers (Conniff, 1990; Struble, 1991).
```

Provide a page number only when you quote the exact words of a source, and *do* use "p." or "pp." with page numbers:

```
Conniff (1990, p. 33) explained that the bureau must

"figure out how to keep the land healthy while also

accommodating cowpokes, strip miners, dirt bikers,

birdwatchers and tree huggers, all vocal, all willing to

sue for their conflicting rights."
```

Put the year immediately after the name of the authority; the page number may appear at the end of the quotation:

```
Jones (1984) found that "these data of psychological

development suggest that retarded adolescents are atypical

in maturational growth" (p. 215).
```

Write a quotation of 40 words or more as a separate block, indented an additional five spaces. (*Note:* MLA style uses 10 spaces.) Because it is set off from the text in a distinctive block, do not enclose it with quotation marks:

```
Albert (1983) reported the following:

        Whenever these pathogenic organisms attack the human
```

five-character indent

```
        body and begin to multiply, the infection is set in

        motion.  The host responds to this parasitic invasion

        with efforts to cleanse itself of the invading agents.

        When rejection efforts of the host become visible

        (fever, sneezing, congestion), the disease status

        exists.  (pp. 314-315)
```

When one work has two or more authors, use "&" in citations only, not in the text:

> It has been reported (Werner &| Throckmorton, 1990) that
> toxic levels exceeded the maximum allowed levels each year
> since 1983.

> Werner |and| Throckmorton (1990) offered statistics on their
> analysis of water samples from six rivers and announced
> without reservations that "the waters are unfit for human
> consumption, pose dangers to swimmers, and produce
> contaminated fish that may cause salmonella" (pp. 457–458).

For three to six authors, name them all in the first entry, "(Torgerson, Andrews, Smith, Lawrence, & Dunlap, 1989)," but thereafter use "(Torgerson et al., 1989)." For seven or more authors, employ "(Fredericks et al., 1989)" in the first and in all subsequent instances.

Use small letters (a, b, c) to identify two or more works published in the same year by the same author; for example, "Thompson (1986a)" and "Thompson (1986b)." Then use "1986a" and "1986b" in your list of references (see 285 for an example). If necessary, specify additional information:

> Horton (1986; cf. Thomas, 1982, p. 89) suggested an
> intercorrelation of these testing devices. But after
> multiple-group analysis, Welston (1989, esp. p. 211)
> reached an opposite conclusion.

If you make an in-text citation to an article or chapter of a textbook, casebook, or anthology, use the in-text citation to refer only to the person(s) you cite:

> One writer stressed that two out of every three new jobs in
> the 1990s will go to women (Bailey, 1988).

The list of references will clarify the nature of this reference to Bailey (see "Textbook, Casebook, Anthology," 286).

Corporate authors may be abbreviated after a first, full reference:

> One source has questioned the results of the use of aspirin
> for arthritis treatment in children (American Medical
> Association [AMA], 1991).

Thereafter, refer to the corporate author by initials: (AMA, 1991).

When a work has no author listed, cite the title as part of the in-text citation (or use the first few words of the material):

> The cost per individual student has continued to rise
> rapidly ("Money Concerns," 1991, p. 2).

10c PREPARING THE LIST OF REFERENCES

Use the title "References" for your bibliography page. Alphabetize the entries and double-space throughout. Every reference used in your text should appear in your alphabetical list of references at the end of the paper. Type the first line of each entry flush left, and indent succeeding lines three (3) spaces. (*Note:* MLA style uses five spaces.) Use two spaces after each period in a reference (except between initials of names).*

Books

Book (Basic Format)

> Carter, J. (1988). An outdoor journal: Adventures and
> reflections. New York: Bantam.

List the author (surname first with initials for given names), year of publication within parentheses, title of the book underlined and with only the first word of the title and any subtitle capitalized (but *do* capitalize proper nouns), place of publication, and publisher. In the publisher's name, omit the word *Publishing, Company,* or *Inc.,* but otherwise give a full name: Harcourt Brace Jovanovich; Florida State University Press; HarperCollins.

List chronologically two or more works by the same author; for example, Fitzgerald's 1989 publication would precede his 1991 publication:

> Fitzgerald, R. F. (1989). Controlling oil spills.
> Fitzgerald, R. F. (1991). Alaska and its oil reserves.

References with the same author in the same year are alphabetized and marked with lowercase letters (a, b, c) immediately after the date:

> Fitzgerald, R. F. (1990a). Water purification systems.
> Fitzgerald, R. F. (1990b). Water waste today.

---

*Some confusion exists in the matter of spacing after periods. The sample paper in the *Publication Manual of the American Psychological Association* appears to use a single space after each period; however, Leslie Cameron, director of the APA manual, has assured this author that the rule of two (2) spaces after periods (APA manual, page 140) remains in force.

Entries of a single author precede multiple-author entries beginning with the same surname without regard for the dates:

```
Fitzgerald, R. F.  (1990).  Water purification systems.

Fitzgerald, R. F., & Smithson, C. A.  (1988).  Water maps.
```

References with the same first author and different second or third authors should be alphabetized by the surname of the second author:

```
Fitzgerald, R. F., & Smithson, C. A.  (1988).  Water maps.

Fitzgerald, R. F., & Waters, W. R.  (1989).  Alaska

    pipelines.
```

Part of a Book

```
Hartley, J. T., Harker, J. O., & Walsh, D. A.  (1980).

    Contemporary issues and new directions in adult

    development of learning and memory.  In L. W. Poon

    (Ed.), Aging in the 1980s: Psychological issues (pp.

    239-252).  Washington, DC: American Psychological

    Association.
```

List author(s), date, chapter or section title, editor (with name in normal order) preceded by "In" and followed by "(Ed.)" or "(Eds.)," the name of the book (underlined), page numbers to the specific section of the book cited (placed within parentheses), place of publication, and publisher.

Textbook, Casebook, Anthology   Make a primary reference to the anthology:

```
Vesterman, W.  (Ed.) (1991).  Readings for the 21st

    century.  Boston: Allyn & Bacon.
```

Thereafter, make cross-references to the primary source, in this case to Vesterman. *Note:* These entries should be mingled with all others on the reference pages in alphabetical order so that cross-references may appear before or after the primary source. The year cited should be the date when the cited work was published, not when the Vesterman book was published; such information is usually found in a headnote, footnote, or list of credits at the front or back of the anthology.

```
Bailey, J.  (1988).  Jobs for women in the nineties.  In

    Vesterman, pp. 55-63.

Fallows, D.  (1982).  Why mothers should stay home.  In

    Vesterman, pp. 69-77.
```

```
Steinem, G.  (1972).  Sisterhood.  In Vesterman, pp. 48-53.

Vesterman, W. (Ed.)  (1991).  Readings for the 21st

    century.  Boston: Allyn & Bacon.
```

The alternative to the style shown above is to provide a complete entry for every one of the authors cited from the casebook (in which case you do not need a separate entry to Vesterman):

```
Bailey, J.  (1988).  Jobs for women in the nineties.  In W.

    Vesterman (Ed.), (1991), Readings for the 21st century

    (pp. 55-63).  Boston: Allyn & Bacon.

Fallows, D.  (1982).  Why mothers should stay home.  In W.

    Vesterman (Ed.), (1991), Readings for the 21st century

    (pp. 69-77).  Boston: Allyn & Bacon.

Steinem, G.  (1972).  Sisterhood.  In W. Vesterman (Ed.),

    (1991), Readings for the 21st century (pp. 48-53).

    Boston: Allyn & Bacon.
```

Book with Corporate Author, Third Edition

```
American Psychiatric Association.  (1980).  Diagnostic

    statistical manual of mental disorders (3rd ed.).

    Washington, DC: Author.
```

Encyclopedia

```
Woodley, D. J.  (1990).  Acne.  World book encyclopedia.

    Chicago: World Book.
```

List author, year, title of the article, title of the encyclopedia (underlined), place, and publisher. If no author is listed, begin with the title of the article.

```
Brazil.  (1970).  Harper encyclopedia of the modern world.

    New York: Harper.
```

Periodicals

Journal

```
Mielke, K. W.  (1988).  Television in the social studies

    classroom.  Social Education, 52, 362-365.
```

List author, year, title of the article without quotation marks and with only the first word capitalized, name of the journal underlined and with all major words capitalized, volume number underlined, inclusive page numbers *not* preceded by "p." or "pp."

Magazine

```
Conniff, R.  (1990, September).  Once the secret domain of
     miners and ranchers, the BLM is going public.
     Smithsonian, pp. 30-47.
```

List author, date of publication (year, month without abbreviation, and the specific day for weekly and fortnightly magazines), title of the article without quotation marks and with only the first word capitalized, name of the magazine underlined with all major words capitalized, and inclusive page numbers preceded by "p." or "pp."

Newspaper

```
Raymond, C.  (1990, September 12).  Global migration will
     have widespread impact on society, scholars say.  The
     Chronicle of Higher Education, pp. A1, A6.
```

List author, date (year, month, and day), title of article with only the first word and proper nouns capitalized, complete name of newspaper in capitals and underlined, and the section with all discontinuous page numbers.

Abstract *(Citing from an Abstract Only)*   An abstract of a published article is cited as follows:

```
Misumi, J., & Fujita, M.  (1982).  Effects of PM
     organizational development in supermarket organization.
     Japanese Journal of Experimental Social Psychology, 21,
     93-111.  (From Psychological Abstracts, 1982, 68,
     Abstract No. 11474)
```

An abstract of an unpublished work is cited as follows:

```
Havens, N. B.  (1982).  Verbalized symbolic play of
     pre-school children in two types of play environments.
     Abstract of doctoral dissertation, Temple University.
     (From Dissertation Abstracts International, 1982, 42,
     5058A)
```

Review

```
Jones, S. L.  (1991, January 6).  The power of motivation
     [Review of Body heat].  Contemporary Film Review, p. 18.
```

Report

Lance, J. C. (1990). Housing regulations (KU No. 90–16). Lawrence, KS: Media Center.

Nonprint Material

Corborn, W. H. (1990, November 3). "On facing the fears caused by nightmares" [Interview]. Lexington, KY.

Purple, W. C. (Producer). (1990). Hitting the backhand [Videotape]. Nashville: Sports Network.

Landers, J., Woolfe, R. T., & Balcher, C. (1990). Geometry games: Level two [Computer program]. Emporia, KS: Mediaworks.

10d WRITING THE ABSTRACT

You should provide an abstract with every paper written in APA style. An abstract is a quick but thorough summary of the contents of your paper. It is read first and may be the only part read, so it must be:

1. *Accurate* in order to reflect both the purpose and content of the paper.
2. *Self-contained* so that it (a) explains the precise problem and defines terminology, (b) describes briefly both the methods used and the findings, and (c) gives an overview of your conclusions.
3. *Concise and specific* in order to remain within a range of 80 to 150 words.
4. *Nonevaluative* in order to report information, not to appraise or assess the value of your work.
5. *Coherent and readable* in a style that uses an active, vigorous syntax and that uses the present tense to describe results ("the findings confirm") but the past tense to describe testing procedures ("I attempted to identify")

For theoretical papers, the abstract should include:

the topic in one sentence
the purpose, thesis, and scope of the paper
the sources used (e.g., published articles, books, personal observation)
your conclusions and the implications of the study

For a report of an empirical study (see also Section 3b, 78), the abstract should include:

the problem and hypothesis in one sentence if possible
the subjects (e.g., species, number, age, type)
the method, including procedures and apparatus
the findings
your conclusions and the implications of the study

For a model abstract in APA style, see 291.

10e SAMPLE PAPER IN APA STYLE

The following paper demonstrates the format and style of a paper written to the standards of APA style. It requires a title page that establishes the running head, an abstract, in-text citations to name and year of each source used, and a list of references. Marginal notations explain specific requirements.

Number the title page.

Autism

1

Autism: Cause and Treatment

Pat Bracy

Austin Peay State University

This heading will appear at the top of each page.

Running Head: AUTISM

Abstract

Autism has been reported as a neurological dysfunction of the brain that afflicts infants before age 30 months. Theories about the causes and the necessary treatment have differed ever since Kanner (1943) reported his findings that autism differed from other childhood disorders. Two theories have existed side by side since that time—the behavioral bias and the pharmacological bias. The majority of psychiatrists now defend a biochemical imbalance as the major cause. Treatment has accordingly shifted to pharmacological methods, yet researchers continue to enlist the parents as therapists in response to evidence that behavioral treatment has benefited the autistic child. The findings demonstrate that medical treatment, in harmony with behavioral treatment, may enhance the lives of some autistic persons.

Place the abstract separately on page 2.

Do not indent the first line of the abstract.

The abstract should be 100-200 words in length.

Autism

Autism, a neurological dysfunction of the brain which

Cite the year immediately after the name of the source. commences before the age of 30 months, was identified by Kanner (1943), who studied 11 cases, all of which showed a specific type of childhood psychosis that was different from other childhood disorders, although each was similar to childhood schizophrenia. Kanner described the

See 78 for a discussion of the paradigm for the scientific paper. characteristics of the infantile syndrome as:

1. Extreme autistic aloneness

2. Language abnormalities

3. Obsessive desire for the maintenance of sameness

4. Good cognitive potential

5. Normal physical development

Use past tense or present perfect tense when citing the sources. 6. Highly intelligent, obsessive, and cold parents

Rutter (1978) has reduced these symptoms to four criteria: onset within 30 months of birth, poor social development, late language development, and a preference for regular, stereotyped activity. In the United States, autism affects one out of 2,500 children, and is not usually diagnosed

Use "&" in citations, not in the text. until the child is between two and five years of age (Koegel & Schreibman, 1981).

Kanner (1943) labeled the disorder as "early infantile autism" (p. 249). He determined that cold parenting, "the

Add page numbers when you quote a source. refrigerator mother syndrome," was a primary cause for autism. Today autism is viewed as a distinct developmental disability that can be diagnosed differently from psychoses, retardation, and other childhood disorders (Rutter, 1968). "Causal theories of autism are quite

List three authors in the citation. diverse and range in essence from a fragile chromosome to a fragile parent" (Gallagher, Jones, & Byrne, 1990, p. 935).

Accordingly, two possible theories have existed side by side--the behavioral bias and the pharmacological bias.

One set of scientists has manipulated the child's
environment in order to test and treat the child's
behavior; another set of scientists has administered
medication to affect the child's brain. Both methods have
demonstrated positive effects. Schreibman (1988) and also
Groden and Baron (1988) surveyed the behavioral approaches
(cited in Mesibov, 1989). Gallagher, Jones, and Byrne
(1990) have provided a survey of biogenic theories.

Use underlined
side headings to
mark divisions
of a paper in
APA style. You
may triple-space
before side
headings to
improve
appearance and
readability of
the typed
manuscript.

Cause

Rutter (1968) listed three possible causes: behavioral
syndrome, organic brain disorder, or a range of biological
and psychosocial factors. Herman et al. (1986) have shown
that autism may be caused by abnormally high levels of
brain chemicals, called opioids, which have been found to
decrease pain perception and inhibit motivation in much the
same way as morphine and heroin (Herman et al., 1986).
When a person is born, the opioid level is 100 times
greater than later in life, "perhaps to protect the newborn
from birth trauma" (Herman et al., 1986, p. 1172). It has
been proposed that opioid levels may not drop quickly in
some infants, and this may lead to autism (see Herman et
al., 1986, & Herman et al., 1987).

For seven or
more authors,
use "et al." in
the first and all
subsequent
instances.

Autism also may be caused by an underdevelopment of
the cerebellum. "Autism is a disorder of brain
development," according to Eric Courchesne (cited in Fay,
1987, p. 85). Courchesne and his team of researchers used
a scanning technique called magnetic resonance imaging
(MRI). This scanning method is more revealing than x-rays
for soft tissue like the brain. Eighteen autistic and
18 normal brains were scanned. In most examinations of the
autistic subjects, MRI showed a 25% deficit in the vermis
of the cerebellum, while the 18 normal subjects had brains

Use this form
for a double
reference when
one source cites
another.

Use Arabic
numbers in
the text.

that were fully developed. Autism may be linked to the
underdeveloped brain. The condition might appear
immediately, even before birth, or discovered between age
one and two (Fay, 1987).

     Gallagher, Jones, and Byrne (1990) surveyed

Explain tables in the text.

professionals in the mental health field for opinions about
the causes of autism. Gallagher et al. explained the study
in this manner:

Indent long quotations of 40 words or more five additional spaces and omit the quotation marks.

     The results of the segment of the analysis exhibited

     in Table 1 [see below] can be summarized

     straightforwardly: Biogenic factors clearly dominate

     psychiatrists' current attitudes toward etiological

     theories of infantile autism. Among the biogenic

     factors, by far the prominent choice is "biochemical

Page numbers go outside the final period after a long quotation.

     imbalance," with a perceived strength-of-relationship

     mean value about midway between "related" and

     "strongly related." (p. 936)

Behavior

     The behavior of the autistic child has been reported
(Fay, 1987; Rimland, 1984; Rutter, 1968; Vandershaf, 1987).
A typical autistic child withdraws into self-imposed
privacy, avoids social contact, and avoids the touching
hands of others. The child often rocks rhythmically and
silently. He or she cannot or will not answer questions,
and many autistics cannot or will not speak. Some of them
senselessly copy the voices of others, a syndrome called
echolalia. Others only emit a few sounds. They speak "at"
people, not "to" them, and they usually avoid eye contact.
Many autistic children are hyperactive. They fling their
hands, flick their fingers, blink their eyes repeatedly,

Establish abbreviations before you use them alone.

and commit self-injurious behavior (SIB), especially when
placed in an unfamiliar area. Self-inflicted pain "may
afflict eighty percent of autistic children sometime during

Autism

6

Table 1

Psychiatrists' Attitudes Toward Etiological Theories of
Infantile Autism

See 216–219 for information on using illustrations and tables.

Etiological theory	Mean value	Rank
Biochemical imbalance	3.491	1
Genetic inheritance	3.078	2
Brain lesion	3.014	3
Metabolic dysfunction	2.832	4
Prenatal factors	2.821	5
Chromosomal mutation	2.623	6
Maternal deprivation	1.933	7
Cold "intellectualized" parenting	1.752	8
Immune system deficiency	1.718	9
Maternal age	1.714	10
Birth order	1.361	11

Note. From "A National Survey of Mental Health
Professionals Concerning the Causes of Early Infantile
Autism" by B. J. Gallagher and B. J. Jones, 1990, Journal
of Clinical Psychology, 46, p. 936.

Use this form to cite the source of a table.

Triple-space before and after a table.

their lives" (Vandershaf, 1987, p. 16). Rutter (1968) has
reported four ritualistic behaviors commonly seen with
autism:

1. Autistic children may select toys of a specific
   shape or structure and play.
2. An autistic child may become overattached to a
   certain toy. The child will want that toy with
   him or her at all times. Should it be taken away,
   the child will usually throw a tantrum.
3. The child may have unusual concern for numbers,
   geometric shapes, and colors.

   4. The child maintains a specific routine and order,
       and the child gets perturbed if it is changed.
       (pp. 139-40)

    Psychologically, an autistic child cannot understand
other people's feelings (Perner, Firth, Leslie, & Leekam,
1989; Baron-Cohen, 1991; Mason, McGee, Farmer-Dougan, &
Risley, 1989). An important concern is the mother-child
attachment. Many of the autistics' actions may be linked
with the lack of nurturing from the autistics' mothers.
Bowlby (1968) was commissioned by the United Nations World
Health Organization to study the effects of maternal
separation, and he reported: "It is sufficient to say that
what is believed to be essential for mental health is that
the infant and young child should experience a warm,
intimate, and continuous relationship with his mother (or
permanent mother substitute)" (p. 11). An autistic child,
deprived of a mother's love, could lose the ability to form
relationships with any person.

Pharmacological Treatment

    Experimental treatments to help the autistic child are
under way. Most treatments are drug-related. Naltrexone,
a drug that blocks the opioid receptors in the brain, has
been tested with success. Herman et al. (1986)
administered naltrexone on five autistic children, 3 to 13
years old, for eight weeks. The drug decreased autistic
behavior--hand flapping, body whirling, babbling, and
nonsense words--both in their homes and at the laboratory.
Before taking naltrexone, the children could not look
someone directly in the eyes for lengthy periods, but after
taking it, they could make eye contact 15 times longer.
The children also enjoyed hugging more, so Herman et al.

(1986) offered the theory that "parental comforting may release opioids in children's brains" (p. 1172).

Herman et al. (1987) also experimented with three boys, two autistic males and one nonautistic male. The scientists administered naltrexone to each boy to see if it would lessen their attempts to injure themselves. The naltrexone decreased the autistic boys' attempts to injure themselves. Before the drug was administered, one of the autistic children had tried to hurt himself 200 times in one five-minute session. He even had to wear a helmet for protection. The naltrexone reduced this behavior significantly (Herman et al., 1987). The other autistic child also improved, but the third (nonautistic) child did not, probably because he did not have high opioid levels to begin with. This last finding supports the idea that naltrexone is not a universal panacea, neither for SIB nor for autism, because some children may not have an excessive presence of opioids (Rutter, 1978).

Use past tense to cite the work of a scientist.

Use present tense for established knowledge.

Walters, Barrett, Feinstein, Mercurio, and Hole (1990) treated a 14-year-old male whose SIB had been treated unsuccessfully since autism was diagnosed at age 3. Walters et al. administered naltrexone and a placebo alternately for 21 days at a time. The frequency of SIB decreased dramatically during the periods of naltrexone treatment and increased under the placebo. "Results indicated a pronounced favorable clinical response to the use of naltrexone" (Walters et al., 1990, pp. 172-73).

Another test administered varying dosages of naltrexone to four autistic males, ages from 5 to 21 (Panksepp & Lensing, 1991). Researchers observed a decrease in aggressive behavior and SIB in each patient, an increase in eye contact and social behavior, and improved language skills.

For three to six
authors, list all
authors at first
use and
thereafter use
"et al." with
the lead
author's
name.
Another drug thought to be helpful for treating autism
is an antihypertensive "beta-blocker," which eases
aggression and limits impulsive behavior. It interferes
with the nervous stimulation of specific receptors in the
heart. Psychiatrist John J. Ratey at Massachusetts Mental
Health Center prescribed propranolol, a beta-blocker, at
Summarize
experiments
and testing
procedures
in your text.
low doses to adult autistics (see Bower, 1986). The dosage
was raised every one to two weeks if problems continued.
The treatment lasted an average of 14 months. Ratey
reported that adult autistics showed moderate to marked
drops in aggressive behavior. As their aggression
decreased, their friendliness increased. The study also
showed a decrease in discomfort of autistic persons when
faced with social confrontations (cited in Bower, 1986).

Behavioral Treatment

    Rather than pharmacological treatment, researchers
also have enlisted the parents to be therapists for
behavioral treatment in the home. Bower (1989) reported,
"Most behavioral researchers accept the biological
hypothesis, but they attempt to treat autism by
manipulating the child's environment with the parents'
help" (p. 136).

    The work of Perner, Frith, Leslie, and Leekam (1989)
showed that "autistic children are grossly delayed in their
acquisition of a theory of mind" (p. 698). Human contact
may contribute to the autistic child's understanding of
knowledge.

    Another behavioral test used nonverbal and verbal play
skills to treat autistic children (Coe, Matson, Fee,
Manikam, & Linarello, 1990). Both physical and verbal
responses to a game were studied. The three subjects
learned the game and executed multiple tasks.

    Bower (1989) has reported that three behavioral

treatment centers continue their work: the University of
California, where Ivar Lovass in 1970 established a pioneer
program; TEACCH, an outpatient program in North Carolina
for autistics; and LEAP, a preschool in Pittsburgh.

Discussion

The two schools of treatment need not be at odds with
each other. Cold parenting can be dismissed as a causal
force, but warm parenting can certainly serve the child.
Pharmacological treatment has gained support because of
evidence that "autism stems from such biological phenomena
as biochemical imbalance, genetic inheritance, brain
lesion, metabolic dysfunction, prenatal factors, and
chromosomal mutation, in that order" (Gallagher et al.,
1990, p. 938). Drugs and behavioral treatment together may
enhance the lives of many autistic persons.

The discussion should evaluate and interpret the implications of your study.

Most autistic persons are withdrawn from the world,
but a few do seem to enjoy a special gift of geniusness.
They are considered idiot savants; that is, they specialize
in a particular field, such as mathematics or music. Their
memories are unusually exceptional and they are able to
recall almost anything from years past. The movie Rain Man
brought the illness to national attention.

There is hope in the future that both the cause and
the cure for autism will be found. For the present, new
drug therapies and behavior modification offer some hope
for the abnormal, SIB actions of autistics. Since autism
is sometimes outgrown, childhood treatment offers the best
hope for the autistic person who must try to survive in an
alien environment.

References

Baron-Cohen, S. (1989). Do people with autism understand what causes emotion? Child Development, 60, 689-700.

Bower, E. B. (1986). Betablocking autistics' aggression. Science News, 129, 344.

Bower, E. B. (1989). Remodeling the autistic child. Science News, 136, 312-313.

Bowlby, J. (1966). Maternal care and mental health. New York: Schocken.

Coe, D., Matson, J., Fee, V., Manikam, R., & Linarello, C. (1990). Teaching nonverbal and verbal play skills to mentally retarded and autistic children. Journal of Autism and Developmental Disorders, 20, 177-187.

Fay, M. (1986, September). Child of silence. Life, pp. 84-89.

Gallagher, B. J., Jones, B. J., & Byrne, M. M. (1990). A national survey of mental health professionals concerning the causes of early infantile autism. Journal of Clinical Psychology, 46, 934-939.

Herman, B., Hammock, M., Arthur-Smith, A., Egan, J., Chatoor, I., Zelnik, N., Corradine, M., Appelgate, K., Boeck, R., & Shar, S. (1986). Role of opioid peptides in autism: Effects at acute administration of naltrexone. Neuroscience Abstracts, 12, 1172.

Herman, B., Hammock, M., Arthur-Smith, A., Egan, J., Chatoor, I., Werner, A., & Zelnick, N. (1987). Naltrexone decreases self-injurious behavior. Annals of Neurology, 22, 550-552.

Kanner, L. (1943). Autistic disturbances of affective contact. Nervous Child, 2, 217-250.

Journal article.

Book.

Five authors.

Magazine article.

Ten authors.

Koegel, R. L., & Schreibman, L. (1981). Teaching autistic
and other severely handicapped children. Austin:
Pro-ed.

Mason, A. M., McGee, G. G., Farmer-Dougan, V., & Risely, T.
R. (1989). A practical strategy for ongoing reinforcer
assessment. Journal of Applied Behavioral Analysis, 22,
171-179.

Mesibov, G. B. (1989). [Review of Autism by L. Schreibman
and of Autism: Strategies for change by G. Groden & M.
G. Baron]. Journal of Clinical Child Psychology, 18,
273-274.

Panksepp, J., & Lensing, P. (1991). Brief report: A
synopsis of an open-trial of naltrexone treatment of
autism with four children. Journal of Autism and
Developmental Disorders, 21, 243-249.

Perner, J., Frith, U., Leslie, A. M., & Leekam, S. R.
(1989). Exploration of the autistic child's theory of
mind: Knowledge, belief, and communication. Child
Development, 60, 689-700.

Rimland, B. (1984). Infantile autism. New York:
Appleton-Century-Crofts.

Rutter, M. (1978). Diagnosis and definition of childhood
autism. Journal of Autism and Childhood Schizophrenia,
8, 139-161.

Vandershaf, S. (1987, March). Autism: A chemical excess?
Psychology Today, pp. 15-16.

Walters, A. S., Barrett, R. P., Feinstein, C., Mercurio,
A., & Hole, W. T. (1990). A case report of naltrexone
treatment of self-injury and social withdrawal in
autism. Journal of Autism and Developmental Disorders,
20, 169-176.

Review article.

Use "p." or
"pp." with page
numbers to
magazines to
prevent
confusion with
volume
numbers of a
journal.

11   *Form and Style for Other Disciplines*

Guide, by Discipline

Every academic discipline has distinctive forms for displaying scholarship, as shown in Chapters 1 through 9 for literature and modern languages and in Chapter 10 for psychology. When writing papers in physics, biology, music, and other fields, you may need to cite works according to one of these additional formats:

1. The **name and year** system for use in the social sciences, biological and earth sciences, education, linguistics, and business.
2. The **number** system for use in the applied sciences, such as chemistry, computer science, mathematics, physics, and medicine.
3. The **footnote** system for use with papers in the fine arts (art, theater, and music) and humanities (history, philosophy, and religion, but excluding language and literature, which use the MLA style).

11a USING THE NAME AND YEAR SYSTEM

When writing research papers by the name and year system, conform to the following rules (see also Section 10b, 282–85):

1. Place the year within parentheses immediately after the authority's name:

```
Smith (1991) ascribes no species-specific behavior to man.

However, Adams (1992) presents data that tend to be

contradictory.
```

2. If you do not mention the authority's name in your sentence, insert the name, year, and even page numbers in parentheses:

```
Hopkins (1991) found some supporting evidence for a portion

of the questionable data (Marr & Brown, 1990, pp. 23-32)

through point bi-serial correlation techniques.
```

3. For two authors, employ both names: "(Torgerson & Andrews, 1992)." For three to six authors, name them all in the first entry, as ("Torgerson, Andrews, & Dunlap, 1992)," but thereafter use "(Torgerson et al., 1992)." For seven or more authors, employ "(Fredericks et al., 1992)" in the first and all subsequent instances.

4. Use lowercase letters (a, b, c) to identify two or more works published in the same year by the same author; for example, "Thompson (1992a)" and "Thompson (1992b)." Then use "1992a" and "1992b" in your list of references (see 284 for an example).

5. If necessary, specify additional information:

```
Horton (1991; cf. Thomas, 1990, p. 89) suggests an

intercorrelation of these testing devices.  But after

multiple-group analysis, Welston (1992, esp. p. 211)

reached an opposite conclusion.
```

6. In the case of direct quotation or paraphrase to a specific page, you must include the author, year, *and* page number(s), as follows:

a. Quotation or paraphrase in the middle of the sentence:

```
He stated, "These data of psychological development suggest

that retarded adolescents are atypical in maturational

growth" (Jones, 1991, p. 215), but he failed to clarify

which data were examined.
```

b. A quotation or paraphrase that falls at the end of a sentence:

```
Jones (1992) found that "these data of psychological

development suggest that retarded adolescents are atypical

in maturational growth" (p. 215).
```

c. A long quotation set off from the text in a block (and therefore without quotation marks):

```
Albert (1992) found the following:

    Whenever these pathogenic organisms attack the human

    body and begin to multiply, the infection is set in

    motion.  The host responds to this parasitic invasion

    with efforts to cleanse itself of the invading agents.

    When rejection efforts of the host become visible

    (fever, sneezing, congestion), the disease status

    exists.  (pp. 314-315)
```

7. Every reference used in your text should appear in your alphabetical list of references at the end of the paper. The format differs for almost every discipline, so find the instructions for your discipline (see the list above, 302).

11b USING THE NAME AND YEAR SYSTEM FOR PAPERS IN THE SOCIAL SCIENCES

Education   Geography   Home Economics
Linguistics   Physical Education Political Science
Psychology   Sociology

The disciplines of the social sciences employ the name and year system. In general, the stipulations of the APA *Publication Manual* (see Chapter 10) have gained wide acceptance, but variations exist by discipline.

Education

In-Text Citation   Use the name and year system, as explained above in Section 11a, 303–04, or in Section 10b, 282–85.

List of References   Label the list as "References." Use APA style as described in Section 10c, 285–89. A sample list follows:

References

Casella, V. (1988). Computers-in-the-curriculum workshop. Instructor, 97, 128–129.

Dahlberg, L. A. (1990). Teaching for the information age. Journal of Reading, 34, 199–200.

Edelwich, J., & Brodsky, A. (1980). Burnout. New York: Human Services Press.

Maslach, D. (1978a). Job burnout: How people cope. Public Welfare, 36, 56–58.

Maslach, D. (1978b). The client role in staff burnout. Journal of Social Issues, 34(4), 111–124.

Note: **The form of these entries is based in general on the style and format of several education journals, such as *Journal of Educational Research, Educational Administration Quarterly, Educational Communication & Technology,* and *Education Research Quarterly.***

Geography

See the form and style for Sociology, 308.

Home Economics

Use the name and year system as explained above in Section 11a, 303–04, or in Section 10b, 282–85.

Linguistics: LSA Style

In-Text Citation   In-text citations for linguistic studies include almost always a specific page reference to the work along with the date, separated by a colon; for example, "Jones 1983: 12–18" or "Gifford's recent reference (1982: 162)." Therefore, follow basic standards for the name and year system (see 303–04) with a colon to separate year and page number(s).

List of References   As shown below, label the list as "References" and alphabetize the entries. Place the year immediately after the author's name. For journal entries, use a period rather than a colon or comma to separate volume and page. There is *no* underlining. Linguistic journals are abbreviated, others are not. A sample list follows:

```
                        References
Beal, Carole R., and Susan L. Belgrad.  1990.  The
     development of message evaluation skills in young
     children.  Child Development 61.705-713.
De Boysson-Bardies, Bénédicte, and Marilyn M. Vihman.
     1991.  Adaptation to language: Evidence from babbling
     and first words in four languages.  Lg.  67.287-319.
Bresnan, Joan.  1970.  On complementizers: Toward a
     syntactic theory of complement types.  Fd. of Lg.
     6.297-321.
Burnam, Tom.  1988.  A misinformation guide to grammar.
     Writer's Digest 68.36-39.
Chomsky, Noam.  1965.  Aspects of the theory of syntax.
     Cambridge, MA: MIT Press.
```

————. 1975. Reflections on language. New York: Pantheon.

Jacobsson, Bengt. 1988. Should and would in factual that-clauses. English Studies 69.72–81.

Keenan, Edward, and Bernard Comrie. 1977. Noun phrase accessibility and universal grammar. LI 8.63–99.

————, ————. 1979. Noun phrase accessibility revisited. Lg. 44.244–266.

Ross, John R. 1967. Constraints on variables in syntax. MIT dissertation.

> *Note:* **The form of these entries conforms in general to that advocated by the Linguistic Society of America, LSA Bulletin, No. 71 (December 1976), 43–45; the December issue annually; and the form and style practiced by the journal** *Language.*

Physical Education

In-Text Citation   Use the name and year system as explained above in Section 11a, 303–04, or in Section 10b, 282–85.

List of References   Follow the stipulations of APA style as explained and demonstrated in Chapter 10, 285–89.

Political Science

In-Text Citation   Use the name and year system as explained above in Section 11a, 303–04, or in Section 10b, 282–85.

List of References   Follow the stipulations of APA style as explained and demonstrated in Chapter 10, 285–89.

Psychology: APA style

See Chapter 10.

Sociology and Social Work

In-Text Citation Use the name and year system as explained above in Section 11a, 303–04, or in Section 10b, 282–85.

List of References Use APA style as explained and demonstrated in Chapter 10. APA style is used in many sociology journals, such as *Journal of Social Psychology, Journal of Social Work and Human Sexuality,* and *Journal of Social Issues.* However, your instructor may prefer the style used by the prestigious *American Journal of Sociology.* If so, modify APA style in this manner:

1. List the author's full name.

2. List year without parentheses.

3. Capitalize all major words in titles.

4. Enclose journal titles within quotation marks.

5. Do not underline volume number.

6. Follow volume number with a colon, not a comma, with no space between the colon and the page number(s).

A sample list follows to show the style of the *American Journal of Sociology:*

References

Adamny, David W., and George E. Agree. 1975. <u>Political Money</u>. Baltimore: Johns Hopkins University Press.

Alwin, Duane F., and Jon A. Krosnick. 1991. "Aging, Cohorts, and the Stability of Sociopolitical Orientations over the Life Span." <u>American Journal of Sociology</u> 97:169–195.

Epstein, Edwin M. 1980. "Business and Labor under the Federal Election Campaign Act of 1971." Pp. 107–151 in <u>Parties, Interest Groups, and Campaign Finance Laws</u>, edited by Michael J. Malbin. Washington, DC: American Enterprise Institute for Public Policy Research.

Waldman, Steven. 1992. "Deadbeat Dads." <u>Newsweek</u> May 4:46–52.

11c USING THE NAME AND YEAR SYSTEM FOR PAPERS IN THE BIOLOGICAL AND EARTH SCIENCES

Agriculture   Anthropology   Archaeology   Astronomy
Biology   Botany   Geology   Zoology

The disciplines of this major grouping employ the name and year system. In general, the rules of APA style (Chapter 10) match the documentation standards of these disciplines, especially for the in-text citations, but stylistic variations do exist for the reference lists, as explained and demonstrated below.

Agriculture

In-Text Citation   Use the name and year system as explained above in Section 11a, 303–04, or in Section 10b, 282–85.

List of References   In general, the agriculture form follows that of the *Council of Biology Editors Style Manual* (CBE) style as mentioned below, 311–12, except that second and succeeding lines of each entry are indented five rather than two spaces. A sample list follows:

References

Brotherton, I. 1990. On the voluntary approach to
    resolving rural conflict. Environ. & Plan. A.
    64:923.

Celis, William. 1988. Tax changes hit groups in land
    conservation. Wall Street J. Jan. 26:38.

Corring, T., A. Aumaitre, and G. Durand. 1978.
    Development of digestive enzymes in the piglet from
    birth to 8 weeks. Nutr. Metab. 22:231.

Cranwell, P. D. 1974. Gastric acid secretion in newly
    born piglets. Res. Vet. Sci. 16:105.

Cranwell, P. D. 1976. Gastric secretion in the young pig.
    Proc. Nutri. Soc. 35:28A (Abstr.).

Kmenta, J. 1971. Element of econometrics. New York:
    Macmillan.

> *Note:* **The form of these entries conforms, in general, to that found in agriculture journals, especially *Journal of Animal Science* and *Journal of the American Society for Horticultural Science*.**

Anthropology and Archaeology

In-Text Citation Use the name and year system as explained above in Section 11a, 303–04, or in Section 10b, 282–85.

List of References Label the list "References Cited" and set the author's name and the date to the left, as shown next:

```
                    References Cited
Austin, James H.
   1978  Chase, Chance, and Creativity: The Lucky Art of
         Novelty.  New York: Columbia University Press.
Bastien, Joseph
   1978  Mountain of the Condor: Metaphor and Ritual in an
         Andean Ayllu.  American Ethnological Society Monograph
         64.  St. Paul: West Publishing Co.
Binford, Louis R.
   1962  Archaeology as Anthropology.  American Antiquity
         28:217-225.
Briody, Elizabeth K., and Marietta L. Baba
   1991  Explaining Differences in Repatriation Experiences:
         The Discovery of Coupled and Decoupled Systems.
         American Anthropologist 93:322-344.
Dubinskas, F. A.
   1988a  [ed.] Making Time: Ethnographies of
          High-Technology Organizations.  Philadelphia:
          Temple University Press.
   1988b  Janus Organizations: Scientists and Managers in
          Genetic Engineering Firms.  In Making Time:
          Ethnographies of High-Technology Organizations.  Pp.
          170-232.  Philadelphia: Temple University Press.
```

Dye, Daniel S.

   1949 A Grammar of Chinese Lattice. 2nd ed.

      Harvard–Yenching Monograph Series VI. Cambridge:

      Harvard University Press.

Jennings, J. D.

   1978 Origins. <u>In</u> J. D. Jennings, ed. Ancient Native

      Americans, pp. 1–41. San Francisco: Freeman.

McLaren, Peter L.

   1988 The Liminal Servant and the Ritual Roots of

      Critical Pedagogy. Language Arts 65:164–180.

> *Note:* **The form of these entries is based on the stylistic format of the journal *American Anthropologist.***

Astronomy

See format of Geology, 312–14.

Biology/Botany/Zoology: CBE Style

The new 1993 edition of *CBE Style Manual,* an official guide published by the Council of Biology Editors in association with the American Institute of Biological Sciences, advocates two reference styles. For general biological studies, use the name and year system, shown next. For bio-medical papers use the number system (see Section 11g, "Using the Number System for Papers in the Medical Sciences," 322–28).

In-Text Citation   Use the name and year system as explained above in Section 11a, 303–04, or in Section 10b, 282–85, and as demonstrated with this example:

> This fact would ensure their continued presence in the
> cell as a screen mechanism (McClure 1976). Kirk and
> Tilney–Bassett (1976, pp. 83–84) suggest that "many of the
> other plants that have these air blisters are also shade
> plants, indicating that such structures may be safeguards
> against loss of the shading cover and subsequent

photo–oxidation of the photosynthetic pigments" (cf. Downs et al. 1980).

List of References   Alphabetize the list and label it "Literature Cited." Type the first line of each entry flush left; indent the second line and other succeeding lines two spaces.

For journals, list name(s) of the author(s), year, title of the article, name of the journal, volume number, and inclusive page numbers. Do not underline the title of the journal, and capitalize only the first word and proper nouns in the article's title.

For books, list author(s), year, title, city of publication, and publisher. Do not underline the title of the book, and capitalize only the first word and proper nouns in the book's title.

Literature Cited

Argyres, A.; Schmitt, J. 1991. Microgeographic structure of morphological and life history traits in a natural population of Impatiens capensis. Evolution 45: 178–189.

Bateson, P. 1978. Sexual imprinting and optimal outcrossing. Nature 273: 659–660.

Bertin, R. I. 1982. Paternity and fruit production in trumpet creeper (Campsis radicans). American Naturalist 119: 694–709.

Ephron, B. 1982. The jackknife, the bootstrap, and other resampling plans. Philadelphia: Society for Industrial and Applied Mathematics.

Handel, S. 1983. Pollination ecology, plant population structure, and gene flow. In L. Real (ed.), Pollination biology, 163–211. Orlando: Academic Press.

> *Note:* **The form of these entries conforms in general to the new *CBE Style Manual,* 6th ed., to be released sometime in 1993.**

Geology

The United States Geological Survey sets the standards for geological papers, as explained below.

In-Text Citation   Use the name and year system as explained above in Section 11a, 303–04, or in Section 10b, 282–85, and as demonstrated with this example:

> In view of Niue's position as a former volcanic island
> rising from a submarine plateau (Schofield, 1959), it might
> be further speculated that it has a late-stage, silicic,
> peralkaline phase (Baker, 1974, pp. 344–45). Such melts
> readily lose significant amounts of uranium and other
> elements on crystallization (Rosholt et al., 1971; Haffty
> and Nobel, 1972; Dayvault, 1980), which are available to
> contemporary or later hydrothermal systems (Wallace, 1980).

List of References   Label the bibliography as "Literature Cited," and list only those works mentioned in the paper. If you list references not used in the paper, label the page "Selected Bibliography." Alphabetize the list. For books, list author, followed by a comma; year, followed by a comma; title of the work with only the first word and proper names capitalized, followed by a colon; the place of publication, followed by a comma; publisher, followed by a comma; and total pages, followed by a period. For journals, list author, followed by a comma; date, followed by a comma; title of the article with only the first word and proper nouns capitalized, followed by a colon; name of the journal, abbreviated but not underlined, followed by a comma; the volume number with a lowercase "v.," as in "v. 23," followed by a comma; the inclusive page numbers preceded by one "p." Add other notations for issue number maps, illustrations, plates, and so forth (see the Mattson entry below). A sample list follows:

Literature Cited

Alavi, M., 1991, Sedimentary and structural characteristics
   of the Paleo-Tethys remnants in northeastern Iran:
   Geol. Soc. Amer. Bull., v. 103, p. 983–992.

Bowler, S., 1990a, Unprecedented damage as earthquake
   occurs close to surface: New Scientist, v. 126, 30
   June, p. 31.

-----, 1990b, When will a big quake hit eastern US?: New
   Scientist, v. 127, 29 Sept., p. 26.

-----, 1991, Alaska quake spurs huge wave: New York Times
   22 Feb., p. A18.

Donath, F. A., 1963, Strength variation and deformational behavior in anisotropic rock, p. 281–297 <u>in</u> Judd, Wm. R., Editor, State of stress in the earth's crust: New York, American Elsevier Publishing Co., Inc., 732 p.

Friedlander, G., Kennedy, J. W., and Miller, J. M., 1964, Nuclear and radiochemistry: New York, John Wiley and Sons, 585 p.

Heard, H. C., Turner, F. J., and Weiss, L. E., 1965, Studies of heterogeneous strain in experimentally deformed calcite, marble, and phyllite: Univ. Calif. Pub. Geol. Sci., v. 46, p. 81–152.

Hill, M. L., and Troxel, B. W., 1966, Tectonics of Death Valley region, California: Geol. Soc. America Bull., v. 77, p. 435–438.

Mattson, Peter H., 1979, Subduction, buoyant braking, flipping, and strike–slip faulting in the northern Caribbean: J. of Geology, v. 87, no. 3, p. 293–304, 3 figs., map.

Thorpe, R. S., 1974, Aspects of magnetism and plate tectonics in the Precambrian of England Wales: Geol. J., v. 9, p. 115–136.

> *Note:* **The form of these geology entries conforms to** *Suggestions to Authors of the Reports of the United States Geological Survey,* **7th ed. (Washington, DC: Dept. of the Interior, 1991), and to** *The Journal of Geology* **and** *Journal of Geological Education.*

11d USING THE NAME AND YEAR SYSTEM FOR PAPERS IN BUSINESS AND ECONOMICS

In-Text Citation   Use the name and year system as explained above in Section 11a, 303–04, or in Section 10b, 282–85.

List of References Consult with your instructor. Many business instructors endorse APA style (see Section 10c, 285–89) because it is used in many business journals, such as *Journal of Marketing Education, Applied Financial Economics,* and *Applied Economics.* For other instructors, you may need to modify APA style to conform with another set of business journals, such as *Journal of Marketing* or *Journal of Marketing Research.* Modify APA style in this manner:

1. Use full names of authors; separate two authors with "and," not "&."

2. Use capitals for all major words in titles.

3. Enclose the title of an article within quotation marks.

4. Use a comma after the date.

5. Use commas to separate all items in a journal reference.

6. Do not underline the volume number.

7. Do not precede page number(s) with "p." or "pp."

References

Addison, James T., and B. Thomas Hirsch (1989), "Union
    Effects on Productivity, Profits and Growth: Has the
    Long Run Arrived?" Journal of Labor Economics, 7,
    72-105.

Anderson, James E. (1981), "Cross-Section Tests of the
    Hackscher-Ohlin Theorem: Comment," American Economic
    Review, 71, 1037-1039.

Carter, Allen (1970), Structural Change in the American
    Economy. Cambridge: Harvard University Press.

Celis, William. (1991), "Study Urges a Preschool Role for
    Businesses," New York Times (March 1), A2.

Deardorff, Alan V. (1979), "Weak Links in the Chain of
    Comparative Advantage," Journal of International
    Economics, 9, 197-209.

-------- (1980), "The General Validity of the Law of
    Comparative Advantage," Journal of Political Economy,
    88, 941-957.

Dooley, Michael, and Peter Isard (1979), "The
    Portfolio-Balance Model of Exchange Rates,"
    International Finance Discussion Paper (No. 141, May),
    Federal Reserve Board.

"An Updated Yardstick for GNP Growth" (1985), <u>Business
    Week</u> (June 10), 18.

Zufryden, Fred S. (1986), Multibrand Transition
    Probabilities as a Function of Explanatory Variables:
    Estimation by a Least-Squares-Based Approach," <u>Journal
    of Marketing Research</u>, 23 (May), 177-183.

> *Note:* **The form of these business/economics entries is based in general on the style and format of** *Journal of Marketing* **and** *Journal of Marketing Research.*

11e USING THE NUMBER SYSTEM

The number system is used in the applied sciences (chemistry, computer science, mathematics, and physics) and in the medical sciences (medicine, nursing, and general health). In simple terms, it requires an in-text *number,* rather than the year, and a list of works cited with each entry numbered to correspond to the in-text citation. Writers in these fields conform to several general regulations that apply to all applied sciences.

After completing a list of references, assign a number to each entry. Use one of two methods for numbering the list: (1) arrange references in alphabetical order and number them consecutively (in which case, of course, the numbers will not appear in consecutive order in the text), or (2) forgo an alphabetical arrangement and number the references consecutively as they appear in the text, interrupting that order when entering references cited earlier.

The bibliography entries are always preceded by a numeral. When writing a rough draft, use the numbers as in-text citations. You can, of course, use the number with the name of the authority. In both cases, the number serves as key reference to the source, as listed at the end of the paper. If you quote a source, add specific page numbers to the bibliography entry (see examples in the reference lists below) or add page numbers to your in-text citations. Conform to the following regulations:

1. Place the number within parentheses (1) or brackets [2] alone or with the name(s) of the source:

> In particular, the recent paper by Hershel, Hobbs, and
> Thomason (1) raises many interesting questions related to
> photosynthesis, some of which were answered by Skelton (2).

However, several disciplines and their journals use a raised superscript number:

> In particular, the recent paper by Hershel, Hobbs, and
> Thomason[1] raises many interesting questions related to
> photosynthesis, some of which were answered by Skelton.[2]

2. If the sentence construction does not require the use of the authority's name, employ one of the following methods:

a. Insert the number only, enclosing it within parentheses (or brackets) or use a raised superscript:

> It is known (1) that the DNA concentration of a nucleus
> doubles during interphase.

> It is known[1] that the DNA concentration of a nucleus
> doubles during interphase.

b. Insert both name and number within parentheses:

> Additional observations include alterations in carbohydrate
> metabolism (Evans, 3), and changes in ascorbic acid
> incorporation into the cell (Dodd and Williams, 11) and
> adjoining membranes (Holt and Zimmer, 7).

3. If necessary, add specific data to the entry:

> "The use of photosynthesis in this application is crucial
> to the environment" (Skelton,[8] p. 732).

> The results of the respiration experiment published by
> Jones (3, Table 6, p. 412) had been predicted earlier by
> Smith (5, Proposition 8).

11f USING THE NUMBER SYSTEM FOR PAPERS IN THE APPLIED SCIENCES

Chemistry   Computer Science   Mathematics   Physics

The disciplines of the applied sciences employ the number system, but variations by field exist in both textual citations and in entries of the list of references.

Chemistry: American Chemical Society (ACS) Style

In-Text Citation   You may use one of two styles. Check with your chemistry instructor for his or her preference.

1. Use raised superscript numerals as references occur:

> The stereochemical features of arene molecules chemisorbed on metal surfaces cannot be assessed precisely.[3-5]

2. Place the reference numbers within parentheses:

> However, composite statistics from theoretical calculations (6) and chemical studies (7-10) indicate that benzene is often chemisorbed.

Number your references in consecutive order as used, *not* in alphabetical order. If a reference is repeated, use the original number, not a new one.

List of References   Label the list "References." List entries as they occur in the text, not in alphabetical order. The basic forms for chemical entries are demonstrated below. Titles of journal articles are not listed at all. Dates of journals only are set in boldface; if you cannot print in boldface, use a wavy line under the date (e.g., 1992). A sample list follows:

References

(1) Blatter, F.; Schumacher, E. J. Chem. Ed. **1990**, 67, 519–521.

(2) Norrby, L. J. J. Chem. Ed. **1991**, 68, 110–114.

(3) "Selected Values of Chemical and Thermodynamic Properties." Natl. Bur. Stand. (U.S.) Circ. **1950**, No. 500.

(4) Humphries, R. B. In High School Chemistry, 3rd ed.; Lamm, Nancy, Ed.; Lumar Press: New York, 1984; Vol. III, Chapter 6.

(5) Terrel, L. J. Chem. **1960**, 34, 256; Chem. Abstr. **1961**, 54, 110a.

(6) Cotton, F. A. J. Am. Chem. Soc. **1968**, 90, 6230.

(7) (a) Sievert, A. C.; Muetterties, E. L. Inorg. Chem.
    1981, 20, 489. (b) Albright, T. A., unpublished data,
    1984.

The in-text citation may refer to 7, 7a, or 7b.

(8) Jones, R. C. Modern Chemistry; Zurtcher: New York,
    1991; pp 152–198.

Note: **The form of these chemistry entries conforms to the *ACS Style Guide: A Manual for Authors and Editors*. Ed. Janet S. Dodd (Washington, DC: American Chemical Society, 1986).**

Computer Science

In-Text Citation   Use raised superscript numerals (as above for chemistry, like this[12]), and then number them in consecutive order by appearance in the paper, not by alphabetical order.

List of References   Label the list "Works Cited." Number the references according to their appearance in the text, not by alphabetical order. For books, titles are underlined, publisher precedes city of publication, and specific page(s) of books need not be listed, but in-text citation should specify pages for paraphrases and direct quotations. For journals, the title of the article is provided within quotation marks and with first word only of the title capitalized; title of the journal is underlined; volume number is underlined; issue number is provided, when available, preceding the date and page number(s). A sample list follows:

Works Cited

1. Stonebraker, M. Readings in Database Systems, Morgan,
    Kaufmann, San Mateo, Calif., 1988.

2. Stonebraker, M. "Future trends in database systems."
    IEEE Trans. Knowledge and Data Eng. 1 (1) (Mar. 1989),
    33–44.

3. Aho, A. V.; Hopcroft, J. E.; and Ullman, J. D. The
    Design and Analysis of Computer Algorithms.
    Addison-Wesley, Reading, Mass., 1974.

4. Gligor, V. D.; Shattuck, S. H. "On deadlock detection in distributed systems." <u>IEEE Trans</u>. <u>Softw. Eng.</u> <u>SE-6</u> <u>5</u> (Sept. 1980), 435–40.

5. Sklansky, J.; Wassel, G. N. <u>Pattern Classifiers and Trainable Machines</u>. Springer-Verlag, New York, 1981.

6. Holt, R. C. "Some deadlock properties of computer systems." <u>Computer Surv</u>. <u>4</u> (3) (Sept. 1972), 179–96.

7. Nelson, T. "On the Xanadu project." <u>Byte</u> <u>15</u> (Sept. 1990), 298–99.

Engineering

See the form and style for Physics, 321–22.

Mathematics: AMS Style

In-Text Citation   First alphabetize and then number the list of references. Label the list "References." All in-text citations are then made to the reference number, which you should place in your text within brackets with boldface type (use a wavy line, [5], if you cannot achieve boldface), as in the following example:

In addition to the obvious implications it is already known from **[5]** that every <u>d</u>-regular Lindelof space is <u>D</u>-normal. Further results on <u>D</u>-normal spaces will appear in **[8]**, which is in preparation. The results obtained here and in **[2]**, **[3]**, and **[5]** encourage further research.

List of References   For books, titles are underlined, publisher precedes city of publication, and specific page(s) of books need not be listed. For journals, title of the article is underlined, journal title is *not* underlined, volume is set in boldface (but use a wavy line, 38, if you cannot achieve boldface), year of publication follows within parentheses, then complete pagination of the article. A sample list follows:

References

1. R. Artzy, <u>Linear geometry</u>, Addison-Wesley, Reading, Mass., 1965.

2. I. M. Isaacs and D. S. Passman, Groups with representations of bounded degree, Canad. J. Math. **16** (1964), 299–309.

3. ——————, Characterization of groups in terms of the degrees of their characters, Pacific J. Math. **15** (1965), 877–903.

4. K. Krusen, A historical reconstruction of our number system, Arith. Teacher **38** (1991), 46–48.

5. L. J. Meconi, Number bases revisited, Sch. Science & Math. **90** (1990), 396–403.

6. O. Solbrig, Evolution and systematics. Macmillan, New York, 1966.

> *Note:* **The form of these entries conforms to *A Manual for Authors of Mathematical Papers*, rev. ed. (Providence: American Mathematical Society, 1990).**

Physics: American Institute of Physics (AIP) style

In-Text Citation Use raised superscript numerals, like this.[12] Number the list of references in consecutive order of in-text usage, not in alphabetical order. Label the list "References."

List of References For books, titles are underlined, publisher precedes place of publication, and specific page references *should* be provided. For journals, the title of the article is omitted entirely, the title of the journal is abbreviated and *not* underlined, the volume is set in boldface (use a wavy line under the volume to indicate boldface, if necessary, 44), and the year within parentheses follows the pagination. A sample list follows:

References

[1] T. Fastie, W. G. Rouch, Phys. Today **44**, 37–44 (1991).

[2] C. D. Motchenbacher and F. C. Fitchen, Low-Noise Electronic Design (Wiley, New York, 1973), p. 16.

[3] L. Monchick, S., Chem. Phys. **71**, 576 (1979).

[4] F. Riesz and Bela Nagy, Functional Analysis (Ungar, New York, 1955), Secs. 121 and 123.

[5]G. E. Brown and M. Rho, Phys. Lett. **82B**, 177 (1979); G. E.
Brown, M. Rho, V. Vento, Phys. Letts. **84B**, 383 (1979);
Phys Rev D **22**, 2838 (1980; Phys Rev. D **24**, 216 (1981).
[6]Marc D. Levenson, Phys. Today **30**(5), 44–49 (1977).

> *Note:* **The form of these entries conforms to** *Style Manual
> for Guidance in the Preparation of Papers for Journals
> Published by the American Institute of Physics,* **3rd ed.
> (New York: American Institute of Physics, 1978).**

11g USING THE NUMBER SYSTEM FOR PAPERS IN THE MEDICAL SCIENCES

Health   Medicine   Nursing   Bio-medical

Like other applied sciences, the medical sciences, as a general rule,
employ the number system. Variations among medical journals do exist, so
consult with your instructor about the proper format.

In-Text Citation   Number your citations as they occur in the text, like
this (1) or like this.[1] See the explanation and examples above, Section 11e,
316–17.

List of References   Label the list "References." Do not alphabetize the
list; rather, number it to correspond to sources as you cite them in the text.
For books, list author; title, underlined and with all major words capitalized; place; publisher; and year. For journals, list author; title of the article,
without quotation marks and with only the first word capitalized; name of
the journal, underlined and with major words capitalized and abbreviated
without periods (but followed by a period); year, followed by a semicolon;
volume, followed by a colon and page number(s). A sample list follows:

References

1. Woodley, D. T., Zelickson, A. S., Briggaman, R. A.,
Hamilton, T. A., Weiss, J. S., Ellis, Charles N., Voorhees,
J. J. Treatment of photoaged skin with topical tretinoin
increases epidermal–dermal anchoring fibrils: A preliminary
report. JAMA. 1990;263:3057–3060.

2. Angell, M. Juggling the personal and professional life. J Am Med Wom Assoc. 1982;37:64–68.

3. Antonovsky, A. Health, Stress, and Coping. San Francisco, Jossey-Bass, 1979.

4. Ayman, D. The personality type of patients with arteriolar essential hypertension. Am J Med Sci. 1983;186:213–233.

5. Nash, Paul. Authority and Freedom in Education. New York, Wiley, 1966.

6. Green, M. I., Haggery, R. J. (eds). Ambulatory Pediatrics. Philadelphia, W. B. Saunders, 1968.

> *Note:* **The form of these entries represents a general standard as established by the American Medical Association,** *Style Book: Editorial Manual,* **6th ed. (Acton, MA: Publishing Sciences Group, Inc., 1976), and as used in numerous medical journals, such as** *JAMA, Nutrition Reviews, Journal of American College Health,* **and others.**

Sample Paper Using the Number System

The following paper demonstrates the format for a paper in the applied sciences. It is recommended that you use numbers within parentheses rather than raised index numbers in order to simplify the task of typing the paper. However, your instructor may require a different format.

Pat Bracy

May 8, 1991

Autism: Questions of Cause and Treatment

Autism has been reported as a neurological dysfunction of the brain that afflicts infants before age 30 months. Theories about the causes and the necessary treatment have differed ever since Kanner (1) reported his findings that autism differed from other childhood disorders. Two theories have existed side by side since that time--the behavioral bias and the pharmacological bias. The majority of psychiatrists now defend a biochemical imbalance as the major cause. Treatment has accordingly shifted to pharmacological methods, yet researchers continue to enlist the parents as therapists in response to evidence that behavioral treatment has benefited the autistic child. The findings demonstrate that medical treatment in harmony with behavioral treatment may enhance the lives of some autistic persons.

Kanner (1) described the six basic characteristics of the infantile syndrome as:

1. Extreme autistic aloneness

2. Language abnormalities

3. Obsessive desire for the maintenance of sameness

4. Good cognitive potential

5. Normal physical development

6. Highly intelligent, obsessive, and cold parents

Rutter (2) has reduced these symptoms to four criteria: onset within 30 months of birth, poor social development, late language development, and a preference for regular, stereotyped activity. In the United States, autism affects one out of 2,500 children, and it is not usually diagnosed until the child is between two and five years of age (3).

Kanner (1, p. 249) labeled the disorder as "early

Margin notes:

Cite a number immediately after the name of the source.

Repeat a number if you make a reference to the same source a second or third time.

Add a page number if you quote the source.

Autism 2

infantile autism." He determined that cold parenting, "the
refrigerator mother syndrome," was a primary cause for
autism. His theory is subject to dispute. Today autism is
viewed (4-7) as a distinct developmental disability that
can be diagnosed differently from psychoses, retardation,
and other childhood disorders. "Causal theories of autism
are quite diverse and range in essence from a fragile
chromosome to a fragile parent" (5, p. 86).

Accordingly, two possible theories have existed side
by side--the behavioral bias and the pharmacological bias.
One set of scientists has manipulated the child's
environment in order to test and treat the child's
behavior; another set of scientists has administered
medication to affect the child's brain. Both methods have
demonstrated positive effects. Mesibov (8) has reported on
the behavioral approaches of Schreibman and also Groden and
Baron. In addition, Gallagher, Jones, and Byrne (5) have
provided a survey of biogenic theories.

Cause

Rutter (2) listed three possible causes: behavioral
syndrome, organic brain disorder, or a range of biological
and psychosocial factors. It has been shown that autism
may be caused by abnormally high levels of brain chemicals,
called opioids, which have been found to decrease pain
perception and inhibit motivation in much the same way as
morphine and heroin (9). When a person is born, the opioid
level is 100 times greater than later in life, "perhaps to
protect the newborn from birth trauma" (9, p. 1172). It
has been proposed that opioid levels may not drop quickly
in some infants, and this may lead to autism (9, 15).

> Refer to several sources in one citation by citing more than one number.

> Separate two source numbers by a comma.

Omitted pages of this essay can be found in the full essay in APA style
in Chapter 10, 290-301.

Bower (18) has reported that behavioral treatment centers continue their work at the University of California where Ivar Lovass in 1970 established a pioneer program, at TEACCH, an outpatient program in North Carolina for autistics, and at LEAP, a preschool in Pittsburgh.

Discussion

The two schools of treatment need not be at odds with one another. Cold parenting can be dismissed as a causal force, but warm parenting can certainly serve the child. Pharmacological treatment has gained support because of evidence that "autism stems from such biological phenomena as biochemical imbalance, genetic inheritance, brain lesion, metabolic dysfunction, prenatal factors, and chromosomal mutation, in that order" (5, p. 938). Drugs and behavioral treatment together may enhance the lives of many autistic persons.

Although ninety-five percent of autistic persons require institutionalization, some are capable of leading productive, self-fulfilling lives. Their symptoms may change and even disappear with age. Most autistic persons are withdrawn from the world, but a few do seem to enjoy a special gift of geniusness. They are considered idiot savants; that is, they specialize in a particular field, such as mathematics or music. Their memories are unusually exceptional and they are able to recall almost anything from years past. The movie Rain Man brought the illness to national attention.

There is hope in the future that both the cause and the cure for autism will be found. For the present, new drug therapies and behavior modification offer some hope for the abnormal, self-destructive actions exhibited by autistics. Since autism is sometimes outgrown, childhood treatment offers the best hope for the autistic person who must try to survive in an alien environment.

Autism 13

References

1. Kanner, L. Autistic disturbances of affective contact. Nerv Child. 1943;2:217–250.

2. Rutter, M. Diagnosis and definition of childhood autism. J of Autism and Child Schizo. 1978;8:139–161.

3. Koegel, R. L., Schreibman, L. Teaching Autistic and Other Severely Handicapped Children. Austin: Pro-Ed, 1981.

4. Rimland, B. Infantile Autism. New York: Appleton-Century-Crofts, 1984.

5. Gallagher, B. J., Jones, B. J., Byrne, M. M. A national survey of mental health professionals concerning the causes of early infantile autism. J of Cli Psy. 1990;46:934–939.

6. Walters, A. S., Barrett, R. P., Feinstein, C., Mercurio, A., Hole, W. T. J of Autism and Dev Dis. 1990;20:169–176.

7. Fay, M. Child of silence. Life. Sept.1986:pp. 84–89.

8. Mesibov, G. B. [Rev of Autism by L. Schreibman and of Autism: Strategies for Change by G. Groden & M. G. Baron]. J of Cli Child Psy. 1989;18:273–274.

9. Herman, B, Hammock, M., Arthur-Smith, A., Egan, J., Chatoor, I., Zelnik, N., Corradine, M., Appelgate, K., Boeck, R., Shar, S. Role of opioid peptides in autism: Effects at acute administration of naltrexone. Neurosci Abs. 1986;12:1172.

10. Vandershaf, S. Autism: A chemical excess? Psy Today. Mar.1987:15–16.

11. Perner, J., Frith, U., Leslie, A. M., Leekam, S. R. Exploration of the autistic child's theory of mind: Knowledge, belief, and communication. Child Dev. 1989;60:689–700.

12. Baron-Cohen, S. Do people with autism understand what causes emotion? Child Dev. 1991;62:385–395.

The reference list is numbered by appearance of the source in the text, not by alphabetical order.

The citations on this page conform to the style of JAMA and other medical journals.

Autism 14

13. Mason, A. M., McGee, G. G., Farmer-Dougan, V. Risley, T. R. A practical strategy for ongoing reinforcer assessment. <u>J of Appl Behav Anal</u>. 1989;22:171–179.

14. Bowlby, J. <u>Maternal Care and Mental Health</u>. New York, Schocken, 1966.

15. Herman, B., Hammock, M., Arthur-Smith, A., Egan, J., Chatoor, I., Werner, A., Zelnick, N. Naltrexone decreases self-injurious behavior. <u>Ann of Neuro</u>. 1987;22:550–552.

16. Panksepp, J., Lensing, P. Brief report: A synopsis of an open-trial of naltrexone treatment of autism with four children. <u>J of Autism and Dev Dis</u>. 1991;21:243–249.

17. Bower, E. B. Betablocking autistics' aggression. <u>Sci News</u>. 1986;129:344.

18. Bower, E. B. Remodeling the autistic child. <u>Sci News</u>. 1989;136:312–313.

19. Coe, D., Matson, J., Fee, V., Manikam, R., Linarello, C. Teaching nonverbal and verbal play skills to mentally retarded and autistic children. <u>J of Autism and Dev Dis</u>. 1990;20:177–187.

11h USING THE FOOTNOTE SYSTEM

The fine arts and some fields in the humanities (but not literature) employ traditional footnotes, which should conform to standards set by the *Chicago Manual of Style,* 13th ed., 1982. With this system, you must employ superscript numerals within the text (like this[15]) and place documentary footnotes on corresponding pages. Usually, no list of works cited will be necessary; however, some instructors will ask for one at the end of your paper; if so, see below (335). The discussion below assumes that notes will appear as footnotes; however, some instructors accept endnotes (that is, all notes appear together at the end of the paper, not at the bottom of individual pages; see 331).

In-Text Citation: Superscript Numerals Use Arabic numerals typed slightly above the line (like this[12]). Place this superscript numeral at the end of quotations or paraphrases, with the number following immediately without a space after the final word or mark of punctuation, as in this sample:

```
        Colonel Warner soon rejoined his troops despite severe

pain.  He wrote in September of 1864: "I was obliged to

ride at all times on a walk and to mount my horse from some

steps or be helped on.  My cains [sic] with which I walked

when on foot were strapped to my saddle."6  Such heroic

dedication did not go unnoticed, for the Washington

Chronicle cited Warner as "an example worthy of

imitation."7  At Gettysburg Warner's troops did not engage

in heavy fighting and suffered only limited casualties of

two dead and five wounded.8
```

The superscript numbers go outside the marks of punctuation. The use of "[sic]" indicates exact quotation, even to the point of typing an apparent error. Avoid placing one superscript at the end of a long paragraph because readers will not know if it refers to the final sentence only or to the entire paragraph. If you introduce borrowed materials with an authority's name and then place a superscript numeral at the end, you direct the reader to the full extent of the borrowed material.

Footnotes   Place footnotes at the bottom of pages to correspond with superscript numerals (see immediately above). Some papers will require footnotes on almost every page. Follow these conventions:

1. **Spacing.** Single-space footnotes, but double-space between notes.
2. **Indention.** Indent the first line five spaces, use a raised superscript numeral with no space between it and the first word of the note.
3. **Numbering.** Number the notes consecutively throughout the entire paper.
4. **Placement.** Collect at the bottom of each page all footnotes to citations made on that page.
5. **Distinguish footnotes from text.** Separate footnotes from the text by triple-spacing or, if you prefer, by a twelve-space bar line from the left margin.
6. **Footnote form.** Basic forms of notes should conform to the following:

For a Book.

```
    1Bill Moyers, A World of Ideas, ed. Betty Sue Flowers
(New York: Doubleday, 1989), 28.
```

For a Journal Article.

²Duane F. Alwin and Jon A. Krosnick, "Aging, Cohorts, and the Stability of Sociopolitical Orientation over the Life Span," <u>American Journal of Sociology</u> 97 (1991): 169–75.

For a Collection.

³Lonne Elder, "Ceremonies in Dark Old Men," in <u>New Black Playwrights: An Anthology</u>, ed. William Couch, Jr. (Baton Rouge: Louisiana State University Press, 1968), 62–63.

For an Edition with Multiple Authors.

⁴Albert C. Baugh, et al. <u>A Literacy History of England</u>. 2nd ed. (New York: Appleton, 1967), 602–11.

For a Magazine Article.

⁵Nicholas von Hoffman, "The White House News Hole," <u>The New Republic</u>, 6 September 1982, 19–23.

For a Newspaper Article.

⁶Karen Grassmuck, "More Small Colleges Merge with Larger Ones, But Some Find the Process Can Be Painful," <u>The Chronicle of Higher Education</u>, 18 September 1991, A1, A37–A39.

For a Review Article.

⁷John Gardner, review of <u>Falconer</u>, by John Cheever, <u>Saturday Review</u>, 2 April 1977, 20.

7. **Subsequent footnote references** after a first full reference should be shortened to author's name and page number. When an author has two works mentioned, employ a shortened version of the title: "³Jones, *Paine*, 25." In general, avoid latinate abbreviations, such as *loc. cit.* or *op. cit.;* however, whenever a note refers to the source in the immediately preceding note, you may use "*Ibid.*" with a page number, as shown next (note especially the difference between notes 4 and 6):

[3]S. C. Kleene, Introduction to Metamathematics (Princeton, NJ: Van Nostrand, 1964), 24.

[4]Ibid., 27.

[5]Abraham J. Heschel, Man Is Not Alone: A Philosophy of Religion (New York: Farrar, Straus, and Young, 1951), 221.

[6]Kleene, 24.

[7]Ibid., 27.

8. **Endnotes.** With permission of your instructor, put all your notes together as a single group of endnotes to lessen the burden of typing the paper. Follow these conventions:

a. Begin notes on a new page at the end of the text.

b. Entitle the page "Notes," centered, and placed one inch from the top of the page. This page is unnumbered, but number all other pages of endnotes.

c. Indent the first line of each note five spaces, type the note number slightly above the line, begin the note with no intervening space, and use the left margin for succeeding lines.

d. Double-space the notes and double-space between the notes.

e. Triple-space between the heading and the first note.

Conform to the following sample:

Notes

[1]W. V. Quine, Word and Object (Cambridge, MA: MIT Press, 1966), 8.

[2]G. S. Boolos, "On Second-Order Logic," Journal of Philosophy, 72 (1975): 509–510.

[3]S. C. Kleene, Introduction to Metamathematics (Princeton, NJ: Van Nostrand, 1964), 24.

[4]Ibid., 27.

[5]Abraham J. Heschel, Man Is Not Alone: A Philosophy of Religion (New York: Farrar, Straus, and Young, 1951), 221.

[6]Kleene, 24.

[7]Ibid., 27.

[8]Heschel, 222.

[9]Boolos, 509.

11i USING THE FOOTNOTE SYSTEM FOR PAPERS IN THE HUMANITIES

History   Philosophy   Religion   Theology

In-Text Citation   Use the form of raised superscript numerals as explained above, Section 11h, 328–29.

List of References   Place the references at the bottom of each page on which a citation occurs. See explanation above, 329–31, and duplicate the form and style of the following footnotes:

Footnotes for a Paper on Religion

¹Jo Ann Hackett, "Can a Sexist Model Liberate Us? Ancient New Eastern 'Fertility' Goddesses," Journal of Feminist Studies in Religion, 5 (1989): 457–58.

²E. E. Evans-Pritchard, Nuer Religion (Oxford: Clarendon Press, 1956), 84.

³Claude Lévi-Strauss, The Savage Mind (Chicago: University of Chicago Press, 1966), chap. 9, esp. p. 312.

⁴Ibid., 314.

⁵Ibid.

⁶E. E. Evans-Pritchard, Theories of Primitive Religion (Oxford: Clarendon Press, 1965), chap. 2.

⁷Evans-Pritchard, Nuer, 85.

⁸Evans-Pritchard, Primitive Religion, 46.

⁹Humphries, P. T., "Salvation Today, Not Tomorrow," Sermon (Bowling Green, KY: First Methodist Church, 1984).

¹⁰Rom. 6:2.

¹¹1 Cor. 13:1–3.

¹²The Church and the Law of Nullity of Marriage, Report of a Commission Appointed by the Archbishops of Canterbury and York in 1949 (London: Society for Promoting Christian Knowledge, 1955), 12–16.

Footnotes for a History Paper

¹G. E. Thomas, "Puritans, Indians, and the Concept of Race," New England Quarterly 48 (1975): 3–27.

[2]Thomas Jefferson, Notes on the State of Virginia (1784), ed. William Peden (Chapel Hill, NC: University of North Carolina Press, 1955), 59.

[3]Harold Child, "Jane Austen," in The Cambridge History of English Literature, ed. A. W. Ward and A. R. Waller (London: Cambridge University Press, 1927), 12:231–44.

[4]Encyclopaedia Britannica: Macropaedia, 1974 ed., s.v. "Heidegger, Martin."

Note: "s.v." means *sub verbo,* "under the word(s)."

[5]Henry Steele Commager, The Nature and Study of History, Social Science Seminar Series (Columbus, OH: Merrill, 1965), 10.

[6]Dept. of the Treasury, "Financial Operations of Government Agencies and Funds," Treasury Bulletin (Washington, DC: GPO, June 1974), 134–41.

[7]Constitution, Art. 1, sec. 4.

[8]Great Britain, Coroner's Act, 1954, 2 & 3 Eliz. 2, ch. 31.

[9]State v. Lane, Minnesota 263 N. W. 608 (1935).

[10]Ibid., clipping from the Washington Chronicle.

[11]Dan Beaver, "Conscience and Context: The Popish Plot and the Politics of Ritual, 1678–1682," Historical Journal 34 (1991): 297–327.

[12]Papers of Gen. A. J. Warner (P–973, Service Record and Short Autobiography), 1968(?) Western Reserve Historical Society.

Note: The use of a question mark in parentheses after the year means the accuracy of the date is uncertain, even though portions of the papers can be dated with some accuracy.

11j USING THE FOOTNOTE SYSTEM FOR PAPERS IN THE FINE ARTS

Art   Dance   Music   Theater

Documentation for a research paper in the fine arts uses superscript numerals in the text; see Section 11h, 328–29, and footnotes or endnotes, 329–31.

Endnotes for a Paper in the Fine Arts

Notes

[1]Natasha Staller, "Melies's 'Fantastic' Cinema and the Origins of Cubism," <u>Art History</u> 12 (1989): 202–03.

[2]There are three copies of the papal brief in the archives of the German College, now situated on Via S. Nicola da Tolentino. The document is printed in Thomas D. Culley, <u>Jesuits and Music</u> (Chicago: Jesuit Historical Institute Press, 1970), 1: 358–59.

[3]Staller, 214.

[4]Denys Hay, ed., <u>The Age of the Renaissance</u>, 2nd ed. (London: Guild, 1986), 286.

[5]Aristophanes, <u>The Birds</u>, in <u>Five Comedies of Aristophanes</u>, trans. Benjamin B. Rogers (Garden City, NY: Doubleday, 1955), 1.2.12–14.

[6]Jean Bouret, <u>The Life and Work of Toulouse Lautrec</u>, trans. Daphne Woodward (New York: Abrams, n.d.), 5.

[7]Cyrus Hoy, "Fathers and Daughters in Shakespeare's Romances," in <u>Shakespeare's Romances Reconsidered</u>, ed. Carol McGinnis Kay and Henry E. Jacobs (Lincoln: University of Nebraska Press, 1978), 77–78.

[8]Lionello Venturi, <u>Botticelli</u> (Greenwich, CT: Fawcett, n.d.), plate 32, p. 214.

Note: Add "p." for page only if needed for clarity.

[9]Cotton Vitellius ms, A., 15. British Museum.

[10]<u>Ham.</u> 2.3.2.

[11]George Henry Lewes, Review of "Letters on Christian Art," by Friedrich von Schlegel, <u>Athenaeum</u> No. 1117 (1849): 296.

[12]Ron Stoppelmann, "Letters," <u>New York</u>, 23 August 1982, 8.

[13]<u>The World Book Encyclopedia</u>, 1976 ed., s.v. "Raphael."

[14]<u>The Last Tango in Paris</u>, United Artists, 1972.

¹⁵Wolfgang A. Mozart, <u>Jupiter</u>, Symphony No. 41.

¹⁶William Blake, <u>Comus</u>, a photographic reproduction in Irene Taylor, "Blake's <u>Comus</u> Designs," <u>Blake Studies</u> 4 (Spring, 1972): 61, plate 4.

¹⁷Lawrence Topp, <u>The Artistry of Van Gogh</u> (New York: Matson, 1983), transparency 21.

¹⁸Eric Sevareid, <u>CBS News</u> (New York: CBS-TV, 11 March 1975); Media Services Videotape 1975-142 (Nashville: Vanderbilt Univ., 1975).

¹⁹Zipperer, Daniel, "The Alexander Technique as a Supplement to Voice Production," <u>Journal of Research in Singing</u> 14 (June 1991): 1-40.

11k WRITING A BIBLIOGRAPHY PAGE FOR A PAPER THAT USES FOOTNOTES

In addition to footnotes or endnotes, you may need to supply a separate bibliography page that lists sources used in developing the paper. Use a heading that represents its contents, such as "Selected Bibliography," "Sources Consulted," or "Works Cited." *Note:* If you write completely documented footnotes, the bibliography is redundant. Check with your instructor before preparing one because it may not be required. Separate the title from the first entry with a triple space. Type the first line of each entry flush left; indent the second line and other succeeding lines five spaces. Alphabetize the list by last names of authors. List alphabetically by title two or more works by one author. The basic forms are:

For a Book.

Mapp, Alf J., Jr. <u>Thomas Jefferson: A Strange Case of Mistaken Identity</u>. New York: Madison, 1987.

For a Journal Article.

Aueston, John C. "Altering the Course of the Constitutional Convention." <u>Yale Law Journal</u> 100 (1990): 765-783.

For a Newspaper.

Stephenson, D. Grier, Jr. "Is the Bill of Rights in Danger?" <u>USA Today</u> 12 May 1991: 82+.

See also the bibliographies to the sample papers, 236 and 248-49.

Appendix*

Index to the List of Reference Sources, by Discipline

*Revised and annotated by Anne May Berwind, head of Library Information Services, Austin Peay State University.

List of Reference Sources, by Discipline

The double asterisk (**) before an entry is a signal to the most important sources within a discipline. A brief annotation explains the nature of these special reference works.

Art

Basic Sources and Guides to Art Literature

American Art Directory. New York: Bowker, 1952–present.

**Arntzen, E., and R. Rainwater. *Guide to the Literature of Art History.* Chicago: ALA, 1980.

A comprehensive listing of sources in art history worldwide. A section on general reference sources is followed by sections on individual arts (e.g., sculpture), which are organized by time period and by country. Has a subject index.

Art Education: A Guide to Information Sources. Detroit: Gale, 1977.

Art Library Manual: A Guide to Resources and Practice. Ed. Philip Pacey. New York: Bowker, 1979.

Art Research Methods and Resources: A Guide to Finding Art Information. Ed. L. S. Jones. Dubuque, IA: Kendall/Hunt, 1985.

A Biographical Dictionary of Women Artists in Europe and America Since 1850. Ed. P. Dunford. Philadelphia: U of Penn. P, 1990.

Britannica Encyclopaedia of American Art. Ed. M. Rugoff. Chicago: Encyclopaedia Britannica, 1973.

Contemporary Architects. 2nd ed. Chicago: St. James, 1987.

Contemporary Artists. 3rd ed. New York: St. James, 1989.

Contemporary Designers. 2nd ed. Chicago: St. James, 1988.

Contemporary Photographers. 2nd ed. Chicago: St. James, 1988.

De La Croix, Horst, and Richard G. Tansey. *Art Through the Ages.* 7th ed. 2 vols. New York: Harcourt, 1980.

Dictionary of American Painters, Sculptors, and Engravers. Ed. Mantle Fielding. Poughkeepsie, NY: Apollo, 1986.

Dictionary of Contemporary American Artists. 5th ed. New York: St. Martin's, 1988.

Encyclopedia of American Art. New York: Dutton, 1981.

Encyclopedia of Architecture. Ed. S. A. Wilkes and R. T. Packard. New York: Wiley, 1988–90.

**Encyclopedia of World Art.* 15 vols. New York: McGraw, 1959–68. Supplements, 1983 and 1987.

An international, scholarly encyclopedia covering all aspects of art. Articles are historical (e.g., baroque art), conceptual (e.g., biblical subjects), and geographical (e.g., the Americas), so it is best to use the index volume to determine where a particular subject or artist will be found.

Fine and Applied Arts Terms Index. Detroit: Gale, 1983.

Fletcher, Bannister. *A History of Architecture.* 18th ed. New York: Macmillan, 1975. [Lists vital information on every important building.]

Guide to Art Reference Books. Chicago: ALA, 1959.

Guide to Basic Information Sources in the Visual Arts. Ed. Gerd Muehsam. Santa Barbara: ABC/Clio, 1977.

Historical Art Index A.D. 400–1650: People, Places, and Events Depicted. Jefferson City, NC: McFarland, 1989.

How to Find Out in Architecture and Building: A Guide to Sources of Information. Riverside, NJ: Pergamon, 1967.

Larousse Dictionary of Painters. New York: Larousse, 1981.

Macmillan Encyclopedia of Architects. 4 vols. New York: Free, 1982.

The New International Illustrated Encyclopedia of Art. 24 vols. New York: Greystone, 1967.

Oxford Companion to Twentieth Century Art. New York: Oxford UP, 1981.

Oxford Illustrated Encyclopedia of the Arts. New York: Oxford UP, 1990.

Pelican History of Art. 50 vols. in progress. Baltimore: Penguin, 1953–present.

Print Index: A Guide to Reproductions. Comp. P. J. Parry and Kathe Chipman. Westport, CT: Greenwood, 1983.

Random House Library of Painting and Sculpture. 4 vols. New York: Beazley, 1981.

Research Guide to the History of Western Art. Chicago: ALA, 1982.

Who's Who in American Art. New York: Bowker, 1935–present. Annually.

Bibliographies to Art Books and Other Sources

Annotated Bibliography of Fine Art. 1897; rpt. Boston: Longwood, 1976.

Applied and Decorative Arts: A Bibliographic Guide. Ed. D. L. Ehresmann. Englewood, CO: Libraries Unlimited, 1977.

Art Books. 1876–1949. New York: Bowker, 1981. Supps. cover 1950–79 and 1980–84.

Arts in America: A Bibliography. Ed. Bernard Karpel. 4 vols. Washington: Smithsonian, 1979–80.

Bibliographic Guide to Art and Architecture. Boston: Hall, 1977–85.

Fine Arts: A Bibliographic Guide. Ed. D. L. Ehresmann. 2nd ed. Littleton: Libraries Unlimited, 1979.

Electronic Sources to Art Information

ACADEMIC INDEX
ARCHITECTURE DATABASE (RILA)
ARTBIBLIOGRAPHIES MODERN
ART LITERATURE INTERNATIONAL (RILA)
ARTS & HUMANITIES SEARCH
WILSONDISC: ART INDEX

Indexes to Journal Articles

ARTbibliographies Modern. Santa Barbara: ABC/Clio, 1969–present.

**Art Index.* New York: Bowker, 1929–present.

Indexes most art journals, such as *American Art Journal, Art Bulletin, Artforum, Design, Sculpture Review,* and many others.

RILA. Repertoire International de la Literature de l'Art. Williamstown, MA: RILA, 1975–present.

Biological Sciences

Basic Sources and Guides to the Literature

Biolexicon: A Guide to the Language of Biology. Springfield, IL: Thomas, 1990.

Biology Data Book. Ed. P. L. Altman and Dorothy S. Dittmer. 2nd ed. 3 vols. Madison: FASEB, 1972–74.

Dictionary of Biology. 6th ed. Baltimore: Penguin, 1978.

Encyclopedia of Bioethics. 2 vols. New York: Macmillan, 1982.

Encyclopedia of the Biological Sciences. Ed. Peter Gray. 2nd ed. New York: Reinhold, 1970.

Grzimek's Encyclopedia of Mammals. 5 vols. New York: McGraw, 1990.

Guide to the Literature of the Life Sciences. Ed. R. C. Smith and W. M. Reid. 9th ed. Minneapolis: Burgess, 1980.

Guide to Sources for Agricultural and Biological Research. Berkeley: U of California P, 1981.

Henderson's Dictionary of Biological Terms. Ed. E. Lawrence. 10th ed. New York: Wiley, 1987.

**Information Sources in the Life Sciences.* Ed. H. V. Wyatt. 3rd ed. London: Butterworth, 1987.

Consists of in-depth bibliographic essays on the literature of biology. Includes chapters focusing on subspecialties, such as microbiology.

Library Research Guide to Biology: Illustrated Search Strategy and Sources. Ann Arbor: Pierian, 1978.

Magill's Survey of Science: Life Science Series. Ed. F. Magill. 6 vols. Englewood Cliffs, NJ: Salem, 1991.

Bibliographies to Books and Other Sources in the Biological Sciences

Bibliography of Bioethics. Detroit: Gale, 1975–present.

Biological Abstracts. Philadelphia: Biological Abstracts, 1926–present.

Botanical Bibliographies: A Guide to Bibliographical Materials Applicable to Botany. Monticello: Lubrecht & Cramer, 1974.

Electronic Sources to Biology Literature

ACRICOLA
AGRIS INTERNATIONAL
AQUACULTURE
BIOSIS PREVIEWS
LIFE SCIENCES COLLECTION
SCISEARCH
WILSONDISC: BIOLOGICAL & AGRICULTURAL INDEX
ZOOLOGICAL RECORD

Indexes to Journal Articles in the Biological Sciences

**Biological Abstracts.* Philadelphia: Biological Abstracts, 1926–present.

Indexes and gives brief descriptions of books and journal articles, especially journals such as *American Journal of*

Anatomy, American Zoologist,
Biochemistry, Journal of Animal
Behavior, Quarterly Review of Biology,
Social Biology, and many others.

**Biological and Agricultural Index. New
York: Wilson, 1964–present.

Indexes about 275 periodicals, including
*American Journal of Physiology, Field
Crops Research, Human Biology, Journal
of Bacteriology,* and *Quarterly Review of
Biology.*

General Science Index. New York: Wilson,
1978–present.

Covers about 100 science periodicals,
including *American Naturalist,
Biological Bulletin,* and *Human Biology.*

Business

See also Economics, 342–43.

Basic Sources and Guides to Business Literature

AMA Management Handbook. Ed. William
K. Fallon. 2nd ed. New York: AMA, 1983.

*American Economic and Business History:
Information Sources.* Detroit: Gale,
1971.

Basic Business Library: Core Resources.
Ed. Bernard S. Schlessinger. 2nd ed.
Phoenix: Oryx, 1989.

Business Information Desk Reference. New
York: Macmillan, 1991.

A Business Information Guidebook. Ed. O.
Figueroa and C. Winkler. New York:
AMA, 1980.

**Business Information Sources. Ed. L. M.
Daniells. Berkeley: U of California P,
1985.

A selective guide to business sources,
arranged by subject area (e.g.,
insurance). Within each subject area are
listed several recommended reference
sources, by type (e.g., handbooks).

Business Rankings and Salaries Index.
Detroit: Gale, 1988.

Dictionary for Business and Finance. 2nd
ed. Fayetteville: U of Arkansas P, 1990.

*Dow Jones-Irwin Business and Investment
Almanac.* New York: Dow Jones-Irwin,
annually.

*Encyclopedia of American Business
History and Biography.* 50 vols. Ed.
W. H. Baker. New York: Facts on File,
1987–present (in progress).

Encyclopedia of Banking and Finance. 9th
ed. Boston: Bankers, 1991.

*Encyclopedia of Business Information
Sources.* 7th ed. Ed. J. Woy. Detroit:
Gale, 1988; supp. 1989.

Encyclopedia of Management. Ed. Carl
Heyel. 3rd ed. New York: Van Nostrand,
1982.

Handbook of Business Information.
Englewood, CO: Libraries Unlimited,
1988.

The Real Estate Industry. Phoenix: Oryx,
1987.

*Use of Management and Business
Literature.* Ed. K. D. C. Vernon. London:
Butterworth, 1975.

Where to Find Business Information. 2nd
ed. New York: Wiley, 1982.

Bibliographies to Business Books and Other Sources

*Bibliographic Guide to Business and
Economics.* 3 vols. Boston: Hall,
1975–present. Annually.

Business Publications Index and Abstracts.
Detroit: Gale, 1983–present. Annually.

Core Collection. Cambridge, MA: Harvard,
1971–present. Annually.

*Historical Bibliography of Administration,
Business, and Management.* Ed. D. D.
Van Fleet. Monticello: Vance Biblios.,
1978.

Electronic Sources to Business Information

ABI/INFORM
ACADEMIC INDEX
AGRIBUSINESS U.S.A.
BUSINESSWIRE
CENDATA
D&B DUN'S FINANCIAL RECORDS
D&B ELECTRONIC YELLOW PAGES
DISCLOSURE
ECONOMIC LITERATURE INDEX
FINIS (Financial Industry National
Information Service)
LABORLAW
MANAGEMENT CONTENTS
MOODY'S CORPORATE NEWS
PTS F&S INDEXES
PTS PROMPT
STANDARD & POOR'S NEWS
TRADE AND INDUSTRY INDEX
WILSONDISC: BUSINESS PERIODICALS
INDEX

Indexes to Business Journal Articles

**Accountants' Index. New York: AICPA,
1921–present.

Indexes accounting and tax subjects in
journals such as *Accountants' Digest,*

Accounting Review, Banker's Magazine, CA Magazine, Journal of Finance, Tax Adviser, and many others.

Business Periodicals Index. New York: Wilson, 1958–present.

Indexes journals such as *Business Quarterly, Business Week, Fortune, Journal of Business, Journal of Marketing, Personnel Journal,* and many others.

Personnel Literature. Washington, DC: OPM Library, 1942–present.

Indexes articles on personnel management.

The Wall Street Journal Index. New York: Dow Jones, 1958–present. Annually.

Indexes the *Wall Street Journal* and *Barron's.*

Chemistry and Chemical Engineering

Basic Sources and Guides to Chemistry Literature

Chemical Engineers' Handbook. 6th ed. New York: McGraw, 1984.

Chemical Industries Information Sources. Ed. T. P. Peck. Detroit: Gale, 1979.

Chemical Publications, Their Nature and Use. New York: McGraw, 1982.

The Chemist's Companion: A Handbook. Ed. A. J. Gordon and R. A. Ford. New York: Wiley, 1972.

CRC Handbook of Chemistry and Physics. Boca Raton: CRC, annually.

Dictionary of Chemistry. 2 vols. New York: International, 1969.

Encyclopedia of Chemistry. 4th ed. New York: Van Nostrand, 1977.

Guide to Basic Information Sources in Chemistry. Ed. Arthur Antony. New York: Wiley, 1979.

Handbook for Authors. Washington, DC: ACS, 1978.

How to Find Chemical Information: A Guide for Practicing Chemists, Teachers, and Students. Ed. R. E. Maizell. 2nd ed. New York: Wiley, 1987.

A detailed overview of selected sources in chemistry. Good explanations of how to use major sources (e.g., *Chemical Abstracts*). Also covers online searching and patents.

How to Find Out in Chemistry. Ed. C. R. Burman. 2nd ed. Elmsford, NY: Pergamon, 1967.

Literature of Chemical Technology. Ed. T. E. Singer and J. F. Smith. Washington, DC: ACS, 1968.

Research in the Chemical Industry. Ed. A. Baines. Englewood Cliffs, NJ: Burgess, 1969.

Riegel's Handbook of Industrial Chemistry. 8th ed. New York: Reinhold, 1983.

Searching the Chemical Literature. Washington: ACS, 1961.

Use of Chemical Literature. Ed. R. T. Bottle. 3rd ed. London: Butterworth, 1979.

Using the Chemical Literature: A Practical Guide. New York: Dekker, 1974.

Bibliographies to Chemistry Books and Other Sources

Chemical Abstracts. Columbus, OH: ACS, 1907–present. Weekly.

Chemical Titles. Columbus, OH: ACS, 1960. Biweekly.

Selected Titles in Chemistry. 4th ed. Washington, DC: ACS, 1977.

Electronic Sources to Chemical Literature

BEILSTEIN ONLINE
CA SEARCH
CHEMICAL INDUSTRY NOTES
CHEMNAME
CHEMSIS
CLAIMS/U.S. PATENTS ABSTRACTS
COMPENDEX
HEILBRON
INSPEC
NTIS
SCISEARCH
WILSONDISC: GENERAL SCIENCE INDEX

Indexes of Journal Articles to Chemistry and Chemical Engineering

Chemical Abstracts: Key to the World's Chemical Literature. Easton: ACS, 1907–present. Weekly.

Indexes such journals as *Applied Chemical News, American Chemical Society Journal, Chemical Bulletin, Chemist, Journal of the American Chemical Society,* and many more. Provides a good abstract even if your library does not house the journal.

General Science Index. New York: Wilson, 1978–present.

Covers about 100 science periodicals, including *Analytical Chemistry, Inorganic Chemistry,* and *Journal of Organic Chemistry.*

Computer Science

Basic Sources and Guides to Computer Science Literature

Computer Dictionary and Handbook. 4th ed. Indianapolis: Sams, 1985.
Computer Dictionary for Everyone. Ed. Donald Spencer. New York: Scribner's, 1981.
Computer Sciences Resources: A Guide to Professional Literature. Ed. D. Myers. White Plains, NY: Knowledge Industries, 1981.
Dictionary of Computing. 3rd ed. New York: Oxford UP, 1990.
Encyclopedia of Computer Science and Technology. Ed. Jack Belzer. 21 vols. New York: Dekker, 1975–89.
McGraw-Hill Personal Computer Programming Encyclopedia. 2nd ed. New York: McGraw, 1989.
***Scientific and Technical Information Sources.* Ed. C. Chen. 2nd ed. Cambridge, MA: MIT P, 1988.

A useful source for identifying sources to consult in this field. Includes computer science as a section within each chapter on types of sources (e.g., bibliographies, handbooks).

Bibliographies to Computer Books and Other Sources on Data Processing

ACM Guide to Computing Literature. 1978–present. Annually.
Bibliographic Guide to the History of Computing, Computers, and the Information Processing Industry. Westport, CT: Greenwood, 1990.
Computer-Readable Bibliographic Data Bases: A Directory and Data Sourcebook. Washington, DC: ASIS, 1976–present.

Electronic Sources to Computer Information

BUSINESS SOFTWARE DATABASE
COMPENDEX PLUS
COMPUTER DATABASE
COMPUTER-READABLE DATABASES
INSPEC

MICROCOMPUTER INDEX
WILSONDISC: APPLIED SCIENCE AND TECHNOLOGY

Indexes to Journal Articles on Computers

***Applied Science and Technology Index.* New York: Wilson, 1958–present.

Indexes articles in *Byte, Computer Design, Computers in Industry, The Computer Journal, Computer Methods, Computer, Data Processing,* and *Microcomputing.*

Computer Abstracts. Great Britain: Technical Information, 1957–present.
Computer Literature Index. Phoenix: ACR, 1971–present.

Ecology

Basic Sources and Guides to Environmental Literature

Atlas of United States Environmental Issues. New York: Macmillan, 1991.
Earth Care Annual. Emmaus, PA: Rodale, 1990.
Encyclopedia of Community Planning and Environmental Protection. Ed. Marilyn Schultz and Vivian Kasen. New York: Facts on File, 1983.
Energy Information Guide. Ed. David R. Weber. Santa Barbara: ABC/Clio, 1982–83.
Environment Information Access. New York: EIC, 1971–present.
The Last Rain Forest: A World Conservation Atlas. New York: Oxford UP, 1990.
***World Resources.* New York: Oxford UP, 1986–present. Annually.

Contains chapters on conditions and trends in the environment worldwide (e.g., energy). Also provides statistical tables (e.g., "net additions to the greenhouse heating effect").

Bibliographies to Environmental Books and Other Sources

Energy Abstracts for Policy Analysis. Oak Ridge, TN: TIC, 1975–89.
Environment Abstracts. New York: EIC, 1971–present.
Pollution Abstracts. Washington, DC: Cambridge Scientific Abstracts, 1970–present.
Selected Water Resources Abstracts. Springfield, VA: NTIS, 1968–present.

Electronic Sources to Environmental Literature

ACADEMIC INDEX
BIOSIS PREVIEWS
COMPENDEX
ENVIRONLINE
ENVIRONMENTAL BIBLIOGRAPHY
GEOBASE
POLLUTION ABSTRACTS
TOXLINE
WATER RESOURCES ABSTRACTS
WILSONDISC: APPLIED SCIENCE AND
TECHNOLOGY
WILSONDISC: BIOLOGICAL AND
AGRICULTURAL INDEXES

Indexes to Journal Articles on Environmental Issues

***Biological Abstracts.* Philadelphia:
Biological Abstracts, 1926–present.

Indexes articles on environmental issues
in journals such as *American Forests,
The Conservationist, Florida Naturalist,
Journal of Soil and Water Conservation,
The Living Wilderness, Sierra, Ambio,
Ecology, Environmental Pollution,* and
others.

***Biological and Agricultural Index.* New
York: Wilson, 1964–present.

Includes coverage of *Ecology,
Environmental Pollution, Forest Ecology
and Management,* and *Journal of
Environmental Biology,* as well as
others.

Ecological Abstracts. Norwich, England:
Geo Abstracts, 1974–present.

***Environmental Index.* New York: EIC,
1971–present.

Gives additional indexing of other
journals, such as *Environment,
Environmental Ethics, Journal of
Applied Ecology, Solar Age,* and others.

***General Science Index.* New York:
Wilson, 1978–present.

Covers about 100 science periodicals,
including *Ecologist, Ecology,* and
Environmental Science and Technology.

Economics

See also Business, 339–40.

Basic Sources and Guides to Economics Literature

American Dictionary of Economics. Ed.
Douglas Auld et al. New York: Facts on
File, 1983.

*Dictionary of Banking and Financial
Services.* Ed. J. M. Rosenberg. New York:
Wiley, 1985.

Economic Handbook of the World. Ed.
A. S. Banks et al. New York: McGraw,
1981.

Emory, C. William. *Business Research
Methods.* 4th ed. Homewood, IL: Irwin,
1990.

Encyclopedia of Economics. New York:
McGraw, 1982.

***Information Sources in Economics.* Ed.
J. Fletcher. 2nd ed. London:
Butterworth, 1984.

Covers research sources, by type (e.g.,
databases) and also by different subject
areas of economics (e.g.,
macroeconomics). Describes and
evaluates the sources listed.

***The New Palgrave: A Dictionary of
Economics.* Ed. J. Fletcher. 4 vols. New
York: Stockton, 1987.

A scholarly, thoroughly documented
work that covers all aspects of economic
theory and thought. The bibliographies
following each article will be very
helpful.

*Studies in Economics and Economic
History.* Ed. Marcelle Kooy. Durham,
NC: Duke UP, 1972.

Who's Who in Hard Money Economics.
Mill Valley, CA: Matlock-Silber, 1981.

*Bibliographies to Economics Books
and Other Sources*

*Bibliographic Guide to Business and
Economics.* Boston: Hall, 1975–present.
Annually.

Business and Economics Book Guide. 2
vols. Boston: Hall, 1974. Supplements.

*Economics: Bibliographic Guide to
Reference Books and Information
Resources.* Ed. Peter Melnyk. Englewood,
CO: Libraries Unlimited, 1971.

Economics Books. Clifton, NJ: Kelley,
1974–present. Annually.

*Select Bibliography of Modern Economic
Theory: 1870–1929.* Ed. Harold E.
Batson. Clifton, NJ: Kelley, 1930.

*Special Bibliography in Monetary
Economics and Finance.* Ed. J. Cohen.
New York: Gordon, 1976.

*Electronic Sources to Economics
Literature*

ACADEMIC INDEX
ECONBASE: TIME SERIES AND
FORECASTS

ECONOMIC LITERATURE INDEX
FOREIGN TRADE AND ECONOMIC
  ABSTRACTS
PTS INTERNATIONAL FORECASTS
PTS U.S. FORECASTS

Indexes to Economic Journal Articles

Index of Economic Articles. Homewood,
  IL: Irwin, 1961–present.
**Journal of Economic Literature.*
  Nashville: AEA, 1964–present.

  Indexes such journals as *American
  Economist, Applied Economics, Business
  Economics, Economic History Review,
  Economic Journal, Federal Reserve
  Bulletin, Journal of Economic Issues,*
  and many more.

The Wall Street Journal Index. New York:
  Dow Jones, 1958–present.

Education

Basic Sources and Guides to Education Literature

***Education: A Guide to Reference and
  Information Sources.* Englewood, CO:
  Libraries Unlimited, 1989.

  Lists a variety of reference sources in
  education and sources in other related
  fields (e.g., social work). Each source is
  described and evaluated.

Education Journals and Serials. Ed. M. E.
  Collins. Metuchen, NJ: Scarecrow, 1988.
Educator's Desk Reference. New York:
  Macmillan, 1989.
The Encyclopedia of Education. Ed. L. C.
  Deighton. 10 vols. New York: Macmillan,
  1971.
Encyclopedia of Education. New York:
  Philosophical Library, 1970.
Encyclopedia of Educational Research. Ed.
  H. E. Mitzel. 5th ed. 4 vols. New York:
  Free, 1982.
*A Guide to Sources of Educational
  Information.* Ed. M. L. Woodbury. 2nd
  ed. Arlington: Information Resources,
  1982.
Handbook of Research on Teaching. Ed. M.
  C. Wittrock. 3rd ed. New York:
  Macmillan, 1986.
International Encyclopedia of Education.
  Ed. T. Husen and T. N. Postlethwaite. 10
  vols. Elmsford, NY: Pergamon, 1985.
International Yearbook of Education.
  Paris: UNESCO, 1948–present.

Library Research Guide to Education. Ed.
  J. R. Kennedy. Ann Arbor, MI: Pierian,
  1979.
Multicultural Education: A Source Book.
  New York: Garland, 1989.
*Philosophy of Education: A Guide to
  Information Sources.* Ed. C. A. Baatz.
  Detroit: Gale, 1980.
*Second Handbook of Research on
  Teaching.* Ed. R. M. W. Travers. Chicago:
  Rand, 1973.
World Education Encyclopedia. 3 vols.
  New York: Facts on File, 1988.

Bibliographies to Education Books and Other Sources

Bibliographic Guide to Education. Boston:
  Hall, 1978–present.
*Bibliographic Guide to Educational
  Research.* Ed. D. M. Berry. 2nd ed.
  Metuchen, NJ: Scarecrow, 1980.
Resources in Education (formerly *Research
  in Education*). Washington, DC: ERIC,
  1956–present.
*Subject Bibliography of the History of
  American Higher Education.* Westport,
  CT: Greenwood, 1984.

Electronic Sources to Education Literature

ACADEMIC INDEX
A-V ONLINE (nonprint educational
  materials)
ERIC
EXCEPTIONAL CHILD EDUCATION
  RESOURCES
WILSONDISC: EDUCATION INDEX

Indexes to Journal Articles in Education

***Current Index to Journals in Education.*
  Phoenix: Oryx, 1969–present.
***Education Index.* New York: Wilson,
  1929–present.

  Both titles above index articles in such
  journals as *Childhood Education,
  Comparative Education, Education
  Digest, Educational Forum, Educational
  Review, Educational Studies, Journal of
  Educational Psychology, Review of
  Education,* and many more.

Exceptional Child Education Resources.
  Reston, VA: CEC, 1968–present.
State Education Journal Index.
  Westminster, CO: SEJI, 1963–present.

Electronics

Basic Sources and Guides to Electronics Literature

Buchsbaum's Complete Handbook of Practical Electronics Reference Data. 2nd ed. Englewood Cliffs, NJ: Prentice, 1987.

Dictionary of Electronics. Ed. S. W. Amos. 2nd ed. Boston: Butterworth, 1987.

Electronic Properties of Materials: A Guide to the Literature. 3 vols. New York: Plenum, 1965–71.

Electronic Properties Research Literature Retrieval Guide. 4 vols. New York: Plenum, 1979.

Electronics Style Manual. Ed. John Markus. New York: McGraw, 1978.

Encyclopedia of Computer Science and Technology. Ed. Jack Belzer. 21 vols. New York: Dekker, 1975–89.

Encyclopedia of Electronics. 2nd ed. Ed. E. S. Gibilisco and N. Sclater. Blue Ridge Summit, PA: TAB, 1990.

***A Guide to the Literature of Electrical and Electronics Engineering.* Ed. S. B. Ardis. Englewood, CO: Libraries Unlimited, 1987.

A listing of research sources in engineering, this guide is useful for choosing where to start looking for information.

Handbook of Modern Electronics and Electrical Engineering. New York: Wiley, 1986.

International Encyclopedia of Robotics: Applications and Automation. 3 vols. New York: Wiley, 1988.

Modern Dictionary of Electronics. Ed. R. Graf. 6th ed. Indianapolis: Sams, 1984.

Scientific and Technical Information Sources. Ed. C. Chen. 2nd ed. Cambridge, MA: MIT, 1987.

Bibliographies to Electronics Books and Other Sources

Bibliography of the History of Electronics. Ed. George Shiers. Metuchen, NJ: Scarecrow, 1972.

Electronics: A Bibliographical Guide. Ed. C. K. Moore and K. J. Spencer. 3 vols. New York: Plenum, 1961–73.

Electronic Sources to Electronics Literature

COMPENDEX
INSPEC
SCISEARCH
SUPERTECH
WILSONDISC: APPLIED SCIENCE AND TECHNOLOGY

Indexes to Journal Articles in Electronics

***Applied Science and Technology Index.* New York: Wilson, 1958–present. Indexes electronics articles in journals such as *Bell System Technical Journal, Electrical Communication, Electrical Engineer, Electrical Review, Electronic News, Electronics, Electronics Letters,* and many more.

Engineering Index. New York: Engineering Information, 1906–present.

Ethnic Studies

Basic Sources and Guides to Ethnic Studies

Allen, James, and E. Turner. *We the People: An Atlas of America's Ethnic Diversity.* New York: Macmillan, 1988.

An Annotated Guide to the Ethnic Experience in the United States. Ed. J. Barton. Cambridge, MA: Langdon, 1976.

Dictionary of American Immigration History. Ed. F. Cordasco. Metuchen, NJ: Scarecrow, 1990.

The Ethnic Almanac. Garden City, NY: Doubleday, 1981.

Ethnic Periodicals in Contemporary America: An Annotated Guide. Ed. S. Ireland. Westport, CT: Greenwood, 1990.

Ethnic Theatre in the United States. Ed. Maxine Seller. Westport, CT: Greenwood, 1983.

Harvard Encyclopedia of American Ethnic Groups. Ed. S. Thernstrom. Cambridge, MA: Belknap/Harvard UP, 1980.

Johnson, Harry. *Ethnic American Minorities: A Guide to Media and Materials.* New York: Bowker, 1976.

Kinloch, Graham. *Race and Ethnic Relations: An Annotated Bibliography.* New York: Garland, 1984.

Kinton, Jack. *American Ethnic Groups and the Revival of Cultural Pluralism.* 4th ed. Aurora, IL: Social Science and Sociological Resources, 1974.

Miller, Wayne C., et al. *A Comprehensive Bibliography for the Study of American Minorities.* 2 vols. New York: New York UP, 1976.

Minority Organizations: A National Directory. 3rd ed. Garrett Park, MD: Garrett Park Press, 1987.

*Multi-Ethnic Media: Selected
Bibliographies in Print.* Ed. D. Cohen.
Chicago: ALA, 1975.

Guides and Bibliographies to American Indian Studies

*American Indian Novelists: An Annotated
Critical Bibliography.* New York:
Garland, 1982.
***Guide to Research on North American
Indians.* Ed. Arlene Hirschfelder.
Chicago: ALA, 1983.

Lists basic sources of information for
researching North American Indians.
Chapters cover a variety of aspects,
including history, economics, society,
religion, the arts, and literature.

Handbook of North American Indians. 20
vols. Washington, DC: Smithsonian Inst.,
1978–present (in progress).
*Indians of North America: Methods and
Sources for Library Research.* Hamden,
CT: Library Professional Pubs., 1983.
Ruoff, L. *American Indian Literature: An
Introduction, Bibliographic Review, and
Selected Bibliography.* New York: MLA,
1990.
*Studies in American Indian Literature:
Critical Essays and Course Designs.* New
York: MLA, 1983.

Guides to Asian American Studies

***Asian American Studies.* Ed. H. Kim.
Westport, CT: Greenwood, 1989.

A bibliography of books and articles
about Asian Americans. Includes
historical and cultural/sociological
studies as well. Most items listed have
brief descriptions.

Chen, Jack. *The Chinese of America.* New
York: Harper, 1982.
Cheung, K. *Asian American Literature.*
New York: MLA, 1988.
Melendy, Henry Brett. *Asians in America:
Filipinos, Koreans, and East Indians.*
New York: Hippocrene, 1981.
Montero, Darrel. *Vietnamese Americans:
Patterns of Resettlement and
Socioeconomic Adaptation in the United
States.* Boulder: Westview, 1979.
Wilson, Robert A., and Bill Hosokawa. *East
to America: A History of the Japanese in
the United States.* New York: Quill, 1980.

Guides and Bibliographies to Black American Studies

See also Black Literature, 355.

***Afro-American Reference.* Ed. N. Davis.
Westport, CT: Greenwood, 1985.

A selective listing of sources on all
aspects of the African American
experience. Lists other reference sources
as well as recommending individual
books on particular subjects (e.g.,
"blacks in motion pictures").

Bibliographic Guide to Black Studies.
Boston: Hall, 1975–present.
*A Bibliography of the Negro in Africa and
America.* Ed. M. N. Work. New York:
Octagon, 1966.
*Black Index: Afro-Americans in Selected
Periodicals 1907–1949.* New York:
Garland, 1981.
Blacks in the Humanities, 1750–1984. Ed.
D. F. Joyce. Westport, CT: Greenwood,
1986.
Blacks in Science and Medicine. Ed. V. O.
Sammons. New York: Hemisphere, 1989.
Contributions of Black Women to America.
Ed. M. W. Davis. 2 vols. Columbia, SC:
Kenday, 1982.
Dictionary of American Negro Biography.
Ed. R. W. Logan and M. R. Winton. New
York: Norton, 1982.
Encyclopedia of Black America. Ed. W. A.
Low. New York: McGraw, 1981.
Hughes, Langston, et al. *A Pictorial History
of Black Americans.* 5th rev. ed. New
York: Crown, 1983.
***In Black and White.* Ed. M. M.
Spradling. 3rd ed. Detroit: Gale, 1980.
Supplement, 1985.

A bibliography of magazine and
newspaper articles and books on 15,000
African American individuals and
organizations, past and present.

*Index to Periodical Articles by and About
Blacks.* Boston: Hall, 1973–present.
Annually.
The Negro Almanac. Ed. H. A. Ploski and
J. Williams. 5th ed. Venice, CA:
Bellwether, 1989.
*Negro in the United States: A Research
Guide.* Ed. E. K. Welsch. Bloomington:
Indiana UP, 1965.
Statistical Record of Black America.
Detroit: Gale, 1990.
Who's Who Among Black Americans.
Detroit: WWABA, 1976–present.

Guides and Bibliographies to Hispanic American Studies

Chicano Literature: A Reference Guide.
Ed. J. A. Martinez and F. A. Lomeli.
Westport, CT: Greenwood, 1985.

Hispanic American Periodicals Index. Los Angeles: UCLA Latin American Center, 1974–present.

Hispanic Americans Information Directory. Detroit: Gale, 1989.

Hispanics in the United States: A New Social Agenda. Ed. P. S. J. Cafferty and W. McCready. New Brunswick: Transaction, 1984.

Literature Chicana. Comp. R. G. Trujillo. Encino, CA: Floricanto Press, 1985.

Manual of Hispanic Bibliography. Ed. D. W. Foster and V. R. Foster. 2nd ed. New York: Garland, 1976.

¿Quien Sabe?: A Preliminary List of Chicano Reference Materials. Los Angeles: U of California Chicano Studies Research Center, 1981.

***Sourcebook of Hispanic Culture in the United States.* Chicago: ALA, 1982.

Essays surveying Mexican American, Puerto Rican American, Cuban American, and Hispanic American literature, education, sociolinguistics, and music. Each essay concludes with lengthy, evaluative bibliographies of recommended books and periodical articles, many in English.

Spanish-American Women Writers: A Bibliographical Research Checklist. Ed. L. E. R. Cortina. New York: Garland, 1982.

Statistical Handbook on U.S. Hispanics. Phoenix: Oryx, 1991.

Who's Who among Hispanic Americans. Detroit: Gale, 1991.

Electronic Sources to Ethnic Studies

ACADEMIC INDEX
AMERICA: HISTORY AND LIFE
POPULATION BIBLIOGRAPHY
SOCIAL SCISEARCH
SOCIOLOGICAL ABSTRACTS
WILSONDISC: SOCIAL SCIENCES AND HUMANITIES INDEXES

Indexes to Journal Articles on Ethnic Issues

MLA International Bibliography. New York: MLA, 1921–present.

Indexes ethnic languages and literatures.

***Social Sciences Index.* New York: Wilson, 1974–present.

Indexes articles on many minority topics in such journals as *American Journal of Physical Anthropology, Aztlan, Black Scholar, Ethnic Groups, Ethnic and Racial Studies, Ethnohistory, Ethnology, Journal of Black Studies, Journal of Ethnic Studies, Japan Quarterly, Modern Asian Studies,* and others.

Sage Race Relations Abstracts. London and Beverly Hills: Sage, 1976–present.

Sociological Abstracts. LaJolla, CA: Sociological Abstracts, 1952–present.

Foreign Languages

Basic Sources and Guides to the Literature

French

Concise Bibliography of French Literature. Ed. Denis Mahaffey. New York: Bowker, 1976.

Concise Oxford Dictionary of French Literature. Ed. J. Reid. Oxford: Clarendon, 1976.

Critical Bibliography of French Literature. Syracuse: Syracuse UP, 1947–85 (in progress).

Dictionnaire étymologique de la langue française. New York: French and European, 1975.

Dictionnaire de la litterature française contemporaine. New York: French and European, 1977.

***French Language and Literature: An Annotated Bibliography.* Ed. F. Bassan et al. 2nd ed. New York: Garland, 1989.

A listing of reference books, periodicals, and other books to consult when researching French. Includes historical and cultural aspects of French language and literature in France and other French-speaking countries.

French Literature: An Annotated Guide to Selected Bibliographies. Ed. R. Kempton. New York: MLA, 1981.

French Twenty Bibliography: Critical and Biographical References for the Study of French Literature Since 1885. Ed. D. W. Alden. New York: French Institute, 1969–present. Annually.

Grand larousse encyclopedique. 12 vols. Elmsford, NY: Maxwell, 1964. Supplements.

Modern French Literature. Ed. D. Popkin. 2 vols. New York: Ungar, 1977.

New History of French Literature. 2 vols. Cambridge, MA: Harvard UP, 1989.

Oxford Companion to French Literature. Ed. Paul Harvey and Janet Heseltine. Oxford: Clarendon, 1959.

German

Critical Bibliography of German Literature in English Translation: 1481–1927. 2nd ed. Metuchen, NJ: Scarecrow, 1965. Supplements.

Der Grosse Duden. Ed. R. Duden. 10 vols. New York: Adler's, 1971.

Deutsches Woerterbuch. Ed. Jacob Grimm and Wilhelm Grimm. 32 vols. New York: Adler's, 1973.

German Literature: A Reference Guide. Ed. U. K. Faulhaver and P. B. Goff. New York: Garland, 1979.

German Periodical Publications. Ed. G. Erdelyi and A. F. Peterson. Stanford: Hoover, 1967.

***Introduction to Library Research in German Studies.* Ed. L. Richardson. Boulder: Westview, 1984.

A listing of reference sources for research on German language, literature, art, and civilization (history, folklore, philosophy and religion, music, and cinema). Includes descriptive and evaluative comments.

Lese der Deutschen Lyrik: Von Klopstock bis Rilke. Ed. Friedrich Burns. New York: Irvington, 1961.

Oxford Companion to German Literature. Ed. H. Garland. 2nd ed. New York: Oxford UP, 1986.

Reallexikon der deutschen Literaturgeschichte. Ed. W. Kohlschmidt and W. Mohr. 3 vols. New York: DeGruyter, 1958–77.

Selected Bibliography of German Literature in English Translation: 1956–1960. Ed. M. F. Smith. Metuchen, NJ: Scarecrow, 1972.

Wer Ist Wer. 20th ed. New York: IPS, 1973. Supplements.

Latin

***Ancient Writers: Greece and Rome.* Ed. T. J. Luce. 2 vols. New York: Scribner's, 1982.

Detailed information on 47 classical authors and their works. Each article is followed by a selective listing of recommended reading.

Cambridge History of Classical Literature. New York: Cambridge UP, 1982–present (in progress).

The Classical World Bibliography of Roman Drama and Poetry and Ancient Fiction. New York: Garland, 1978.

Mackail, John W. *Latin Literature.* New York: Ungar, 1966.

McGuire, Martin R., and Hermigild Dressler. *Introduction to Medieval Latin Studies: A Syllabus and Bibliographical Guide.* 2nd ed. Washington, DC: Catholic UP, 1977.

Oxford Companion to Classical Literature. Ed. M. C. Howatson. 2nd ed. New York: Oxford UP, 1989.

Oxford Latin Dictionary. Ed. P. G. Glare. New York: Oxford UP, 1982.

Repertoire des index et lexiques d'auteurs latins. Ed. Paul Faider. 1926; rpt. New York: Burt Franklin, 1971.

Wagenvoort, Henrik. *Studies in Roman Literature, Culture and Religion.* New York: Garland, 1978.

Russian

Basic Russian Publications: A Bibliographic Guide to Western-Language Publications. Ed. P. L. Horecky. Chicago: U of Chicago P, 1965.

Basic Russian Publications: A Selected and Annotated Bibliography on Russia and the Soviet Union. Ed. P. L. Horecky. Chicago: U of Chicago P, 1962.

Bibliography of Russian Literature in English Translation to 1945. Ed. M. B. Line. 1963; rpt. Totowa, NJ: Rowman, 1972.

Bibliography of Russian Word Formation. Ed. D. S. Worth. Columbus, OH: Slavica, 1977.

Dictionary of Russian Literature. Ed. W. E. Harkins. 1956; rpt. Westport, CT: Greenwood, 1971.

Dictionary of Russian Literature since 1917. New York: Columbia UP, 1988.

Guide to Bibliographies of Russian Literature. Ed. S. A. Zenkovsky and D. L. Armbruster. Nashville: Vanderbilt UP, 1970.

Guide to Russian Reference Books. Ed. Korol Maichel. 5 vols. Stanford: Hoover, 1962–67.

***Introduction to Russian Language and Literature.* Ed. R. Auty and D. Obolensky. New York: Cambridge UP, 1977.

A survey of the history of Russian, with chapters on linguistics, printing, prose, poetry, and theater. Each chapter presents a chronological overview and includes selective bibliographies of resources, many of them in Russian.

Literature of the Soviet Peoples: A Historical and Biographical Survey. Ed. Harri Junger. New York: Ungar, 1971.

Modern Encyclopedia of Russian and Soviet Literature. Gulf Breeze, FL: Academic International, 1971–present (in progress).

Russia, the USSR, and Eastern Europe: A Bibliographic Guide to English Language Publications, 1975–1980. Englewood, CO: Libraries Unlimited, 1982. Supplements, 1981–85; 1987.

Who Was Who in the U.S.S.R. Metuchen, NJ: Scarecrow, 1972.

Spanish

Anderson-Imbert, E. *Historia de la literatura hispanoamericans.* 2 vols. Mexico: Fondo, 1974.

Bibliography of Old Spanish Texts. Ed. Anthony Cardenas et al. 3rd ed. Madison: Hispanic Seminary, 1984.

Biographical Dictionary of Hispanic Literature in the United States. Westport, CT: Greenwood, 1989.

**Bleznick, Donald W. *A Sourcebook for Hispanic Literature and Language.* 2nd ed. Metuchen, NJ: Scarecrow, 1983.

Lists a selection of reference sources and other recommended reading on the literatures of Spain and Spanish America. Includes some sources written in English.

Diccionario de la literature latinoamerica. Washington, DC: OAS, 1958.

Dissertations in Hispanic Languages and Literatures: An Index of Dissertations Completed in the United States and Canada. Ed. J. R. Chatham and Carmen C. McClendon. Lexington: UP of Kentucky, 1981.

Handbook of Latin American Literature. Comp. D. W. Foster. New York: Garland, 1987.

Handbook of Latin American Studies. Gainesville: UP of Florida, 1935–present.

Historia de la literature espanola and hispanoamerica. Spain: Aguilar, 1983.

Latin American Writers. Ed. C. A. Solé. 3 vols. New York: Scribner's, 1989.

The Literature of Spain in English Translation: A Bibliography. Comp. Robert S. Rudder. New York: Ungar, 1975.

Manual of Hispanic Bibliography. 2nd ed. New York: Garland, 1977.

Modern Spanish and Portuguese Literatures. Ed. M. J. Schneider and I. Stern. New York: Ungar, 1988.

Oxford Companion to Spanish Literature. Ed. F. Ward. Oxford: Clarendon, 1978.

Spanish and Spanish-American Literature: An Annotated Guide to Selected Bibliographies. Ed. H. C. Woodbridge. New York: MLA, 1983.

Spanish American Women Writers. Ed. D. Marting. Westport, CT: Greenwood, 1990.

Electronic Sources to Foreign Language Studies

ACADEMIC INDEX
ARTS AND HUMANITIES SEARCH
LIBA (LINGUISTICS AND LANGUAGE BEHAVIOR ABSTRACTS)
MLA BIBLIOGRAPHY
WILSONDISC: HUMANITIES INDEX

Indexes to Journal Articles on Foreign Languages and Literatures

Humanities Index. New York: Wilson, 1974–present.

**MLA International Bibliography.* New York: MLA, 1921–present.

Indexes articles in journals such as *Yale French Studies, German Quarterly, Philological Quarterly, Journal of Spanish Studies,* and many others. It features special indexes to foreign language studies of the literature of the foreign country.

Geography

Basic Sources and Guides to Geography Literature

Geography and Cartography: A Reference Handbook. 3rd ed. Hamden, CT: Shoe String, 1976.

Goode's World Atlas. Ed. B. Rodner. 17th ed. Chicago: Rand, 1987.

Guide to Information Sources in the Geographical Sciences. London: Croom Helm, 1983.

**Illustrated Encyclopedia of Mankind.* 22 vols. Freeport, NY: M. Cavendish, 1989.

Good starting place for background information on the cultures of 500 different peoples of the world. Also includes articles giving cross-cultural overviews (e.g., marriage).

**The Literature of Geography: A Guide to Its Organization and Use.* 2nd ed. Hamden, CT: Shoe String, 1978.

An introductory overview of geographical research methods and materials. Includes chapters on specific areas of geography (e.g., regional) with lists of sources for research.

Modern Geography: An Encyclopedic Survey. Ed. G. S. Dunbar. New York: Garland, 1991.

Research Catalogue of the American Geographical Society. 15 vols. Boston: Hall, 1962. Supplements, 1962–76.

Source Book in Geography. Ed. George Kish. Cambridge, MA: Harvard UP, 1978.

The Times Atlas of the World. 2nd ed. New York: Times Books, 1983.

Bibliographies to Geography Books and Other Sources

Geographers: Bio-Bibliographical Studies. Ed. T. W. Freeman et al. London: Mansell, 1977–present. Annually.

Geographical Bibliography for American Libraries. Ed. C. D. Harris. Washington, DC: AAG, 1985.

Geography and Local Administration: A Bibliography. Ed. Keith Hoggart. Monticello, IL: Vancy, 1980.

International List of Geographical Serials. 3rd ed. Chicago: U of Chicago P, 1980.

Electronic Sources to Geography Information

ACADEMIC INDEX
GEOBASE
SOCIAL SCISEARCH
WILSONDISC: SOCIAL SCIENCES INDEX

Indexes to Geography Journal Articles

Geo Abstracts. Norwich, England: Geo Abstracts, 1966–present.

***Social Sciences Index.* New York: Wilson, 1974–present.

Indexes articles in such journals as *American Cartographer, Cartographic Journals, Cartography, Economic Geography, Geographical Analysis, Geographical Journal, Geographical Magazine, Geographical Review, Geography, Journal of Geography, Journal of Historical Geography,* and others.

Geology

Basic Sources and Guides to Geology Literature

Challinor's Dictionary of Geology. 6th ed. New York: Oxford UP, 1986.

***Encyclopedia of Field and General Geology.* Ed. C. W. Finkle. New York: Van Nostrand, 1982.

One volume of the Encyclopedia of Earth Sciences series. Gives technical, documented information and references to other sources.

Geologic Reference Sources: A Subject and Regional Bibliography. Ed. D. C. Ward, M. Wheeler, and R. Bier. 2nd ed. Metuchen, NJ: Scarecrow, 1981.

Glossary of Geology. Ed. R. L. Bates and J. A. Jackson. 3rd ed. Falls Church, VA: AGI, 1987.

Guide to Information Sources in Mining, Minerals, and Geosciences. Ed. S. R. Kaplan. New York: McGraw, 1978.

Magill's Survey of Science. Earth Science Series. 5 vols. Englewood Cliffs, NJ: Salem, 1990.

McGraw-Hill Encyclopedia of the Geological Sciences. New York: McGraw, 1978.

Sourcebook in Geology: Fourteen Hundred to Nineteen Hundred. Ed. K. F. Mather. Cambridge, MA: Harvard UP, 1970.

***Use of Earth Sciences Literature.* Ed. D. N. Wood. New York: Archon, 1973.

Discusses types of information sources (e.g., maps and review publications) and then provides extensive bibliographies in specific areas of geology (e.g., stratigraphy).

Bibliographies to Geology Books and Other Sources

Bibliography and Index of Geology. Boulder: GSA, monthly with annual indexes.

Bibliography of North American Geology. 49 vols. Washington, DC: Geological Survey, 1923–71.

Catalog of the U.S. Geological Survey Library. Boston: Hall, 1964. Supplements.

Geological Reference Sources: A Subject and Regional Bibliography. Ed. D. Ward, M. Wheeler, and R. Bier. Metuchen, NJ: Scarecrow, 1981.

***Publications of the Geological Survey.* Washington, DC: GPO, 1979.

An annual listing of USGS publications, updated by their monthly *New Publications of the Geological Survey.*

Strategic Minerals: A Bibliography. Waterloo, ON: U of Waterloo P, 1987.

Electronic Sources to Geology Literature

APILIT (American Petroleum Institute)
COMPENDEX
GEOARCHIVE
GEOBASE
GEOREF
INSPEC
WILSONDISC: APPLIED SCIENCE AND
TECHNOLOGY and GENERAL SCIENCE
INDEXES

Indexes to Geology Journal Articles

**Bibliography and Index of Geology.
Boulder: AGA, 1933–present.

Indexes geology journals, such as
*American Journal of Science, American
Mineralogist, Chemical Geology, Earth
Science, Geological Magazine,
Geological Society of America Bulletin,
Geology, Journal of Geology,* and others.

Bibliography and Index of Geology.
Boulder: GSA, monthly with annual
indexes.

**General Science Index. New York:
Wilson, 1978–present.

Covers about 100 science periodicals,
including *Earth Science, Geological
Society of America Bulletin,* and
Mineralogical Record.

Health and Physical Education

See also Education, 343, and Medical
Studies, 359–60.

Basic Sources and Guides to the Literature

*Author's Guide to Journals in the Health
Field.* New York: Haworth, 1980.
****Biographical Dictionary of American
Sports.** Westport, CT: Greenwood,
1987–89.

Features four separate volumes on
baseball, basketball, football, and other
outdoor sports.

Columbia Encyclopedia of Nutrition. New
York: Putnam, 1988.
*Consumer Health Information Source
Book.* 3rd ed. Phoenix: Oryx, 1989.
Encyclopedia of Sports. New York: Barnes
and Noble, 1978. Supplements.
Food and Nutrition Information Guide.
Englewood, CO: Libraries Unlimited,
1988.

*Foundations of Physical Education and
Sport.* Ed. C. A. Bucher. St. Louis:
Mosby, 1986.
*Health Maintenance Through Food and
Nutrition: A Guide to Information
Sources.* Ed. H. D. Ullrich. Detroit: Gale,
1981.
*Health Statistics: A Guide to Information
Sources.* Detroit: Gale, 1980.
****Introduction to Reference Sources in
Health Sciences.** Ed. F. Roper and J.
Boorkman. 2nd ed. Chicago: Medical
Library, 1984.

Discusses and lists health science
reference materials, bibliographic
sources, and other specialized sources
(e.g., statistical). Explains how to use
many of the sources described.

Research Processes in Physical Education.
2nd ed. Englewood Cliffs, NJ: Prentice,
1984.
****Sports and Physical Education: A Guide
to the Reference Resources.** Ed. B.
Gratcher et al. Westport, CT:
Greenwood, 1983.

Lists biographical, statistical, and other
sources on physical education and many
individual sports. Briefly describes each
source.

Vitamin and Mineral Encyclopedia. New
York: Simon, 1990.

Bibliographies to Books and Other Sources

*Annotated Bibliography of Health
Economics.* Ed. A. J. Culyer et al. New
York: St. Martin's, 1977.
*Bibliography of Research Involving Female
Subjects.* Washington, DC: AAHPER,
1975.

Electronic Sources to Literature in Health and Physical Education

ACADEMIC INDEX
ERIC
MEDLINE
SOCIAL SCISEARCH
SPORT
WILSONDISC: EDUCATION and GENERAL
SCIENCE INDEXES

Indexes to Journal Articles in Health and Physical Education

See also Education, 343, and Medical
Studies, 359–60.

Current Index to Journals in Education.
Phoenix: Oryx, 1969–present.

***Education Index.* New York: Wilson, 1929–present.

Both index articles on physical education and health education in such journals as *Journal of Physical Education and Recreation, Journal of School Health, Physical Educator, Research Quarterly for Exercise and Sport,* plus many others.

***General Science Index.* New York: Wilson, 1978–present.

Indexes 100 science journals, including *American Journal of Public Health, Health, JAMA, The Physician,* and *Sportsmedicine.*

Physical Education Index. Cape Giradeau, MO: Oak, 1978–present.

Physical Fitness and Sports Medicine. Washington, DC: GPO, 1978–present.

History

General Guides to Historical Literature

Britannica Book of the Year. Chicago: Encyclopaedia Britannica, 1938–present.

***Dictionary of American History.* 8 vols. New York: Scribner's, 1976.

Although dated, this encyclopedia is a well-documented, scholarly source for background information on the people, places, and events in U.S. history. Most of the articles include brief bibliographies of recommended sources.

Dictionary of the Middle Ages. Ed. J. R. Strayer. 13 vols. New York: Scribner's, 1982–89.

Encyclopedia of American History. Ed. Richard Morris. 6th ed. New York: Harper, 1982.

Encyclopedia of Asian History. 4 vols. New York: Scribner's, 1988.

Encyclopedia of Colonial and Revolutionary America. New York: Facts on File, 1989.

Encyclopedia of the Renaissance. New York: Facts on File, 1987.

Encyclopedia of World History. 5th ed. Boston: Houghton, 1972.

Facts on File Yearbook. New York: Facts on File, 1946–present.

Grum, B. *Timetables of History.* New York: Simon, 1979.

Guide to American Foreign Relations Since 1700. Ed. R. D. Burns. Santa Barbara: ABC/Clio, 1983.

Guide to Historical Method. Ed. R. J. Shafer. 3rd ed. Chicago: Dorsey, 1980.

***Library Research Guide to History.* Ed. E. Frick. Ann Arbor, MI: Pierian, 1980.

Step-by-step guide to using reference sources in American history. Does not list many sources, but thoroughly explains and analyzes all of the major tools in history. Good source for the beginning researcher.

McCoy, F. N. *Researching and Writing in History: A Practical Handbook for Students.* Berkeley: U of California P, 1974.

Narrative and Critical History of America. Ed. Justin Winsor. 8 vols. 1889; rpt. of 1889 ed. New York: AMS, 1978.

***Prucha, F. P. *Handbook for Research in American History.* Lincoln: U of Nebraska P, 1987.

Lists sources of information, arranged by type of material and then by subject. A good resource for comprehensive research in American history when the basic sources are exhausted.

Pulton, H. J., and M. S. Howland. *The Historian's Handbook.* Norman: U of Oklahoma P, 1986.

Research in Archives: The Use of Unpublished Primary Sources. Ed. P. C. Brooks. Chicago: U of Chicago P, 1968.

Writing History Papers. Ed. J. D. Bennett and L. H. Harrison. St. Louis: Forum, 1979.

Bibliographies to History Books and Other Sources

American: History and Life. Santa Barbara: ABC/Clio, 1964–present.

Bibliographer's Manual of American History. 5 vols. Philadelphia: Henkels, 1907–10.

Bibliography of British History. Oxford: Clarendon, 1928–77.

Combined Retrospective Indexes to Journals in History: 1838–1974. 11 vols. Woodbridge, CT: Research Publication, 1977.

English Historical Reviews.

This journal regularly features valuable bibliographies.

Goldentree Bibliographies in History. Northbrook: AHM, series.

Harvard Guide to American History. Ed. F. Freidel. Cambridge, MA: Harvard UP, 1974.

Historical Abstracts. Santa Barbara:
ABC/Clio, 1955–present.
Historical Bibliography. Ed. D. Williamson.
Hamden: Shoe String, 1967.
*International Bibliography of Historical
Sciences.* New York: Wilson,
1930–present.
Wars of the United States. New York:
Garland, 1984–present.

Series of annotated bibliographies.

Writings on American History.
Washington, DC: AHA, 1902–present.

Electronic Sources to History Literature

ACADEMIC INDEX
AMERICA: HISTORY AND LIFE
HISTORICAL ABSTRACTS
WILSONDISC: HUMANITIES INDEX

Indexes to Journal Articles in History

America: History and Life. Santa
Barbara: ABC/Clio, 1964–present.
**American Historical Association.
Recently Published Articles.**
1976–present.

Both works above index articles on
American history in journals such as
*American Historical Review, Civil War
History, Journal of American History,
Journal of the West, Reviews in
American History,* and many others.

Historical Abstracts, 1955–present.

Provides international coverage of
European and world history.

Humanities Index. New York: Wilson,
1974–present.

Indexes world history and American
history in *Canadian Journal of History,
English Historical Review, European
Historical Quarterly, Journal of Modern
History,* and many others.

Journalism/Mass Communications

Basic Sources and Guides to the Literature

*The Associated Press Stylebook and Libel
Manual.* Rev. ed. New York: AP, 1987.
Broadcast Communications Dictionary.
Ed. L. Diamant. Westport, CT:
Greenwood, 1989.

Broadcast Television: A Research Guide.
Ed. F. C. Schreibman. Los Angeles: AFI
Education Services, 1983.
Broadcasting Cablecasting Yearbook.
Washington, DC: Broadcasting
Publications, 1982–present. Annually.
**Cates, S. A. *Journalism: A Guide to the
Reference Literature.* Englewood, CO:
Libraries Unlimited, 1990.

An extensive listing of sources of use in
researching print and other mass media.
Provides evaluative, descriptive
comments on each of the 700 sources
included.

Encyclopedia of American Journalism. Ed.
D. Paneth. New York: Facts on File,
1983.
*Encyclopedia of Twentieth-Century
Journalists.* Ed. William H. Taft. New
York: Garland, 1984.
Galvin, Kathy. *Media Law: A Legal
Handbook for the Working Journalist.*
Berkeley: Nolo, 1984.
Halliwell's Film and Video Guide. 6th ed.
New York: Scribner's, 1987.
*Historical Guides to the World's Periodicals
and Newspapers* (series). Westport, CT:
Greenwood (in progress).
**International Encyclopedia of
Communications.* Ed. E. Barnouw et al.
4 vols. New York: Oxford UP, 1989.

A very scholarly, thorough treatment of a
great variety of subjects. Includes
articles on key people in mass
communications (e.g., Charlie Chaplin)
as well as concepts and issues (e.g.,
copyright, cybernetics).

Les Brown's Encyclopedia of Television.
New York: Zoetrope, 1982.
Media Research: An Introduction. Ed.
R. D. Wimmer and J. R. Dominick.
Belmont, CA: Wadsworth, 1982.
Nelson, Harold L., and Dwight L. Teeter,
Jr. *Law of Mass Communications.* 5th ed.
Mineola, NY: Foundation, 1981.
The Reporter's Handbook. New York: St.
Martin's, 1990.
**Rubin, Rebecca B., et al. *Communication
Research.* 2nd ed. Belmont, CA:
Wadsworth, 1986.

Along with chapters providing guidance
in library research plans and the sources
needed for them, it also contains useful
information on conducting formal
research studies.

*U.S. Television Network News: A Guide to
Sources in English.* Comp. M. J. Smith,
Jr. Jefferson, NC: McFarland, 1984.

World Press Encyclopedia. Ed. G. T. Kurian. 2 vols. New York: Facts on File, 1982.

Bibliographies to Journalism Books and Other Sources

American Journalism History. Ed. W. D. Sloan. Westport, CT: Greenwood, 1989.

An Annotated Journalism Bibliography: 1958–1968. Minneapolis: U of Minnesota P, 1970.

Annotated Media Bibliography. Ed. B. Congdon. Washington, DC: ACC, 1985.

Black Media in America: A Resource Guide. Ed. G. H. Hill. Boston: Hall, 1984.

Broadcasting Bibliography: A Guide to the Literature of Radio and Television. Rev. ed. Washington, DC: National Association of Broadcasters, 1989.

Journalism Biographies: Master Index. Detroit: Gale, 1979. Supplements.

The Journalist's Bookshelf. Ed. R. F. Wolseley and I. Wolseley. 8th ed. Atlanta: Berg, 1986.

Law of Mass Communications: Freedom and Control of Print and Broadcast Media. Mineola, NY: Foundation Press, 1989.

The Literature of Journalism: An Annotated Bibliography. Ed. Warren C. Price. Minneapolis: U of Minnesota P, 1959.

Mass Media Bibliography. Ed. E. Blum et al. Champaign: U of Illinois P, 1990.

Mass Media and the Constitution: An Encyclopedia of Supreme Court Decisions. Ed. R. F. Hixson. New York: Garland, 1989.

Multi-Media Reviews Index. Ed. C. E. Wall and P. B. Northern. Ann Arbor: Pierian, 1972.

News Media and Public Policy: An Annotated Bibliography. Ed. J. P. McKerns. 2 vols. New York: Garland, 1985.

Radio and Television: A Selected, Annotated Bibliography. Metuchen, NJ: Scarecrow, 1978. Supplements to 1982.

Violence and Terror in the Mass Media: An Annotated Bibliography. Westport, CT: Greenwood, 1988.

Electronic Sources to Journalism Literature

ACADEMIC INDEX
AP NEWS
ARTS AND HUMANITIES SEARCH
COURIER PLUS
MAGAZINE INDEX
NATIONAL NEWSPAPER INDEX
NEWSEARCH
REUTERS
SOCSCI SEARCH
UPI NEWS
WILSONDISC: BUSINESS, HUMANITIES, and the READERS' GUIDE INDEXES

Indexes to Journalism Articles

**Business Periodicals Index.* New York: Wilson, 1958–present.

Indexes such industry periodicals as *Broadcasting, Communications News, Television/Radio Age,* and *Telecommunications.*

Communications Abstracts. Beverly Hills, CA: Sage, 1978–present.

Indexes approximately 100 journals and selected books.

**Humanities Index.* New York: Wilson, 1974–present.

Indexes journalism articles in such journals as *Journalism History, Journalism Quarterly, Columbia Journalism Review, Commentary, Quill, Encounter, Communications Quarterly, Journal of Broadcasting,* and others.

**Readers' Guide to Periodical Literature.* New York: Wilson, 1900–present.

Indexes news and general interest magazines, such as *Nation, Newsweek, New York Review of Books, New Republic, Saturday Review, U.S. News and World Report,* and others.

Language and Literature

Basic Sources, Guides, and Bibliographies to the Literature

Concise Bibliography for Students of English. Stanford: Stanford UP, 1972.

Contemporary Authors. Detroit: Gale, 1962–present.

Contemporary Literary Criticism. Detroit: Gale, 1973–present.

The Critical Temper: A Survey of Modern Criticism on English and American Literature. New York: Ungar, 1969. Supplements, 1981 and 1989.

**Dictionary of Literary Biography* (series). Detroit: Gale, 1978–present (in progress).

Already comprising over 100 volumes, this is an excellent, well-documented encyclopedia of authors. Includes writers from England, France, Canada, and Germany, as well as the United States, and also has volumes on major journalists, historians, and screenwriters. The best source for finding background information and selected bibliographies on individual authors.

Essay and General Literature Index. New York: Wilson, 1900–present.

Fiction Catalog. New York: Wilson, 1980. Supplements annually.

Goldentree Bibliographies in Language and Literature. Series. Northbrook, IL: AHM, 1968–79.

**Holman, C. H., and W. Harmon. *Handbook to Literature.* 6th ed. New York: Macmillan, 1992.

An excellent dictionary of the words and phrases used in the study of English and American literature. Uses many literary examples for each major term.

***Literary Criticism Index.* Ed. A. R. Weiner and S. Means. Metuchen, NJ: Scarecrow, 1984.

Although the title may be misleading, this is nonetheless a very useful work. It indexes about 85 standard bibliographies of literary criticism, many of them listed in the sections below. When looking up a particular literary writer, one will find the name and page number in a bibliography where listings of criticisms of that writer and of his or her specific works will be found.

***Magill's Bibliography of Literary Criticism.* Ed. F. Magill. 4 vols. Englewood Cliffs, NJ: Salem, 1979.

A handy source when looking for selected critical articles, books, or chapters in books that deal with specific works of Western literature. Includes listings for 2,500 works of literature by 600 different authors.

**Patterson, C. *Literary Research Guide.* 2nd ed. New York: MLA, 1984.

A comprehensive guide to major literary reference tools and other sources for literature worldwide. Provides descriptive information about each source.

Reference Guide for English Studies. Ed. M. J. Marcuse. Berkeley: U of California P, 1990.

Research Guide for Undergraduate Students: English and American Literature. New York: MLA, 1985.

Selective Bibliography for the Study of English and American Literature. Ed. R. D. Altick and A. Wright. 6th ed. New York: Macmillan, 1979.

American Literature

See also Ethnic Studies, 344–46.

American Bibliography. Ed. Charles Evans. 14 vols. Magnolia, MA: Smith, 1967.

American Literary Scholarship. Durham: Duke UP, 1963–present.

American Novel: 1789 to 1968. Ed. D. Gerstenberger and George Hendrick. Chicago: Swallow, 1961 and 1970.

American Writers. 4 vols. New York: Scribner's, 1961–81. Supplements.

Articles on American Literature. (Separate titles covering 1900–50, 1950–67, and 1968–75). Durham: Duke UP, 1954, 1970, and 1979.

Backgrounds of American Literary Thought. Ed. R. W. Horton and H. W. Edwards. 3rd ed. New York: Meredith, 1974.

Bibliographical Guide to the Study of Literature of the USA. Ed. C. Gohdes. 5th ed. Durham: Duke UP, 1984.

A Bibliographical Guide to the Study of Western American Literature. Ed. R. W. Etulain. Lincoln: U of Nebraska P, 1982.

Bibliography of American Literature. New Haven: Yale UP, 1955–present.

Bibliography of Bibliographies in American Literature. Ed. Charles H. Nilon. New York: Bowker, 1970.

Cambridge Handbook of American Literature. Ed. J. Salzman. New York: Cambridge UP, 1986.

Eight American Authors: A Survey of Research and Criticism. Ed. James Woodress. Rev. ed. New York: Norton, 1971.

Guide to American Literature and Its Backgrounds Since 1890. Ed. J. M. Jones and R. M. Ludwig. 4th ed. Cambridge, MA: Harvard UP, 1972.

Kazin, Alfred. *An American Procession.* New York: Random, 1984.

Literary History of the United States. Ed. R. E. Spiller et al. 4th ed. 2 vols. New York: Macmillan, 1974.

Mathiessen, F. O. *American Renaissance: Art and Expression in the Age of Emerson and Whitman.* London: Oxford UP, 1968.

Modern American Literature. Ed. D.
Nyren. 4th ed. New York: Ungar,
1969–76. Supplements.
*Oxford Companion to American
Literature.* Ed. J. D. Hart. 5th ed. New
York: Oxford UP, 1983.
*Sixteen Modern American Authors: A
Survey of Research and Criticism.* Ed.
J. R. Bryer. New York: Norton, 1969.
*The Transcendentalists: A Review of
Research and Criticism.* Ed. Joel
Myerson. New York: MLA, 1984.

Black Literature

See also Ethnic Studies, 355.

Bibliographic Guide to Black Studies. New
York: Hall, 1980. Supplements.
*A Bibliography of Neo-African Literature
from Africa, America, and the
Caribbean.* New York: Grove, 1966.
*Black American Fiction Since 1952: A
Preliminary Checklist.* Ed. F. Deodene
and W. P. French. Metuchen, NJ:
Scarecrow, 1970.
Black American Fiction: A Bibliography.
Ed. C. Fairbanks and E. A. Engeldinger.
Metuchen, NJ: Scarecrow, 1978.
*Black American Writers: Bibliographic
Essays.* 2 vols. New York: St. Martin's,
1978.
*Black American Writers Past and Present:
A Biographical and Bibliographical
Dictionary.* Ed. T. G. Rush et al. 2 vols.
Metuchen, NJ: Scarecrow, 1975.
*Black Americans in Autobiography: An
Annotated Bibliography of
Autobiographies and Autobiographical
Books Written Since the Civil War.*
Durham: Duke UP, 1984.
Black Literature Resources. New York:
Dekker, 1975.
Blacks in America: Bibliographic Essays.
Ed. James P. McPherson et al. New York:
Doubleday, 1971.
*Conjuring: Black Women, Fiction, and
Literary Tradition.* Bloomington:
Indiana UP, 1985.
Davis, Arthur. *From the Dark Tower:
Afro-American Writers from 1900 to
1960.* Washington, DC: Howard UP,
1974.
Gilkin, R. *Black American Women in
Literature.* Jefferson, NC: McFarland,
1989.
*The Negro in American Literature and a
Bibliography of Literature by and about
Negro Americans.* Ed. Abraham
Chapman. Oshkosh: Wisconsin Council
of Teachers of English, 1966.

Poetry of the Negro: 1746–1970. Ed.
Langston Hughes and Arna Bontemps.
New York: Doubleday, 1970.
Werner, Craig. *Black American Women
Novelists.* Englewood Cliffs, NJ: Salem,
1989.
Whitlow, Roger. *Black American
Literature: A Critical History.* Totowa,
NJ: Littlefield, 1974.

British Literature

*Anglo-Irish Literature: A Review of
Research.* Ed. Richard J. Finneran. New
York: MLA, 1976. Supplement, 1983.
Baker, Ernest A. *History of the English
Novel.* 11 vols. New York: Barnes, 1975
(reprint of 1924–67 ed.).
*Bibliographical Resources for the Study of
Nineteenth Century English Fiction.* Ed.
G. N. Ray. Folcroft, PA: Folcroft, 1964.
British Writers. Ed. Ian Scott-Kilvert. 8
vols. New York: Scribner's, 1979–83.
Supplement, 1987.
British Writers and Their Works. 10 vols.
Lincoln: U of Nebraska P, 1964–70.
*Cambridge Bibliography of English
Literature.* Ed. G. Wilson. 5 vols. New
York: Cambridge UP, 1965.
Cambridge Guide to English Literature.
Ed. M. Stapleton. New York: Cambridge
UP, 1983.
Cambridge History of English Literature.
15 vols. Cambridge, England: Cambridge
UP, 1961.
*A Descriptive Catalogue of the
Bibliographies of Twentieth Century
British Poets, Novelists, and Dramatists.*
Ed. E. W. Mellown. 2nd ed. Troy, NY:
Whitston, 1978.
Encyclopedia of Victorian Britain. Ed.
Sally Mitchell. New York: Garland, 1987.
*The English Romantic Poets: A Review of
Research and Criticism.* 4th ed. New
York: MLA, 1985.
Evans, Gareth L., and Barbara Evans. *The
Shakespeare Companion.* New York:
Scribner's, 1978.
Garland Shakespeare Bibliographies. New
York: Garland, 1980–present (in
progress).
McGraw-Hill Guide to English Literature. 2
vols. Ed. K. Lawrence, B. Seifter, and L.
Ratner. New York: McGraw, 1985.
Modern British Literature. 4 vols. Literary
Criticism Series. New York: Ungar,
1966–75.
*New Cambridge Bibliography of English
Literature.* 5 vols. New York: Cambridge
UP, 1969–77.

Oxford Companion to English Literature.
Ed. M. Drabble. 5th ed. Oxford:
Clarendon, 1985.

Oxford History of English Literature.
Oxford: Clarendon, 1945–present.

*Romantic Movement: A Selective and
Critical Bibliography.* New York:
Garland, 1980–present.

Victorian Fiction: A Guide to Research.
New York: MLA, 1980. [Covers research
through 1962.]

*Victorian Fiction: A Second Guide to
Research.* Ed. G. H. Ford. New York:
MLA, 1978. [Covers research 1963–74.]

Victorian Prose: A Guide to Research. Ed.
David J. DeLaura. New York: MLA, 1973.

Drama and Theater

*American Drama Criticism: Interpretations,
1890–1977.* Ed. F. E. Eddleman.
Hamden, CT: Shoe String, 1979.
Supplements 1984 and 1989.

Bailey, J. *A Guide to Reference and
Bibliography for Theatre Research.* 2nd
ed. Columbus: Ohio State UP, 1983.

Cambridge Guide to World Theatre. Ed. E.
Banham. New York: Cambridge UP,
1989.

*Catalog of the Theatre and Drama Collec-
tions.* Boston: Hall, 1967. Supplements.

Cheshire, David F. *Theatre: History,
Criticism, and Reference.* Washington,
DC: Archon, 1967.

Chicorel Index Series. Ed. M. Chicorel. 27
vols. New York: Chicorel Library,
1970–78.

Contemporary Dramatists. Ed. J. Vinson.
4th ed. New York: St. Martin's, 1987.

Critical Survey of Drama. Ed. F. N. Magill.
6 vols. Englewood Cliffs, NJ: Salem,
1982. Supplement, 1987.

Cumulated Dramatic Index: 1909–1949. 2
vols. Boston: Hall, 1965.

Cumulated Dramatic Index. 2 vols. Ann
Arbor, MI: Faxon, 1965.

Drama Criticism. 2 vols. Denver: Swallow
Hill, 1970.

Dramatic Criticism Index. Ed. P. F. Breed
and F. M. Sniderman. Detroit: Gale,
1972.

Drury's Guide to Best Plays. 4th ed.
Metuchen, NJ: Scarecrow, 1987.

Index to Full Length Plays: 1895–1964. 3
vols. Ann Arbor, MI: Faxon, 1956–65.

Index to Plays in Periodicals. Metuchen,
NJ: Scarecrow, 1979; 1977–87.
Supplement, 1990.

*McGraw-Hill Encyclopedia of World
Drama.* 2nd ed. 5 vols. New York:
McGraw, 1983.

Modern Drama: A Checklist. Metuchen, NJ:
Scarecrow, 1967.

Oxford Companion to the Theatre. 4th ed.
New York: Oxford UP, 1984.

Play Index. New York: Wilson,
1953–present.

*A Survey and Bibliography of Renaissance
Drama.* 4 vols. Lincoln: U of Nebraska
P, 1975–78.

Language Studies

*American Literature and Language: A
Guide to Information Sources.* Detroit:
Gale, 1982.

Cambridge Encyclopedia of Language. Ed.
D. Crystal. New York: Cambridge UP,
1988.

*A Concise Bibliography for Students of
English.* 5th ed. Stanford: Stanford UP,
1972.

*A Dictionary of American English on
Historical Principals.* Ed. W. Craigie and
J. R. Hulbert. 4 vols. Chicago: U of
Chicago P, 1938–44.

Dictionary of American Regional English.
Ed. F. Cassidy. Cambridge, MA: Harvard
UP, 1985–present (in progress).

International Encyclopedia of Linguistics.
4 vols. New York: Oxford UP, 1991.

Oxford English Dictionary. 2nd ed. Ed.
J. A. Simpson et al. 20 vols. New York:
Oxford UP, 1989.

The World's Major Languages. Ed. B.
Comrie. New York: Oxford UP, 1987.

Mythology and Folklore

American Folklore: A Bibliography.
Metuchen, NJ: Scarecrow, 1977.

The Arthurian Encyclopedia. Ed. N. J.
Lacy. New York: Garland, 1984.

*Arthurian Legend and Literature: An
Annotated Bibliography.* 2 vols. New
York: Garland, 1983.

Ashlimar, D. L. *Guide to Folktales in the
English Language.* Westport, CT:
Greenwood, 1987.

Bullfinch's Mythology. New York: Avenel,
1978.

Campbell, Joseph. *Historical Atlas of World
Mythology.* New York: Harper Collins,
1988.

Dictionary of Classical Mythology Ed. R. S.
Bell. Santa Barbara: ABC/Clio, 1982.

*Fable Scholarship: An Annotated
Bibliography.* Ed. Pack Carnes. New
York: Garland, 1982.

*Facts on File Encyclopedia of World
Mythology and Legend.* Ed. A. S.
Mercatante. New York: Facts on File,
1988.

Folklore and Literature in the United States: An Annotated Bibliography. Ed. S. S. Jones. New York: Garland, 1984.

Frazer, Sir James. *The Golden Bough*. New York: St. Martin's, 1955.

Grimal, P. *Dictionary of Classical Mythology*. New York: Blackwell, 1986.

Index to Fairy Tales, Myths, and Legends. Ed. M. H. Eastman. 2nd ed. Ann Arbor, MI: Faxon, 1926. Supplements.

Index to Fairy Tales, 1949–1972. Ed. N. O. Ireland. Metuchen, NJ: Scarecrow, 1973.

Mythological and Fabulous Creatures: A Source Book and Research Guide. Westport, CT: Greenwood, 1987.

Storyteller's Sourcebook. Detroit: Gale, 1982.

Tale Type—and Motif—Indexes: An Annotated Bibliography. Ed. D. S. Azzolina. New York: Garland, 1987.

The Novel

American Fiction: A Contribution Toward a Bibliography. Ed. Lyle H. Wright. 3 vols. San Marino: Huntington Library, 1969, 1979.

American Fiction 1900–1950: A Guide to Information Sources. Ed. James Woodress. Detroit: Gale, 1974.

The American Novel 1789–1959: A Checklist of Twentieth Century Criticism. Denver: Swallow Hill, 1961.

The American Novel. Ed. Christof Wegelin. New York: Macmillan, 1977.

The American Novel: A Checklist. Vol. 2: Criticism Written 1960–68. Ed. D. Gerstenberger and G. Hendrick. Chicago: Swallow, 1970.

Chase, Richard. *American Novel and Its Tradition*. Baltimore: Johns Hopkins, 1980.

The Contemporary English Novel: An Annotated Bibliography of Secondary Sources. Ed. H. W. Drescher and Bernd Kahrmann. New York: IPS, 1973.

The Contemporary Novel: A Checklist of Critical Literature on the British and American Novel Since 1945. Ed. I. Adelman and R. Dworkin. Metuchen, NJ: Scarecrow, 1972.

The Continental Novel: A Checklist of Criticism in English, 1900–1960. Metuchen, NJ: Scarecrow, 1968.

Critical Survey of Long Fiction. Ed. F. N. Magill. 8 vols. Englewood Cliffs, NJ: Salem, 1983. Supplement, 1987.

English Language Criticism on the Foreign Novel. Athens, OH: Swallow Press, 1989.

English Novel: 1578–1956: A Checklist of Twentieth Century Criticism. Ed. J. F. Bell and D. Baird. Denver: Swallow Hill, 1958.

English Novel Explication: Criticism to 1972. Ed. Helen Palmer and Jane Dyson. Hamden, CT: Shoe String, 1973. Supplement, 1976–present.

Holman, C. Hugh. *American Novel Through Henry James*. Arlington Heights, IL: Harlan Davidson, 1973.

Watt, Ian. *British Novel: Scott through Hardy*. Arlington Heights, IL: Harlan Davidson, 1973.

Wiley, Paul L. *British Novel: Conrad to the Present*. Arlington Heights, IL: Harlan Davidson, 1973.

Poetry

American and British Poetry: A Guide to the Criticism. Athens, OH: Swallow Press, 1984.

Columbia Index to Poetry. Ed. W. J. Smith. 9th ed. New York: Columbia UP, 1990.

Critical Survey of Poetry. Ed. F. N. Magill. 8 vols. Englewood Cliffs, NJ: Salem, 1982.

English Poetry: Select Bibliographical Guides. Ed. A. E. Dyson. New York: Oxford UP, 1971.

Guide to American Poetry Explication. 2 vols. Boston: Hall, 1989.

Pearce, Roy Harvey. *The Continuity of American Poetry*. Princeton, NJ: Princeton UP, 1961.

Poetry Explication: A Checklist of Interpretations since 1925 of British and American Poems Past and Present. Boston: Hall, 1980.

Subject Index to Poetry for Children and Young People. Ed. D. B. Frizzell-Smith and Eva L. Andrews. Chicago: ALA, 1977.

Waggoner, Hyatt H. *American Poetry: From the Puritans to the Present*. Boston: Houghton, 1968.

Short Story

American Short-Fiction Criticism and Scholarship, 1959–1977: A Checklist. Ed. Joe Weixlmann. Athens: Ohio UP, 1982.

Critical Survey of Short Fiction. Ed. F. N. Magill. 7 vols. Englewood Cliffs, NJ: Salem, 1981. Supplement, 1987.

Short Story Index. Ed. D. E. Cook and I. S. Monro. New York: Wilson, 1953. Supplements.

Twentieth-Century Short Story Explication. Ed. W. S. Walker. 3rd ed. Hamden, CT: Shoe String, 1977. Supplements.

World Literature

Benet's Reader's Encyclopedia. 3rd ed. New York: Harper, 1987.

Columbia Dictionary of Modern European Literature. Ed. Jean-Albert Bede and William Edgerton. New York: Columbia UP, 1980.

Dictionary of World Literary Terms. Ed. J. T. Shipley. Boston: Writer, 1970.

Encyclopedia of World Literature in the 20th Century. New York: Ungar, 1967 and 1981 editions.

Reader's Companion to World Literature. Ed. L. H. Horstein. Rev. ed. New York: NAL, 1956.

Electronic Sources to Literature and Language Studies

ACADEMIC INDEX
ARTS AND HUMANITIES SEARCH
BOOK REVIEW INDEX
LLBA (Linguistics and Language Behavior Abstracts)
MLA BIBLIOGRAPHY
WILSONDISC: HUMANITIES INDEX

Indexes to Articles in Literary Journals

***Abstracts of English Studies.* Urbana, IL: NCTE, 1958-present.

Provides abstracts to monographs and journal articles. The 10th issue each year features a subject index.

Abstracts of Folklore Studies. Austin: U of Texas P, 1962-75. (Ceased publication)

Indexes folklore journals, such as *Dovetail, Kentucky Folklore Record, Relics,* and others.

Book Review Digest. New York: Wilson, 1905-present.

Book Review Index. Detroit: Gale, 1965-present.

***Humanities Index.* New York: Wilson, 1974-present.

Provides general indexing to literary and language topics in several key journals.

Index to Book Reviews in the Humanities. Detroit: Thompson, 1960-present.

***MLA International Bibliography of Books and Articles on the Modern Language and Literatures.* New York: MLA, 1921-present. Annually.

The best overall index to major literary figures and language topics. Although it is not kept current, it nevertheless has comprehensive coverage of the field.

Law

See also Political Science, 363-64.

Basic Sources and Guides to the Literature

American Jurisprudence. 2nd ed. Rochester, NY: Lawyers Cooperative, 1962-present (continuously revised and supplemented).

Black's Law Dictionary. 6th ed. St. Paul, MN: West, 1990.

Corpus Juris Secundum. New York: American Law Book, 1936-present (continuously revised and supplemented).

Dictionary of Modern Legal Usage. New York: Oxford UP, 1987.

Encyclopedia of Legal Information Sources. Ed. P. Wasserman et al. Detroit: Gale, 1988.

***Guide to American Law.* 12 vols. and annual yearbooks. St. Paul, MN: West, 1985.

An encyclopedia of law written for the nonspecialist. Provides background and explanations of legal topics and issues (e.g., abortion, civil rights).

Guide to the Supreme Court. 2nd ed. Washington, DC: Congressional Quarterly, 1990.

Legal Research and Writing. 3rd ed. St. Paul, MN: West, 1986.

Legal Research in a Nutshell. 4th ed. St. Paul, MN: West, 1985.

Bibliographies to Law Books and Other Sources

Index to Legal Books. 6 vols. New York: Bowker, 1989.

The U.S. Supreme Court: A Bibliography. Washington, DC: Congressional Quarterly, 1990.

United States Supreme Court Decisions. 2nd ed. Metuchen, NJ: Scarecrow, 1983.

Electronic Sources to Law Materials

CRIMINAL JUSTICE PERIODICALS INDEX
LABORLAW
LEGAL RESOURCE INDEX
LEXIS
NCJRS (National Criminal Justice Reference Service)
WILSONDISC: INDEX TO LEGAL PERIODICALS

Indexes to Articles in Law Journals

***Index to Legal Periodicals.* New York: Wilson, 1909-present.

Indexes such journals as *American Bar Association Journal, Harvard Law Review,* and *Trial.*

**PAIS International In Print* (formerly *PAIS Bulletin*). New York: PAIS, 1915–present.

Indexes government publications and other books, as well as such journals as *High Technology Law Journal, Labor Law Journal, Law and Contemporary Problems,* and *Real Estate Law Journal.*

Mathematics

Basic Sources and Guides to Mathematics Literature

CRC Handbook of Mathematical Sciences. Ed. W. Beyer. 6th ed. West Palm Beach, FL: CRC, 1987.

Encyclopaedia of Mathematics. 10 vols. Norwell, MA: Reidel/Kluwer, 1988–present (in progress).

**Encyclopedic Dictionary of Mathematics.* Ed. K. Ito. 2nd ed. 4 vols. Cambridge, MA: MIT P, 1987.

Provides thorough but concise coverage of 450 different concepts and phenomena of mathematics (e.g., algebraic groups). Also includes bibliographies listing important sources of research.

**How to Find Out in Mathematics.* Ed. J. E. Pemberton. 2nd ed. Elmsford, NY: Pergamon, 1970.

A description of the resources available for research, including reference books, periodicals, and monographs. Also includes sections on careers, education, and the history of math.

International Catalogue of Scientific Literature: 1901–1914. Section A: Mathematics. Metuchen, NJ: Scarecrow, 1974.

Mathematics Encyclopedia: A Made Simple Book. Garden City, NY: Doubleday, 1977.

Use of Mathematics Literature. Ed. A. R. Darling. Boston: Butterworth, 1977.

Using the Mathematical Literature: A Practical Guide. Ed. B. K. Schaefer. New York: Dekker, 1979.

The VNR Concise Encyclopedia of Mathematics. Ed. W. Gellert. 2nd ed. New York: Van Nostrand, 1989.

Bibliographies to Mathematics Books and Other Sources

Annotated Bibliography of Expository Writing in the Mathematical Sciences.

Ed. M. P. Gaffney and L. A. Steen. Washington, DC: Mathematics Association, 1976.

Bibliography and Research Manual of the History of Mathematics. Ed. K. L. May. Toronto: U of Toronto P, 1973.

Current Information Sources in Mathematics: An Annotated Guide to Books and Periodicals: 1960–72. Ed. E. M. Dick. Englewood, CO: Libraries Unlimited, 1973.

Omega Bibliography of Mathematical Logic. Ed. G. H. Muller and W. Lenski. 6 vols. New York: Springer, 1987.

Schaaf, William I. *A Bibliography of Recreational Mathematics.* 4 vols. Reston, VA: NCTM, 1970.

Schaaf, William I. *The High School Math Library.* 8th ed. Reston, VA: NCTM, 1987.

Vestpocket Bibliographies. Ed. William L. Schaaf. [See miscellaneous issues of the *Journal of Recreational Mathematics,* 1983–present.]

Electronic Sources to Mathematics Literature

MATHSCI
WILSONDISC: GENERAL SCIENCE INDEX

Indexes to Journal Articles in Mathematics

**General Science Index.* New York: Wilson, 1978–present.

Covers about 100 science periodicals, including *American Mathematical Monthly, Journal of Recreational Mathematics,* and *Mathematics Magazine.*

Mathematical Reviews. Providence: AMS, 1940–present.

Medical Studies

Basic Sources and Guides to Medical Literature

American Medical Association Encyclopedia of Medicine. New York: Random, 1989.

Author's Guide to Journals in the Health Field. Ed. D. Ardell and J. James. New York: Haworth, 1980.

Core Collections in Nursing and Allied Health Sciences. Phoenix: Oryx, 1990.

Health Statistics: A Guide to Information Sources. Ed. F. O. Weise. Detroit: Gale, 1980.

Information Sources in the Medical Sciences. Ed. L. T. Morton and S.

Godbolt. 3rd ed. London: Butterworth, 1984.

International Dictionary of Medicine and Biology. 3 vols. New York: Wiley, 1986.

***Introduction to Reference Sources in Health Sciences.* Ed. Fred Roper and JoAnne Boorkman. 2nd ed. Chicago: MLA, 1984.

Discusses and lists health science reference materials, bibliographic sources, and other specialized sources (e.g., statistical). Explains how to use many of the sources described.

Logan, C., and M. K. Rice. *Logan's Medical and Scientific Abbreviations.* Philadelphia: Lippincott, 1987.

Polit, Denise, and Bernadette Hungler. *Nursing Research: Principles and Methods.* 3rd ed. Philadelphia: Lippincott, 1987.

**Stauch, K., et al. *Library Research Guide to Nursing.* Ann Arbor, MI: Pierian, 1989.

Provides guidance in formulating a research plan, as well as information on finding and using specific research tools. Also has a listing of recent sources in major areas of nursing (e.g., "community health issues").

Bibliographies to Medical Books and Other Sources

AIDS Information Sourcebook. Phoenix: Oryx, 1988.

An Annotated Bibliography of Health Economics. Ed. A. J. Culyer et al. New York: St. Martin's, 1977.

Medical Reference Works, 1679–1966. Ed. J. Blake and C. Roos. Chicago: Medical Library Assn., 1967. Supplements.

Nursing Studies Index. Ed. Virginia Henderson. 4 vols. Philadelphia: Lippincott, 1957–72.

Resources for Third World Health Planners: A Selected Subject Bibliography. Buffalo: Conch, 1980.

Electronic Sources to Medical Literature

ACADEMIC INDEX
AIDSLINE
BIOSIS PREVIEWS
EMBASE
MEDLINE
NURSING AND ALLIED HEALTH
SCISEARCH
WILSONDISC: GENERAL SCIENCE INDEX

Indexes to Journal Articles in Medicine

***Cumulated Index Medicus.* Bethesda: U.S. Department of Health and Human Services, 1959–present.

Provides indexing to most medical journals published worldwide.

***Cumulative Index to Nursing and Allied Health Literature.* Glendale: CINAHL, 1956–present.

Indexes nursing literature in journals such as *Cancer Nurse, Current Reviews for Recovery Room Nurses, Journal of Practical Nursing, Journal of Nursing Education,* and many more.

International Nursing Index. New York: AJN, 1970–present.

Music

Basic Sources and Guides to Music Literature

Baker's Biographical Dictionary of Musicians. 7th ed. New York: Schirmer, 1984.

Dictionary of Music. Ed. Alan Isaacs and Elizabeth Martin. New York: Facts on File, 1983.

***Druesdow, S. *Library Research Guide to Music.* Ann Arbor, MI: Pierian, 1982.

An easy-to-follow guide to starting, planning, and carrying out library research in music. Explains how to use the sources, as well as listing a variety of periodical indexes, bibliographies, and other reference tools.

Encyclopedia of Pop, Rock, and Soul. Ed. Irwin Stambler. New York: St. Martin's, 1977.

Information on Music: A Handbook of Reference Sources in European Languages. 3 vols. Englewood, CO: Libraries Unlimited, 1975–84.

International Cyclopedia of Music and Musicians. Ed. Bruce Bahle. 11th ed. New York: Dodd, 1985.

International Encyclopedia of Women Composers. Ed. A. Cohen. 2nd ed. 2 vols. New York: Books and Music USA, 1988.

***Music Reference and Research Materials.* Ed. V. Duckles and M. Keller. 4th ed. New York: Schirmer, 1988.

A comprehensive and thorough bibliography of sources for research in music, including recordings and music history. Provides brief comments on many of the 3,200 sources listed.

New College Encyclopedia of Music. New York: Norton, 1981.

New Grove Dictionary of American Music. Ed. H. Hitchcock and S. Sadie. 4 vols. New York: Grove, 1986.

***New Grove Dictionary of Music and Musicians.* Ed. Stanley Sadie. 20 vols. New York: Macmillan, 1980.

A very scholarly, comprehensive, and international encyclopedia for music and music history. Includes bibliographies of important resources for each major topic.

New Harvard Dictionary of Music. Ed. Willi Apel. Cambridge, MA: Harvard UP, 1986.

New Oxford Companion to Music. New York: Oxford UP, 1983.

New Oxford History of Music. London: Oxford, 1957–74.

World's Encyclopedia of Recorded Music. London: London Gramophone Corp., 1952. Supplements, 1953–57.

Bibliographies to Music Books and Other Sources

Bibliographic Guide to Music. Boston: Hall, 1976–present. Annually.

General Bibliography for Music Research. Ed. K. E. Mixter. 2nd ed. Detroit: Information Coordinators, 1975.

General Index to Modern Musical Literature in the English Language Including Periodicals for the Years 1915–1926. 1927; rpt. New York: DaCapo, 1970.

Musicalia: Sources of Information in Music. Ed. J. H. Davies. 2nd ed. Elmsford, NY: Pergamon, 1969.

Popular Music: An Annotated Index of American Popular Songs. Detroit: Gale, 1963–present.

Source Readings in Music History. Ed. Oliver Strunk. 5 vols. New York: Norton, 1950.

Electronic Sources to Music Literature

ACADEMIC INDEX
ARTS & HUMANITIES SEARCH
RILM ABSTRACTS (Repertoire Internationale de Litterature Musicale)
WILSONDISC: HUMANITIES INDEX

Indexes to Journal Articles in Music

***Humanities Index.* New York: Wilson, 1974–present.

Indexes topics in music in such journals as *American Music, Early Music, Journal of Musicology,* and *Musical Quarterly.*

***Music Article Guide.* Philadelphia: Information Services, 1966–present.

Indexes music education and instrumentation in such journals as *Brass and Wind News, Keyboard, Flute Journal, Piano Quarterly,* and many more.

***Music Index.* Warren, MI: Information Coordinations, 1949–present.

Indexes music journals such as *American Music Teacher, Choral Journal, Journal of Band Research, Journal of Music Therapy, Music Journal, Musical Quarterly,* and many others.

RILM (Repertoire Internationale de Litterature Musicale) New York: City U of New York, 1967–present.

Indexes international music information.

Philosophy

Basic Sources and Guides to Philosophy Literature

Bynago, H. E. *Philosophy: A Guide to the Reference Literature.* H. E. Bynago. Englewood, CO: Libraries Unlimited, 1986.

Dictionary of the History of Ideas. Ed. P. Winer. 5 vols. New York: Scribner's, 1974.

A Dictionary of Philosophy. Ed. P. A. Angeles. New York: Harper, 1981.

Dictionary of Philosophy. Ed. A. R. Lacey. New York: Paul/Methuen, 1987.

Dictionary of Philosophy. Ed. Dagobert D. Runes. Rev. ed. New York: Philosophical Library, 1984.

***Encyclopedia of Philosophy.* Ed. P. Edwards. 8 vols. New York: Macmillan, 1967–68.

Although dated, this is still an excellent source for background information on concepts (e.g., analytic and synthetic statements), movements (e.g., Darwinism), issues (e.g., certainty), and philosophers. Includes brief

bibliographies of important works for
each major article.

*Fifty Major Philosophers: A Reference
  Guide.* Ed. D. Collinson. New York:
  Routledge, 1987.
*A Guide to Philosophical Bibliography and
  Research.* Ed. R. T. DeGeorge. New
  York: Appleton, 1971.
Handbook of Western Philosophy. Ed.
  G. H. R. Parkinson et al. New York:
  Macmillan, 1988.
A History of Philosophy. 9 vols. Garden
  City, NY: Doubleday, 1977.
The Philosopher's Guide. Ed. R. T.
  DeGeorge. Lawrence, KS: Regents, 1980.
***Research Guide to Philosophy.* Ed. T. N.
  Tice and T. P. Slavens. Chicago: ALA,
  1983.

Consists of 30 bibliographic essays on
sources in the history of philosophy
(e.g., 17th century) and various areas of
philosophy (e.g., logic). Concludes with
a bibliography of reference works.

Research in Philosophy. Ed. H. J. Koren.
  Atlantic Highlands, NJ: Duquesne, 1966.
Who's Who in Philosophy. 1942; rpt.
  Westport, CT: Greenwood, n.d.
*World Philosophy: Essay Reviews of 225
  Major Works.* Ed. Frank Magill. 5 vols.
  Englewood Cliffs, NJ: Salem, 1982.

Bibliographies to Philosophy Books and Other Sources

*A Bibliographical Survey for a Foundation
  in Philosophy.* Ed. F. E. Jordack.
  Lanham, MD: U of America P, 1978.
*A Bibliography of Philosophical
  Bibliographies.* Ed. Herbert Guerry.
  Westport, CT: Greenwood, 1977.
*The Classical World Bibliography of
  Philosophy, Religion, and Rhetoric.* New
  York: Garland, 1978.
Philosophers Index: A Retrospective Index
  [1940–66]. Bowling Green: Bowling
  Green UP, 1978.
*Philosophy and Psychology: Classification
  Schedule, Author and Title Listing.* 2
  vols. Cambridge, MA: Harvard UP, 1973.
*Philosophy: A Select, Classified
  Bibliography of Ethics, Economics, Law,
  Politics, Sociology.* Ed. S. A. Matczak.
  Jamaica, NY: Learned Publishers, 1970.

Electronic Sources to Philosophy Literature

ACADEMIC INDEX
ARTS & HUMANITIES SEARCH
PHILOSOPHER'S INDEX
WILSONDISC: HUMANITIES INDEX

Indexes to Journal Articles in Philosophy

***Humanities Index.* New York: Wilson,
  1974–present.

Provides a general index to
philosophical topics in journals such as
*British Journal of Philosophy,
Environmental Ethics, International
Philosophy Quarterly, Journal of the
History of Ideas, Journal of Philosophy,*
and many others.

***Philosopher's Index.* Bowling Green:
  Bowling Green UP, 1967–present.

Indexes philosophy articles in journals
such as *American Philosophical
Quarterly, Humanist, Journal of the
History of Ideas, Journal of Philosophy,
Philosophical Review, Philosophy Today,*
and many more.

Physics

Basic Sources and Guides to Physics Literature

American Institute of Physics Handbook.
  Ed. D. E. Gray. New York: McGraw,
  1972.
Annual Review of Neuroscience. Palo Alto:
  Annual Rev., 1952–present.
*Dictionary of Effects and Phenomena in
  Physics.* Ed. J. Schubert. New York: VCH,
  1987.
Encyclopedia of Physics. 2nd ed. New
  York: Van Nostrand, 1974.
Encyclopedia of Physics. 54 vols. New
  York: Springer, 1956–present.
Encyclopedia of Physics. Ed. Rita G. Lerner
  and George L. Trigg. Reading, MA:
  Addison, 1980.
A Guide to the Literature of Astronomy.
  Ed. R. A. Seal. Englewood, CO: Libraries
  Unlimited, 1977.
How to Find Out About Physics. Ed. Bryan
  Yates. Elmsford, NY: Pergamon, 1965.
*An Introductory Guide to Information
  Sources in Physics.* Ed. L. R. A. Melton.
  Bristol: Inst. of Physics, 1978.
Physics Literature: A Reference Manual.
  Ed. R. H. Whitford. 2nd ed. Metuchen,
  NJ: Scarecrow, 1968.
Space Almanac. New York: Arcsoft, 1989.
Use of Physics Literature. Ed. H. Coblans.
  Boston: Butterworth, 1975.

Bibliographies to Physics Books and Other Sources

***Physics Abstracts.* London: IEE,
  1898–present. Bimonthly.

A guide to the most recent work in physics worldwide. It provides an abstract that you can use in your research even though the journal itself might be unavailable.

Solid State Physics Literature Guides. New York: Plenum, 1972–present.

Sources of History of Quantum Physics. Ed. T. S. Kuhn et al. Phildelphia: APS, 1967.

Electronic Sources to Physics Literature

INSPEC
SCISEARCH
SPIN (Searchable Physics Information Notices)
WILSONDISC: GENERAL SCIENCE INDEX

Indexes to Journal Articles in Physics

***Applied Science and Technology Index.* New York: Wilson, 1958–present.

Indexes general physics topics in *Laser Focus, Monthly Weather Review, Physics Today,* and others.

Current Papers in Physics. London: IEE, 1966–present. Bimonthly.

***Current Physics Index.* New York: American Institute of Physics, 1975–present. Quarterly.

Consult this work for indexing to most articles in physics journals, such as *Applied Physics, Journal of Chemical Physics, Nuclear Physics, Physical Review, Physics Letters,* and many more.

Political Science

Basic Sources and Guides to Political Science Literature

Blackwell Encyclopedia of Political Institutions. Ed. V. Boddanor. Oxford: Blackwell, 1987.

Communism in the World Since 1945. Ed. S. K. Kimmel. Santa Barbara: ABC/Clio, 1987.

Congress A to Z. Washington, DC: Congressional Quarterly, 1988.

Congress and Lawmaking: Researching the Legislative Process. 2nd ed. Santa Barbara: ABC/Clio, 1989.

Dorsey Dictionary of American Government and Politics. Belmont, CA: Dorsey, 1988.

Encyclopedia of Public Affairs Information Sources. Ed. P. Wasserman et al. Detroit: Gale, 1988.

Encyclopedia of the United Nations and International Relations. 2nd ed. New York: Taylor and Francis, 1990.

A Guide to Library Sources in Political Science: American Government. Ed. C. E. Vose. Washington, DC: APSA, 1975.

Guide to Official Publications of Foreign Countries. Chicago: ALA, 1990.

***Information Sources of Political Science.* Ed. F. L. Holler. 4th ed. Santa Barbara: ABC/Clio, 1986.

Covers all forms of information sources (books, periodicals, and data bases) for research on American politics and government, international relations, and the study of foreign governments.

Morehead, Joe. *Introduction to United States Public Documents.* 3rd ed. Englewood, CO: Libraries Unlimited, 1983.

Political Handbook of the World. Ed. A. S. Banks. New York: McGraw, annually.

Political Research and Political Theory. Ed. O. Garceau. Cambridge, MA: Harvard UP, 1968.

Political Science: A Guide to Reference and Information Sources. Ed. H. York. Englewood, CO: Libraries Unlimited, 1990.

State Yellow Book: A Directory. New York: Monitor, 1989–present. Semi-annually.

The Statesman's Yearbook. New York: St. Martin's, 1964–present. Annually.

Webb, W. H. *Sources of Information in the Social Sciences.* 3rd ed. Chicago: ALA, 1986.

Yearbook of the United Nations. Lake Success: United Nations, 1947–present. Annually.

Bibliographies to Political Science Books and Other Sources

Bibliography on the American Left. Comp. L. M. Wilcox. Kansas City: ERS, 1980.

Free-thought in the United States: A Descriptive Bibliography. Westport, CT: Greenwood, 1978.

International Bibliography of Political Science. New York: IPS, 1979. Supplements.

The Literature of Political Science: A Guide for Students, Librarians, and Teachers. New York: Bowker, 1969.

Monthly Catalog of U.S. Government Publications. Washington, DC: GPO, 1895–present.

Political Science: A Bibliographical Guide to the Literature. Metuchen, NJ: Scarecrow, 1965. Supplements, 1966–present.

Russia and Eastern Europe, 1789–1985: A Bibliographical Guide. Manchester: Manchester UP, 1989.

Electronic Sources to Political Science Literature

ACADEMIC INDEX
ASI
CIS
CONGRESSIONAL RECORD ABSTRACTS
FEDERAL REGISTER ABSTRACTS
GPO MONTHLY CATALOG
NATIONAL NEWSPAPER INDEX
PAIS
UNITED STATES POLITICAL SCIENCE DOCUMENTS
WASHINGTON PRESSTEXT
WILSONDISC: SOCIAL SCIENCES INDEX
WORLD AFFAIRS REPORT

Indexes to Political Science Journal Articles

***ABC: Pol Sci.* Santa Barbara: ABC/Clio, 1969–present.

Indexes the tables of contents of about 300 international journals in the original language.

***PAIS International In Print* (formerly *PAIS Bulletin*). New York: PAIS, 1915–present.

Indexes government publications and books, as well as such journals as *Annals of the American Academy of Political and Social Science* and *International Studies Quarterly.*

***Social Sciences Index.* New York: Wilson, 1974–present.

Indexes articles in such journals as *American Journal of Political Science, American Political Science Review, British Journal of Political Science, Political Quarterly, Political Science Quarterly,* and many others.

Psychology

Basic Sources and Guides to the Literature

Alsip, J. E., and D. D. Chezik. *Research Guide in Psychology.* Morristown, NJ: General Learning Press, 1974.
American Handbook of Psychiatry. Ed. S. Arieti. 2nd ed. 8 vols. New York: Basic, 1974–81.
Bachrach, A. J. *Psychological Research: An Introduction.* 4th ed. New York: Random, 1981.

Borchardt, D. H. *How to Find Out in Philosophy and Psychology.* Elmsford, NY: Pergamon, 1986.
Diagnostic and Statistical Manual of Mental Disorders. 3rd ed. Washington, DC: American Psychiatric Assn., 1987.
Dictionary of Behavioral Science. 2nd ed. New York: Academic, 1989.
***Encyclopedia of Psychology.* Ed. R. J. Corsini. 4 vols. New York: Wiley, 1984.

A scholarly, thorough introduction to all aspects of psychology, including its major theorists. Most of the articles include references to other sources, all of which are listed in the extensive bibliography in the index volume.

Encyclopedia of Psychology. 3 vols. New York: Seaburg, 1979.
Encyclopedic Dictionary of Psychology. Eds. G. Harre and R. Lamb. Cambridge, MA: MIT P, 1983.
International Handbook of Psychology. Westport, CT: Greenwood, 1987.
Library Research Guide to Psychology. Ann Arbor, MI: Pierian, 1984.
***Library Use: A Handbook for Psychology.* Ed. J. C. Reed and R. M. Baxter. Washington, DC: APA, 1983.

A thorough overview of the research process in psychology. Provides guidance in choosing and narrowing topics, as well as suggesting research sources to consult in psychology and such related fields as education and management. Also explains how to use sources such as *Psychological Abstracts.*

Oxford Companion to the Mind. Ed. R. Gregory. New York: Oxford UP, 1987.
Research Guide for Psychology. Ed. R. G. McInnis. Westport, CT: Greenwood, 1982.

Bibliographies to Psychology Books and Other Sources

Annual Reviews of Psychology. Palo Alto: Annual Reviews, 1950–present.
Bibliographical Guide to Psychology. Boston: Hall, 1982. Supplements.
Bibliography of Aggressive Behavior: A Reader's Guide to the Research Literature. Ed. J. M. Crabtree and K. E. Mayer. New York: Liss, 1977.
Coping and Adapting: A Behavioral Science Bibliography. New York: Basic, 1974.
The Index of Psychoanalytic Writings. Ed. A. Grinstein. 14 vols. New York: International Universities, 1956–71.

Psychoanalysis, Psychology, and Literature: A Bibliography. Ed. Norman Kiell. 2nd ed. 2 vols. Metuchen, NJ: Scarecrow, 1982.

Psychological Abstracts. Lancaster, PA: APA, 1927–present.

Psychological Index. 42 vols. Princeton, NJ: Psychological Review, 1895–1936. Superseded by *Psychological Abstracts.*

Electronic Sources to Psychology Studies

ACADEMIC INDEX
CHILD ABUSE AND NEGLECT
ERIC
MENTAL HEALTH ABSTRACTS
PSYCINFO
SOCIAL SCISEARCH
SOCIOLOGICAL ABSTRACTS
WILSONDISC: SOCIAL SCIENCES INDEX

Indexes to Journal Articles in Psychology

Child Development Abstracts and Bibliography. Chicago: U of Chicago P, 1927–present.

**Psychological Abstracts.* Arlington, VA: APA, 1927–present.

Indexes and provides brief abstracts to psychology journals such as *American Journal of Psychology, Behavioral Science, Journal of Abnormal and Social Psychology, Psychological Review,* and many more.

**Sociological Index.* New York: International Sociological Assn., 1952–present.

Indexes such journals as *American Journal of Community Psychology, Journal of Drug Issues, Sex Roles,* and many others.

Religion

Basic Sources and Guides to the Literature

Concise Encyclopedia of Islam. Ed. C. Glasse. San Francisco: Harper, 1989.

Encyclopedia Judaica. Ed. C. Roth. 16 vols. New York: Macmillan, 1972. (Annual yearbooks serve to supplement.)

**Encyclopedia of Religion.* Ed. M. Eliade. 16 vols. New York: Macmillan, 1987.

A scholarly, thorough treatment of worldwide religions, religious thinkers, and religious issues (e.g., the afterlife). Useful bibliographies follow nearly all articles.

Encyclopedia of American Religions. Ed. G. J. Melton. 2 vols. Wilmington, NC: McGrath, 1978.

Encyclopedia of the American Religious Experience. Ed. C. Lippy and P. Williams. 3 vols. New York: Scribner's, 1987.

Guide to Hindu Religion. Ed. D. J. Dell. Boston: Hall, 1981.

Harper Atlas of the Bible. Ed. J. Pritchard. New York: Harper, 1987.

The International Standard Bible Encyclopedia. Ed. Geoffrey W. Bromley. 4 vols. Grand Rapids: Eerdmans, 1979–88.

Introduction to Theological Research. Ed. Cyril J. Barber. Chicago: Moody, 1982.

**Library Research Guide to Religion and Theology.* Ed. James Kennedy. 2nd ed. Ann Arbor, MI: Pierian, 1984.

A good, step-by-step introduction to the basic sources in religious studies. Also includes a bibliography of sources in specific areas (e.g., the Bible, comparative religion).

Lives of the Saints. Ed. Thurston Attwater. 4 vols. Westminster: Christian Classics, 1976.

Nelson's Complete Concordance to the Revised Standard Version of the Bible. Ed. John W. Ellison. New York: Nelson, 1978.

New Catholic Encyclopedia. 17 vols. New York: McGraw, 1977–79.

New Dictionary of Theology. Ed. J. Komonchak et al. Wilmington: Glazier, 1987.

Oxford Dictionary of the Christian Church. New York: Oxford UP, 1974.

Philosophy of Religion: A Guide to Information Sources. Ed. Donald Capps et al. Detroit: Gale, 1976.

Research Guide to Religious Studies. Ed. J. F. Wilson and Thomas Slavens. Chicago: ALA, 1982.

A Reader's Guide to the Great Religions. Ed. C. J. Adams. 2nd ed. Riverside, NJ: Free, 1977.

Who's Who in Religion. Chicago: Marquis, 1975/76–present.

Yearbook of American and Canadian Churches. New York: Abingdon, annually.

*Bibliographies to Religion Books
and Other Sources*

*A Critical Bibliography of Writings on
Judaism.* Lewiston, NY: Mellen, 1989.
***Humanities Index.* New York: Wilson,
1974–present.

Indexes religious journals such as
*Church History, Harvard Theological
Review,* and *Muslim World.*

***Index of Articles on Jewish Studies.*
Jerusalem: Jewish National and U
Library P, 1969–present.

Indexes 10,000 periodicals for all phases
of Jewish religion and studies.
Guide to Indexed Periodicals in Religion.
Metuchen, NJ: Scarecrow, 1975.
Index Islamicus. Vols. covering 1665–1905
(Millersville, PA: Adiyok, 1989);
1906–50 (Cambridge: Cambridge UP,
1958); and 5-year cumulations since
1971 (London: Mansell, 1972–present).
*Reference Works for Theological Research:
An Annotated Selective Bibliographical
Guide.* Ed. Robert Kepple. 2nd ed.
Lanham, MD: UP of America, 1981.
Religious Books and Serials in Print. New
York: Bowker, annually.
Religions: A Select, Classified Bibliography.
Ed. J. F. Mitros. New York: Learned,
1973.
*Religion and Society in North America: An
Annotated Bibliography.* Ed. R.
Brunkow. Santa Barbara: ABC/Clio,
1983.
A Theological Book List. Ed. R. P. Morris.
Cambridge: Hadden, 1971.
Warden, Jacques. *Classical Approaches to
the Study of Religion: Aims, Methods,
and Theories of Research.* Part 2:
Bibliography. Hawthorne, NY: Mouton,
1974.
Wiersbe, Warren W. *A Basic Library for
Bible Students.* Grand Rapids: Baker,
1981.

*Electronic Sources to Religion
Studies*

ACADEMIC INDEX
RELIGION INDEX
WILSONDISC: HUMANITIES INDEX

Indexes to Journal Articles

*The Catholic Periodical and Literature
Index.* New York: Catholic Library Assn.,
1934–present.

Indexes 170 Catholic periodicals.

***Religion: Index One: Periodicals,
Religion and Theological Abstracts.*
(Formerly *Index to Religious Periodicals
Literature.*) Chicago: ATLA,
1949–present.

Indexes religious articles in journals
such as *Biblical Research, Christian
Scholar, Commonweal, Harvard
Theological Review, Journal of Biblical
Literature,* and many others.

Sociology and Social Work

*Basic Sources and Guides to
Sociology Literature*

DeSola, R. *Crime Dictionary.* Rev. ed. New
York: Facts on File, 1988.
Encyclopedia of Child Abuse. New York:
Facts on File, 1989.
*Encyclopedia of Marriage, Divorce, and
the Family.* New York: Facts on File,
1989.
Encyclopedia of Social Work. Ed. A.
Minahan. 18th ed. 3 vols. New York:
NASW, 1988. Supplement, 1989.
Encyclopedia of Sociology. Ed. G. Johnson.
Guilford, CT: Dushkin, 1974.
Handbook of Sociology. Ed. N. Smelser.
Newbury Park, CA: Sage, 1988.
McMillan, P., and S. R. Kennedy. *Library
Research Guide to Sociology.* Ann Arbor,
MI: Pierian, 1980.
***Sociology, A Guide to Reference and
Information Sources.* Ed. S. Aby.
Englewood, CO: Libraries Unlimited,
1987.

A very good starting place when trying
to find which indexes, bibliographies,
and other reference books might be
relevant. Covers 600 major resources in
sociology and related fields, giving
descriptive and evaluative information
for each.

***Student Sociologist's Handbook.* Ed.
P. B. Bart and L. Frankel. 4th ed. New
York: McGraw, 1986.

Along with listing recommended
sources for researching sociological
topics, also includes sections on trends
in the field and on writing different
types of sociology papers.

*Bibliographies to Sociology Books
and Other Sources*

American Homelessness. Ed. M. E. Hombs.
Santa Barbara: ABC/Clio, 1990.

Families in Transition. Ed. J. Sadler. Hamden, CT: Anchor, 1988.

Index to Sociology Readers: 1960–1965. Ed. H. J. Abramson and Nicholas Sofios. 2 vols. Metuchen, NJ: Scarecrow, 1973.

Reference Sources in Social Work: An Annotated Bibliography. Ed. James H. Conrad. Metuchen, NJ: Scarecrow, 1982.

Sociological Aspects of Poverty: A Bibliography. Ed. H. P. Chalfant. Monticello, IL: Vance, 1980.

Sociology: Classification Schedule, Author and Title Listing, Chronological Listings. 2 vols. Cambridge, MA: Harvard UP, n.d.

Electronic Sources to Sociological Literature

ACADEMIC INDEX
CHILD ABUSE AND NEGLECT
FAMILY RESOURCES
NCJRS (National Criminal Justice Reference Service)
SOCIAL SCISEARCH
SOCIOLOGICAL ABSTRACTS
WILSONDISC: SOCIAL SCIENCES INDEX

Indexes to Journal Articles

Popular Periodical Index. Roslyn, PA: PPI, 1973–present.

Indexes contemporary and regional issues in magazines such as *GEO, Life, Ohio Magazine, Playboy, Rolling Stone, Texas Monthly,* and others.

***Social Sciences Index.* New York: Wilson, 1974–present.

Indexes articles in such journals as *Child Welfare, Families in Society,* and *Social Problems.*

Social Work Research and Abstracts. New York: NASW, 1964–present.

Indexes social work periodicals.

***Sociological Abstracts.* New York: Sociological Abstracts, 1952–present.

Indexes and provides brief descriptions of articles in journals such as *American Journal of Sociology, Environment and Behavior, Journal of Applied Social Psychology, Journal of Marriage and the Family, Social Education, Social Research, Sociological Inquiry, Sociology,* and many others.

Speech

See also Drama and Theater, 356, and Journalism/Mass Communications, 352–53.

Basic Sources and Guides to the Literature

Index to Speech, Language, and Hearing: Journal Titles, 1954–78. San Diego: College Hill, n.d.

***Research Guide in Speech.* Ed. G. Tandberg. Morristown, NJ: General Learning Press, 1974.

Dated, but nevertheless it is a very useful source for guidance on all stages of preparing oral presentations. Also includes a brief history of oratory and a selective listing of recommended sources for research in various subject areas as well as the field of speech.

Bibliographies to Speech Books and Other Sources

American Orators Before 1900: Critical Studies and Sources. Westport, CT: Greenwood, 1987.

Bibliography of Speech and Allied Areas, 1950–1960. Westport, CT: Greenwood, 1972.

Radio and Television: A Selected Annotated Bibliography. Metuchen, NJ: Scarecrow, 1978.

Rhetoric and Public Address: A Bibliography: 1947–1961. Madison: U of Wisconsin P, 1964. (Continued annually in *Speech Monographs.*)

Table of Contents of the Quarterly Journal of Speech, Speech Monographs, and Speech Teacher. Ed. John McPhee. New York: Farrar (in association with the Speech Association of America), 1985.

Electronic Sources to Speech Literature

ACADEMIC INDEX
ERIC
LLBA (Language and Language Behavior Abstracts)
MLA BIBLIOGRAPHIES
SOCIAL SCISEARCH
WILSONDISC: HUMANITIES INDEX

Indexes to Journal Articles to Speech Literature

***Humanities Index.* New York: Wilson, 1974–present.

Indexes such speech journals as *Communication, Journal of Communication, Quarterly Journal of Speech, Speech Monographs,* and *Studies in Public Communication.*

MLA International Bibliography. New York: MLA, 1921–present.

Indexes rhetorical subjects.

Women's Studies

Basic Sources and Guides to the Literature

Fishburn, Katherine. *Women in Popular Culture: A Reference Guide.* Westport, CT: Greenwood, 1982.

Guide to Social Science Resources in Women's Studies. Ed. E. H. Oakes and K. E. Sheldon. Santa Barbara, CA: ABC/Clio, 1978.

Lerner, Gerda. *Black Women in White America.* New York: Pantheon, 1972.

Index-Directory of Women's Media. Washington, DC: Women's Institute for Freedom of the Press, 1975–present.

Index to Women of the World from Ancient to Modern Times: Biographies and Portraits. Ann Arbor, MI: Faxon, 1970.

**Searing, S. *Introduction to Library Research in Women's Studies.* Boulder: Westview, 1985.

A multidisciplinary listing of sources for researching women's issues and problems in the social sciences.

Statistical Handbook on Women in America. Phoenix: Oryx, 1991.

Who's Who of American Women. Chicago: Marquis, 1958–present.

Womanhood Media: Current Resources About Women. Chicago: Marquis, 1958–date.

Women Today: A Multidisciplinary Approach to Women's Studies. Ed. M. A. Baker et al. Monterey, CA: Brooks/Cole, 1979.

Women's Action Almanac: A Complete Resource Guide. Ed. J. Williamson et al. New York: Morrow, 1979.

**Women's Studies Encyclopedia.* 3 vols. Westport, CT: Greenwood, 1989–present (in progress).

A multidisciplinary reference source on all issues relating to women. Vol. 1 covers "views from the sciences" (1989); vol. 2 deals with "literature, arts, and learning" (1990).

Bibliographies to Books and Other Sources

American Women and Politics: A Selected Bibliography and Research Guide. New York: Garland, 1984.

American Women Writers: An Annotated Bibliography. Ed. B. A. White. New York: Garland, 1976.

Annotated Bibliography of Feminist Criticism. Ed. M. Humm. Boston: Hall, 1987.

Annotated Bibliography of Twentieth Century Critical Studies of Women and Literature: 1660–1800. New York: Garland, 1977.

Bibliographic Guide to Studies on the Status of Women: Development and Population Trends. Paris: UNESCO, 1983.

Bibliography on Women Workers: 1961–1965. 2nd ed. Washington, DC: International Labor Office, 1974.

Biographies of American Women. Santa Barbara: ABC/Clio, 1990.

Feminist Companion to Literature in English. Ed. V. Blain et al. New Haven: Yale UP, 1990.

Feminist Resources for Schools and Colleges: A Guide. Ed. A. Chapman. New York: Feminist Press, 1986.

New Feminist Scholarship: A Guide to Bibliographies. Ed. Jane Williamson. New York: Feminist Press, 1979.

Older Women in 20th-Century America: A Selected Annotated Bibliography. New York: Garland, 1982.

The Status of Women: A Selected Bibliography. New York: United Nations, n.d.

Women and Work: Paid and Unpaid: A Selected Annotated Bibliography. Ed. M. A. Ferber. New York: Garland, 1987.

Women in America: A Guide to Information Sources. Ed. V. R. Terris. Detroit: Gale, 1980.

Women's Studies: A Recommended Core Bibliography. Ed. E. Stineman and C. Loeb. Englewood, CO: Libraries Unlimited, 1979.

Electronic Sources to Women's Studies

ACADEMIC INDEX
ERIC
SOCIAL SCISEARCH
SOCIOLOGICAL ABSTRACTS
WILSONDISC: SOCIAL SCIENCES INDEX and HUMANITIES INDEX

Indexes to Journal Articles on Women's Studies

**Social Sciences Index.* New York: Wilson, 1974–present.

Indexes such journals as *Feminist Studies, Ms., Signs, Womanpower, Woman Activist, Woman's Journal, Women and Literature, Women's Studies,* and *Women's World.*

Women's Studies Abstracts. Rush, NY: Rush, 1972–present.

Index